Planning and Federalism

**THE UNIVERSITY OF QUEENSLAND PRESS
SCHOLARS' LIBRARY**

Planning and Federalism

Australian and Canadian Experience

KENNETH WILTSHIRE

University of Queensland Press

ST LUCIA • LONDON • NEW YORK

in association with
The Centre for Research on Federal Financial Relations

First published 1986 by University of Queensland Press
Box 42, St Lucia, Queensland, Australia

Typeset by University of Queensland Press
Printed by Silex Enterprise & Printing Co., Hong Kong

Distributed in the UK and Europe by University of Queensland Press
Dunhams Lane, Letchworth, Herts. SG6 1LF England

Distributed in the USA and Canada by University of Queensland Press
250 Commercial Street, Manchester, NH 03101 USA

Cataloguing in Publication Data

National Library of Australia

Wiltshire, Kenneth W. (Kenneth William), 1944–
  Planning and federalism.

  Includes index.

  1. Federal government — Australia. 2. Federal government
  — Canada. 3. Australia — Politics and government — 20th
  century. 4. Canada — Politics and government — 20th
  century. I. Australian National University. Centre for
  Research on Federal Financial Relations. II. Title.
  (Series: University of Queensland Press
  scholars' library).

321.02'0994

British Library (data available)

Library of Congress

Wiltshire, Kenneth W.
  Planning and federalism.

  (Scholars' library/University of Queensland Press)
  Bibliography: p.
  Includes index.

  1. Federal government — Australia. 2. Federal government — Canada. 3. Planning — Australia. 4. Planning —
  Canada. I. Title. II. Series: Scholars' library.

JQ4020.S8W55   1986   321.02'0994   85-16521

For Christopher

Contents

Tables

Publisher's Note

This book is in a series designed by the University of Queensland Press to make reference and specialist works available. Titles in the series normally will not be stocked by booksellers and may be obtained by writing directly to the publisher.

Foreword

There certainly has not been any surfeit of published writings specifically bearing on the detail of comparative federalism of Australia and Canada. There has been a great deal written about federalism in each country but the comparative treatment has been usually cursory. In any case federalism in recent decades has had to cope with a pace of change that very quickly leaves outdated all but the most basic and elementary treatises.

Dr Wiltshire identifies and updates the marked similarities between the two countries (and they are many and remarkable) as well as the common features of the two federalisms. In some instances where the two constitutions provide for a difference of treatment the actual arrangements have evolved in rather a converging way. Whether because of the realities of geography, size, distance, resource development, the presence of major city corridors of political influence, common historical influences, etc., life with these two federal states is so similar as to make for instant recognition and adaptation. Except for climate and its effect on life style the degree of similarity is greater than that between any other two countries and peoples elsewhere.

Delve into the detail of federal-state fiscal relations; budget sizes and allocation. You may temporarily be dismayed by the immensity of detail; the apparent differences in priorities of expenditure. Even though the Canadian provinces may appear to control greater revenues and expenditures than do the Australian states relative to the commonwealth government, that difference may easily be given exaggerated weight. It is only in the last decade that the Canadian provinces agreed to "restyling" of a part of the previous massive federal transfer payments to provinces to provide for a tax field responsibility along with the revenue. Had it not been for that event Australian and Canadian fiscal federalism would not even appear to be very different. Then again, perhaps federalism is not meant to be clearly understood — at least not in our two countries' style of it. It has become too much of a blood sport — in both places. It may well be the only blood sport in which players of the same uniform attack each other at least once per year.

Dr Ken Wiltshire is to be commended for both the timeliness and the substance of his most recent published work *Planning and Federalism: Australian and Canadian Experience*.

Edward Schreyer
Canadian High Commissioner to Australia

Acknowledgments

The material for this book has been dependent to a significant extent on responses of interviewees, most of whom were Australian and Canadian public servants. The necessary anonymity of viewpoints has been achieved by aggregation of responses, which means that identification of sources of argument has not always been possible. It has also meant, regrettably, that it has not been possible to single out each respondent for acknowledgment of cooperation, without which the exercise would not have been possible.

The following organizations provided funding or resources for the conduct of this study and their assistance is gratefully acknowledged:

Reserve Bank of Australia
Government of Canada
Canadian High Commission, Canberra
Canadian Consulate, Sydney
Centre for Research on Federal Financial Relations, Canberra
Institute of Intergovernmental Relations, Kingston, Ontario
Australian Advisory Council for Inter-government Relations
Royal Australian Institute of Public Administration
Institute of Public Administration of Canada
Royal Institute of Public Administration, London
Political and Economic Planning, London
Committee for Economic Development of Australia
Centre for the Study of Federalism, Philadelphia, USA
US Advisory Commission on Intergovernmental Relations
Canadian Federal-Provincial Relations Office
HM Treasury, London

For assistance in typing I am indebted to Ruth Forrest, Irene Saunderson, Jane Parslow, Sandy Henderson, and Carol Parker. My colleagues, Colin Hughes, Ron Lane, Ken Kernaghan, Bill Hull, Cheryl Saunders, Ken Knight, Richard Simeon, John Hayes, Jean Holmes, and Campbell Sharman provided guidance which was greatly appreciated.

My greatest debt of gratitude is to Professor Russell Mathews, Director of the ANU Centre for Research on Federal Financial Relations, who has been a never-ending source of encouragement througout the duration of this project.

Introduction

The aim of this book is to determine to what extent it is possible for the units of the Australian and Canadian federations to engage in public sector planning. It has been in gestation for many years and its origins lie in the author's experience as a state public servant during the 1960s — the so-called "decade of development" — when it became readily apparent that there was a complete lack of forward planning by the various levels of government in Australia, and the minimum of harmonization of objectives between the levels of government.

In 1970 and 1971 the opportunity arose to study at first hand the experience with indicative planning of various nations in Western Europe in the postwar period. Other developments included public sector planning following the Plowden Report in 1961 in Great Britain, and the Planning Programming Budgeting System experiments in North America which had followed the Johnson initiatives of the mid 1960s.

It was only a short step to a posing of the question as to why public sector planning of at least one of these kinds had not taken hold in Australia. Arising out of research, which is elaborated upon in the text of this study which follows, it became apparent that there were many hindrances to the adoption of such planning processes in Australia, some of them "natural" (that is, related to the nature of the country and its people), and many of them "artificial" (that is, man-made or heavily influenced by the political and social structures which had been contrived). As in most countries, many of those hindrances were relevant to each level of government separately, but the most fundamental hindrance was the federal form of government itself.

To some extent it seemed natural that planning should be more difficult in a federation. After all, if one level of government, the national government, has to pass a large share of its resources to other levels of government (state and local), and is unable to determine the uses to which that share is devoted, then that is a monumental constraint upon that level of government in its forward thinking and in its determination of its own priorities. On the other hand, consider a level of government (state or local) which must receive a very large share of its resources from another level of government (national), and it becomes clear that forward thinking and priority determination are severely curtailed for that recipient government, especially when a proportion of the transferred resources it receives is earmarked by the donor government.

There were, of course, many other elements of a federal form of government which, superficially at least, promised to be impediments to planning by its component units. For example, the fact that there are more sovereign units of government involved than in a unitary system spells trouble in itself, as does the potential conflict of those jurisdictions which requires the presence of an umpire (the High Court) to arbitrate between them. Large families find it harder to plan their activities than smaller ones, or childless couples, especially if the parents of those larger families are liberal in their attitude to the rest of the family.

Nevertheless it was clear from the literature and recounted experiences of other federations that planning was possible to some extent in a federal situation. West Germany seemed to have achieved sufficient harmonization between the Federal and Lander governments to achieve coordination of priorities and formulation of plans for the whole public sector of that country; India had seemingly successfully grafted a national planning process onto its modern federal political system; and even the United States had managed, for a time, to absorb the Planning Programming Budgeting System (PPBS) into the public sector of the national and some subnational units of government, albeit with varying degrees of success.

Why then could there not be similar reforms in Australia? Why indeed, had none of the post-Plowden reforms in Great Britain[1] (which had introduced public sector planning into that country with its strong local and county structure), been copied in Australia, when past history had revealed a tendency for all budgetary changes and most other Westminster modifications to be copied in Australia within a very short space of time?

These questions and many others prompted the question as to why there had been no large scale moves to implement public sector planning in Australia, and whether that federal system was really so severe an obstacle to any reform in this direction.

Thus, the central hypothesis to be examined here is that planning, in concept and practice, is compatible with federalism in concept and practice. The methodology to test this hypothesis is quite simple. Firstly, a model (more accurately — a system) of planning has been derived by a synthesis of theoretical material on planning and the experience of those countries which have introduced forms of public sector planning. Secondly, the system has been placed over, or applied to, the Australian and Canadian federations to see how well it fits. Thirdly, the obstacles or hindrances which have emerged have been identified and analysed in an effort to determine whether they are fundamentally incompatible with the planning system, or whether with some rethinking and modification they could be adapted to become partially or completely compatible with it. Naturally enough, it was realized from the outset that if enough incompatibilities or hindrances were found with the planning system which had been contrived, doubts would have to be cast on the integrity and relevance of that planning system itself.

Now if one wants to determine the validity of one's hypotheses or model one can apply it to the behaviour of a system and watch the reaction — in other words one can set up an empirical test. That was achieved in this study by attempting to fit the planning framework to the political, legal, administrative, and above all financial structures which comprise the Australian federal system, together with the actual processes or functions or behaviour which take place within that structure. In that sense this is a structural/functional approach. The primary resources which have been used for this approach have included government publications, files, documents, agreements, statistics, addresses, articles, etc., and some secondary sources based on these primary ones.

However, in the social sciences one has another method of testing the validity of a model, and that is to apply it to the *perceptions* of the actors who form part of the system under review. If one wants to test a theory about where the incidence of fire is greatest in a metropolis one can:

1.   set up a method of monitoring the incidence of fires over a period of time; or
2.   rigorously question fire brigade chiefs with long years of service as to where most fires occur; or
3.   both.

It is not possible to employ the first method in this analysis because there is no public sector planning in evidence to enable any empirical testing; instead we have attempted to make a notional application of a "synthetic" planning system by reviewing available literature. The second method was pursued by means of comprehensive interviews over a period of six years, predominantly of national, state/provincial, and local public servants intimately involved in federal relations and priority determination for their own level of government, together with politicians, fellow academics, and others with relevant expertise. The emphasis has been upon public servants because they are in a unique position to perceive political influences at work and the manner in which those political influences are translated into resource allocation, which lies at the heart of priority determination.

Although Australia is the main focus of attention, this is also a comparative study. Material from other federations has been incorporated, where relevant, but the main comparison is with Canada. It was decided early in the project to adopt this approach mainly because, when each of the major hindrances to public sector planning in Australia were identified, it became important to know whether that hindrance was peculiar to the Australian federal experience or whether it was common to similar federations. As will be argued later, Canada has a federal system which is most like that in Australia, particularly in that it operates as a federation within a Westminster-derived model of government at both national and subnational levels. Consequently Canada was used as a comparison.

However, it must be stressed that no attempt is being made to create a new comparative model. This study simply compares Australia with Canada using the framework of the "Westminster model" and the concept of federalism. What is understood to comprise the elements of that framework is elaborated upon as the study progresses. The aspect claimed to be original, in particular, is the delineation of the main theoretical and practical features of the federalism concept, of significance for the introduction of public sector planning.

To recapitulate, the approach used here has been to develop a planning system, to attempt to apply it to the Australian and Canadian federal system, to consider the concepts "planning" and "federalism" in the abstract, and in practice, to identify any basic conceptual incompatibilities. Then we identify the main hindrances which emerge and single them out for more detailed analysis, in each case attempting to discover just what it is about that hindrance that frustrates the implementation of the planning system. Our planning system is, in effect, a model derived from the literature and experience of single units of government. This means that we are using a planning system spawned from intragovernmental experience, and we are then attempting to apply it to an intergovernmental situation. That is to say, we are posing the question whether public sector planning, as it is known and practised within individual political units, can be applied overall in a federal environment with its essential interaction of such units. This makes it essential to appreciate that the definition, or concept, of planning employed in this study remains constant throughout.

A few other aspects of this study need to be mentioned at the outset. It is meant to be an analysis of the *public* sector; but it should be realized that the public/private sector dichotomy is often a blurred one in most democracies, especially as public sector planning involves very close relations with, influences, and is profoundly influenced by events in, the private sector. The emphasis in the study is more on the state or provincial governments than either the national or local governments. There are two reasons for this emphasis. The first is that the problems for local governments in most federations are basically similar to those which state/provincial governments face in relation to the national government. The second is that the problems posed by federations for national governments in their public sector planning are more self-evident than those for the lower levels. For example, it is obvious that the Australian or Canadian national governments face many more difficulties than the national government of any unitary system simply because they do not have as much control over priority determination within the public sector of the whole nation. To put it another way, it is the state/provincial governments which are the far more interesting elements for a study on this topic because they are more constrained — being the middle level of a three-tiered structure having two other levels of government, with the potential to interfere more directly with their priority determination, and therefore interfering with their capacity to think ahead.

This study assumes that the reader has a complete familiarity with the history and institutions of Australian, and to a lesser extent Canadian, federalism. Given the confines of the length allowed it has simply not been possible to give a full account of each institution or process being described.

Finally, this exercise broaches a number of disciplines. Its main orientation is in the literature and concepts of public administration, although it borrows heavily from the realms of public finance, political science, economics (theoretical and applied), and even accounting. But then public administration is itself a predatory discipline.

The first chapter defines "planning" as a system, and the second traces Australian experience in public sector planning with some observations also on Canadian experience. The third chapter analyses various theories of federalism and the principal features of various federal systems, in an effort to identify those characteristics which are basically compatible or incompatible with the concept of planning as defined in the first chapter. The fourth chapter examines the actual practice of federalism in Australia and Canada using the framework of the preceding chapter, to identify in an empirical way the hindrances which emerge when the planning concept meets the reality of a federal situation. Each of the three subsequent chapters takes up one of the major hindrances for a more detailed examination, and chapter 8 discusses conditional funding.

The concluding chapter examines the basis of the hindrances which emerge in an effort to determine their validity and intractability. Suggestions are then made for reforms which might overcome any basic hindrances to public sector planning. In order to be practical and realistic, the only reforms contemplated are those possible within the existing constitutional context of both federations.

The basic assumption of the exercise throughout is that the essential features of a public sector planning system can be applied in concept and practice in democratic federations. The case study of Australia compared with Canada is used in an attempt to prove or disprove that assumption.

Identifying the Hindrances

As already intimated, the methodology employed in pursuing our objective includes an examination of the concept of federalism to ascertain aspects of that concept which appear, superficially at least, to be at odds with the components of our planning concept. This proceeds to a survey, at least in a broad sense, of the Australian and Canadian federal systems, using our own distillation of the theories of federalism, to isolate any features of these two particular systems which seem, on the face of it, to pose obstacles of a greater or lesser kind to the superimposition of our planning framework upon them. However, this is not adequate for our purpose, and in order to assess the true consequences of these seemingly incompatible aspects, and, indeed, to identify the hindrances to the meshing of the two concepts in practice, we need to translate them into actual, tangible aspects of the federal systems we are studying. For example, it is one thing to recognize that the principle of divided sovereignty (one of the main elements of the federalism concept) is basically at odds with the process of coordination of hierarchy or resource allocation (elements of our planning system), but to analyse the degree and nature of that juxtaposition we have to study what happens "on the ground", through the expression of these concepts in the actual functioning of the federal systems. Ideally we should scrutinize all characteristics of these two countries for a complete inventory of the practicalities associated with our basic objective. However, as space and time preclude this, our method will be to identify the *major* aspects of the operation of the two federations which appear to present the most serious obstacles; "serious" in this case meaning those of lasting duration and magnitude in terms of the volume and significance of the resources involved. What is the best method we could use?

Our methodology incorporates two approaches:

1.   a review of all the available literature on the operation of these federal systems to determine whereabouts in the functioning of those systems the elements of our planning system breaks down; and
2.   interviews of a large number of participants intimately involved in these federal systems.

In the first approach we are, in effect, looking to find which portions of the federal political process are likely to pose the most obstacles for the achievement of such public sector processes as forecasting, harmonization of priorities, resource allocation, implementation and review, and also what is most likely to impede coordination within the system, particularly coordination which is democratically accountable. Our source material for this exercise includes government documents, the recorded words of politicians and other actors in the process, statistics of various kinds, description and analysis by third parties including academics who have observed the federal systems in action, and the results of related litigation.

In the light of all this literature it is impossible to escape the conclusion that the centre of our attention should be upon the margin between the levels of government, that is, the very point of interaction or interface at which problems of forecasting, priority harmonization, and coordination come into the sharpest focus, because it is at this point that the conflicts of federalism arise. There has been more written about this element of federalism than any other and, indeed, it is symptomatic of the nature of federalism itself. Moreover, if one accepts the argument advanced in a later chapter, that divided sovereignty is the main political hallmark of federalism, the logical place to assess the problems of operating a federal system is at the point where such sovereignty clashes; and that is unquestionably at the interface of the two levels of government. Naturally, there are faults within each of the discrete units of a federal system which hinder the attainment of public sector planning, just as there are in a unitary system of government, and we shall also examine those; but in a federal system it is the interaction between the sovereign levels which is more dominant. There are many perspectives of the interaction between levels of government, including the political, legal, administrative, and financial. The distinction between these perspectives is in some senses a false one because, for example, all activity is political activity, and an administrative action may well have financial and legal ramifications. Nonetheless, it is the case that the relationships between levels of government in federations, and especially in Australia and Canada, tend to be conducted within those categories represented by particular institutions and actors portraying each perspective, for example, politicians, lawyers, and public administrators of various kinds.

Studies of a comparable nature to this one in either Australia or Canada are rare, and as mentioned later, comparative studies of these two countries are also particularly scarce. One major piece of research which is comparable in its content and methodology is Simeon's study of federal-provincial negotiation in Canada on three major policy issues.[2] In that study Simeon combined a theoretical perspective based on literature review (especially the analogous field of international diplomacy), with empirical observations by means of interviews. Simeon's method was to interview in depth those who were most intimately involved in the particular issues. On this basis, his interviews concentrated heavily on public servants and particularly those in the central agencies, for example, finance and intergovernmental affairs. Clearly this involved the national government, but he found it adequate to study five provinces as representative of all provinces, those five being Quebec, Ontario, Manitoba, British Columbia, and New Brunswick.

The criteria used for selection of these provinces were:
1. the need for a regional distribution;
2. a distribution according to party in power;
3. size and relative wealth (size apparently being in terms of both geography and population, and wealth referring to per capita income per province)

Simeon's five provinces accounted for eighty per cent of Canada's population.

The methodology employed here is basically similar in that firstly, there is a blend of literature review and empirical analyses; secondly, the concentration is on those intimately involved in the process under consideration, which means a heavy emphasis on public servants; and third, there is a representative group of subnational government units. However, as this is also a comparative study, a further criterion has to be added to those used by Simeon in his choice of provinces, namely, that there has to be a similarity in the "profiles" of the Australian states and Canadian provinces being chosen for analysis whenever and wherever possible. It is to be noted that there has never been a *comparative* study (of this kind) undertaken.

In the Australian case the criterion of representativeness is relatively easy to satisfy because there are only six states. Interviews were conducted in five of them, Western Australia being the only one excluded (and the two territories).

The provinces chosen in Canada for intensive interviews were British Columbia, Alberta, Ontario, Quebec, New Brunswick, and Nova Scotia; but some interviews were also conducted in Saskatchewan and Manitoba. This selection of provinces meets Simeon's criteria, and it also complies with the comparative requirement because the sample in both countries includes:

1. the largest and second largest state/province in terms of population;
2. resource-rich states/provinces;
3. rurally-oriented states/provinces;
4. maritime states/provinces;
5. small states/provinces in respect of both population and geographical size.

It must be emphasized that the initial access to Canadian interviewees was made possible predominantly through the Canadian "Special Visitors' Programme", which had the effect of gaining access to the most senior officials involved (inevitably permanent heads and ministers). It also meant that they were prepared to close their doors, order all telephone calls to be diverted, and continue the interview until it was completed to the satisfaction of the interviewer. It was possible for written material to be readily available (all interviewees had been given prior notice in writing of the sorts of questions and issues to be discussed), including a considerable amount of confidential and internal documentation. In this respect, one should also make some observation about the readier access gained by researchers from another country compared with domestic prophets. All of these factors were equally in evidence for a series of follow-up interviews conducted on a second Canadian visit. It should be emphasized that the interviewing process in total took six years, and about half of the Canadian interviewees in 1977 were reinterviewed in 1979. Table 1 gives an indication of the state of domicile of the interviewees.

The bulk of these interviewees came from finance departments and/or treasuries; policy coordination departments or prime minister's departments or the Privy Council office; Coordinator-General's Department; Public Service Boards or Commissions; and especially departments and agencies responsible for intergovernmental relations (entities which have appeared increasingly in both countries in the 1970s).

Interviews on the subject matter of this study were not suitable for any highly structured questions or quantitative responses. The basic aim was to have respondents stipulate what they saw as the main hindrances to the implementation of this planning system and ask them to apply it to their own situation — not a difficult mental exercise since nearly all respondents were permanent heads (deputy ministers) or divisional heads, or cabinet ministers themselves, and they would be the very people responsible for the operation of such a planning system if it were introduced. The interviews were never less than one and a half hours and were often three to

Table 1   Interview participants

Australia	
Government	Number of interviewees
National	31
New South Wales	14
Victoria	8
Queensland	11
South Australia	5
Tasmania	4
Others*	11
Total	84

Canada	
Government	Number of interviewees
National	22
Ontario	8
Quebec	8
British Columbia	7
Alberta	6
New Brunswick	8
Nova Scotia	7
Saskatchewan	2
Manitoba	4
Others*	16
Total	88

* "Others" includes academic, local government officials, political party officials, and pressure group representatives.

four hours, without any interruption, so that time was available for deep probing of verbal responses and requests for explanatory and backup material. It must be said that the interview process was slightly easier in Canada where all levels of government have been involved in various attempts to introduce forward planning and rationalization of priority determination in the recent past. Also, most of the Canadian interviewees were familiar with the European and North American planning techniques referred to earlier. Thus they were able to grasp the concepts immediately and readily understand the object of the exercise. Indeed, some had themselves been concerned about the lack of forward thinking and rational resource allocation in intergovernmental relations. In any event, virtually all the Canadian interviewees grasped the aim of the exercise very readily. The situation was a little more difficult in Australia where, as already outlined, there has been little experience with public sector planning within either the national or state levels, and almost most of the officials have extremely limited knowledge of the attempts at planning for the public sector made in other countries. This is especially true of the state governments in Australia. There is another basic difference between Australian public servants and their Canadian counterparts, which will be examined more deeply later, but which does have a bearing on the interview process. A great many senior Canadian civil servants have served in both national and provincial governments, that is, there is a high degree of mobility amongst middle to top civil servants between the two levels of government. This is not so in Australia, and it means, among other things, that Canadian civil servants have a readier appreciation of the role of their counterparts in the other level of government, and even in other units at the same level in the case of the provinces. Both these factors were responsible for a somewhat smoother process of interview amongst Canadians than Australians although Australian respondents, for the most part, had no difficulty grasping the intention of the exercise once it was elaborated upon in more detail. In the case of all officials from both countries cooperation was readily forthcoming.

The detailed views of the respondents appear in the following chapters, aggregated to preserve confidentiality. Here we can observe which broad aspects of the federal process were regarded as providing the severest obstacles to the introduction of the planning system envisaged. Amongst the numerous suggestions made by respondents four aspects in particular were regarded as being so vital as to dominate all others. They were:

1. fiscal transfers from the national to subnational level — in particular, the mixture of unconditional and conditional funding;
2. the allocation of functions and roles between levels of government and the difficulty of preserving a stable pattern in this respect;
3. working with intergovernmental agreements, including their political, constitutional, and legal uncertainties;
4. the difficulty of maintaining accountability to the public through all aspects of intergovernmental relations, and especially if planning processes were to be introduced.

We examine the first three of these aspects in separate chapters, and the issue of accountability is raised within each chapter. The technique is to research what available literature has to say on the subject and augment that by the responses of interviewees, followed in a concluding chapter by analysis of the main arguments which emerge.

It will be noticeable that the elements outlined are all concerned with the interface of the levels of government in these two federations, and this accords with our earlier observations. However, both the literature and the interview responses indicate that there are also aspects of the internal functioning of each unit within the federation which are not conducive to public sector planning. Some of these do become involved in the intergovernmental process, because a unit of government that cannot plan its own activities is going to find it quite difficult to participate in public sector planning on an intergovernmental basis. Consequently this element also features in the discussion within each of the subsequent chapters. It must be stressed that no claim is being made that these areas/issues (namely, financial transfers, allocation of functions, and intergovernmental agreements), encompass all of the hindrances to the attainment of public sector planning in these federations. What *is* being asserted is that these are the major ones, and that a reasonably intensive study of them will produce a reliable indication of the nature and scale of the impediments which federalism creates for any attempt to introduce the sort of comprehensive planning envisaged. The concluding chapter considers the intractability or otherwise of these impediments.

1

Planning

In the Australian context planning is no longer a neutral word, mainly because it has become too closely associated in the mind of the public with the policies and experience of totalitarian regimes in second world countries in the 1950s and 1960s. This association resulted mainly from constant use of the word in that context by conservative political forces which, in appearance at least, were violently opposed to any form of government intervention in the economy, and laid stress on reduction of the size of the public sector. For this reason alone, the word needs to be carefully defined whenever it is used.

Another reason for careful definition is the fact that many disciplines have claimed the term "planning" for their own and have prefixed it with their own adjectives. Every one of those disciplines and its associated profession has its own body of theory, knowledge, and technique, often purporting to be *the* superior framework for planning a whole society. Thus there is economic planning, town planning, regional planning, manpower planning, social planning, and so on. The literature on each of these is now immense. However, what they all have in common, is that planning is really a process, irrespective of the field in which it is practised or the resource to which it is directed. This study will use the word planning to mean a process, or more accurately a *system*.

Systems Theory

It is most useful to define planning as a system for a number of reasons. In the first place, the task before us is particularly amenable to the application of systems theory itself. We are seeking to apply a concept, namely, planning, to an environment, namely, federalism, in an effort to determine whether that concept can survive in that environment; if not, then why not. If the concept of planning can be conceived systematically, it can also provide a rigid tool for comparative analysis across the two federal countries under review. Systems theory is acknowledged to be particularly useful for comparative purposes.[1] It is also regarded as being particularly useful for empirical analysis. As Young states, in the context of systems thinking, the key elements of "an approach", and specifically a scientific approach, include:

(a) A systematic orientation and perspective for cutting into a subject area,

(b) Some statements concerning the central questions or types of questions that should be posed,

(c) Criteria of relevance for mapping out and selecting data for analysis, and

(d) Some guidelines for hierarchical ordering of both questions and data in terms of significance in any given analysis.[2]

Characteristics of various approaches to systems theory include such focuses as concepts that are primarily descriptive, factors that regulate or maintain systems, and dynamic but nondisruptive change either through internally generated processes or responses to altered environmental conditions. Young sees two fundamental points of view regarding the basic notions of systems theory, one being as an integrated and generalized set of concepts, hypotheses, and validated propositions; and the second being as a set of techniques and as a framework for a systematic process of analysis. The various definitions of system, he maintains, embody "the idea of a group of objects or elements standing in some characteristic structural relationship to one another and interacting on the basis of certain characteristic processes".[3]

Other advantages claimed for systems theory, which are of particular relevance for this study, include its capacity to cope with dynamic patterns of interaction and not just static relationships; to achieve explicitness of categories so that the framework of reference will not shift as new "facts are introduced; to integrate variables that don't fall within a single discipline; to attain a degree of explicitness which helps to reveal incompleteness; and to generate hypotheses by indicating structural similarities to other subject matters".[4]

Of course the use of systems theory by political scientists is really a relatively recent phenomenon, although Spiro traces the origin of the use of systems theory in political theory back to Hobbes, and says that he does this "to emphasize that anyone who attempts to study politics scientifically must at least implicitly think of politics as though it were functioning as some sort of system. That is, he must assume that more or less regular relationships can be discerned among various aspects of politics and between phenomena he describes as political, and certain other phenomena not so described."[5]

Systems theory has found considerable use in political science in recent times for studies ranging from the very broad overview of politics itself, as, for example, when Miller employs the approach to analyse what he calls "recurrent political situations" which include both situations and personalities; to the formulation of models for understanding international relations; and the clarification of the functioning of single political systems, such as David Easton's extremely useful input/output model.[6] This provides in turn a springboard for attempts (with varying degrees of success), at international comparative studies of the structural/functional kind.[7] It has also found a ready application in theory designed to explain the behaviour of organizations operating within the environment of the political system itself.[8]

Naturally it is difficult for us to predict what kind of system the one we shall define will prove to be, especially whether it will be homeostatic, but it must be stressed, at this early stage, that the methodology being employed in this study is in many ways the reverse of that generally encountered in systems theory. Here we are constructing a system, a planning·system, and then endeavouring to place it in an environment, or two environments, to assess its adaptability, pattern maintenance, stability, and especially its relationship with its environment, so that boundary maintenance will be of significance. With respect to the last mentioned factor, it is of relevance to note that systems theorists have conceded that the concept of "boundary" can also be used to apply to geographical, that is, spatial boundaries (spatial considerations are embedded in the structure and functioning of federations).

Since our analysis will also seek to be longitudinal in its time sequence it needs the capacity, which systems theory gives, to handle historical change through the allowance of a dynamic relationship between the elements of the system. Of particular use in historical analysis is the by-product of systems theory — communications models. The chief exponent in this field, Karl Deutsch, has a number of important points to make for a study of his kind when he clarifies the difference between his feedback (dynamic) and equilibrium (static) approaches. In a feedback approach the goal situation being sought is outside the goal seeking system and not inside it; the system itself is not isolated from its environment but, on the contrary, depends for its functioning upon a constant stream of information from the environment, as well as a constant stream of information concerning its own performance. Moreover, the goal may be a changing one, and it may change both its position and even its speed and direction. The goal may be approached indirectly by a course, or a number of possible courses, around a set of obstacles. As Deutsch observes, in politics, it appears as the problem of maintaining a *strategic purpose* throughout a sequence of changing tactical goals.[9]

Needless to say, there are some shortcomings of systems analysis which have to be recognized by those who seek to apply it. There is, for example, a strong tendency to become overwhelmed by the internal relationship of the system itself, and thereby lose sight of its relationship with its environment, which is akin to a preoccupation with means rather than ends. The goals of the system should be kept constantly in view, and this is related to the warning, given by many systems theorists, that the analyst should never overlook the fact that the system exists in an environment, leading to the attendant difficulty of boundary maintenance.[10]

Attention has been focused on the concept of boundary maintenance here because it is of special relevance to the methodology of this study. In systems theory, boundary maintenance means, in its simplest expression, the difficulty of defining a system in such a way that the limits of that system are identifiable and are capable of being sustained when that system is examined within its environment. In other words, the degree to which the boundaries of the system can be maintained is a major indicator of the degree of integrity of the system itself. Thus the usefulness of the concept in this study becomes apparent, in that we have to define a planning system whose integrity is established so that its boundaries can be maintained when it is applied to the federal environment. This is especially important when the planning system is going to be applied to two federal environments. In this context it can be seen to be imperative that the boundaries of the planning system remain discrete and clear, or else its use as a comparative tool will be reduced. In short, our planning model will be the system, the two federations will be the environment, and the model will have to be formulated in such a way that it corresponds to systems theory, including the important requirement that its boundaries are capable of being maintained when it is applied.

Other Theoretical Strands

Whilst the rise of systems theory in political science has become more prevalent, it has been other strands of the progressive refinement of the discipline which have actually analysed planning as a process. Until recently this has been a feature predominantly of public administration, which is regarded here as one element of the more all-embracing discipline of political science. Whilst it is something of an oversimplification, it is nonetheless true, that until relatively recently political scientists were more concerned with the ends of politics, and those who regarded public administration as their speciality, emphasized the means of government. Both "camps" are now moving into theories of public choice and public policy formulation, which have served as the catalyst towards demonstrating that neither politics nor administration can be concerned solely with means but must take account of ends, and acknowledging the fact that political actors (which include government administrators) are positive elements in the political system of which they form a part.

The most interesting way to trace this development is within the evolution of the literature of public administration, and that, in twentieth century terms, begins with organization theorists like the Frenchman, Fayol — an industrialist who generalized from his own long and successful experience. For Fayol administration was but one (albeit the most important one) of the six basic operations which occur in business, the other five being technical, commercial, financial, security, and accounting. This function of administration was then fragmented into five main aspects, that is, to plan, to organize, to command, to coordinate, and to control. Thus planning was for him but part of the function of administration. However, as Urwick points out, the word Fayol used — "purveyance" — has been translated as "to plan" but it really covers two functions — to foretell the future as well as to prepare for it. It is unmistakably clear from his formulation that he conceived of forecasting leading to a plan. A similar view of the place of planning in a scientific management approach was provided by Taylor; and it also found expression in Gulick and Urwick's classic *Papers on the Science of Administration*, which contained their well-known acronym for the work of a chief executive — PODSCORB, or Planning, Organising, Directing, Staff, Coordinating, Reporting, and Budgeting. The definition of planning within this pattern is: "Planning, that is working out in broad outline the things that need to be done and the methods for doing them to accomplish the purpose set for the enterprise".[11] A little later in their theoretical formulation Gulick and Urwick speak of the need to aggregate work units and the principles which can be used in this task. Each worker in each position could, they believe, be characterized by (1) the *major purpose* he was serving, (2) the *process* he was using, (3) the *person* or things being dealt with or served, and (4) the *place* where the service was rendered. They acknowledge a need at times for a selection to be made as to which of the principles should be given precedence. Each principle had its own inherent advantages, and in respect of organization by major purpose, the advantages are claimed to be that it makes more certain the accomplishment of any given broad purpose or project; from the standpoint of self-government, organization by purpose seems to conform best to the objectives of government as they were recognized and understood by the public; and it apparently "served as the best basis for eliciting the energies and loyalties of the personnel and for giving a focus and central device to the whole activity, because purpose is understandable by the entire personnel down to the last clerk and inspector".[12]

Some of the dangers of organizing according to major purpose include the impossibility of clearly dividing all the work of governments into a few such major purposes which do not overlap extensively; that the thought of purpose will downplay emphasis on process to an extent that the organization will not keep up to date with new technology; that the contribution of single elements will be lost in preoccupation with the overall single purpose; the tendency to overcentralization within the organization; and the danger of self-sufficiency with the potential to drift towards independence and "even from democratic control itself".[13]

Urwick, writing just a little later (in the period of the second world war), speaks of planning in danger of becoming a "blessed word — one of the major curses of society" (thereby reflecting the keen interest in planning as a panacea for postwar development). But for Urwick "forecasting enters into process, with a plan or planning. The administrator, having made up his mind what the future holds, has got to do something about it",[14] unlike the postwar utopians who, he says, seem as if they couldn't make the arrangements for a school treat without muddling up the buns and the tennis balls. Clearly then, planning encompasses forecasting plus action, the latter being dependent on the former. His observations about the nature of forecasting hold significance for us too in our exercise. It was Urwick's belief that investigation or research was the principle which must underlie the process of forecasting, but investigation itself had to be conducted in the light of certain intellectual principles, which included:

* *The Principle of Determinism.* Every social phenomenon is the result of definite and ascertainable causes.
* *The Principle of Relation.* Facts which are to form the basis of action must be in terms of the environment in which the action takes place. This involves
* *The Principle of Analysis.* The scheme of classification must be appropriate to the activity investigated.
* *The Principle of Definition.* The facts must be stated in terms which correspond with the underlying sciences on which the activity investigated is based.
* *The Principle of Measurement.* The facts must be stated in terms of definite units or standards.[15]

It was probably during the period prior to the Depression and New Deal activities in the United States, that the politics-administration dichotomy was perceived to be both a valid description of government activity and a normative statement as well. As long as administration was regarded as a self-contained activity it was easy for principles of organization, such as those enumerated, to evolve free from any "political interference". No wonder that planning, along with all the other so-called activities or functions of administrators, could be regarded as a completely rational process. Although the Chicago School, and even Gulick himself, questioned the validity of the politics/administration dichotomy through the late 1930s, that emphasis continued to hold sway (particularly in other countries like Australia where many would contend that it still predominates academic and practical discussion in the discipline).

It was out of this questioning of the so-called principles of public administration that yet another stream of the discipline arose, which has an important bearing on our attempts to understand the lineage of the planning concept. Writing in the late 1940s Herbert Simon attacked the "principles" as being superficial and pointed out that they occurred in pairs, like proverbs. "For almost every principle one can find an equally plausible and acceptable contradictory principle".[16] Amongst other things, Simon then discounted the possibility of separating the means from the ends of government, and in so doing confronted the concept of rational decision making in government. For various reasons, said Simon, it was simply not possible to achieve a perfectly rational process of decision making in the traditional Weberian sense of means/ends relationships. Because of the nature of the situation, and the limited capacity of the actors, what could occur was only "bounded rationality" whereby decision makers would "satisfice" rather than maximize in their choice of a course of action. Speaking specifically of planning, Simon distinguishes between "substantive planning", where the individual or organization makes broad decisions about the values being aimed at, the methods to be employed, and the information needed to be able to make particular decisions within the limits of the prescribed policy to implement the decisions; and "procedural planning", which involves the establishment of mechanisms to direct attention and information in such a way as to cause specific routine decisions to conform with the "substantive plan". In other words there is, here again, the link between desired goals and actual action taken to achieve those goals. As Simon puts it elsewhere: "In the practical world, plans are characterized as 'utopian' whose success depends on wished-for behaviour on the part of many individuals, but which fail to explain how this wished-for behaviour will, or can, be brought about".[17] Ultimately Simon speaks of a planning *process*, which he describes as a series of psychological processes which consist in selecting general criteria of choice, and then particularizing them by application to specific situations. Using examples drawn from engineering, he concludes that the planning procedure is a compromise whereby only the most plausible alternatives are worked out in detail.

As is now well known, Simon's emphasis on decision making as the central element in administrative behaviour produced a veritable minefield of criticism which gradually built up into a body of decision making theory. Self, for example, claims that Simon's model is not all that different from the logic of ends-means analysis,[18] and it is certain that latter day critics saw little distinction either. Caiden assesses Simon's efforts as an attempt to "reform the discipline of public administration on rationality, as opposed to the folklore of scientific principles, and on a logical positivist bent to behaviouralism centred on the concept of rational decision making that minimized nonrationality content".[19]

Caiden also makes the extremely important observation that Simon's concern with the end product of administration — decision making — coincided with the redefinition of public administration as a study of public policy making and application. Taken together, these two streams of the discipline represent a force of considerable importance to an understanding of the likely operation of any system of planning in a political environment, because decision making and/or policy making lie at the heart of the planning process.

The contribution of the decision making theorists has been substantial, and each consecutive addition to theory has further refined our understanding of this process. Thus, for example, Lasswell writing in the mid-1950s, identified seven functional stages through which, he claimed, all decisions are processed:

1. information (problem identification and information search);
2. recommendation (formulation of alternatives);
3. prescription (sanctioned selection of alternatives);
4. invocation (provisional enforcement);
5. application (specific implementation);
6. appraisal (monitoring, and review of the decision and its effects);
7. termination (renewal, revision, or repeal).[20]

This process can be seen to possess a logical sequence reminiscent of the sort of rational decision making which Simon explored and found to be possible in only a limited sense. By contrast, Braybrooke and Lindblom believe that the obstacles confronting political decision makers frustrate any attempts by them to approximate the synoptic ideal, and instead, such actors exploit, in quite systematic ways, adaptive strategies for decision making. The most important and commonplace of these strategies, they claim, is that of "disjointed incrementalism". The key variable for them is whether change is large or small. They conclude:

> It becomes clearer now why political policy, in its focus on increments of change, also shows other characteristics — it is remedial, serial, and exploratory ... To pursue incremental changes is to direct policy towards specific ills — the nature of which is continually being re-examined — rather than toward comprehensive reforms; it is also to pursue long-term changes through sequences of moves. Avoiding social cleavage along ideological lines, which is exacerbated when issues of ultimate principle are raised, incremental politics explores a continuing series of remedial moves on which some agreement can be developed even among members of opposing ideological camps.[21]

Space prevents a full analysis of this theory, but it is sufficient, anyway, for our purpose to focus on what Braybrooke and Lindblom call the "Margin-Dependent choice" in their strategy, where they distinguish three salient features:

1. only those policies are considered whose known or expected consequent social states differ from each other incrementally;
2. only those policies are considered whose known or expected consequences differ incrementally from the status quo;
3. examination of policies proceeds through comparative analysis of no more than the marginal or incremental differences in the consequent social states rather than through an attempt at more comprehensive analysis of the social states.[22]

Consequently, they conclude that "incremental evaluation is quite clearly different from the construction of a rational-deductive system".

Actually, the essence of this approach is probably presented more clearly in Lindblom's work on the policy-making process. He says that whilst one is tempted to think that policy is made through a sequence of steps (of the kind put forward by Lasswell), this tends to view policy making as though it were the product of one governing mind, which is clearly not the case. According to Lindblom it "fails to evoke or suggest the distinctively political aspects of policymaking, its apparent disorder, and the consequent strikingly different ways in which policies emerge".[23] Some of the constraints which operate on rational decision making are later listed by Lindblom as including defining the policy problem, complexity and inadequate information, difficulties in organizing goals and values, the difficulty of agreement on criteria for policy, the public interest criterion, resistances to analysis (including the irrationality of mankind and the bias of analysts), and the question of who can be trusted.

The proliferation of public policy studies and attempts to establish a policy science are now so numerous as to prohibit a comprehensive evaluation. Each has a different perspective, and many fall somewhere on a continuum from the notion of the completely rational policy process, through the highly incremental "partisan-mutual adjustment" model, offered again by Braybrooke and Lindblom, to the so-called science of "muddling through" which is the focus of other studies by Lindblom. Another author in this stream, Dror, seeks to stress that all forms of process may be involved in decision making, including the most intuitive as well as the most rational or scientific. Etzioni attempts to put a similar viewpoint, and offers his "mixed scanning" model as a compromise, and more comprehensive description of policy-making processes.[24]

So we have come full circle, as it were, although it must be acknowledged that most contributors do have fresh insights to offer — such as Vickers's concept of the "multi-valued choice" and the need for a "balancing" as well as an optimizing function in all decision making. Vickers's concepts of "appreciative judgement" and the *art* of judgment, stress his central belief that such appreciative behaviour involves making judgments of value no less than judgments of reality.[25] In other words, to borrow another of his phrases — "science is human". Friedrich sums up the view of many other theorists when he says that "every decision is a response to a change in environment of the decision maker", and he goes on to make a clear distinction between public decisions and individual or group decisions.[26] Writing in the mid 1960s, Dye explained that neither traditional (that is, structural and philosophical) political science, nor modern (behavioural) political science, had dealt directly with the content of public policy, whereas political scientists were currently shifting their attention to public policy — to the description and explanation of the causes and consequences of government activity, that is, what governments do, why they do it, and what difference it makes. Whereas the policy maker is decision-oriented, the policy scientist is theory-oriented. According to Dye, one factor contributing to these differing perspectives is the symbolic use of policy (or the fact that individuals have perceptions of government action and consequent attitudes towards it). What governments *say* is as important as what they *do*, and policy analysts must acknowledge this fact so that they don't become solely preoccupied with examining the actions of government. This is an element which Edwards and Sharkansky are also at pains to emphasize. For them it is *public opinion* which serves as just as important a constraint on policy makers as all the other aspects which have already been outlined by other authors.[27]

In a preface to a comparative analysis of public policies, Rose formulates a model of political change which bears reasonably close resemblance to processes we have already encountered. Public policy, he says, is best conceived in terms of a *process* rather than in terms of policy making, because the policy-making framework is narrow. He concentrates upon the decision-making stage of the policy process. His model involves the following:

1. the initial state;
2. placing a condition on the agenda of political controversy;

3. the advancement of demands;
4. reviewing resources and constraints;
5. shifting from nondecision to decision;
6. the content of choice;
7. implementing policies;
8. the production of outputs;
9. impact upon society;
10. the routinization of feedback;
11. deroutinizing a stable state (the second step in another cycle of the policy process), thereby once again placing a condition on the agenda of political controversy.

He then builds on this framework to develop four models of public policy — the static, cyclical, linear, and discontinuous. Thus it can be seen that the key element of his process is that it is sequential and systemic.[28]

One difficulty with most of these theorists of decision making and policy making, is that one cannot be sure whether they are, at all times, simply describing a process which they believe to be empirically observable, or whether they are not also making a normative judgment, and arguing that the process they identify is the one which *ought* to be employed. This is a familiar problem in the social sciences, and whilst it doesn't matter for our purposes, it can be important if one is tempted to assume that theories abstracted from certain political systems or cultures or situations or policy "fields" can be transplanted into others.

One more recent school of thought which confronts this question of polemic versus analytic ("what ought" rather than "what is") is the "new public administration". We have not the space to analyse all aspects of this product of the 1970s, but suffice to say that it rejects strongly the public administration "as means" approach, and argues that analysts ought to pay careful attention to the impact of public policies and not just their processes. It is also, they claim, important to recognize that the values of the policy maker (including the administrator) are an important ingredient in determining the policy outcome. As one prominent American writer put it: "To define public administration as 'the management of men and materials in the accomplishment of the purposes of the state' will not do for a number of reasons".[29] We might say that the overwhelming concern of the new public administration is that government bureaucrats are enmeshed in their environment to such an extent that they are irrevocably bound to a continuous but flexible quest for policy that is in the public interest. It is also necessary to recognize that public servants should have goals, and these goals should be related to efficacy rather than solely equity and/or efficiency. This leads to the assertion that the goals of government bureaucracies will correspond automatically, as it were, with the public interest or the social optimum.[30]

It is also this concern over the intermingling of means and ends in public policy which has led political scientists to venture into association with other disciplines. (The old associations with concepts of scientific management have already been mentioned, as well as analogies and models borrowed from engineering, natural science, and psychology.) The most recent example of this phenomenon is the "public choice" school, comprised of: economists who realize the imperfections of their models of economic behaviour caused by political intrusions; and political scientists who have long been on a quest for more rigorous conceptualizations of terms like "the public interest", "optimum resource allocation", and "flexibility". Some people would no doubt argue that this merely represents an inevitable eventual return of the two "disciplines" to the fold of "political economy" itself, from which they were hived off over two centuries ago, but whatever else the movement may represent, its significance for this analysis is that it is an attempt to understand the nature of the processes of resource and value allocation, and therefore the determination of priorities, which lies at the heart of any planning process.[31]

It is clear from the above résumé, albeit a brief one, that a significant body of theory exists of relevance to the concept of planning. Some of the characteristics of interest about this theory include the fact that it tends to be culture-bound in the sense that each author portrays policy making, or decision making, according to the manner in which it takes place within his own political system. There is also a certain uneasiness about whether each author is merely describing a process, or engaging also in polemic and advocating that the process outlined ought to be the one adopted. One discernible trend in the sequence of this theoretical refinement is that writers have come to acknowledge more explicitly the political nature of the environment within which their particular model or system is to operate. This leads to another highly significant factor — that the distinction between means and ends is becoming much more blurred, and that theorists have recognized the effects of the process of policy making upon the content, or outcome, of that policy. In particular, the old dichotomy between politics and administration, so prominent a feature of the literature of public administration, is now all but forgotten.

In any event, the key terminology nowadays in the disciplines which relate to this study includes words like priorities, choice, optimal, public interest, functional, goals, etc. These words in themselves convey an impression of order or system or purpose, and bear testimony to the usefulness of speaking about government in the systems context. All the world's a stage and the men and women are the players, and all the world is also a system — a social system — of which the public sector is a subsystem with its own players and resources. In that subsystem it is financial resources which are usually paramount, especially as other resources, notably human and physical, become translated eventually into fiscal terms. Hence, this study is about a system — a planning system — and that system lays particular emphasis on finance; and so for the most part we shall be using data and language related to money. What has to be recognized is that social systems, unlike those of the natural sciences, are open rather than closed systems. In other words, it is precisely because we are dealing with human activity, that the activity will not always be completely rational, in the sense that it will not always conform to patterns or laws. For this reason our planning system, like all systems derived in the social sciences, cannot be expected to be infallible in its predictive capacity.

Comparative Studies

It can be demonstrated empirically that those governments (or political systems) which have entered into *and sustained* some form of planning, be it planning for the whole society or just for the public sector, have ultimately refined their planning processes until they resemble *systems* of action. The countries which have entered into this form of planning can be divided fairly clearly into four categories. (There would be five categories if we also considered countries which adopted planning processes in wartime, but our concern here is with planning attempts which have been sustained.)

The first group comprises those with command economies, for example, USSR, China, and the Soviet bloc. They began the modern day process of planning for fixed periods, in the sense of establishing targets and manipulating the society towards the achievement of those targets. Having complete political control over all resources is the unique feature of these countries, and they have gradually settled into regular cycles of planning, usually for five year periods. Then there are the third world or developing countries which have desired rapid economic and social development and have employed planning as a means towards that end. In these cases the objectives are clear, limited, and strongly desired, creating the necessary preconditions for coordination and unity of effort to allow for government coercion in planning mechanisms. Moreover, planning in developing countries has often been encouraged by developed donor countries, who want to see some sort of blueprint for future progress in the countries to whom they are giving aid. Whatever the reasons, various developing countries now have clearly identifiable *systems* of planning which have lasted over many planning periods, even when the targets of the plan have not been met. Apart from the actual experience of developing countries, the theories which have been developed to describe their process of development portray the planning experience in a systemic manner.[32]

Next there are the countries of Western Europe which have experimented with indicative planning. France is probably the most notable example although there are others such as the Netherlands, Belgium, and Sweden. In the case of France it is not without significance that the impetus for such planning began when the French economy was devastated in World War II, the goal of reconstruction was of major importance, and Marshall funds were on hand to assist. It was in that environment that Jean Monet was able to translate earlier theories about the role of the state into a positive and coherent planning framework in a democratic free enterprise context. The significance of this development is that prior to the advent of Monet-style indicative planning, there were only two choices or models available in respect of planning — one being the command economy and the other being some sort of extension of traditional annual budgeting. Indicative planning was a new middle way and in France, after three planning periods, the system of planning emerged — incorporating a preparation phase, an elaboration phase, and an implementation phase. Even when the plans missed their targets and various participants disagreed with the content of the plan, and even as it became transformed from the narrow economic first plan to the broad social seventh plan, the natural process or system of planning remained intact, based as it was on Monet's belief that it is necessary to raise people's expectations and remove uncertainty to ensure that resources go into pursuits that will be productive in the long term. A planning process in which there is widespread participation gives that assurance.

Speaking in the context of the experience of economic planning experiments in developed democratic countries, Friedrich makes the observation that:

> The clamour for planning, misunderstood as technicalization of value-related decisions and policies, is ill-conceived. *Planning only makes sense, to repeat it once more, within the context of rational decision making based upon prevailing, in other words, communal, values and beliefs.*[33]

Friedrich also addresses himself to the question of the potential for democratic planning and concludes that it is feasible, given basic common objectives in the society, and mechanisms to ensure the accountability of the planners. Shonfield expresses the same sentiment when he says that economic planning, of the kind adopted in France, is the most characteristic expression of the new capitalism, and whilst it reflects the determination to take charge rather than be driven by events, it has democratic elements built into it — "the recognition of certain limits which the spontaneous choices of free people necessarily impose on the activity of planning however benevolent and wise its intent". These limitations, he says, are of two kinds: limits on the range of behaviour that can be regulated and limits on the manner in which these decisions can be translated into fact. Shonfield's definition of planning is "the attainment of specific objectives of a long range character" and by long range he means four to five years.[34]

Finally, there are those countries like Britain, and occasionally the United States, that have endeavoured to inject more forward thinking into their public sector by way of an extension of the annual budgeting cycle. Notionally it is these examples which hold most interest for us because it is a public sector planning model we are endeavouring to construct, rather than one which spans the whole economy. In Britain, whilst attempts to introduce an indicative planning system for the whole economy during the

1960s failed rather miserably, more success has been achieved in the public sector as witnessed by the report of the Plowden Committee in 1961, marking a turning point in thinking about allocation of resources and priority determination.[35] The Committee recommended that each annual appropriation should be considered not so much in the light of last year's apportionment but in relation to the *total* amount of public resources available for the coming year and for subsequent years. The "forward looks" in public expenditure, spanning a rolling quinquennium, are not really a plan, it is true, because they are only projections and not commitments, but they do represent a regular cycle or system of forward projection, which came as a result of British Treasury initiatives plus the stimulus of a 1969 House of Commons Select Committee. They are now embodied in the PESC (Public Expenditure Survey Committee) and PAR (Programme Analysis Review). This is quite definitely a system of public sector forecasting which gets close to being a planning system, because it is intimately linked to the political process itself through the Select Committees on Expenditure, who use the projections for their deliberations on the annual budget, and feed some sort of information about political priorities into the executive, and its administration, which prepares the forecasts. Interviews conducted in Britain in association with this study revealed that the five year public expenditure projections definitely influence annual budgetary frameworks, and that a healthy relationship has developed between the British Treasury and the members of parliament. Moreover, the long term has now become a much stronger aspect of resource allocation (although it is not terribly evident from records of parliamentary proceedings), and it is clear that when politicians are presented with a long term picture which reflects priorities between components of the public sector, they are capable of adapting to a perspective longer than the current week. The British PESCPAR can be regarded very much as a model for public sector planning in Westminster-style governments.

The fundamental elements of the system outlined by Clarke in 1971 remain basically unchanged:

> PAR and PESC should be seen as one very large operation, consisting of a number of stages, designed to enable the government to:
> (a)   create an overall strategy across the whole range of those of its policies which involve significant use of resources.
> (b)   establish the objective of each department and the priorities between them, considered over a five year period, and in particular to determine which are the marginal objectives, affected by small changes up or down in the resources allocated to the department.
> (c)   determine the allocations between the departments, and so provide the resource framework within which each department can work.
> (d)   ensure that departments keep within their allocations, both of money and of civil service manpower.
> (e)   have an effective means of making day-to-day decisions within this

framework of overall strategies, departmental objectives and priorities, and departmental allocations.[36]

The systematic nature of the process is clear from Clarke's description. Similarly, the PPBS (Planning Programming Budgeting System), as it became fully fledged in the United States between 1965 and 1971 on a mandatory basis, and afterwards on a voluntary basis, was very definitely a *systematic* attempt at projection and resource commitment for the public sector, despite the polemic which has ensued attacking it and in its defence. Similarly, the surprising revival of zero base budgeting under the Carter administration, although short of the comprehensiveness of the former PPB concept, is nonetheless evidence of a desire for systematic thought about priority determination reflected through resource allocation. Indeed PPBS, in its conceptual framework, is probably the best example of a *system* of planning for the public sector yet devised, at least for democratic conditions. Perhaps the nature of PPBS is still most clearly understood from the words of President Johnson who, in introducing the system on a mandatory basis throughout the executive of the United States government in the mid 1960s, expressed the hope that the system would enable public decision makers to:

(1) Identify our national goals with precision and on a continuing basis;
(2) Choose among the goals the ones that are most urgent;
(3) Search for the alternative means of reaching those goals most effectively at the least cost;
(4) Inform ourselves not merely on next year's costs, but on the second, and third, and subsequent years' cost of our programmes;
(5) Measure the performance of our programmes to ensure a dollar's worth of service for each dollar spent.[37]

The programme budget, as it evolved, came to comprise a number of features which I have described elsewhere.[38] They include presentation on functional lines, concern with outputs rather than inputs, expression as far as possible in quantitative terms, a "zero-base" or fresh exercise in resource allocation each cycle, and most importantly, allocations projected over a number of years (multi-year costing). It is a *planning* system, and this means it is concerned with the formulation of long-term strategies for public expenditure. It is also a *programming* system, which entails the grouping of governmental outputs into classifications so that programmes with common objectives are considered together. The vital aspect of being a *budgetary* process means that having established plans, and structured programmes according to their outputs, those aspects are then related to the budgetary process; it is here that policy is translated into fiscal action. It is also a *system*, a continuing process, which persistently reviews past results, formulates new plans, and translates them into another annual budget.

A Planning System

In our attempts to build a planning system we have been assisted materially by the theory and practice of government as revealed in the literature and experience of a number of comparative countries. In this respect, Friedrich's portrayal of the symbiotic nature of the theory/practice relationship is particularly attractive:

> ... decision making, policy and planning are closely tied and ... under contemporary conditions of advanced industrial society, as well as in underdeveloped countries, these three processes cannot be considered in isolation. All depend upon a considerable measure of rationality, but it seems important not to overestimate this aspect. Whether it is a matter of individual decisions or group decisions, and whether they are public decisions or not, decisions are related to known alternatives, and tend in the last analysis to become dichotomic ... Planning procedures are, of course, particularly striking evidence of the complex character of nondichotomic decision-making. Public policy also is usually adopted in facing a multi-faceted reality in which a number of alternative ways of dealing with environmental challenges are handled. Planning is often involved in effective policy-making as the very process of sorting out such alternatives. And the opinion which sees an insoluble conflict between planning and democracy is untenable. Experience has shown further that the voters have a sense of appreciation for objective achievements. The electorate at the same time recognizes that there are other technical problems, and it reacts sharply when the values and beliefs of the community are at stake. If the often heard claim that planning is incompatible with democracy or with a free society is therefore untenable, contemporary evidence suggests that they both presuppose planning under contemporary conditions. Hence planning and public policy are least likely to be defective under such conditions as only democracy and freedom can provide.[39]

It is true that we have examined none of the polemic surrounding the planning notion, but this is simply because we are committed to the development of a planning concept that can be applied to the processes of federalism within two federal polities. It may well be that various authors can demonstrate the fallacy, or even danger, of planning attempts with all sorts of political hindrances, and it is clear that all political systems present obstacles of varying degrees of significance for planning. But our sole concern here is with the hindrances to planning which are found in federalism. So we require a definition of planning that is rigid in its construct, but capable of meaningful analysis of its environment.

The ideal solution would have been to utilize a definition of planning which had already been formulated, especially if it had been derived from practical experience. Since there has been no sustained planning, of the kind we have outlined, in either Australia or Canada, we cannot look to those sources for such a construct. To borrow the framework of the experiments of the most similar political systems, for example, Britain with its PESC/PAR concept and America with its PPBS, is not appropriate because those models are narrower than the framework we require.

A search through the literature for such an operational definition also proved fruitless because the definitions which are offered are either too vague or not sufficiently comprehensive to be of use in the rigorous analysis of the Australian and Canadian federations — which is our objective. For example, F.A. Bland called his textbook (the first public administration text in Australia) *Planning the Modern State*, but nowhere in that book did he provide an operational definition of planning; rather he seemed to equate it with forecasting. Andrew Shonfield, in his significant work, *Modern Capitalism*, which still contains the best description of indicative planning mechanisms in Western European countries, gives no actual definition of the planning concept. We might take the definition of planning provided by the best authority on PPBS, David Novick, because PPBS was actually introduced in Canada, albeit for a short period. Novick says: "Planning is the production of the range of meaningful potentials for selection of courses of action through a systematic consideration of alternatives". A little later he adds: "In planning one seeks a continual review of objectives and the means for their attainment".[40] Consider, for example, Friedrich himself, whose arguments have provided an enormously valuable underpinning for our understanding of the concept of planning. He barely offers any actual definition of planning and the closest he comes is to say that ". . . planning is a policy of very great complexity. Planning seeks to inter-relate various aspects of a field of public policy or maybe several aspects, an obvious example being economic and social planning".[41] A similar definition is offered by Lindblom, who calls planning "the interrelation of policies". David Easton's monumental work on systems theory does not even mention planning; Urwick, who places great emphasis on planning and its virtues, regards it mainly as a method; and Herbert Simon just calls planning a "complex chain of activities". Rather than prolong this point, we can turn to one of the best synthesizers of administrative theories, Peter Self, who discusses planning in relation to decision making, in relation to theories of polycentricity, and in relation to particular parts of the public sector. The closest he comes to a definition is when he is contrasting the planning process with the political process. He says: "Planning requires a harmonisation of interests along systematic lines and on a fairly durable basis".[42]

The Planning System

It becomes obvious that no available operational or theoretical definition is adequate for our purposes. Therefore one has been constructed. It has been conceived as a system and it purports to draw from the twin strands of (1) related theory, especially as it has emerged in the twentieth century, and (2) practical experience of governments in various parts of the world, predominantly in the post–World War II period. So, when the word planning is used hereafter, it refers to the following system.

1.   Forecasting

The first element in any planning system is forecasting. Unfortunately there is a tendency to equate forecasting with planning. Thus when government agencies prepare population projections or likely economic trends, they often speak as if these are plans. They are not; they are merely forecasts. It is worth noting that forecasting is not necessarily a neutral or objective exercise. The values of the expert performing the projection can be built into the techniques used, the population growth rates and family sizes thought likely to eventuate, the period over which debt charges and interest rates should be discounted, etc. Therefore care needs to be taken that any value judgments on which forecasts are based are made explicit.

2.   Formation of Priorities

After forecasts have been completed an attempt can be made to form priorities in the light of that data. Often forecasts are prepared on a number of sets of assumptions. One of them assumes no deliberate attempt to change natural phenomena, and the forecasts are made on the basis that natural trends will be allowed to continue. Other sets of projections can then be prepared assuming different scales and different types of intervention in natural developments. It is not necessary for the forecasts to have been prepared on these alternative patterns but it does aid the formation of priorities by narrowing the options. Naturally the forecasters need some guidance upon which to base the projections which involve intervention, and this is discussed in the review section (5). The formation of priorities is an "all-in" exercise which also contains heavy overtones of value judgment. In a democratic system it ought to be carried out by representative and accountable politicians rather than by bureaucrats alone; otherwise valid accusations of technocracy (government by public servants predetermining public policy) will follow.

3.   Allocation of Resources

Once broad priorities or objectives are determined, it remains to secure the means of attainment of those priorities, and the manner in which governments do this is to allocate financial resources. This is very definitely a political function because it is in the actual process of resource allocation that values-become most explicit. It is interesting to note that one definition of economics is the allocation of limited resources to unlimited ends, whereas a definition of political science is the *authoritative* allocation of values. A corollary is that in any society the allocation of public resources reflects the values of that society, and in a democracy that allocation must be an authoritative one. In a Westminster system that authority comes, in principle at least, from the elected representatives, who remain subject to dismissal if their allocation of resources does not find favour with the majority of the population. (We shall examine the practical flaws in the Westminster model as they affect this process later.)

4.   Implementation

It is only when forecasts, priorities, and ultimately resource allocation are implemented that they can be called a plan. Forecasts or projections that are never implemented, or acted upon, remain solely as forecasts or projections. In long term planning it is essential to consider what means will be used to implement the plan. When it is public sector planning that is being considered the obvious pattern is that the annual financial appropriation procedures should be the method used to implement the various phases of the long term plan. Thus it becomes largely a function for administrators with political oversight.

5.   Review

This final element is what moulds all of the foregoing processes into a system. There has to be a review mechanism which is brought to bear, either continuously or sporadically, to ensure that the system is heading towards the set objectives, that the objectives are still worthwhile and realistic, and that there are no better alternative means of reaching those objectives. Again, in relation to the public sector of any particular government system, the best review technique is to monitor the progress of the plan continuously in the light of public sector activity (especially the annual budget), and also to engage in a wholesale review of the components of the plan after each year's appropriation of resources. This process can be performed by administrators and politicians acting in concert. The review then provides feedback to the forecasters who are involved in drawing up the projections for the next phase of the planning cycle — forecasting (1), and so the whole system continues dynamically.

The planning system I have outlined thus comprises five processes each of which is performed in sequence and is linked to the subsequent process. It could be questioned whether each of them is necessarily mutually exclusive. Clearly, for example, the review process will take account of developments in all of the previous four processes. It is not necessary for each element to be discrete for the system to be valid, but, for the most part, each of them should be visible as a separate entity, if only because of the different posture of the actors in each process, irrespective of whether they are the same actors throughout. It is contended that this planning system can be applied to any resource or sector or organization. In this study it is used mainly in relation to financial resources of the public sector. It has been used in the analysis of events in the Australian, Canadian, and other federal systems. It is the concept which has been used in all the interviews associated with this study. In other words, in the effort to determine whether the political units of the federation could engage in public sector planning — this system is what is meant by the word "planning". It is the fixed element in this study, the independent variable.

Planning and Democracy

As we have already observed, there is one further element of planning which is worth dwelling upon, albeit briefly; planning is a concept which is often painted as being antidemocratic.[43] It is true that most planning processes tend to concentrate an undue amount of policy making in the hands of a progressively declining number of people, unless this tendency is checked. Most of the western countries referred to earlier have found considerable difficulty in maintaining a high level of public participation, and indeed interest, in planning processes. There are many reasons for this and most of them relate to the fact that the required expertise to make informed judgments about the future is not distributed widely amongst the community, especially given the growing complexity of society, and the commensurate complexity of government required to regulate that society. This, and other factors, explain why parliaments have not been particularly effective in this process. However, it appears that there are more fundamental aspects of planning which explain this phenomenon. This is because the inherent nature of planning conceptually produces the following sequence:

1. *Planning means coordination.* Aspects such as priority determination and allocation of resources are by their nature mental and physical constructs, which make coordination of decision making ultimately essential, irrespective of which person or group of persons makes those final choices.
2. *Coordination means hierarchy.* If there is to be coordination inevitably some person or organization must do the coordinating. Normally, this need not necessarily mean a hierarchy of ranking or status in respect of the coordinator versus the coordinated, but when it is a political system about which we are speaking, the very act of coordination symbolizes and indeed institutionalizes, a hierarchical relationship.
3. *Hierarchies tend to produce elites.* Every pyramid must have its apex and wherever there is a hierarchy there must, be definition, be a pinnacle to that hierarchy. That pinnacle is the elite, and whilst it is true that the elite remains connected to its lower members, in political systems there are profound tendencies for each elite to become removed from the other members of the hierarchical relationship.
4. *Elites are fundamentally antidemocratic.* For those reasons previously outlined, the sheer presence of an elite is an inhibition to the attainment of mass participation in decision making or even the supply of information.

The assertion being made here is that coordination *ultimately* produces a hierarchical relationship and institutionalizes that relationship between the actors involved. This need not necessarily mean that the *process* of coordination has to proceed in a totally hierarchical manner, with superior and inferior participants. Indeed, coordination can be achieved through informal as well as formal means and the more informal the mechanism, the less hierarchical the situation will appear. It follows that there can be gradations of the hierarchical relationship thereby affecting the sharpness of the pinnacle referred to in our third aspect of planning, and affecting, in turn, the degree of elitism produced, which in itself determines the degree of democratic participation.

In other words, this four step process should be seen as a framework for describing a relative process rather than an absolute one.

If one follows this reasoning through, then it follows that planning, by its nature, tends to be antidemocratic. However, it is contended here that although this means planning can never be fully democratic (in the ancient Greek sense of the word democratic), it can be more or less democratic. It is axiomatic that democracy should be a time-consuming process involving, as it does, consultation and dialogue. It is therefore inevitable that the more democratic and open a planning system is, the slower and more complex it will be. Now the system of planning which has been formulated earlier does not of itself admit to any particular degree of democratic involvement. Naturally democracy is a desirable end, but in the course of discussion of the topic of this study, namely, planning and federalism, no attempt is made to stipulate any necessary or minimum democratic component, other than to raise the particular problem of accountability which would result from superimposing the planning system we have derived on the federations under review. Nonetheless, this aspect of planning needs to be kept in mind because we shall see, in the next chapter, that it is fundamentally at odds with many of the inherent characteristics of federalism as it is popularly conceived.

The Planning Experience of Australia

As intimated earlier, Australia has had little experience of the comprehensive style of public sector planning being discussed. Nonetheless, there have been various attempts during certain periods of Australian history to plan activity for some portion of the public sector, and they ought to be kept in mind as an important component of the background to our study. We will refer to them in this chapter, albeit in brief terms. However, the impression must not be given that there has been no interest in planning in Australia; indeed, there has always been a lively debate about the concept. But when planning has been the subject of debate in this country, the discussants have inevitably been referring to total planning — most often economic planning for the *whole* economy, and not just for the public sector. This highlights another important factor — that Australians, when speaking about planning, are not always talking the same language. The word "planning" has always meant different things to different groups so that some, for example, simply mean forecasting, whilst others mean the total control of all resources, and yet others are envisaging something in between these extremes. For the purpose of our short historical analysis we will accept all or any of these notions, recognizing that none of them corresponds to the systemic conceptualization of planning which we have defined, and which we shall employ later in this study.

The second half of the nineteenth century is the phase of Australian history which began to see significant moves to establish infrastructure throughout the continent. This was the era of railway development, construction of roads, bridges, harbours, and the various public utilities. A good deal of this infrastructure had to be financed and constructed by public activity because the large size of the nation, together with the relatively small and scattered population, made it an uneconomic proposition for private capital. A good deal of this activity in public works was undertaken by statutory corporations, entities which Australia pioneered and which provided the necessary political and administrative freedom for forward planning. Each of these works projects required a lead time, often up to ten years, and so considerable forethought had to be brought to bear regarding the supply of capital, in the first instance, and then the supply of manpower and materials. However, despite the fact that each of these projects required individual planning, there was no concerted effort to coordinate all of the works projects occurring in each colony. More significantly, there was virtually no coordination of works projects between colonies, and each government conducted its own loan raising and construction programme independently of the others. In relation to current expenditures, and revenue raising, those were the days of small governments and balanced budgets. Governments would fix rates of taxation and other means of revenue raising according to the expected spending for the coming year. Naturally the different desires and wishes of each colony gradually became evident, and by the first world war were reflected in quite different rates of taxation (especially income taxation) and levels of indebtedness between the states. At the time of federation little thought was given to any need for the new national government to engage in forward planning — indeed the expectation in 1901 was that the new national government would remain extremely small, as witnessed by the provisions of the Braddon Clause in the constitution. Under this clause (Section 87 — mistakenly named after the Tasmanian Premier), the expectation was that the new national government would be able to exist on the income from one quarter of customs and excise duties. At the time of federation, the main source of revenue to the colonies was customs and excise duties, and the key question for the draftsmen of the national constitution was what proportion of this revenue should be guaranteed to the states if the commonwealth were given a monopoly over such revenue raising. The Braddon Clause required the commonwealth to distribute to the states three-quarters of its net customs and excise revenues. It was to apply for ten years and then be reviewed.

It was also the case that most of the public sector activities which required large capital expenditure and forethought, remained as state functions under the division of powers, including railways, and the bulk of the provision of economic and social infrastructure, for example, irrigation, harbours, roads, education, and health. The colonies had not wanted to hand over many of these functions because of the potential for pork-barrelling within them, the obvious major exception being defence, although defence expenditure was very small anyway at that time.

The first world war saw some attempts at national coordination of policy making and priority determination, as well as the shifting of resources into the war effort, but it was not a technological war and Australia was not threatened. There was therefore little emphasis on capital expenditure and hence only minor attention to the forward planning of resources.

The period from the first world war to the end of the 1920s in Australia saw a rapid escalation in government borrowing, and progressively more marked differences in rates of taxation and levels of indebtedness between the states and also the commonwealth government, which had begun to enter various fields of taxation and engage in some capital works programmes. The establishment of a voluntary loan council in 1923, and the permanent Australian Loan Council in 1927 (examined in more detail later), provided the most significant move ever made in this country towards the introduction of the sort of planning under discussion. Although the coordinated borrowing programme was formulated for only one year ahead, there was nonetheless for the first time something of a bird's eye view, across the whole nation, of capital resource allocation for the public sector. Moreover, because of the lead time of public works projects, the Loan Council each year had a reasonably accurate picture of the level of future commitment involved in the continued financing of these public works. Allocations of loan funds, however, continued to be on a spatial rather than a sectoral basis, reflecting regional priorities rather than national ones.

Naturally enough, the advent of the Depression shifted thinking away from any long term considerations, and emphasis shifted to short term expedients directed at creating employment, or at least reducing unemployment. Government revenues were cut, public service wages were reduced, and loan programmes contracted. Eventually out of this crisis a number of proposed methods of bringing about recovery were mooted under the guise of being "plans", for example, Premiers Plan, Niemeyer's Plan, and the Lang Plan. The concept which eventually gained sway was in many respects akin to the basic premise of the subsequent theories of John Maynard Keynes. Theodore and others proposed the use of the public sector works programme as the means of generating employment, and even took this theory a step further by proposing that governments keep a string of public works projects at the ready, so that they could be brought into phase at the exact time required (that is, when a lull appeared in employment growth), and also in the exact locations required. The introduction of this sequential and spatial element to the projection of public sector capital expenditure probably represents the first conceptual formulation of a planning framework in Australia, even if it was introduced for pragmatic reasons. Irrespective of the motivation, it worked, and towards the end of the 1930s entities known as Coordinators of Works began to appear in most states of Australia and in the Commonwealth.[1]

Coincidentally there was, during the 1930s, bitter academic debate occurring about planning as a concept. To a large extent it reflected the dispute occurring in Europe between the polemic of Hayek, Wootton, and others. It was clearly associated with the notion of planning for the whole economy, not just the public sector, but its principles were still readily applied to the activities which were occurring in the Australian public sector. It was at this period that the word planning came to be associated with the policies of the Soviet governments and to convey the meaning of government control of the whole society. Amidst that sort of polemic there was little room for any advocacy of planning solely for the public sector. It was all or nothing; planning or free enterprise.

The Australian debate was best recorded in the Shann and Copland volume, *The Battle of the Plans*, which contained documentation of the rival proposals for combating the Depression put before the Premiers Conference in mid 1931.[2] These so-called plans were, of course, only methods of ensuring a return of stability in prices and employment primarily through progress towards a balanced budget. On 25 April 1931 the Loan Council passed a resolution: "That Australia must aim at securing a balanced budget by the end of June 1934". The Loan Council also established a subcommittee to report on action to be taken to achieve this objective. Three premiers and Professors Copland, Giblin, Melville, and Shann were asked to form a Working Committee with the Under Treasurer from all states except New South Wales, which did not participate. The subcommittee presented to a Loan Council meeting and then a Premiers Conference in May and June of 1931.

Most of the debate on these plans was launched in economic terms. One commentator observed that the so-called Battle of the Plans evidenced a "pathetic weakness which a democracy almost inevitably exhibits in a time of crisis and the inability of its rulers to confess that they have made mistakes".[3]

The plan finally adopted by the Premiers Conference of 1931 consisted, amongst other aspects, of five elements relating to reduction of government expenditure, increased taxation, and reduced interest rates (both government and private). Describing the agreed solution, Bland and Mills made a pertinent comment when they stated that:

> hastened by the complexities which the discussion of the proposals revealed, the Conference avoided any decision which would limit the freedom of the several Governments to make the reductions in whatever way they deemed equitable, though they did declare that the carrying out of any one part is dependent on the carrying out of all parts.[4]

The authors also add the pregnant observation that "the action finally taken was belated, and only adopted when it was obvious that a complete breakdown in public finance was imminent".

Lyons objected to the fact that the measures agreed upon at the Premiers Conference had been termed a "National Rehabilitation Plan". He believed that the restoration of budgetary equilibrium, although an important step, could only be the first step in the immense task of national reconstruction. Lyons also saw considerable difficulties with the concept of using public works as the long term remedy:

> Public works programmes as factors in eliminating the worst affects of trade depression require long-range planning. At the present time we are thoroughly unscientific in the manner in which we approach this problem . . . A scientific public economy would ensure that the public works would be planned well in advance of the unemployment emergency, and that a reserve would be created to pay for them.[5]

The debate about planning figured prominently in various conferences held in the 1930s. Fisher, an advocate of economic planning, claimed that the essential ingredients for a plan were (1) that it should have a purpose, and (2) that purpose should be known and understood. Most planners, he argued, became preoccupied with the means of the plan, although he conceded that there was still no universally accepted answer to the question of what the proper purpose should be for a general economic plan. According to Fisher planning also presupposed, in relation to the units whose activities were destined to make the plan effective, a considerable measure of control in so far as their actions impinged upon the plan. This also led to the necessity for the absence of violent change in the methods of work which the plan was likely to require. However, Fisher went on to state unambiguously that planning and economic freedom are incompatible.[6] Many of those sentiments were echoed just a year later by Mauldon, who drew on West European experience, especially with the use of Economic Councils, and observed that: "The relationship between an Economic Council charged with the conscious planning of the country's economic future and the sovereign political legislature will assuredly in no country be settled on the economists' terms alone. Moreover, in the constituting of such a focal agency the vexed question whether expertness or representativeness should give it its dominant character has to be worked out to a workable conclusion".[7] Despite these difficulties, Mauldon was in favour of establishing some sort of Australian body to obtain a coordinated overview of economic knowledge, because he saw existing advisory mechanisms to commonwealth and state governments as too specialized and fragmented for the purpose of considering economic and social problems as a whole. He called it a "focal agency for advice and planning". The question of its representativeness, and how it would span both levels of government, would have to be determined, and it could well be necessary to establish two such groups, one representative and one expert, to advise the commonwealth cabinet in the first instance.

Melville records that at a 1934 conference of the Australian Institute of Political Science, there was general agreement that planning of some kind was inevitable and, on the whole, desirable, but there was no agreement about what kind of planning was needed.[8] At that conference, Salter had presented a picture of a planned society as an "ordered society". Portus suggested that the tests of a planned society were that (1) it involved long range, conscious planning ahead, and its purpose must be clear, (2) it must not be opportunist, and (3) the planning must not be partial. Giblin made the significant remark that planning of the kind which was being espoused was only "better planning". He continued: "We are committed to planning, which in its broadest sense means only applying foresight and reason to our economic activities". For Macmahon, parliament was an inadequate device for debate of planning details, and the actual administration of a fully planned economy could best be achieved through the use of statutory corporations. Ross took the argument a step further by saying that the only planning worth having was socialist planning. For his part, Melville regarded the important question as being what it is that we ask of a planned society. The various things we expect are often incompatible — especially the requirements for an increased standard of living, less economic fluctuation, and complete freedom. More particularly, "some may prefer more political liberty even though it involves less economic liberty. Others would prefer economic liberty to political liberty." No two standards, said Melville, are likely to be the same, and so we cannot expect a society to conform to any particular logical pattern. The conflicts, he felt, would be settled politically either by compromise; tyranny of the majority or a minority; or by the marginal voter in a democracy, who is so unintelligent, apathetic, or shallow that he does not know his own mind on the matter.

The publication of F.A. Bland's *Planning the Modern State* in 1934 did much to advance the cause of public administration as a discipline but very little to refine the Australian concept of "planning". Indeed the choice of title was an unfortunate one for what was essentially a collection of lectures, rather than a treatise on planning. Bland said that his book was an attempt to "sketch plans for the machinery which would give us at once a parliament capable of exerting a 'control on behalf of the people', and a public service quick to appreciate and ready to meet the novel needs of our complex society".[9] Bland canvasses the views of Wooton, Polanyi, and Hayek, and it is clear that he too perceived planning as an all-embracing process of control over the whole community, and he did not consider planning solely for the public sector (which is disappointing given the title of the volume). Bland went some way towards justifying this omission in the second edition, published in 1945, when he explained that in the early 1930s in Australia, planning was held to mean the rationalization of methods and machinery of government to meet the demands of the social service state, whereas in 1945 the word had come to mean "the deliberate choice of the method of central direction of all economic effort".

The second half of the 1930s in Australia, as elsewhere, saw an increasing intellectual and practical concern with the area of public finance, and in particular with the role of the budget in influencing economic activity. In a 1935 review of Australian public finance, Hytten revealed that the Premiers Plan had only been policed closely in the first year or so, and after that each government was left to arrive at its deficit as it thought suitable. The superior taxing powers of the commonwealth had made it difficult for the states to tax lower incomes, and the commonwealth super tax made it equally difficult to get much more out of the higher incomes. State public debt charges had risen, and although budgets had not been balanced, these deficits had been reduced to one eighth of the anticipated deficit in 1931–32. Moreover, sinking fund payments had been continued, unlike the situation in other countries. The considerably more favourable result for the commonwealth budget by the mid 1930s, compared with the situation of the states, culminated in a Constitutional Conference in January 1935 at which proposals were discussed to redistribute revenue sources between the commonwealth and the states. The three proposals were to give the states fifty per cent of customs and excise revenue in lieu of existing vertical transfers, to exclude the commonwealth from income tax, and to give the states concurrent powers in respect of excise. All of them failed. Hytten concluded that "for good or ill we are definitely drifting towards an increase in Commonwealth functions at the expense of state functions". Whilst the commonwealth was passing some funds on to the states for unemployment relief and rural rehabilitation, the basis of cooperation seemed to be that "the Commonwealth will find the funds if the states will devise means of spending them, which is surely an insecure foundation for a long range policy".[10]

Other authors also chronicled the trends in public finance during the 1930s, including the conscious move towards deficit financing late in the decade, and it is fair to say that the role of the public sector in a mixed economy gained considerable attention during this period, and the need for government intervention to achieve stability and growth was widely recognized. However, the debate about planning was unresolved, intellectually at least. Some authors passionately took up pro-planning stances, but their support tended to wither as the economy began to recover. Those who opposed planning were, for the most part, less vehement in their viewpoint, and were prepared to concede the need for more rationalization and refinement of existing government/community relationships in order to improve fiscal standards of living, and welfare generally, but stopped short of any strict public controls to achieve these longer term aims. Grattan probably summed up the situation at the end of the decade when delivering an address entitled "The Future in Australia". He said:

> For forty years now Australia has been busy filling up the outlines of the scheme of development laid down more or less unconsciously in the latter quarter of the last century. Since this has been carried forward according to the principles of capitalism, increasingly the tilt of the social balance in this country has been in favour of the owning-producer, and since the world war that tilt has become confirmed.[11]

World War II

The second world war marks a milestone in Australian thinking about public sector planning. It was a technological war and so it required a large amount of capital expenditure. When eventually Australia was directly threatened, it highlighted many of the deficiencies in the country's infrastructure including, in particular, the rail and road transport system, regulated by the states for the most part, and not particularly well coordinated across the nation. But the main effect of this war, in this context, is that it unified the aspirations of the nation towards one purpose and thereby provided the rationale for centralized resource allocation in the public sector — the basic requirement of any planning system. There are, of course, far too many elements in Australian wartime history for us to be able to recount them here, but some of the more significant can be mentioned. Paramount, of course, was the massive planning apparatus established to prosecute the war, including a range of regulatory devices such as price control, rationing, manpower planning, exchange control, capital issues control, and economic stabilization measures.

In the words of Mathews and Jay:

> Australia suffered fewer casualties in World War II than in the first, but the strain on the economy was much greater. The war lasted six years as against four in World War I, and the entry of Japan into the war in December 1941 brought the threat of invasion to Australia. Control of the economy and of the civilian population by the Commonwealth Government was therefore much more rigorous. Australia experienced military and civil conscription, rationing, price control, control of private investment and of production and imports. This was accompanied by very substantial increases in taxation and borrowing to finance defence expenditure and to reduce private expenditure on goods and services. The States were excluded from the field of income tax and had their loan programmes drastically reduced and monitored by the Commonwealth.[12]

They also pointed out that the war and postwar periods saw the commonwealth become heavily involved in direct welfare expenditure.

The year 1940 saw the establishment of the Commonwealth Department of Labour and National Service which had a Reconstruction Division for consideration of the necessary postwar measures which would be required. In 1941 the Joint Parliamentary Committee on Social Security suggested some sort of social plan would be necessary when peace arrived, and the committee quickly moved its emphasis from the planning of social security to the need for economic planning as a whole in order to attain social security. Then came the November 1942 resolution at the Labor Party Conference that there be immediate planning for national postwar reconstruction, and the twin recommendations that the government should appoint a minister whose sole duty would be to proceed immediately with the preparation of a comprehensive scheme of postwar reconstruction, and to coordinate the work of all federal and state government agencies in this field. This was followed by the announcement (by Curtin), in December 1942, that Chifley would be Minister for Postwar Reconstruction as well as Treasurer. In January 1943 Coombs was appointed as Director-General of Postwar Reconstruction, a department assembled mostly by recruitment from outside the public service (Coombs had been director of rationing). Its activities are recounted by Hasluck, who also dwells on the grand concept of a national works programme introduced by Chifley:

> His reference to a national works programme was followed by a discussion with State Ministers and in July a Premiers' Conference decided to establish a National Works Council to determine post-war works policy. Proposals for works from all parts of Australia would be coordinated and fitted into a comprehensive plan to be carried out in various stages, the most urgent being restorative works needed for the civil community to resume activity. "No estimate can be given in broad terms of the money needed", said Chifley, "but the only limit to the operation of Australia's internal economy after the war will be the availability of manpower and materials".

Animating all the planning was the doctrine of full employment. "The primary aim of our post-war economic policy must be a high and stable level of employment", Chifley said on more than one occasion. Work, as well as being available, should be adequately rewarded and directed towards worthwhile ends. It meant raising consumption of those now on low incomes, improving the environment by housing, town and country planning, modern transport and social services. "Above all", he said, "it means placing permanently within the reach of every one of us freedom from basic economic worries, the realisation of some of our ambitions for personal development, and the opportunity of bringing up happy, healthy, well-educated families". This was the yardstick by which he would measure plans coming to him from the commissioners and committees.

For all this there must be planning and there must be some controls, "fairly heavy" tax rates, some regulation of the use of resources to avoid competing demands for materials and labour, and the ending of monopolistic or other restrictions on output.[13]

It was at this time also that a link was announced between the establishment of the postwar reconstruction apparatus and a proposed Constitutional Convention to consider the transfer of powers by the states. Now this attempt at a vertical transfer of powers to the central government is of great importance to the topic of this whole study, because it is a vivid illustration of the hindrances to public sector planning created by the federal division of power in Australia. The incident recurs as an example throughout subsequent pages for this reason — in a time of war a planning system of the sort we are envisaging, becomes imperative, but the required determination of priorities and allocation of resources is slowed down immeasurably. The necessary coordination of decision making is frustrated by the existence of divided sovereignty over the resources required, or in many cases by the fact that the level of government required to make the decisions has no sovereignty at all, short of some sort of full declaration of national emergency powers. Clearly it is not a problem to bedevil a unitary country.

To enable it to have the fourteen powers thought necessary, the national government of the day tried to mount a referendum, but this was initially blocked by a hostile Senate. An effort was then made to have the states transfer the powers, and a couple did, but most wanted substantial amendments or insisted on watering down the proposals. The Constitutional Convention which was held did not help at all, and disintegrated along party lines. Ultimately, after some compromise, a referendum proposal passed through the parliament. The basic issue in the propaganda for the referendum was "plan or chaos". In the words of the case in favour of the referendum: "Do we as a people take our future boldly into our own hands and shape it with the tools we have fashioned in the furnace of war, or do we leave it to the blind forces of economic anarchy?" On 19 August 1944 the referendum was defeated. There was a commonwealth majority for "no"; only South Australia and Western Australia said "yes", and both Queensland and New South Wales said "no", despite the fact that the governments of those two states had earlier adopted the transfer of powers bill.

These events were a significant setback in attempts to transfer powers to the national government. So too were some other subsequent referendums each of which was defeated, namely, organized marketing of primary products (1946), regulation of the terms and conditions of industrial employment (1946), and control of rents and prices (1948). The commonwealth government also failed in its attempts to legislate in certain key areas such as an airline monopoly, free pharmaceutical benefits, and the prevention of private trading banks from acting for state governments or instrumentalities, all in 1945, and the well-known attempt to nationalize the private banks in 1947. Each of these actions was declared unconstitutional by the High Court.

However, there were a number of notable successes as well. Perhaps the most significant of all in relation to national planning was the production of a policy statement which represents the closest Australia has come to the concept of a blueprint for the future of the nation. On 30 May 1945 the national government published its *White Paper on Full Employment*. Amongst other things, it provided for a national housing programme, a plan for land settlement, public works advance planning, training schemes for ex-service personnel, a nationwide employment service, a plan for the restoration or expansion of key industries, controls over scarce resources, and checks on inflationary price rises. The means by which these aims were to be achieved were the various price and quantitative control mechanisms which had been imposed in wartime, including price control, allocation of materials, controls in capital expenditure, import licensing, and some rationing. The institution mainly responsible for overseeing these aspirations was the Department of Postwar Reconstruction.

It was the very retention of these economic and physical control mechanisms which played a large part in the defeat of the Chifley government in 1949, together with other attempts at more national controls mentioned already, especially the bank nationalization attempt. When handed a referendum, the people rejected any changes which would allow a nationalization of banking, and shortly after they also rejected the Chifley government itself, electing the Menzies Liberals who promised, among other things, to dismantle the many control mechanisms which had survived to 1949.

Mathews and Jay provide a catalogue of other government initiatives of this period which "increased the range of its direct participation in the production of goods and services and enabled it to exercise more effective control over the private sector of the economy. These measures included, inter alia, a number of public authorities (Joint Coal Board, Tasmanian Aluminium Authority, Snowy Mountains Authority, TAA, ANL, Qantas takeover, whaling industry, stevedoring industry authorities), the Commonwealth Bank became a central bank, joint Commonwealth/State immigration programmes and various schemes of co-operative federalism, capital issues control, and the use of section 96 payments in education, health, transport and development."[14]

Naturally enough, the wartime period also produced a good deal of literature associated with the concepts of planning, mostly in relation to controls, employment, and curtailment of freedom, with some attention to likely postwar developments. As Prest wrote in 1942: "It is freely asserted, and apparently widely and sincerely believed, that our war-time experience of Government control and economic planning will be of value after the war, when planning for war will be replaced by planning for peace and prosperity, or as some people prefer to put it, by planning for 'full employment' ".[15] In a further contribution to the semantic difficulties surrounding the focus of our study, Prest describes the Australian wartime condition as one in which "centralized bureaucratic planning has replaced individual planning".[16]

Without question the two elements of government activity which were examined most closely in the literature were the full employment objective, and the preparations for postwar reconstruction. Merry and Bruns, in a comparison of the British, Canadian, and Australian white papers on full employment, observe that there was a widespread feeling in the three countries "that there would never again be the marked variations in activity resulting in heavy unemployment", and the three governments had accepted "as a responsibility of government the need to take positive steps to affect any deterioration in business conditions and to set up machinery for providing work for all".[17] They comment that none of the three "plans" was a complete blueprint of postwar adjustment and development; each was little more than a statement of principles. Although they all had a common objective, the means of attaining that objective differed. Nonetheless all three white papers agreed that the items of expenditure most liable to sudden fluctuation, thereby affecting employment levels, were private and public capital expenditure. However, the Australian strategy placed most emphasis on the role of public capital expenditure in encouraging private capital expenditure and maintaining a steady total amount of public expenditure. This, say the authors, was in line with Australia's traditionally heavy emphasis on public capital expenditure. (The Canadian emphasis was on the private sector, and in Britain, public expenditure was seen as a makeweight to step in only when private expenditure declined.) For all its emphasis on public capital expenditure, the Australian white paper did not follow the British concept of a five year plan of capital works projects sufficiently flexible to be brought on stream, when and where necessary, to counteract cycles in private capital expenditure.

Public reaction to the Australian white paper was mostly unfavourable because it depended on continuing restraints. It was painted by some as totalitarian, but was not debated in the parliament. Waters credits Copland as having made the most eloquent statement of opposition to the proposals: "Copland argued that the fundamental conflict between freedom and security should always be kept in the foreground and insisted that people did not want to have their lives planned for them by anyone". Copland also objected to the term "full employment", and claimed "a certain minimum pool of unemployed was the only alternative to labour regimentation, price control, and the fixing of maximum as well as minimum wages".[18]

So much was written and spoken about postwar reconstruction in Australia that it is difficult to do justice to the diversity of opinion which prevailed. We are, of course, only interested in the contribution of this body of literature to conceptions of planning. Coombs spoke of the many problems in postwar absorption of people to civilian life, including various social tensions. He also dwelt on the unity which had typified the Australian people during the war and in one (oft-quoted) passage declared:

> Everybody's vision of the new Jerusalem is, of course, different from his neighbour's, but through them all or at least through the vast majority there run common themes which may be summed up in the objectives of employment, rising standards of living, development and security.[19]

In relation to the second of these three aspirations, Coombs observed: "There is, therefore, an increasing demand that economic organization should be planned consciously to provide a rounded life".[20] Coombs expressed the personal opinion that it would be possible for Australians to be master of their own economic destiny after the war, although there would be many dilemmas to be confronted and a considerable rearrangement of priorities. He concluded thus:

> There are two ways of looking at the post-war problem; the one is to regard the situation as a mass of problems and difficulties to be resolved. The other is to see the very confusion and flexibility of the situation as an opportunity to promote economic and social developments. Opportunity for dramatic steps forward occur but rarely in the lives of men.
>
> The choice before us is to go back or to go on, to attempt to rebuild the so-called "free" economy based here upon individual choice, freedom of enterprise, unemployment, and the alternation of booms and slumps; or to go on, by the use of the knowledge and experience we have built up during the war to an economy, still predominantly one of private ownership and enterprise, but with an increasing responsibility on the Government for the allocation of resources, the prime purpose of which will be the achievement of social objectives of a high and stable level of unemployment [sic], of rising standards of living for all people, of the development of our national resources and security and opportunity for the individual.
>
> My thesis may be summarily stated: The aftermath of war is economic confusion and social instability. But the war, too, has left us an inheritance of experience of economic administration and a consciousness of the power of social effort to achieve. If we are clear upon the objectives we seek and face boldly the dilemmas presented by a changing world, we have an opportunity to move consciously and intelligently towards a new economic and social system.
>
> We have an opportunity to bring within the field of human decision changes which up to now have been brought about by the blind forces of history.

Whether this opportunity will be taken depends upon our boldness in applying our experience and our consciousness of common purpose.[21]

Speaking in the same forum, Copland saw postwar measures of long term economic policy, which placed strong emphasis on a national works programme, each component of which would have a number of objectives and would especially be directed into channels which were socially desirable, but would not be adquately developed by private enterprise. He also saw a concomitant need to develop the administrative ability and economic expertise of the public service to make these longer term strategies possible.[22] The reaction to both Coombs' and Copland's papers showed a marked antipathy to "planning" which was, for the most part, equated with controls and loss of freedom and enterprise.[23]

Just a few years later, reviewing two British books on planning by Jewkes and Harrod, Copland had cause to refute the central argument against planning, namely, that it necessarily implied the state determination of investment and its distribution, of occupation, of consumer's choice, and the destruction of private property leading to national self-sufficiency. (This thesis had its antecedent in Hayek's *Road to Serfdom*.) Copland spoke rather of a "free economy working within the framework of social control". This involved concentration on the frontier between civic and market economies — a moving frontier, which now had to be discussed in the light of advancing techniques of control, of improved administrative machinery, and of the higher social aspirations of all organized communities. Copland actually equated his "system of free enterprise working within the framework of social control" with "planning on broad general principles", and outlined a number of obstacles which would have to be overcome. The problems, he said, raised "questions of political science beyond the realm of pure theory in economics, and it is futile for the economist to endeavour to discuss them in a vacuum".[24]

It was Mauldon, writing in 1949, who produced probably the most lucid overview of the attempts at planning in the 1940s. He used Cole's criterion of planning for his evaluation:

> People are apt to talk as if economic systems must be wholly planned or wholly planless whereas, in fact, no system is either of these things . . . Though planning is a matter of degree, the essential difference between mainly planned and mainly unplanned economies is that in the one case there is a general plan regulating the character, as well as the total amount, of production and employment, whereas in the other there is not.[34]

In the Australian case, Mauldon felt that the debate had crystallized too much into the plan or no-plan stereotype. Eggleston's analysis of government activity in Victoria (*State Socialism in Victoria*) proved in a pragmatic way that Australians did not live in a planless society. Mauldon's general conclusion was that "Australia, during most of the decade before the Second World War, notwithstanding some decisive developments towards comprehensive controls [He listed as examples the Premiers Plan, International Commodity arrangements, the Gentleman's Agreement, and the growth of the Commonwealth Bank's power to control exchange rates and interest rates;] and the resumption of traditional development programmes [including subsidies and other aids to producers], cannot be said to have been an economy guided by any 'general plan regulating the character, as well as the total amount of production and employment'. We doubtless desired opulence, but no case for the use of a 'general plan' as its guarantor had been convincingly accepted on the level of executive action by governments".[26] However, it was Mauldon's view that Australia did have a planned economy for the last two years of the second world war, and in that period there was one overriding purpose in the planning, and that purpose was accorded an overwhelming unanimity of support. It was a pragmatic development and its acceptance did not have to "wait on any doctrinal or theoretical justification of over-all planning". He saw Coombs' Joseph Fisher lecture in June 1944 as the first such theoretical "straw in the wind to indicate how Keynesian doctrine was to play its part in high quarters"; and the white paper on full employment was the first occasion on which there had been set down "the lineaments of general plan for the Australian economy in a time of peace; for, as a prescription for peace, it went far beyond the requirements for the change-over from war to peace".[27] As for the closing few years of the decade, the postwar period, Mauldon observed that it was not possible to answer "yes" or "no" to the question of whether the Australian economy was mainly planned:

> What we have been witnessing in the last three and a half years is an unequal tug-of-war between the will to plan and the forces to be brought into subjection to the plan. The plan was, I believe, on the whole wisely conceived in terms of its objectives, of its recognition of major difficulties to be faced, and most of its prescriptions. But it was essentially an economists' plan. That means it could not embrace the strategy of politics which might, or might not, be necessary for its fulfilment, nor could it be expected to prescribe the psychological and moral adjustments needed if the plan was to control. We have, indeed, had to witness a weakening of the defences of over-all planning since the end of the war. The economy today is much more suffused with governmental interventions than it was before the war, but it would be to put a strain upon the language to say that it is 'mainly planned' in the sense that there is a masterful control of economic forces.[28]

1949 to 1961

From 1949 to 1961 the word planning almost ceased to exist in the vocabulary of the government. The Liberal–Country Party coalition had a strong free enterprise platform aimed at reduction of all forms of government intervention, and reduction of the size of the public sector. It was symbolized by Menzies' efforts to reduce the size of the Commonwealth Public Service by 10,000, a goal which was achieved over five years by nonreplacement of wastage. Clearly, this was an environment hostile to any form of planning, even if confined to the public sector, and Menzies and his colleagues went further, picking up the catch cries of the 1930s and reviving the old association between the word "planning" and totalitarianism, and doing it extremely effectively. The Australian economy was performing very well, especially as a result of the Korean war boom, America and Britain were progressing reasonably well without any elaborate planning mechanisms, and Australia, like most of the western world, spent the 1950s talking of industrialization, economic growth and development, exports, and even decentralization — all of this within the general emotion and economic environment of postwar reconstruction, free of the restrictions of wartime.

Within the arena of federal financial relations Menzies retained the centralized system of uniform taxation, and the 1950s saw most Premiers Conferences centering around often bitter pleas for the "return" of such taxing powers to the states. The Menzies government could see the benefits to themselves and to the people of a system of one government imposing and collecting income tax *at uniform rates* across the nation, although in a fit of pique he once offered the states the return of the power only to find them politely declining the offer. A detailed examination of the federal consequences of uniform income tax is given in chapter 4, but it should be noted here that this created a profound vertical imbalance in the Australian federation which, from the point of view of the states, took away the largest single component of their revenue raising, and, they claimed, caused inevitable difficulties in forecasting and resource allocation. The distribution of the income tax revenue became a frequent issue.

Menzies made a rather uncharacteristic move in 1954. This is of considerable interest because it seemed to fly in the face of his opposition to both centralism and planning. He argued that, in relation to state public works for development, because the commonwealth was responsible for raising large sums of money, it ought to assume some responsibility for its expenditure. The 1954 policy speech contained this statement:

> Just as we claim no right to interfere in state affairs, so do we say that if we, the Commonwealth, are to assume the burden of finding for state works many millions out of the taxpayer's money we have a duty to the taxpayers to see that the selection of works to be done should be guided by their true order of national importance. We will therefore ask the states to cooperate in the creation of a small advisory body of highly expert persons to serve as a national development Commission, acting in association with the Department of National Development, to report to both Commonwealth and States upon the economics and relative importance of particular proposals.[29]

(Interestingly, many of these concepts were repeated by Whitlam in the period 1972–75 and denounced as socialist and centralist.) As Curtis suggests, Menzies' notions struck at the very principle of a federal compact, and in particular the right of states to decide regional interests.[30]

(Commonwealth grants to the states for universities had commenced in 1950.) The idea of determining truly national priorities for public works projects was not new, and it had worked reasonably successfully on a more limited scale in relation to the Development and Migration Commission, and for a short period, through the wartime national Coordinator of Works. Nothing much came of this new proposal, and it faded into the background, but it was not long before the same philosophical basis found its expression in various specific purpose grants to the states originated by the Menzies government a few years later.

The decade of the 1960s produced in Australia quite a different situation. In 1961 an overheated economy produced the response of a credit squeeze from the national government more severe than had been known hitherto. The political result was an election where the Liberal–Country Party Coalition came perilously close to defeat, winning by only one seat, and then only on Communist Party preferences. The Menzies government thus became concerned about the severity of economic fluctuation, and was persuaded to instigate a "Committee of Economic Enquiry" which was appointed in February 1963. The Committee had broad terms of reference and comprised an eminent and influential team headed by James Vernon (chairman). Other members were J.G. Crawford (vice-chairman), P.H. Karmel, D.G. Molesworth and K.B. Myer. The Committee submitted their report but the Menzies government refused to make it public, thereby fuelling speculation about its contents. When it was finally released it became obvious that the Vernon Committee had been extremely impressed by the various indicative planning mechanisms in Western Europe, as well as the role of the Economic Council of Canada. It was the concept of interaction and dialogue between the public and private sectors, which these overseas examples had accommodated, which attracted them, although they were obviously impressed by the economic growth rates of those countries as well — especially France and the EEC in general. So the Vernon report placed strong emphasis on the need for economic growth but not as an end in itself; rather as a means to achieve other economic and social aims. Naturally the report contained many recommendations, but for our purposes the most interesting was proposed machinery for a permanent Advisory Council on Economic Growth, which was quickly construed as a desire for attention to forward thinking and appropriate resource allocation. The Menzies government managed to ignore the report, because when it was finally released, the economy had picked up quite well again and the concerns expressed by the Vernon Committee by that stage gave the appearance of being mere academic debate.

The Vernon Commitee believed that institutional changes since 1945 had helped to fill some of the gaps which had made a national economic policy difficult to carry out before the war, and they mentioned specifically stronger, legally-constituted, central banking, the High Court ruling of 1957 on uniform taxation, cooperation between commonwealth and state governments, and machinery for government consultation with representative bodies of the private sector in the formulation of both general and specific economic measures.[31] In providing the Vernon Committee with its terms of reference, the Menzies government stated its economic objectives as being "a high rate of economic and population growth with full employment, increasing productivity, rising standards of living, external viability, and stability of costs and prices". The Committee regarded economic growth as central to all the other objectives, but strongly emphasized that the seven objectives stated by the government were interrelated in a very complex way. They were quite critical of the government's past emphasis on the short term and its attendant "stop-go" policies. In relation to government expenditure the Committee made this pertinent comment:

> We do not comment at length on the nature of fiscal policy. We think it is generally accepted that government expenditure, by state and commonwealth, cannot easily be quickly adjusted, consistent with efficiency and the interests of long-term development, and it is principally on the revenue side that manipulative steps have to be taken. The difficulty is that under the system of annual budgets in which rates of taxation are fixed for a whole financial year, the possibility for flexibility is limited.[32]

But on public investment they presented a completely different picture:

> As public investment constitutes over one third of total investment, it is essential that it be planned with due regard for economy. There is scope for more coordinated long-term planning of public investment between the states and the commonwealth and for more detailed investigation of the projects involved. Subject to this, we believe that there is room for extension of the "specific purpose" type of commonwealth assistance to the state.[33]

And in respect of the concept of planning:

> We would not, however, suggest anything in the nature of a national economic plan involving individual industry targets for Australia, as this would require elaborate machinery and, in all probability, a considerably higher degree of government intervention in the economy than would be acceptable in this country. . . . Nevertheless we would see merit in periodical statements by the Government that long-term policies will be directed to the achievement of a certain rate of economic growth.[24]

A little later the committee went on to stress the importance of government always taking long term trends into consideration in its decision making, and the experience of other countries was cited in this respect, but nowhere were the means of ensuring that this happened spelt out. Perhaps the nearest they came to this was the recommendation for an Australian Advisory Council somewhat similar to the Canadian Council. They did not comment on the form which such a council would take, but its principal functions would include:

> To report as required on particular subjects.

To prepare an annual review of growth experience and long-term prospects.
To maintain a constant review of and advise on trends in overseas investment,
development problems and any other matters that might be referred to it for
special attention.
To undertake, commission and encourage research bearing on its field of
responsibility, and to publish research papers.[35]

The committee saw the main advantages of such a body being that it
would provide for a constant yet independent review of long term trends,
leading to better public understanding of those trends, and the interdependence of economic factors which must otherwise lead to dissension between various key economic interest groups in the community.
The advisory council, they felt, should be comprised of people chosen for
their ability and not as representatives of groups; it should be small; have
no executive powers or responsibilities; with a strong secretariat; and confine itself to medium and long term matters.

The Vernon Report also made a number of significant observations
about public investment in Australia which went very much unnoticed.
There were major problems in planning and organizing public investment
in the Australian federation, they said. The root of the problem was that
although state and local governments undertook eighty per cent of public
investment, they were responsible for raising only part of this amount,
because a large part of such funds was raised by the commonwealth under
Loan Council borrowing programmes, as well as commonwealth money
provided directly under specific purpose payments. They went on to
make the following pertinent observation:

> 9.44 In our discussions with State Governments, we noted considerable varia-
> tion in the degree of forward planning of public investment by state authorities
> and in the nature of the planning methods adopted. In most cases, state elec-
> tricity, water, railway and road authorities had plans for expenditure for five to
> ten years ahead. However, in some states, even medium term planning for
> education and health appears to be lacking. We do not propose to comment fur-
> ther on state planning, but we felt the need for a greater degree of coordination
> between states and commonwealth in this field.[36]

The Vernon committee thought that because specific purpose grants took
place outside the Loan Council, and involved the commonwealth directly
in the problems of the state, they should therefore provide a basis for joint
commonwealth-state planning of particular projects. However, this in
itself was dangerous from an overall point of view, because a project by
project approach increased the tendency to ad hoc bargaining and
arrangements.

Most of the public response to the Vernon Report focused on the
economic content, and little attention was directed to the machinery
recommendations. Menzies labelled the suggestion for a special project
commission as useless and an advisory council as antidemocratic but, as
was pointed out by at least one author, the existence of these bodies would

have reduced the government's options and forced it to justify taking any actions against those recommended by such bodies.[37]

Although the main attempt of the decade to propagate some thinking about economic planning had fizzled, there were a number of developments occurring quite unobtrusively at this time in the public sector. The Defence Department, like so many of its counterparts in other countries, had moved to five year forward strategies, and the determination of annual fiscal appropriations in the light of those five year forward projections. The post office, late in the decade, introduced its own form of the Planning Programming Budgeting System,[38] and especially in the area of telephone installations, began quite sophisticated projections of population movements and associated industrial and domestic location patterns. Many of the intergovernmental grants and agreements (a lot of them established by the Menzies government itself) moved to either a quinquennial system (for example, roads and housing) or a triennial system (universities) of resource allocation. Even in other areas, such as education and science, annual conditional grants were prepared in the light of longer term frameworks. These intergovernmental arrangements are analysed in later chapters but their planning perspectives should be noted here. Meanwhile the Loan Council continued, as always, to regard annual public works commitments in the light of longer term lead times, although there is substantial evidence to show that capital expenditure grants by the national government were influenced more by political pork-barrelling than by any thought of efficient national resource allocation (especially after the various lessons of the near-election defeat in 1961 where it became clear that there was not a uniform spatial distribution of support for the national government).

There had been some quite pronounced moves by almost all Australian states in the 1960s to promote industrialization, and in some cases decentralization, predominantly by means of carrots rather than sticks. Preferences were given by all state governments in their own tendering to "local" firms, a typical pattern being five per cent for firms in that state over interstate firms, and a further five per cent over international firms. State governments also fiddled with freight rates, road tax charges, and especially the provision of cheap land and government guaranteed finance, in an effort to move industry, but this met with very limited success.[39] It seemed to take a long time for state governments to realize that secondary industry was not particularly mobile and that, in any event, tertiary industry made almost two-thirds of the labour force, and the largest tertiary industry of all was the public sector directly under their own control. Indeed, state government employment in Australia has long comprised over sixty per cent of all government employment. Despite their willingness to intervene in the market place to influence the private sector to move in desired sectoral and spatial directions, state governments rarely seemed to consider the possibility of injecting planning into their own departments and instrumentalities, despite the fact that such action might well have been more readily effective.

Thus the decade of the 1960s can now be seen as the "decade of growth". In Australia it was a period when development, growth, industrialization, and all related concepts, held preeminence in practical and academic discussion. More than one writer pointed out that this growth which was indeed occurring, and being discussed, was taking place without the benefit of any coherent overall policy. Writing in 1965, Davies asked a number of related questions, namely; "Must the Admiral of the Ship of State steer by instinct and tradition, trimming his sails to the political winds of change or can he maintain a relatively steady course to achieve his set objectives?" and "whether it is possible for the Australian community to agree on what is meant by 'national (or public) interest' ". Davies observed (yet again) that there was now no national plan of public works arranged in order of overall priorities, and "The Commonwealth cannot enforce its will on overall priorities (assuming that it possesses a clear conception of such overall priorities, which may be a considerable assumption)". Davies went on to decry the role of the commonwealth's Department of National Development, and demonstrated how it failed to achieve coordinated development strategies across the federal system. In the process he brought to light the fact that the states failed to agree upon the Menzies 1954 election promise (which we encountered earlier) for a National Development Commission to study public works proposals.[40] In another extremely perceptive article, Davies highlighted the hindrances posed by the federal system to national development in Australia. He emphasized that in Australia the states have the main role in development, and much is conveyed by his simple statement that "National development preceded federalism". He effectively conveyed the inconsistent attitude of the non-Labor parties to this question by pointing out that in 1957 the Country Party was advocating in its platform: "Concentration in one planning authority of the Commonwealth and state bodies associated with development, accompanied by machinery to determine the priority of projects"; however, a national government Liberal minister declared in 1965: "In this Federation, it will never be possible for the Commonwealth to set an order of priorities for all developmental works. The States have their own funds and they have the right to say how those will be used".[41] Some other writers analysed one portion of the public sector to demonstrate the manner in which intergovernmental fragmentation of jurisdiction prevented national development in that area. Transport figured largely in this exercise, and Whitlam, in 1968, effectively demonst.ated the political and constitutional difficulties involved in formulating any coherent national transport policy when he pointed out, inter alia, that there were nine federal ministers, six state governments (each with at least six instrumentalities), and hundreds of local authorities involved in regulating the various modes of transport.[42]

Developments of the Seventies

In the 1970s there were a number of developments within both the commonwealth and state governments which represent fragmented moves towards the sort of public sector planning system we are envisaging. The one with perhaps the greatest potential was the introduction of forward estimates by the Commonwealth Treasury. Their origin is difficult to pinpoint from the public record, but their appearance does mark an important step because of previous opposition from the Treasury to forward planning for either public or private sectors. Experience in other countries has shown that, if the Treasury can be converted to planning, the task of introducing a planning framework throughout the public sector is expedited. There had been an informal method of three year projections of public expenditure commenced in 1965, but they were never regarded as firm, and they covered only trends in outlays under existing policies requiring no cabinet involvement. Weller and Cutt trace the beginning of the present forward estimates arrangements to a letter from the Treasurer to his colleagues in March 1971. In that letter, "he emphasized the shortcomings of the budgetary process and the existing schemes and pointed out the need for ministers 'to consider policy and expenditure proposals within a framework of the government's known and anticipated forward commitments and the resources possibly available . . . to meet these commitments' ".[43] It would be unrealistic, however, to presume that the initiative for this move lay personally with the Treasurer. The first collection of more formal forward estimates was made in October 1971, and they differed from their predecessors in that they covered new policies which ministers firmly intended to bring forward, were scrutinized in detail by Treasury divisions, and were updated for policy changes and decisions taken in the annual budget. Most importantly, each minister was now required to indicate that he approved the Estimates as a fair representation of his view. The new forward estimates were prepared on a rolling three year basis, costs and prices were to be assumed as constant at the levels prevailing at the time the estimates were prepared (with the Treasury itself making any necessary adjustments), and the Estimates were not to be regarded as firm or unchangeable, with opportunities being given throughout the year for a review of the figures.[44]

The Whitlam government, after assuming office in December 1972, embraced the concept of forward estimates into its programme and established, in early 1973, a Committee of Ministers to consider reports on forward estimates submitted by the Treasurer and serviced by a new entity called the Priorities Review Staff (which is analysed later). The impetus for reform in this direction was further stimulated in the 1973–74 budget speech which included a statement on changes in budget format and presentation. According to the document, "the principal change was the introduction of a *functional classification* of budget outlays and receipts and its use as the main framework for the detailed discussion of budget policy proposals". In addition, national accounting classifications were consistently adopted in the Budget Speech and in Statements for the definition of outlays and receipts. The aim of the new presentation was stated as being "to improve the presentation of budget data in order to provide better information for decision-making processes of the Government and to provide generally a more useful framework for the consideration of policies and their expenditure implications . . . The basic aim of the new functional classification is to bring together outlays with like *objectives or purposes*. In this way it aims to reveal more fully information on the nature of Government activities, the share of resources devoted to particular objectives and to facilitate assessment of the effectiveness of outlays in meeting objectives."[45]

However, the ostensible purpose of the forward estimates was not made public until the advent of the Royal Commission on Australian Government Administration in 1973, and indeed, the forward estimates themselves have never been made public. In a submission to the Royal Commission on Australian Government Administration the Commonwealth Treasury said:

> The major purposes of the forward estimates are to enable the economic management implications of current and proposed programs for future growth of public spending to be clearly presented to the Treasurer and the government and, secondly, to provide a framework within which a full consideration of longer-term issues of resource allocation (both between the public and private sectors and within the public sector) could be undertaken by government.[46]

Cutt gleaned a third objective from the Treasury papers, namely, "to promote flexibility rather than rigidity in public expenditure policy and decision making. It is clearly felt that the 'incrementalism' of the existing system locks in expenditure decisions, and that greater room for manoeuvre would be obtained under the forward estimates procedure".[47]

In January 1974 the Treasury prepared an internal paper dealing with problems which had been encountered in preparing forward estimates of government outlays.[48] In that paper the Treasury claimed that the basic objective in establishing procedures for the collection of forward estimates was to enable the government to assess, against the background of resources available in the economy, its commitments and priorities, and to take action that would allow expenditures to be directed towards the fulfilment of those priorities and the achievement of its longer term objectives. The paper explained, that under the existing procedures for annual budgeting, the size and shape of total expenditure had always been determined largely by previous decisions. Given the short time available to effect changes in many expenditure programmes, such as payments to the states and other special appropriations, little could be done to make changes which would be effective in the budget year. However, it was not envisaged that forward estimates would ever replace the annual budget, the paper said. It also added that "guidelines that are the outcome of a forward estimates exercise at any one time cannot, and certainly should not, be taken as irrevocable commitments not susceptible to adjustment at relatively short notice".

The key feature of this Treasury paper was the list of problems which had been encountered in the preparation of the forward estimates, and this list is highly instructive for our purposes. The first problem was the lack of "hard" data on likely developments. This had caused line departments to fall back on rough trend analysis usually based merely on an extrapolation of past trends. Mention was also made of the fact that the estimates for capital works were prepared more or less in isolation from estimates from the remainder of each programme, with the consequence that the relation-ship between capital costs and the programme objectives became obscured. Then there was the "taper problem", that is, the tendency for departments to pack everything into year one with lesser estimates for years two and three, reflecting the bargaining nature of the old budgetary process and the mental predisposition of public servants to think only one year ahead. This, in turn, was linked to an organizational dilemma in that the bulk of the estimation task was falling on the shoulders of the finance staff of the departments and, whilst these people were highly skilled in costing and control of expenditures, they were not usually fully informed of the details of policy development, and did not have the time or training to carry out detailed studies of new policy options and the factors underlying expenditure growth. Another difficulty was the timing of forward estimates preparation which clashed with the timing of requests for the budget, especially in December/January, when recreation leave was at its peak! Yet another identifiable technical difficulty was the fact that a proportion of the expenditure of many departments involved requirements to be met by other departments, for example, in office facilities and equipment. A more conceptual difficulty lay in the task of distinguishing between "new" and "continuing" policy expenditure related to a large extent to the difficulty of interpreting cabinet decisions.

These problems notwithstanding, it was only a short time before the Commonwealth Public Service Board introduced a system of manpower forward estimates under the highly deceptive title of "manpower planning". The system was similar to that of the financial forward estimates, but the programme format used for manpower was different from that used by Treasury, and little attempt was made to make them comparable. The Public Service Board, like the Treasury, never attempted to make a formal link between the forward estimates and the upcoming budget, and the manpower forward estimates, in particular, were always seen as something of a sham because the government retained the use of staff ceilings, a very blunt short term instrument, which tended to override any true long term consideration.[49]

Naturally, the new government in December 1972 produced a number of profound changes and some of them are relevant to our analysis. The ALP platform had promised machinery for indicative planning, but nothing came of that in the life of the Whitlam government. What did eventuate was the Coombs Task Force,[50] which conducted a review of the continuing expenditures of the previous government in order to see which programmes had outlived their purpose, and where savings could be made to make room for spending on public sector spending, which Labor was anxious to increase in specific sectors. The report of that committee represents perhaps the most rational reappraisal of government priorities from first principles ever conducted in Australia in modern times, and it found many government programmes whose objectives had either been met long ago, or were no longer relevant or worth pursuing. Another innovation of the Whitlam government was the establishment of a Priorities Review Staff, mentioned previously, which was supposed to be modelled on the Central Policy Review Staff (The Rothschild Think Tank) in Great Britain. However, it was not directly modelled on its British equivalent because it was not tacked on to cabinet as a whole, and so did not really have the macro view of public sector priorities necessary to comment (laterally and objectively about resource allocation over all government activity) on any long term thinking which was capable of being implemented. The positioning of the Priorities Review Staff under the prime minister was a sensible beginning, and its first report *Goals and Strategies*[51] was a good attempt at a think tank role, but it was soon to be shunted to other ministers and given narrower assignments relating to particular parts of the public sector, and so it lost the macro viewpoint and the priority advisory role, as well as the leverage of the prime minister. One of the main difficulties (which is important as it is illustrative of Australian political and administrative culture), was that members of the Labor caucus itself all seemed unable to come to grips with the concept of a government-appointed body engaging in constructive criticism of government policies from first principles, a concept which other countries have found to be essential to public sector planning. A similar fate befell the Whitlam government's attempts at open government, with a media unaccustomed to interpreting internal discussion within government in a sophisticated way, and so painting a picture for the public of disharmony and inability to coordinate policy. This was accentuated by Labor government moves to establish a number of commissions of an advisory nature to supplement advice emanating from the public service — traditionally the exclusive source of policy advice. In those policy areas where the Labor platform was strong and well thought through, programmes with long term aims emerged and often were linked with intergovernmental agreements of the same nature (we examine them in subsequent chapters). By the same token, some of the older established longer term intergovernmental agreements began to break down, especially when non-Labor state governments objected to the changes being made to them by the Labor national government for ideological reasons.

The Whitlam government had also, early in its life, established a number of Royal Commissions including the Royal Commission on

Australian Government Administration chaired by Dr. Coombs. That Royal Commission brought down in 1975 a number of findings which were conducive to public sector planning, including a recommended Department of Industries and the Economy, DINDEC, which would be concerned with the longer term relationships between the public and private sector, and economic development in general. Nothing came of that proposal. The Coombs Commission was also powerfully attracted to the concept of the financial and manpower forward estimates which had by that time been somewhat refined by the Treasury and the Public Service Board. Indeed, they saw these systems as the key to efficient forward planning of resource allocation and recommended their development, together with the cessation of short term expedient controls over public sector growth such as staff ceilings. Towards the end of the Whitlam government, the Jackson committee on manufacturing found a malaise in that sector and dim prospects for the future, and as part of the solution recommended the establishment of tripartite machinery for government, business, and trade unions. A touch of indicative planning was set up independently for the housing sector, and a variety of urban and regional programmes with a strong planning component were well underway, including growth centres, when the Whitlam government suddenly lost office in November 1975.

Whilst in opposition in the national parliament, the Liberal/National parties took the opportunity to formulate some new policies in a comprehensive manner for a number of areas of government activity. One of these was a "new federalism" policy the details of which are examined in the next chapter. This policy provided as its overall thrust for a greater devolution of government activity from the national government to lower levels of government with a commensurate emphasis on increased revenue raising by the lower levels of government as well. In itself this aspect of the new federalism policy was bound to be policy fragmentary, but other aspects such as the continuation of various intergovernmental ministerial conferences, the establishment of some new ones, and provision for an Advisory Council for Inter-government Relations, allowed for a retention of mechanisms for the harmonization of policies between the levels.

On coming to government in 1975, the Fraser government virtually copied the style of the Whitlam government in appointing a committee of review chaired by Sir Henry Bland (and including a state public servant) to advise on rearrangement of national government resource allocation to take account of the policy and ideology of the incoming government. However, unlike the Coombs Task Force, the Bland Expenditure Review Committee's report was never published so it was difficult to know at the time whether the process of their review involved a fresh appraisal of public sector resource allocation from first principles. An analysis of the findings of that committee drew heavily on submissions which were made to it by all the state governments and its basic terms of reference included heavy stress on the Fraser government's desire to shift expenditure to the states and make them more responsible politically for the resources they dispersed. We now know that the main thrust of that Bland Committee Report was to reverse the trend of national domination which had occurred through the use of special purpose grants and advisory commissions.[52]

After 1975 there were very few substantive policy decisions by the Fraser government which bore any resemblance to public sector planning as we have defined it. The findings of many inquiries, each of which pointed towards the injection of more rationality into government priority determination and forward thinking, were ignored or shelved or received slow and cumbersome deliberation by cabinet committees backed up by the usual labyrinth of interdepartmental committees in Canberra. The forward estimates in particular, whilst still continuing, are now regarded by all participants as little more than an academic exercise. Both Labor and non-Labor ministers proved to be unable or unwilling to rank order programmes within their own portfolios, and the Fraser government was at pains to distance itself from any notion of planning, thus maintaining the party's old ideological predispositions. The government also claimed that if the forward estimates were regarded as a planning document, the public would misunderstand the need to alter the estimates from time to time, and falsely accuse the government of missing its targets. The net effect is that there is still only the vaguest of links between the forward estimates and each annual budget, so that the forecasting element is not linked to any implementation device, and so cannot be regarded as planning according to our definition.[53]

An official of the national Department of Finance, speaking in 1978,[54] admitted that the forward estimates had not been used in quite the way that was intended in the textbooks. He claimed that their main purpose then was "to provide a framework in which ministers can take decisions affecting the level and composition of budget outlays", and "the first year's data of these forward estimates have become advanced 'bids' for funds in the year immediately ahead". This was because of the usual bureaucratic difficulties we have observed earlier, but also because, in his words, "Governments have shown no inclination to frame three-year budgets". Interestingly, he saw the new House of Representatives Standing Committee of Expenditure (established in 1976) as having caused greater evaluation of the purposes of government spending; but if one examines the report of that committee it can be seen that such review, though fresh and valuable in its own right, is conducted on a programme or sector review basis and not across the whole public sector.

Part of the difficulty faced by the Fraser government was that the economic situation of the late 1970s produced common thinking in the Western world that public sector cutbacks are one of the key strategies for attacking the inflation rate, and it is very difficult to implement a policy of devolution of public expenditure to lower levels, when the size of that public expenditure has to contract appreciably (according to the government's economic policies at any rate). Nonetheless, there were a number of programmes devolved to the states, strong suggestions of moves to block funding rather than programme funding, and some agreements reached at intergovernmental meetings for responsibility sharing. All of these developments further fragmented public policy making and gave the appearance of "ad hocery", especially when combined with a number of stop/start procrastinations in relation to income tax indexation, temporary income tax surcharges, medibank levy, pension indexation, family trusts, sales tax exemptions, etc. Not all of these have direct federal implications but they provide powerful evidence of a drift well and truly away from rational public policy making and planning.

The Hawke Labor government when elected had as part of its party platform a substantial commitment to long term planning for the Australian economy. Key elements of the platform were a "national strategy", "balanced investment allocation", "regional planning", and the creation of a new body — an Economic Planning Advisory Council (EPAC). A planning division was also promised, within the public service, to prepare forecasts, coordinated strategy development under the direction of cabinet, and monitoring implementation. It was also promised that the forward estimating capacity of departments and instrumentalities would be strengthened. At the time of writing the only tangible evidence of this policy was the creation of EPAC which, however, was given only an advisory role to the government and was not allowed to have any impact on the first Hawke government budget. EPAC is representative of most of the community economic groups including state governments. However, based on its structure and performance, it has been completely misnamed. In no way does it meet the definition of planning outlined in Chapter 1 or any other popular conception of planning for that matter, and in 1985 was even ordered to suppress its medium term economic forecasts.

Developments in the Australian States

During the 1970s there were a number of innovations, introduced by some of the state governments in Australia, designed at least to streamline public policy formulation, and in some cases to engage in forward thinking. The Victorian Treasury has for some time engaged in what it calls "forward looks" in loan expenditure.[55] These are examined in later chapters but the essential feature of them is that government bodies are required each year to project their loan requirements on a three year and six year basis. The forward looks are not published, and are not the subject of executive action by the government, but they serve as a framework for annual allocations despite the fact that there is only limited participation within that state government in such annual allocation. Another significant development in Victoria was the establishment of a State Coordination Council, which comprised the permanent heads of the main state government agencies and was serviced by a secretariat in the premier's office. This body provided at least for communication around the government of coming programmes and their likely impact on various sectors. It had no executive power. The Victorian Treasury in the mid 1970s amalgamated its Consolidated Revenue Fund and its Loan Fund to produce one single Consolidated Fund, thereby reducing the fragmentation in government accounting, and also making it easier to identify complete resource allocation across the public sector, or at least that part of it which comes within the state budget. Despite recommendations from the Bland Committee on Victorian Government Administration,[56] which would have resulted in a reduction in the number and autonomy of independent statutory bodies in that state, and a much greater degree of central coordination especially over entironmental matters, very little action has been taken in this respect, and Victoria still has the lowest proportion of its government workforce under the Public Service Act and a very low proportion of government expenditure coming within the budget subsector. Specifically, the first report of this (Bland) Inquiry had this to say:

6.17   A major issue in the years ahead will be the form and structure of public administration and the machinery of government best designed to secure that the optimum in public administration is achieved.

6.18   If strategic planning has long had a place in the fields of foreign affairs and defence and its importance has in latter years come to be recognized in large scale industrial and commercial enterprises, it has only recently had attention for its application to government at large.

6.19   The shortcomings of the annual budget have long been noted. The predilection of governments to react to day to day pressures is notorious. If there should be well formulated long term objectives, it may often be a matter of chance that the decisions taken in response to temporal and sectional pressures neatly fit into the long term objectives.

6.20   Yet the formulation of long term policy objectives cannot proceed in any abstract way. It depends on the analysis of wide ranging data including available resources — personnel and physical — and calls for selectivity and determination of priorities. Essential are inputs from many disciplines, the weighing of benefits against costs and an overlay of political value judgements. The United Kingdom has responded to this problem by appointing a small multidisciplinary Central Policy Review Staff, housed within the Cabinet Office under the supervision of the Prime Minister, working for Ministers collectively.[57]

Despite the attention which Sir Henry Bland drew to the need for planning in the Victorian public sector, his reports contained no actual recommendation directed towards this end. One particularly significant development in Victoria was the establishment in the late 1970s of a Public Bodies Review Committee, a joint parliamentary committee to review the operations of the numerous nonministerial organizations in the public sector of that state. The committee was given a brief to recommend rationalization of the activities of these organizations, with an unusual power in that its recommended changes would be tabled in the house and would be implemented, unless parliament acted to the contrary within a fixed period of time. The first report of this committee promised considerable changes in the direction of eliminating many of these organizations, reallocating their functions, and making them more accountable. Subsequent reports have confirmed the resultant action by the government in eliminating statutory bodies.[58] The advent of the Cain Labor Government in Victoria in the 1980s has produced further waves in the direction of longer term and coordinated policy making. At the time of writing these measures had included the abolition of the state treasury and creation of an office of management and budget, a form of programme budgeting, more functional portfolio groupings, and moves towards four year parliaments.

In South Australia the Corbett Inquiry Report of 1975 had little to say about public sector planning itself, although it did dwell on some of the prerequisites for such planning, particularly central coordination, reduction of the number of administrative units of government, and establishment of priority overview machinery. The last mentioned factor became crystallized in their recommendation of a broader use of the South Australian Priorities and Planning Advisory Committee, a central body comprised of a minister and the heads of the central government agencies, whose job was ostensibly to advise that government on the macro allocation of resources and hence the determination of priorities. However, in reality, according to most commentators, it fell well short of that ideal.[59] A Department of Economic Planning and Development was established a little later to stimulate the private sector and strengthen the industrial base of that state's economy. The South Australian Treasury moved to the concept of a two-year budget, the only Australian state to do so (although funds are still actually allocated annually), and there were firm intentions to move gradually even further into public sector planning through longer term capital and recurrent spending, as well as the commissioning of studies regarding the possibility of introducing a PPBS system. All of these steps received further impetus from the platform of the new Bannon Labor Government to inject more rationality and forward thinking into decision making, although, at the time of writing, no major specific steps had been implemented which would have matched the steps taken by the new Cain Labor Government in Victoria; other than limited introduction of programme budgeting.

In reviewing developments and systems of procedures in South Australia in the 1970s the Under Treasurer of that state has described them as falling into three main groups:

(a)   Those concerned primarily with improving forecasting with the objective of facilitating planning and getting better use of resources. These involve systems in which Treasury has taken the initiative in respect of both the loan and revenue budgets.

(b)   Broader reviews of government activity bearing on the budget process. These have been introduced in more recent times and involve the participation of departments other than Treasury — those of the Public Service Board, the Auditor-General and the Premier, in particular the Board.

(c)   Those dealing with the review of appropriation and accounting processes, of budget papers and presentation of material to Parliament and of financial legislation.[60]

He saw one of the most important innovations in the first category as being the *Loan Guidelines Document*, which is the name given to the papers which bring together the material relevant in forecasting capital programmes. He described it as "a rolling programme in which each year sets out Treasury's estimates of the capital funds likely to be available to the Government in future years (either through loan programmes approved by Loan Council or from recoveries of moneys spent previously), which has regard to the probable movements on Revenue Account (that is to say whether Revenue Account may support Loan Account or require support from it), which assesses and comments on the departmental requirements as advised, and which sets out proposed allocations for departments within the constraints of the overall funds likely to be available". It was claimed that this process had been useful to cabinet in determining relative priorities for expenditure because it made the options clearer. It had also helped departments in their planning. It eliminated the "end of year syndrome" because funds were allowed to be carried forward from year to year. However, there had been a tendency for the guidelines to be regarded as firm intentions, rather than estimates, and a promise of the allocation of funds. It has been South Australian experience that it is more difficult to forecast their Revenue Account that their Loan Account, and an explanation offered is that whereas available funds for capital purposes can be estimated more confidently, in the recurrent area a state government can influence the total availability of funds by its own efforts in taxes, fees, and charges. It could be that departments who are aware of this find it harder to cut back expanded or new services. It is also true that there is a much greater variety of services to be financed through a Revenue Account. For these and other reasons the South Australian government endeavours to view recurrent and capital funds *together* and not isolated into the two separate accounts.

New South Wales had experienced a review of its machinery of government (borrowing on Canadian experience in Ontario in the early 1970s) under Premier Tom Lewis, and the results promised some rationalization of the cabinet and administrative structure, but the loss of government in the state by the Liberals meant that these reforms were not implemented.[61] The Wran government took some swift action after gaining power in 1976 to strengthen the policy coordination role of the Premier's Department and rein in the statutory corporations, especially in relation to the large sums of money they held in trust funds. Moves were also set in train to begin a slow process of amalgamation of local authorities by means of a Boundaries Commission. To date there has been no wholesale streamlining of the machinery of government or instalment of forward planning processes. The New South Wales Under Treasurer claimed, in 1978, that three or five year programming in both the capital and recurrent areas had been established. The government, he said, had provided two year allocations to departments and authorities on the capital side, thereby giving them a three year forward period with firm allocations for the current year and forecasts for the following two years. However, this procedure had not been adopted for the recurrent budget and he was deeply sceptical of the value of such a concept, although he paid lip service to the usefulness of forward estimates in what he called "planning and preparing for future financial policies and budget strategies". He did make the important observation that many decisions made in one year's budget committed the budgets in future years, and capital expenditure decisions also carried major budget implications for the future, for example, hospitals, goals, and welfare homes. (One example given was a teaching hospital complex whose running costs would exceed its capital costs after only two and a half years.)[62]

However, the greatest promise of reform in the public sector lies in the work of the *Review of New South Wales Government Administration* established by the Wran government soon after coming into office, and being conducted by a single commissioner, Professor Peter Wilenski. An interim report and a final report have been publicly issued[63] and many of their recommendations have already been implemented. Space prevents a comprehensive analysis of this report, but a number of its comments were extremely pertinent to this study and must be mentioned. There was seen to be a major deficiency in the area of policy formulation and programme review, and recommendations were made for a Priorities Review Unit "to examine priorities from the point of view of government as a whole and analyse issues without a vested interest in the outcome". (This recommendation was influenced by the issues of the CPRS and the Australian PRS in providing a macro viewpoint across the whole public sector.) Other recommendations on this aspect included the need for policy units within departments and agencies, the retention of some control and review of policy in the Premier's Department, and the sporadic use of task forces to respond to urgent situations which cross departmental boundaries. In relation to budgeting, the report observed "Not all control and management and planning should take place within the budget cycle" because of the fear of overloading. It suggested that some sort of machinery for review of priorities and evaluation of programmes should be established in close proximity to the budget process so that the results could be fed into budgetary decisions. The report lamented the fragmentation and lack of central control of the New South Wales government budget, as well as the distinct separation of the current and capital elements of the budget, and observed that the budgetary process itself was purely incremental in nature.

The Review made some incisive remarks about forward estimates with a short examination of experience in Britain and at the Australian national government level. The report concluded:

2.41 Foward estimates, i.e., estimates of expenditure in years beyond the current one, are an essential element in good budgetary procedures. They can generally assist the preparation of the current budget by showing the future implications of current decisions, where the government is going, and what room there is likely to be for new programmes.

2.42 Much, however, depends on their method of preparation and presentation. Forward estimates can become simply a "wish list" which gives a distorted picture of likely future trends or they can lock expenditure into ongoing programmes . . .

2.46 With British and Australian experience in mind, it would seem that the simplest and most valuable role for forward estimates in New South Wales would be to provide reliable information to Ministers and officials on the estimated future costs of ongoing programmes of expenditure under existing policies. Providing the government with a clearer picture about the future implications of current activities and intentions under current policies would assist decision making on the current year's expenditures and be a tool for choice rather than a pre-emption of it.[64]

The report also advocated a better presentation of public accounts data for the state including the use of programme and output classifications. In relation to specific recommendations in this area the report of the review stated that there were six areas where change was essential:

* Clearer and more formal expression of government priorities in a form that can give budgetary decisions.
* The development of means to ensure that ongoing programmes compete with new ones for resources.
* The development of a comprehensive State Capital Budget.
* Increased emphasis on policy analysis and programme evaluation to feed into budgetary decisions.
* Moves towards bringing capital and recurrent expenditure budgets closer together.
* Improvements in information systems and better presentation of data.[65]

To achieve these aims the report recommended inclusion of all semi-government bodies in the budget sector, establishment of a special Capital Works Unit in the Treasury, three year forward estimates to cover both capital and recurrent programmes, an earlier budget cycle, and new review and management processes. A little later, especially in relation to public works, the report draws attention to the lack of coordination of policies within the state government and the need for greater physical and economic forecasting, land use and corporate planning. Some caustic remarks were passed about earlier attempts in New South Wales at corporate planning whereby agencies were asked to identify their objectives, the means to achieve those objectives, and the constraints likely in meeting them over the next three, six, and ten years. The exercise had proved fairly useless because there was no overall meaning to the total exercise, the "plans" were extremely variable in quality, and the bulk of them were just platitudinous statements.

There have been very few developments in any other states in the direction of public sector planning. Queensland has had a long history of the existence of separate administrative machinery for capital works expenditure. Commencing with the Bureau of Industry in the depression period, capital works were seen as having a prime role in the stimulation of overall economic development. At the end of the 1930s, a Coordinator General of Works was established, subsuming the Bureau and reinforcing the separation of the overview of public capital expenditure from recurrent expenditure, but with little attention to any firm, forward, coordinated plan. In relation to recurrent expenditure, the Queensland Treasury, like most state treasuries in Australia, has long resisted any attempts at firm forward estimates or other planning processes; although progress has been made on fiscal relationships between central agencies and departments, and effective external and internal auditing, including efficiency audits. For a short while in the 1970s, Queensland instituted a system of regional coordination involving local governments grouped by region in direct communication with the Coordinator General of Works, and hence the Premier, but this was abandoned in 1977.

In 1975 Queensland established a Priorities Review Committee, comprising the permanent heads of the four key central coordinating departments, ostensibly to obtain an overview of the prospective budget before it was finally formulated, but to date that committee has only been concerned with small savings in certain specific items such as travel and the use of government vehicles. In 1982 the Queensland Premier announced what was described as a major reform of central coordination with the merging of the Premier's Department and the Coordinator General's Department, but to date there is little evidence that this has materially affected the coordination of policy making in the state. Queensland remains the only Australian state not to have had a major review of its public administration in the 1970s. Other reviews have taken place in Tasmania (the Cartland review), and Western Australia.

It is highly significant that all of the inquiries into state government administration in Australia in the 1970s have recommended rationalization of the structure of government by means of a reduction in the number of units of government, more central overview of statutory authorities, better communication between various parts of the administration, centralization of priority determination, and the need for more refined advice on broad policy options to cabinets. They have, however, had little to say about federal-state-local relations or, more particularly, the role of parliament in the light of their suggested reforms of the machinery of government. It is true that during the period of the Whitlam Labor national government, the Australian state governments paid much closer attention to their own allocation of resources and tightened up the overview of priority determination across their own public sectors considerably. This was epitomized by the creation of units within the Premier's Departments of all state governments to handle the overview of federal-state relations. This new central overview began as a loose and temporary arrangement in each state, and with the passing of the Whitlam government some of the units and the policy coordination they symbolized fell into relative disuse. The late 1970s and the 1980s have witnessed rather an emergence of Premier's Departments as the strong coordinating force of policy determination for intragovernment relations as well as intergovernment relations. All state premiers in Australia are now supported by very sophisticated departments filled with policy advisors on high classifications, who inject a new coordinating capacity even if they are concerned more with short-term politically expedient issues rather than long-term strategies.

The Lessons of Australian Experience

From this albeit brief consideration of Australian experience it is clear that there has never been a system of planning of the kind we have defined. In relation to Australia as a whole, the nearest situation arose in the second world war when all levels and units of government were drawn into a highly coordinated framework supervised from a central point. When an attempt was made to transfer certain powers between levels of government to provide for a formal centralization of power to facilitate planning for postwar reconstruction, it failed. Thus any coordination and joint priority determination between levels of government in Australia has had to be performed on a cooperative and informal basis. Attempts at planning within each level of government have been limited and sporadic for other reasons. In respect of both relationships between levels of government, and developments within one level of government, the hindrances to the attainment of public sector planning have been as much political as they have been administrative or economic.

There are lessons to be drawn from the planning attempts we have observed arising out of Australian experience:

1. They have all been *piecemeal* attempts in the sense that they have been directed at pragmatic solutions to specific problems, and have never been part of any comprehensive framework for the whole public sector.

2. All of the attempts have been *ad hoc*. Whenever a planning mentality has emerged, and appropriate decision making and administrative structures have been devised, it has always been as if the architects and participants sensed the arrangements would only be temporary and were only required because of "abnormal" circumstances.

3. The vast bulk of planning attempts in Australian history have been *micro* attempts. That is to say, they have been concerned with only one sector of government activity and often only a portion of that sector. The few attempts made on a macro basis, for example, the Priorities Review Staff, or other central priority review mechanisms, have become quietly diverted into one or two sectors, or have only

dabbled in a marginal way across the public sector, or focused on a single resource or item of expenditure.

4. Every move towards public sector planning has been a *short term* consideration. They have either been directed at a problem, or economic or social situation, which was relatively shortlived. Where the system has been established with a permanent intention, it has usually lasted only for a couple of years.

5. Just about all of the planning machinery ever created in Australia has been *advisory*. It has rarely been given any executive powers or, more importantly, linked to any implementation process whereby the forecasts being made could be put into effect.

3

Federalism: The Concept

Here we shall be concerned with the *concept* of federalism, and in particular, whether it seems to possess any conceptual characteristics which would present inherent hindrances to implementation of the planning system previously outlined.

There is no comprehensive theory of federalism although there is a multitude of definitions of "federalism", a score or more of single descriptive frameworks, and a plethora of different "types" of federalism, all of which involve the use of a preceding adjective, for example, "cooperative federalism", "coordinate federalism", and so on. Federalism theory is still evolving and it is interesting to look at some aspects of that evolution.

In the first place each theory has arisen within the confines of a particular discipline. Thus, for many, it was the lawyers and specifically constitutional lawyers who pioneered this area (at least in twentieth century terms). Wheare's classic study is usually the starting point for other modern day theorists, most of whom take great delight in proving his federalism concept inapplicable to particular federations or components of them, or who seek to find internal incompatibilities in the construct of the Wheare formulation, or object to its static two dimensional portrayal. It has been predominantly political scientists and sociologists who have spearheaded this revulsion from the legal perception of federalism as exemplified by writers such as Friedrich, Livingston, Riker, Wildavsky, and most recently Davis. However, these authors have proved just as discipline-bound and their theories sit easily only within the boundaries of their own terminology. They are also just as adept as constitutional lawyers at simply borrowing models derived from other aspects of their discipline, and attempting to bring them to bear (unrefined and unmodified) on federalism. These comments are just as applicable to economists. Here it has been mainly within the subdiscipline of public finance that writers like Musgrave, Scott, Breton, Prest, and Cutt have sought to employ theories of allocation, stabilization and distribution, derived from unitary systems or in relation to only one level of government, to the situation of split levels of public revenue-raising and expenditure typical of federations. This leads to a quite naive approach where most of these economic theorists seem to regard federalism as an aberration from the simple world of centralized resource allocation, and it is, therefore, not surprising that they regard the solution to the federal "problem" as a mere harmonization of allocation and distribution decisions. Other disciplines, notably geography and history, have derived theories of federalism, mostly tangential to the mainstream of their curricula, and certainly with the same "blinkers" strapped firmly in place. Public Administration, to the extent that it is a discipline, is able by its amorphous nature to make use of all of these other bounded approaches, and it rests closely to (or within) political science in claiming to be able to subsume other disciplinary approaches to the extent that the political system can ultimately cap all other subelements of the process of resource and value determination. Nevertheless, there still is no overarching theory of federalism, even from political scientists, and the theoretical literature still consists of a bibliography of remnants each to be found in the call numbers and shelves of discrete disciplines.

A second related aspect is that although federalism theories, like all social science theories, are a blend of intellectual derivation and empirical observation, they tend to comprise more of the latter than the former. That is to say, federalism theories seem to be derived more from abstractions with strong roots in observations of particular federations, than from any logically derived conceptions based on abstract notions of the state or society as a whole. Thus there have been no "ideal-types" presented. Each theory reads more like a comparative framework constructed to fit at least one, but often more, federal systems. This appears to lead to a third feature which is an observable nationalistic streak in many of the theories. Perhaps this is unavoidable because the United States of America is obviously the outstanding example of the modern era of federalism, and few writers on federal theory are able to ignore it, so that any theory derived must at least fit the United States. To a less appreciable extent, most of the theories also reflect something of the characteristics of the system in which the author resides or knows best. Maybe this is simply a reflection of the fact that there is a variety of federal systems throughout the world.

Fourthly there has been, at least in the theories developed in the 1950s and 1960s, an aura of uncertainty about the future and stability of federalism as a practice and as a concept. It has often been described as a temporary phenomenon, a phase through which politics pass on the way towards becoming unitary systems or on the path to structural breakdown. This fear is not to be found in more recent theories, perhaps for the simple reason that federations appear to have established their endurance — most of them at least. But this earlier hesitancy in the literature has led to a fifth, more basic conflict amongst theorists, namely, the question of whether federalism theories ought themselves to be static or dynamic. Now the conceptual stance of Wheare and many other constitutional lawyers is unmistakeably static, in that they saw federalism as a system pervaded by a series of constant relationships between its parts, and clearly delineated formal relationships at that. In all probability this simply reflects a lawyer's view of the world — any world. The contribution of the other social sciences, and particularly political science and sociology, has been to depict federalism as a dynamic concept with relationships which may change in something of a kaleidoscopic manner, those relationships being caused by informal as well as formal aspects of the system, with any necessary equilibrium occurring naturally, but above all, dynamically. Obviously, the dynamic theories lose a little in precision, but they have the advantage of explaining the functioning as well as the structure of the federal system, and thus are able to accommodate descriptions of shifts in the relationships between parts of the system, the question of when a federation ceases to be a federation notwithstanding.

The aspects just outlined seem to be applicable to most theories of federalism, but the decade of the 1970s has seen literature bedevilled by other "problems". Generally speaking, these stem from the desire by authors to attempt to apply general theories of political, economic, or social behaviour to systems which are federal, without taking account of the uniqueness of federalism itself. The most noticeable aspect of this trend is the new literature of "intergovernmental relations" which seeks to provide an umbrella discussion framework which can subsume and even replace the older notion of "federalism". In the process, however, it loses sight of such important features as the divided sovereignty in federal systems between national and subnational units, and since most of the writers in this school are Americans, it tends also to neglect the intrinsic difference between republican and monarchical forms of government, and most importantly, the special problems of reconciling the somewhat irreconcilable conceptual differences between the principles of accountability under the Westminster model of government and the inherent notions of federalism itself. It is perhaps understandable that this last mentioned point escapes an American or European writer, but a Canadian or Australian potential theorist is well aware of the difficulties that are presented in trying to enmesh the separation of powers and the division of powers. That question certainly exercised the grey matter of the founding fathers of those two federations, many of whom might well be regarded as federalism theorists of their day. These factors render any general theories of intergovernmental relations as suspect for our purposes here, especially if they are purporting to relate to central/local or central/regional relationships in unitary countries as well.

However the absence of any single overarching federalism theory need not be a major obstacle in the identification of the characteristics of the federalism concept. It is a relatively straightforward (though tedious) exercise to compare various theories of federalism, irrespective of their origin, and identify a number of aspects common to most of them, and in this way build up a reasonably comprehensive picture. The following seem to be the key common points relevant to our task.

1

Federalism clearly involves divided sovereignty, a concept unknown in a unitary system. It has long been observed that one of the unique characteristics of federalism is that both national and subnational units are elected by the same people, and to the extent that sovereignty can be equated with the "will of the people", this gives rise immediately to a situation where each level can claim a mandate from the same people. The notion is further complicated because federations are typically created in a manner whereby pre-existing subnational units are perceived to spawn a new national unit. (To the best of my knowledge there is no federation where a pre-existing national unit created new subnational units and then voluntarily shared its sovereignty with the new level.)

This aspect of federalism has always caused a great deal of bother to theorists. Davis is of the opinion that the ancient Hellenic civilizations did not represent an association of sovereignty entities in terms of the autonomy which characterizes twentieth century federations.[1] Indeed the very concept of "sovereignty" was still being defined during the time of the medieval leagues, because the meaning of the word as it had evolved during the time of the Holy Roman Empire was no longer applicable. As Davis observes, whilst the power of the King, like that of the Roman Emperor, was indivisible, that was of no use in a more fragmented Empire:

> What is the case, however, when there are two claimants to ultimate power? Plainly, if the power of a gun cannot resolve the matter, or if the force of arms and the force of belief are equally matched, then the ingenuity of a canonical jurisprudence, inspired by a remarkable instinct for survival, composed the rationalizations and the formula of reconciliation in a theory of duality.[2]

The notion of duality has persevered to the present time and there are many modern day theorists who see federalism, for example, as dual citizenship flowing from divided sovereignty. (This of course plays havoc with foreign policy when it is usually required that one government speak on behalf of each nation.)

Naturally enough, the concept of duality or divided sovereignty was anathema to political theorists of the sixteenth and seventeenth centuries, such as Bodin, who saw stability and authority as mainstays of a monarchical system (then being challenged by republicans) — a stability brought about by authority which was centralized, absolute, and indivisible, and personified of course in the sovereign himself. Similar difficulties plagued the philosophical argument of Althusius and his corporate theory of the state. Once again Davis expresses the dilemma very clearly:

> The reconditioning of civic culture from the experience of sovereignty personalized in a monarch to the depersonalized sovereignty of a constitution, and from an indivisible to a divisible sovereignty, however, cannot be affected before time, circumstance, and necessity; and time, circumstance and necessity cannot be replicated in any test tube known to man.[3]

Davis argues that the American situation in the late eighteenth century provided the time, circumstance, and the necessity. Indeed the early years of the American federation saw nationalists arguing for a concept of undivided sovereignty, whilst states-rights advocates preferred to argue that the constitution had effectively divided sovereignty between all the constituent units of the federation — a situation which still prevails very much today (especially in Australia and Canada as we shall see later).

A completely different perspective on this aspect of the question is provided by Friedrich who argues that "sovereignty" is the wrong word to use when speaking of federalism. As he says, "no sovereign can exist in a federal system; autonomy and sovereignty exclude each other in such a political order. To speak of the transfer of part of the sovereignty is to deny the idea of sovereignty which since Bodin has meant indivisibility." For Friedrich, the idea of a compact is inherent in federalism, and the "constituent power" which makes the compact takes the place of the sovereign.[4]

As Sawer points out,[5] the theories of coordinate sovereignty and separate action were powerful in the United States until well into the twentieth century, as symbolized in Bryce's factory analogy in his *American Commonwealth*. The system, Bryce said, was "like a great factory wherein two sets of machinery are at work, their revolving wheels apparently intermixed, their bands crossing one another, yet each doing its own work without touching or hampering the other".[6]

Sawer describes the transition of the sovereignty concept in America by pointing out that the originality of the American solution lay in the fact that under the arrangements of 1787 the centre could operate directly on the citizen, and not merely on the regional governments, as had been the case with the medieval and early Leagues and Confederations. At this time,

> the argument that sovereignty belonged not to any government but to the people — suited the spirit of the Revolution, and accorded well with the natural law and social contract theories which influenced popular attitudes as well as learned commentary in the eighteenth century. . . . In a phrase current at the time, only the people had "perfect sovereignty". If so, then centre and region were in their mutual relations co-ordinate, neither superior to the other, and the Constitution as a whole was valid because of its *popular* basis.

Sawer points out that even in the United States application of this doctrine was ambiguous because the Constitutional Conventions were not a gathering of the people *as a whole* but rather the people organized *in States*.[7]

What then did the English theorists make of the notion of divided sovereignty? The starting point is usually Dicey's attempt to compare unitary and federal systems where he observes, not without a certain degree of wistfulness:

> The distribution of all the powers of the state among coordinate authorities *necessarily* leads to the result that no one authority can wield the same amount of power as under a unitarian constitution is possessed by the sovereign. A scheme again of checks and balances in which the strength of the common government is so to speak pitted against that of the state government leads, on the face of it,

to a certain waste of the energy. A federation therefore will always be at a disadvantage in a contest with unitarian states of equal resources.[8]

This view of the coordinate nature of federalism finds its clearest expression in Wheare's writings, as we shall see shortly, but Wheare rarely directly confronts the divided sovereignty problem. His "federal principle", rather, speaks of a division of *powers*; his "test of a federal government" again speaks only of dividing *powers*; his so-called "prerequisites of federal government" speak in terms of communities which desire division of *government* for different functions; and the word "sovereignty" does not appear at all, although the concept is implied in his discussion of secession, war, foreign relations, and economic affairs. One is forced to conclude that Wheare either regards "sovereignty" as a concept not worth discussing, or else he is equating it with the terms "power" and "government".[9] Indeed, in the writings of most theorists, the sovereignty concept appears indirectly, and later twentieth century writers seem to accept the notion of divided sovereignty without any philosophical equivocation. Thus both Livingston and Duchacek speak of the territorial aspect of federalism and strongly imply that spatial integrity creates a division of sovereignty. Riker speaks of dual citizen loyalties which, he says, maintain the "federal bargain", but that itself, he points out, is a mere tautology.[10] He also employs the concept of "autonomy" in a way which smacks strongly of the notions of sovereignty. Birch uses the term "authority" seemingly as a substitute for "sovereignty".[11] Grodzins says that federalism is a device for dividing *decisions* and *functions* of government, but it is interesting that three of his four causes of dispersed *power* in a federal system are (a) the fact that states existed before the nation, (b) distrust of the central power, and (c) pride in locality and state nurtured by the nation's size and variations of history.[12] (Those factors are now recognized ingredients of modern day tangible expressions of "sovereignty".)

In a detailed attempt to study sovereignty in federal systems Sharma comes to the conclusion that such sovereignty assumes three aspects — the location of sovereign authority, the doctrine of nullification, and the right of seccession of the units from the union. In relation to the first of these, he believes that there is both a theoretical and practical way to answer the question of the location of sovereignty. From a strictly legal point of view, Sharma observes "a federation is the result of the cumulative consent of not only the states but their citizens as well". Without the consent of those citizens the states cannot part with their sovereignty to establish a new government, and this is the view held by the nationalistic theory of federation. Another school, according to Sharma, holds that the parties to the pact that brings the federation into existence are the states, in their capacity as separate communities, and it is these states that are the real source of federal authority. There is a third view, says Sharma, which is that sovereignty lies in the authority authorized to amend the constitution. After canvassing the proponents of each of the three views and their practical experience (especially in the USA), Sharma comes to the conclusion that sovereignty in a federation is located in the individuals of all the states taken as a whole and nowhere else; that there is no division of sovereignty, only a "bifurcation of activities"; and the third viewpoint simply resolves itself into the familiar question of a majority having to respect the rights and wishes of a minority.[13]

Those three views of sovereignty can be reasonably accepted as the basic divisions of opinion about federal sovereignty which prevail in the later twentieth century, even if Sharma's own view of their relative importance is left in the balance, not to mention his delightfully vague expression "bifurcation of activities".

We have spent some time on this aspect of divided sovereignty because it is of the most fundamental importance to our particular exercise to marry the concepts of planning and federalism. The notion of divided sovereignty will recur often throughout this study because it is the basic causal political factor of the major hindrances to attainment of public sector planning in a federation, and the theoretical notion of divided sovereignty will be given practical expression with Australian and Canadian examples. For the moment we can observe that the concept of divided sovereignty also leads to the following concept.

2

The concept of an attempt to delineate areas of jurisdiction for the national and subnational units and so seal them into watertight compartments, more commonly known as the division of powers, has a long history. It is perhaps best crystallized in Wheare's portrayal of the federal units being, as he put it, "within a sphere, coordinate and independent". This is commonly regarded as "coordinate federalism", and although it is the subject of much speculation and attack by other theorists, there are few who would not see some sort of division of powers as characteristic of all federal systems. It is the question of what that division symbolizes, and its precise nature and endurance, which causes most of the debate.

It is true that Wheare admits to the possibility of many variations in the manner in which the powers are divided. In a concluding chapter, he acknowledges the dynamic nature of the power division, for example, "It will have been obvious from the preceding chapters that an ideal division of powers between general and regional governments has not always been achieved in modern federations and that it is difficult to make readjustments in some cases. Yet the federal principle does not prohibit such readjustments. And, if they can be made, then there will be sufficient unity to cope with modern economic life."[14] However, his prescription of the prerequisites for federal government, and the accompanying tests of federal government and model organization, convey a much more static and two-dimensional picture of federalism.

It is this aspect to which other writers, especially nonlegal ones, take exception. Livingston, a sociologist, for example deplores the dominance of the legal view of federalism, stating, as might be expected, that "the essence of federalism lies not in the constitutional or institutional structure but in the society itself. Federal government is a device by which the federal qualities of the society are articulated and protected". For Livingston, federalism is a relative, and not an absolute, term and his "division" of activity is somewhat different:

> Federal government is a form of political and Constitutional organization that unites into a single polity a number of diversified groups or component polities so that the personality and individuality of the component parts are largely preserved while creating in the new totality a separate and distinct political and constitutional unit.[15]

Livingston then observes that the problem of federalism is to make the instrumentalities fit the society beneath, but it is not long before he admits that "the real key to the nature of a federation is in the distribution of powers . . . federalism implies the existence of two coordinates sets of government operating at two different levels in two different spheres".[16]

Sawer has as one of his basic federal principles the following:

> The power to govern is distributed between the centre and the regions in such a way that each set of governmental institutions has a direct impact on the individual citizens and other legal persons within its area of competence.[17]

Friedrich, the political scientist, argues that:

> . . . federalism should not be seen only as a static pattern or design, characterized by a particular and precisely fixed division of power between governmental levels. Federalism is also and perhaps primarily the process of federalizing a political community, that is to say, the process by which a number of separate political communities enter into arrangements for working out solutions, adopting joint policies, and making joint decisions on joint problems and, conversely, also the process by which a unitary political community becomes differentiated into a federally organized whole.[18]

Davis, on the other hand, regards a division of powers as implicit in the concept of federalism itself. He says the division can be viewed qualitatively as well as quantitatively, and argues that it doesn't really matter how the distribution is done, as long as it's done. There is no a priori principle.[19] By contrast, in Riker's concept of federalism as a bargain, he says that the division of powers has little or nothing to do with maintaining that bargain.[20]

Other writers seem to insist that the division of powers must be between levels of government which have territorial dimensions. In other words, it is the fact that powers are being divided spatially as well as jurisdictionally that appears to hold importance for them.[21]

There are, of course, a number of writers who emphasize that the coordinate federalism concept and its division of powers has become greatly out of touch with modern empirical experience, and therefore it is not always possible to have a clear division of functions. Morton Grodzins's culinary image of federalism as a marble cake, rather than a layer cake, is the best example, and we shall be confronting the truth of this phenomenon empirically in later chapters; but even Grodzins still affirms that his main focus is on the "purpose of federalism" which, he says, is the distribution of power between central and peripheral units of government.[22]

These examples drawn from various theorists are sufficient to demonstrate the pervasiveness of the concept of a division of power as a common element of federalism, and for most of them a consequent division of powers are specifically enumerated, although most would agree that there need be no fixed prescription to determine the precise division, or where the residual power should lie. The vast majority favours a flexible division of powers capable of being rearranged according to changing circumstances, and even those who seek to espouse the futility of trying to divide public functions between levels of government are nonetheless admitting the universality of the practice.

We shall devote a major part of this study to the division of powers in the two federations under review because it is clear that the division of powers is the major expression of divided sovereignty, which, as we have commented, appears to stand in clear contradiction to our concept of planning. It is sufficient to note at this stage that the very idea of attempting to create discrete areas of activity for each of the participants in a dynamic federal system obviously and immediately gives rise to the possibility of conflict over jurisdictional territory between those participants, and this leads to the following common theoretical construct.

3

Another construct is the existence of an umpire to resolve questions of sovereignty over disputed claims to functions, revenue, even spatial territory itself, and all other resources. This umpire is usually a court which relies on written documents (a constitution, and possibly other documents), together with customs and conventions; but it need not be a court as long as its role is regarded as legitimate by all the participants and its decisions are binding upon them all.

As might be anticipated, constitutional lawyers stress this factor in the functioning as well as the structure of federalism. Two of Sawer's basic federal principles are the following:

> The constitution provides rules to determine any conflict of authority between centre and regions, where but for the conflict the activity in question would have been within the competence of each of the conflicting authorities. Theoretically the rule could favour either regions or centre, and could vary with the subject of power; in all known cases the general rule is that the centre law prevails.

The distribution of competence between centre and regions is interpreted and policed by a judicial authority which can make authoritative determinations as to the validity of governmental acts (including legislation) where these are alleged to be beyond the competence of the centre or a region, or where the conflict rules referred to . . . have to be applied.[23]

Later Sawer points out that the composition and operation of the court can vary from federation to federation but its function remains the same. The point is that most federal systems accept the principle of judicial review and "the possibility of such review is the most reliable sanction for the preservation of a federal structure. Such review can be effective only if law and the decisions of Courts are habitually observed and treated with respect."[24]

Wheare's view is that the constitution, written or unwritten, must be supreme if a government is to be federal, and by this he means that the terms of the agreement which establishes the general and regional governments, and distributes powers between them, must be binding on those governments. Moreover, the last word in settling disputes about the meaning of the division of powers must not rest either with the general government alone or with the regional government alone. He goes on:

This necessity has been recognized by the founders of most federal systems, but they have not always applied it with complete consistency. Moreover, when they have established some institution with power to decide disputes about the division of powers, they have not confined its jurisdiction merely to that part of the federal Constitution; on the contrary they have given it power to decide the meaning of the whole Constitution — an increase in authority which is not logically necessary for federalism.[25]

Wheare also observes the tendency in most federations for such a dispute-settling body to be appointed and be dismissible by the general government, and this had resulted in Supreme Courts or their equivalent being accused from time to time of undue partiality to the general government.

Other writers have expressed the "umpire" role in slightly different ways. Livingston remarks that the need for such an institution arises because the terms of the distribution of functions can, at best, be only very general, and difficulties will be encountered in applying them to concrete situations.[26] Sharma includes a special position for the judiciary as the third characteristic which, he says, is a natural response of the first two, namely, the supremacy of the constitution and the coexistence of two governments. It is necessary, says Sharma, that there be some agency to "uphold the constitution and keep the two governments within proper limits".[27] Paul Freund expresses the opinion that a federal system presupposes diversity and must cope with corresponding tensions. Once the "general pattern" is validated by the court, he says, "the structure and balance of forces both private and public, which shape the federal system, are left to the working of politics. Thus the courts may be conceived as umpires determining what kinds of contests are permissible, leaving the choice of contests and the detailed rules to be worked out by the immediate participants."[28]

This leads us to a recognition of the fact that the legal process for arbitration of territorial and functional disputes is insufficient for the resolution of all political conflicts.

4

There is also a need for mechanisms for the political allocation of powers and resources, which can be found as for example with conferences of ministers and first ministers, through to the high degree of informality present in pressure groups, parties and the media through which issues are processed, these groups reflecting in turn the federal nature of the system in their own modus operandi. The most forceful writer on this aspect is unquestionably William Riker who attaches vital importance to the party system as the key element in maintenance of a federal system. He says:

> Whatever the general social conditions, if any, that sustain the federal bargain, there is one institutional condition that controls the nature of the bargain in all the instances here examined and in all others with which I am familiar. This is the structure of the party system, which may be regarded as the main variable intervening between the background social conditions and the specific nature of the federal bargain.[29]

Sawer is more cautious about the role of parties. He says that it is exceptional for political parties to have as a genuine independent objective the maintenance of the federal system. They often proclaim support for federalism, Sawer observes, but this is usually because at the particular time the federal distribution of power favours some other objectives which the party wants to achieve. He goes on to point out that in the politics of federalism most parties operating at the centre, or the centre components of parties operating at both the central and regional level, are inevitably driven by circumstances to seek some increase in centre powers. However, "there is an important counter-factor, operating in all federalism, and that is the extent to which national political parties are forced by the mere existence of the federal system to take on a federal shape and be influenced by the vested interests of region governments in their own existence".[30] As part of an investigation into administration in federal systems Watts comes to the conclusion that the effectiveness of a federation depends not just on the constitution, but also on the operation of the political parties and the executives (especially the public services): "the way in which the political parties operate will determine whether interstate cohesion or conflict is accentuated . . . The effectiveness and stability of the federation will depend on whether the public services provide effective administration and upon their leadership in contributing to cohesion and collaboration between levels of government within the federation".[31]

Livingston sums up the origin of these institutions by pointing out that the fractionizing of power that is part of the character of federalism also opens the way for the creation of independent decision-making bodies (conferences of first ministers, royal commissions, fiscal bargaining conferences etc.), which, he observes, appear to be perfectly compatible with federalism but are quite out of harmony with the assumptions of a parliamentary system.[32] We shall have much to say about this aspect in later chapters.

5

Federalism also seems to involve some degree of heterogeneity of the population of the nation. Earlier writers saw cultural differences as the main element of that heterogeneity exemplified by racial, linguistic, and other variations; but more modern theorists see geographical factors as equally divisive aspects, even if the geographical factor is solely one of distance, whereupon, in territorially large federations, spatial considerations can at times prove to be just as significant as cultural ones. The bulk of theorists see the creation of a federal system as a response to the diversity which already exists in the society for which the federation is to be created. (Consider for example Grodzins' causes of dispersed power in a federal system, which was mentioned earlier.) This was the essence of Dicey's description of federalism as being motivated by a desire for *union without unity*.[33] It is reflected in the provisions made in many federations to prevent one regional government from interfering with another, or even in an explicit protection of minority groups, especially when those minority groups happen to be spatially concentrated. For that and other reasons Dikshit believes federalism is the most geographically expressive of all forms of government. It is, he points out, based on the existence of regional differences or a sense of locality. Also, because of the dual political organization and the grant of substantial regional autonomy, the regions remain highly articulate and that means that spatial interactions in a federation, unlike other forms of government, are most clearly recognized. This means that federalism starts with a tacit recognition of the immutability of regional personalities, and spatial political interactions are recognized and provided for.[34]

One of Duchacek's "ten yardsticks of federalism" is the question: "Are the component units immune to elimination of their identity, (outdating or postdating the union), and authority?"[35] But he later refines his so-called model by considering "extraconstitutional reality" and immediately produces what he calls the problem of "federal asymmetry and polyethnicity":

> The component units that the Constitition views as somewhat equal for the purpose of government are now ... highly different in size and population, possessing different economic and political powers, and manifesting unequal interest in the way in which the federal system is supposed to operate. This problem of asymetry may sometimes lead either to intrafederal hegemony or to ex-

plosion, especially if such asymmetry is compounded by linguistic, ethnic, racial or religious differences coinciding with territorial subdivisions. These differences are often exploited by external interference.[36]

A good many writers have commenced their analysis of this heterogeneity in federal systems with the uncompromising statement of Livingston that it is only societies in which social diversities are geographically distributed which can properly be called federal.[37] Watts, for example, takes issue with the logic of this argument and says that even where there are no regionally localized interests, a territorial distribution of power within a federal structure might be advocated simply as a means to limited government and the prevention of tyranny within a plural society. He adds that:

Although all the new federations have contained sectional groups which were geographically distributed rarely have these coincided precisely with the regional political units. In the first place, social diversities have not generally been territorially segregated so exactly that regional political boundaries could mark off completely homogenous units. People just do not arrange themselves like that. (In Canada, he points out, not all the French Canadians live in Quebec). . . . Secondly, even where social diversities are basically regional in their distribution, the geographical location of historical, racial, cultural, economic and other social interests may not coincide precisely with each other. Territorial diversities may operate at several different geographical levels: some may coincide fairly closely with the actual regional political units, others may correspond to groups of states or provinces, while still others may represent divisions within individual territories.[38]

None of this, of course, is to deny our basic proposition which is that federations typically contain some measure of heterogeneity in their populations, however that heterogeneity is expressed or grouped. And, as we observed, the federal structure has usually been tailored with at least some view towards accommodating their diversity. Of course, it may also be true that the federal structure once established serves to reinforce or even ferment such diversity. As Livingston says:

The Constitution, which endows the states with the characteristics of diversity, treats them indiscriminately, and thus tends to create diversity where none previously existed.[39]

6

Perhaps the most crucial aspect of all for the preservation of federal systems, despite the oscillations which occur within them, is the existence of a balance of power. Virtually all modern theorists acknowledge that balance of power to be a dynamic balance, and that means there must exist methods of altering the balance of power. In the words of Friedrich:

Federal relations are fluctuating relations in the very nature of things. Any federally organized community must therefore provide itself with instrumentalities for the recurrent revision of its pattern or design. For only thus can the shifting balance of common and disparate values, interests, and beliefs be effectively reflected in more differentiated or more integrated relations.[40]

Some of the most popular techniques identified in the theory (and practice) of federalism include:

(a) A formal amending process, often by means of referendum, differing in nature between federations, but present in all of them. Livingston argues that in such an amending process the subnational units as separate entities must play a part.[41] This is an ambiguous statement and certainly not in accord with many modern federations. He expresses the thought a little more concisely when he says that it is "generally agreed" that the central legislature cannot be permitted to amend the constitution by itself; and he does raise many pertinent questions. (For example, he asks: Does the fact that a government is federal make necessary a certain kind of amending process? Should it be possible for the constitution to be changed with the consent of less than the whole number of component units? What is the relation between the amendment procedure and the doctrine and practice of majority rule? If democracy be equated with the rule of majorities, can it be said that federalism is inconsistent with democracy?)[42] Sawer expresses it this way in the fourth of his "basic federal principles": "The distribution of competence between centre and regions is affected by a constitution (usually written) having a fair degree of rigidity, so that its basic terms are 'entrenched' — that is, cannot be amended at the sole discretion of the centre or any region or combination of regions".[43] Wheare points out that in virtually all federations the process of amending constitutions is a different process from that of amending their ordinary laws,[44] and McMahon makes the extremely interesting observation that the structure and constitutions of the subnational units themselves are very rigid, and thus rarely amended.[45]

(b) Interpretations of the constitution by the umpire or court can in reality also be a method of altering the balance of power between the levels of government. We have already examined this aspect.

(c) A process whereby the subnational units of government are given representation in the parliament of the national level. This is usually achieved by means of a second chamber spatially elected (or appointed) to represent formally, or through tokenism at least, the wishes of spatial electorates which usually coincide with the boundaries of each subnational unit. Interestingly, this process is not the one through which the reverse flow occurs, and the process of national influence over subnational units is usually through some less formal mechanisms.

Ronald Watts states as his first requirement for federal stability that: "the federal structure must enable the political desires for regional diversity to express themselves adequately. If this opportunity is inadequate secession and fragmentation is likely to result".[46] Duchacek has as the sixth of his ten yardsticks of federalism the following: "Is the collective sharing in federal rule making adequately secured by equal representation of unequal units in a bicameral system?"[47] It should be noted that Duchacek, unlike most writers, raises firmly the spectre of *equal* representation for the subnational units; most writers are content to settle for mere representation. Livingston believes that practice is convenient but not, he argues, essential. He sees it as important that the quality of statehood is represented, and would not agree with writers who believe this feature to be the distinguishing mark of federalism.[48] It does not figure as one of Sawer's basic federal principles, and he notes in passing that this type of upper house has been on the whole a disappointment, at least from the federal point of view.[49] He also makes an astute observation that the failure of the Australian Senate to act as intended is a move towards coordinate federalism, not away from it. Wheare's answer to the question of whether this is an essential feature of federalism is probably the best one for our purposes: "the right answer seems to be that equal representation of the regions in the upper house is not essential logically for a government if it is to be federal, but at the same time it is often essential if federal government is to work well".[50] Wheare's sentiments can be applied equally well to the next concept.

(d) A process whereby the interests of the subnational units in the federation are seen to be represented in the executive of the national government. This is identified as a power brokerage method by only a few writers but as we shall see it has assumed particular importance in Canada and Australia. That is undoubtedly why the second half of Duchacek's sixth yardstick of federalism reads: "What are the Constitutional provisions for collective sharing in the executive and judiciary rule implementation".[51] Livingston observes that although there is no standard type of executive in a federal system nearly all admit some federal qualities,[52] whether it be the electoral college method of selecting an American president, or the deliberate attempts by Canadian and Australian prime ministers to compose a cabinet according to regional and even religious interests.

(e) Provisions for a temporary, and in some cases permanent, interchange of powers, often written explicitly into a constitution and capable of being initiated by either level, that is, by the executives of either level.

(f) Fiscal provisions, usually contained in a written constitution but, more often than not, so vague as to allow a constant ebb and flow of fiscal dominance to take place largely free of the possibility of legal challenge. Davis points out that the dividing of fiscal resources between levels of government is not unique to federalism and every system of territorial delegation involves the distribution of money and criteria for that purpose. What is peculiar to federal systems, he says, is: "the notion that every division of tax sources should keep faith with two ideals: to assure each government sufficient monies to do what it is (or what it is believed to be) constitutionally responsible for, and to assure each government 'independence' (i.e. the independence befitting its 'coordinate' status) in deciding how and in what order to spend its moneys. These are probably irreconcilable expectations . . ."[53] Watts emphasizes the importance of federal finance and says it is significant in three ways: (i) it affects the allocation of administration responsibilities; (ii) it affects the political balance; and (iii) the assignment of fiscal and expenditure powers will determine which governments are able to use those instruments to control the economy.[54] For his part, Wheare is adamant in pointing out that respect for the so-called federal principle requires in practice that both general and regional governments must each have under its own independent control financial resources sufficient to perform its exclusive functions.[55] One can see immediately the difficulty if it is insisted, as Wheare does, that each level must have these resources "under its own independent control". Note that Davis was content that each level should have sufficient resources, the qualitative nature of those resources and the derivation of them notwithstanding. Wheare has here laid down a very harsh condition.

Clearly all analyses of federalism are agreed on the importance of financial relationships to the power balance which is inherent in federalism, even if they differ in their perspectives of it.

(g) Executive or administrative arrangements created in order to secure necessary intergovernmental harmonization of action for a whole variety of purposes. It has only been in recent times that this has been recognized as an important channel for maintaining a power balance in federations and so there is little theoretical material in relation to it. The problem is that most theorists have relegated administrative relations to a passive role as, for example, when Watts says that the administrative relations in each federation are shaped by the character of the society, the institutional structure of the federation, and the political processes in the federation.[56] More recent country studies by Smiley, Simeon, Richardson, Wiltshire,[57] and others, reveal rather that the administrative relationships may affect the political relations and so alter the power balance, that is, they adopt an active role rather than a passive one.

(h) A balance of electoral and pressure group activity. (We shall be making some observations on this aspect in another context.) It is a moot point as to whether this is a cause or consequence of the very federal power relationships which exist, but there can be no doubt that the balance of power in federations, and shifts in it, can be markedly influenced by the electoral process and those who would prey upon it.

(i) The ability to create new subnational units of government or to amalgamate existing ones. Provision is made for this in all federal systems but it is not always a flexible affair. The constitution inevitably prescribes a formal process to achieve these ends.

(j)   Provision for the separation of power for each unit at each level, to keep all the elements of the federation democratic, and to prevent associated intrusions into the division of power. In some federations this concept has been extended so that one level can prevent the infringement of civil liberties in another level. Sawer argues that in some countries the separation of powers affects the division of powers, and he also believes that the effective judicial protection of guaranteed individual liberties is more likely to occur in the federations, like Australia and Canada, because of the control over government activity at even the highest levels which the federal system itself gives to the judiciary.[58] Friedrich recalls an analysis by Montesquieu, which finds expression in Article IV of the American Constitution, that federal republics ought to be composed only of republics.[59] Of course the separation of powers takes on a different form in a Westminster model of government.

Conclusion

These factors then can be regarded as aspects common to most theories of federalism, all of which have a profound bearing on our attempt to reconcile the concept of planning with the concept of federalism. If one reviews these factors it becomes clear that, conceptually at least, "federalism", however defined, theoretically is marked by a number of features which include:

*   a lack of coordination
*   presence of diversity
*   a deliberate lack of unity and uniformity
*   fragmentation
*   a multiplicity of political, legal, and administrative mechanisms, institutions, and processes
*   a balance of power which is dynamic but is emphasized as static
*   separation of powers

At first glance this list, describing what appear to be intrinsic features of the federation concept, would seem to be diametrically opposed to the components of the planning concept formulated in the previous chapter. The very language of federalism is the antithesis of that used in conceptualizing planning, and it may be that we have struck immediately at the root cause of our dilemma.

However, it must immediately be emphasized that the theories of federalism also stress, by contrast, a number of common elements which seem more akin to notions of planning. At the most basic level there is the role of federalism in reconciling diversity in some matters with unity in others; and especially that of reconciling diversity and equality, which is the key factor in distinguishing federal from unitary government. Some more specific elements include at least the following:

1. A guarantee of the mobility of resources is invariably provided which seeks to ensure complete freedom of movement for resources, ideas, concepts, etc., around all parts of the federation. This is seen in its most explicit form in the provisions relating to interregional commerce and trade, but it can also be reflected in the allocation to the national level of functions such as migration, currency, weights and measures, broadcasting, censorship, etc.

2. Although the allocation of responsibility for economic affairs is usually divided between the national and subnational levels, the nature of the economic powers given to the national level is generally broader and superior to those given to the subnational level. Moreover, it is common for some economic powers to be concurrent with an inevitable accompanying proviso that national law will prevail in cases of conflict. This is not to deny some role (and at times a quite significant role) in the regulation of economic activity to the subnational levels — it simply means that the national powers are qualitatively superior. In the words of Watts:

    The sharing of responsibility for economic affairs between levels of government has necessitated a variety of arrangements. Sometimes economic matters have been placed under concurrent jurisdiction. On the other hand, often there have been complex subdivisions spelt out in much detail in legislative lists or in other sections of the constitutions allocating certain aspects exclusively to one tier of government or the other. In most of these federations the central government has been assigned relatively broad or at least concurrent powers over trade, commerce, industry, labour, communications, sources of energy, science, industrial research and statistics. Thus, in most cases, the central governments have possessed sufficient scope for comprehensive planning and for the promotion of economic development.[60]

3. Accompanying the specific division of powers some sort of residual power is indicated so that, other than powers explicitly mentioned, the remaining functions of government are intended to accrue to one level of the federation.

4. A provision is invariably included in the constitution giving one level of government virtually complete dominance in the event of a national emergency (notwithstanding the more difficult question as to which level should have the power to determine when such a national emergency exists, let alone the criteria to be employed).

5. As we have already observed, most federal constitutions invariably contain an inbuilt guarantee preventing any one unit of the federation from destroying other units or the whole system.

6. As also mentioned earlier there is provision made for an umpire in

all federations to resolve disputes between levels of government, but it is significant that there is but one umpire.

7. Then there are the natural factors which led to federation in the first place, and which can reasonably be assumed to retain some impetus, and still point to the need for some degree of central overview. Various authors have differing lists of such factors and each seems to emphasize different aspects, but most tend to include geographical proximity and even contiguity of the units, the need for one voice in international relationships, the fear of external aggression (admittedly weaker in some federations than in others), the expectation of economic advantage, sheer patriotism and national sentiment often coupled with republican or at least independent aspirations, and social and cultural bonds often caused by homogeneity of cultural background.

Some writers have concentrated heavily on this aspect seeking to determine, in particular, why various societies chose to unite in the form of federalism rather than another form. Riker, for example, speaks of two basic predispositions towards the federal "bargain". These are the "expansion condition", caused by politicians who for various reason seek to expand their territorial control, and the "military condition" under which politicians who accept the bargain are willing to do so because of some preconceived external military-diplomatic threat or opportunity.[61] By contrast, Wheare offers a number of suggestions as to why communities have been led to desire union. They include a sense of military insecurity and the consequent need for common defence, a desire to be independent of foreign powers, and a realization that only through union could independence be secured, a hope of economic advantage from union, some prior political association of the communities concerned, geographical neighbourhood, and a similarity of political (and presumably social) institutions.[62] Watts also lists some of these as relevant for most newer federations, and adds the need for administrative efficiency; a community outlook based on race, religion, language or culture; the influence of history; the character of political leadership; the existence of successful older models of federal union; and the influence of the United Kingdom government in constitution-making.[63]

8. A final factor, so often overlooked in federalism theories and admittedly not present in all federal systems, is an attempt to provide an equal standard of government services throughout the federation. Here we are referring mainly to equality in economic terms, although the more general aspect of protection of the interests of minority groups is also relevant. In the former case the most noticeable tangible expressions are the various, often cumbersome, schemes for horizontal fiscal equalization. In the case of the latter, there are often constitutional provisions entrenched in such a way as to prevent minorities

being discriminated against by any unit of the federation or by even all of them acting in concert. It may well be that the dominance of American writers on federalism theory, or writers who look mainly to the American model, has been responsible for the downplay of the concept of spatial equality since that has been much less an issue in the United States than in most other federal systems. We shall examine the phenomenon of equalization in depth in later chapters, but it should be noted at this point that any desire for such spatial equalization has inevitably resulted in more centralization of resource allocation, because it is usually regarded as an appropriate function to be performed by a level of government "higher" than the one to be equalized (West Germany is a notable exception).

In view of all the factors outlined, and no doubt others not considered, it becomes apparent that the attempt to superimpose the concept of planning upon the concept of federalism is fraught with a number of basic difficulties, including the many centrifugal political forces we have observed to be at work in federations. On the other hand we have also encountered a number of countervailing centripetal forces. The question is whether the one can offset the other, but more particularly whether the hindrances inherent in the federalism *concept* to our planning *concept* are so severe as to be impossible to overcome. This will be the prime consideration in the analysis which follows in subsequent chapters, and these conceptual points will be tested in a more empirical manner particularly in relation to the two federations under review. Also, it now becomes easier to understand why no comprehensive definition of "federalism" is possible, and it would seem much more profitable to take Sawer's approach and speak instead of a "federal situation". Whatever else federalism may be, it is certainly a political system characterized by a unique balance of power which in turn is markedly influenced by a diffusion of sovereignty throughout its component units. Friedrich's summation seems the most apt for our purposes:

> Federalism is more fully understood if it is seen as a process, an evolving pattern of changing relationships rather than a static design regulated by firm and unalterable rules.[64]

4

Federalism: Australia and Canada Compared

Having considered the conceptual difficulties involved in meshing the notion of planning and that of federalism, it is now necessary to assess the more specific and tangible hindrances by means of empirical analysis, in this case by way of an overview of these two federal systems.

There have been few attempts to compare Australia and Canada which is surprising in view of the marked similarities which exist between the two countries. Both are large geographical entities with a relatively small population which was originally predominantly from the British Isles; especially the hardy pioneer races from Scotland. The notable difference of course is the presence, in Canada, of a distinctive French province, and the need for accommodation of different cultures; a factor which Australia does not share. Both countries, however, have built up their populations by a deliberate and aggressive immigration effort concentrating mainly on European nations. Both paid little respect to the worth of the indigenous races of their lands. In the two countries the population is scattered and natural geographic features, including distance itself, serve to create a feeling of isolation from the main nucleus of activity, which in Canada is the "Torontreal" axis, and in Australia is the Melbourne-Sydney axis. Both countries span about forty degrees in latitude and over forty degrees of longitude. More than three-quarters of the area of both countries is not settled.

Economically there are many similarities as both countries are rich in rural and mineral resources, reasonably industrialized, but with a concentration of secondary and tertiary industry in the axes mentioned, which is often established behind protective tariff barriers. Transportation is a major problem in both countries, with extremely long distances involved in transporting primary and secondary commodities from source to market. Canada has the added disadvantage that, whilst the nation is basically an east-west conglomerate, the natural flow of economic activity would often be north-south with close trading relationships between bordering areas of the USA. These factors also make mass communications a difficult and expensive operation leading again to the feeling of isolation between parts of the country. Such aspects have been accentuated in both countries in the latter part of the twentieth century as many of the new discoveries of mineral resources have been in relatively remote areas, or at least in areas which possessed only a minimum amount of existing infrastructure.

Naturally it is the aspect of government which holds most interest for us here. The fundamental similarity is that both countries are federations seeking to function with a Westminster model of government. It is this combination which lies at the heart of many of the aspects we shall be considering subsequently and, indeed, it is this very factor which is the reason for the comparison of the two systems. In both countries there is a relatively small number of basic subnational units (six states and two territories in Australia, ten provinces and two territories in Canada), although there is a proliferation of local government units. The size of the states/provinces varies enormously, the most populous state in Australia having about eight times the population of the smallest state, and in Canada a comparable ratio of seventy to one. In terms of geographic areas there are enormous variations between the size of the Australian states, and also of the Canadian provinces.

The Canadian federation is thirty-four years older than the Australian, which accounts for one significant difference between the federations, in that all the present Australian states existed in the form of colonies at federation, whereas in Canada, more than half the existing provinces came into being as legal entities after federation in 1867. In present day terms it is possible to compare various Australian states with Canadian provinces, in a superficial way at least. New South Wales and Victoria have a close parallel with Ontario, all being large in population and containing the bulk of the nation's industrial activity and tending to take a "supportive" attitude to smaller states/provinces. Western Australia has many similarities with British Columbia in the sense of a feeling of isolation, and western isolation at that, including a lagging time zone. Western Australia and Queensland are also economically similar to Alberta and to a lesser extent Saskatchewan because of their large areas and rich mineral deposits, and their attendant desire to exploit them and claim full jurisdiction over them. The problems of Tasmania are akin to those of the maritime or even the Atlantic provinces in the sense of depressed economic activity; and also charm, resulting in part from the fact that in both countries these were areas of early settlement. It can be argued that there is no strict Australian equivalent of Quebec, although in respect of relationships with the national government Western Australia, South Australia, Tasmania and in recent years Queensland, have formed a close parallel.

These, however, are superficial aspects. It is necessary to consider features of the two countries in greater depth, not only to understand the dynamic of the two federal systems, but also to identify the elements of both systems which bear upon our attempts to identify the characteristics of each or both that would serve to hinder or help the attainment of some degree of public sector planning. We shall begin by using the comparative framework derived in the previous chapter from a synthesis of various theories of federalism.

Like all modern federations both Australia and Canada have written constitutions, although there are some differences in the content of the two documents which will shortly become apparent. They are also slightly different in nature, the *British North America Act* being a formal Act of the parliament of the United Kingdom whilst the Australian Constitution although also a statute, stands more as a constitutional document in its own right in the sense that formal constitutional changes are reflected in changes to that text. The *British North America Act* is, strictly speaking, only the dominant constitutional enactment, especially in the light of the package of reform measures introduced in conjunction with the patriation of the Canadian Constitution, including a Charter of Rights and Freedoms, Aboriginal Rights, Equalization and Regional Disparities, and provisions relating to provincial control over natural resources.

Sovereignty in these two federations is split between the national and subnational units. Both levels of government are elected on a common basis of universal suffrage, with compulsory voting in Australia. The Australian Senate is elected popularly whilst the Canadian Senate is appointed, and five of the six Australian states have upper houses most of which are democratically elected, whereas all Provincial parliaments in Canada are now unicameral. All of the provinces/states in the two systems have their own constitutions over which they remain the virtually unrestricted custodians. Whilst the Lieutenant Governors of the Canadian Provinces have been formally appointed by the Governor General, and constitutional provisions exist for the Governor General to disallow provincial legislation, the situation has been, in reality, more akin to that of the Australian states where the Queen appoints the Governors on the recommendation of the state government, and there are no powers of reservation or disallowance for the Governor General over the state governors. An attempt is made in both countries to divide powers between the two levels of government, and we shall examine this shortly. In both cases local government is the constitutional preserve of the states/provinces. However it has been factors other than these formal constitutional provisions which have drawn attention to the divided sovereignty of the two nations, and in this respect the issues which have arisen have been remarkably similar in the two countries. They include disputes over resources; especially mineral resources where the subnational units are able to present a legally based case for ownership and/or control. It is also reflected in attempts by the subnational units to forge international links of various kinds with other nations with, and more often without consultation with their own national government. In Australia there is also a constant reversion by the states to the argument that they pre-existed the national government and indeed created it (an argument not legally valid but politically persuasive). In Canada a similar situation has arisen when Ontario and Quebec and more recently Alberta have sought to demonstrate, rather effectively at times, that "their" economic management is becoming nearly as important as the economic management exercised by the national government. But the sovereignty argument reaches the point of crescendo when it is land which is being discussed and here the states/provinces maintain a jealous and even mystical attachment to the two-dimensional contents within their legal boundaries. It is in the third dimension that their claims to sovereignty are more limited, and in both countries attempts by subnational units to assert sovereignty over resources below the land, below the sea and in the air, have met with only partial success. Nonetheless, on the ground, their sovereignty has been well recognized in theory and in practice. We could go on through numerous examples drawn from the two federations to demonstrate the point, but sufficient has now been said to demonstrate that the concept of divided sovereignty exists in these two federations, and as will be seen later, it is a fundamental stumbling block to the basic ingredients of our planning system. That can be seen in the extreme in the Australian case when the states have claimed sovereignty over such things as the hours of daylight, meteorites that fall from the sky, and the morals and values of their population.

As is the case with most modern federations, both the Australian and Canadian constitutions attempt to create a division of powers between the two levels of government. This is examined in detail in a subsequent chapter because it has proved to be one of the major hindrances to harmonization of priority determination between the two levels of government. Here we can note that the attempted power division is neater in the Australian case than in the Canadian. In the Australian Constitution, section 51 is the major focus for the delineation of powers, and the founding fathers tried to follow the American example by specifying the powers of the new national government, as well as some concurrent powers, and then leaving the residual powers to the states. As will be explained later, this attempt to secure the levels of government into watertight compartments has not really worked for a variety of reasons, but it has been at least more explicit than the Canadian attempts under sections 91 and 92 of the *British North America Act* because the Canadian founding fathers, in their "wisdom", virtually spelt out a list of powers for each level of government. Their admonition that the national list was to be by way of example only has done nothing to resolve the resulting confusion. There are also concurrent powers and the residual powers accrue to the national government. This is held to be an outcome of the belief in mid-nineteenth century Canada, that a strong national government was necessary to militate against the possibility of an American-style civil war which the Canadian founders believed had come about because of the fact that too much power had been given to the American states under that constitution. A further complicating factor in the Canadian case lies in the preamble to section 91 of the *British North America Act* which allows the national government to "make Laws for the Peace, Order and good Government of Canada", and then in the preamble to section 92 the provinces are able, inter alia, to oversee "all matters of a merely local or private nature in the Province". One does not have to be a constitutional lawyer to see the difficulties that both these nebulous phrases would pose when conflict was occurring about authority over particular government functions.

However, the net result is that there is not really a great difference in the way the powers are formally divided in the two federations. In both federations the main state/provincial functions are education, health and welfare, law and order, and various facets of industry regulation, industrial relations, and industrial development. Immigration and agriculture are concurrent fields in Canada, but in agriculture the situation is similar to that in Australia in that the states share policy determination with the national government, albeit in an extra-constitutional manner. Only a few of the differences are major but even they do not involve control of large-scale public resources likely to affect public sector planning. The main differences are the national control of rail transport in Canada compared with predominantly state control in Australia, the national control of criminal law in Canada compared with state control in Australia, and the more unified judicial system in Canada.

An overview of the main government functions which fall to the subnational units of both federations reveals some important characteristics. (1) Those functions are more likely to effect the *daily* lives of the people. (2) They are more *visible* functions and therefore more political. (3) Thus they are functions more amenable to pork-barrelling. (4) They are items which involve heavy capital expenditure as well as recurrent expenditure. (5) Much capital expenditure is not capable of generating income to service its repayment (for example, schools, hospitals, and jails are not in normal circumstances highly revenue-producing). (6) It follows that these functions will be debt-producing ones for the states/provinces. (7) The functions of the subnational governments are intimately involved with the provision of infrastructure, and it has been the provision of infrastructure which has been the burden of the twentieth century for governments of both countries (and, it might be added, has furnished the major opportunity for public sector planning).

If the allocation of government expenditure functions is basically similar between the two federations, the same cannot be said in relation to the allocation of revenue-raising potential. The differences will be explored in more depth in later chapters, and here we shall note only the major differences in terms of their practical effect at the present time.

The basic point to be made is that the Canadian provinces are more financially independent than are the Australian states. This lesser degree of vertical imbalance comes about primarily because the Canadian provinces have direct access to a broader range of revenue measures. Statistics presented later show that, on average, the Canadian provinces are dependent on the national government for about one-quarter of their total funding compared with the average figure of over one-half for the Australian states. The difference in the degree of imbalance can be explained by two main characteristics. (1) the Canadian provinces apply their own income taxes, both personal and corporate. (Australian states still have the power in theory to levy income taxes but the operation of the uniform taxation arrangements since World War II has seen the practice of the national government levying all income tax, personal and corporate, on a uniform basis, and transferring a portion of the tax pool to the states.) (2) the Canadian provinces are able to levy some taxes at the point of wholesale/retail, which in Australia would fall foul of the exclusive jurisdiction of the national government over "customs and excise duty". (There has been some inconsistency in the Australian High Court's judgments. One view now accepted in Australia is that state governments cannot levy taxes which fall at the point of wholesale, because such taxes or levies are deemed to constitute excise duties, an exclusive power of the commonwealth government under the constitution.) Indeed it is these two factors which give the Australian federation a higher degree of fiscal vertical imbalance than most other federations of the world. Reasons for this situation will be examined in subsequent chapters but it can be noted here, in a preliminary way, that public sector planning in the systematic way we are contemplating, can be expected to be more difficult for subnational units of a federation the greater their dependence on handouts from a higher level, particularly in relation to the mixture of conditional and unconditional funding in the fiscal transfers between the levels of government. By contrast centralized financing should make national level planning easier to implement.

Both Australia and Canada have an "umpire" in the form of a High Court which, inter alia, hears dispute of various kinds between the levels of government, especially disputes about sovereignty over functions, resources, and revenues. The courts in both countries are appointed in effect by the national government. (Strictly speaking, they are appointed by the national parliaments.) However, there is nowadays at least an informal practice of consulting with the states/provinces before appointments are made, and in Canada this practice will now be formalized under the recent constitutional reforms. It is now virtually legally correct to say that the High Courts are the final arbiter of constitutional disputes, and, in practice, very few attempts have been made to appeal beyond them on matters of intergovernmental disputes. Legal historians point to clearly defined periods in the history of both countries when the High Courts showed a consistent leaning towards one or other level of government, and this has formed the basis of one of the main criticisms levied at the courts. Another criticism, which is examined in more depth in a later chapter, is the inconsistency of High Court judgments; and yet other criticisms relate to the failure of both courts to give advisory opinions or depart from the text of the constitutional document in seeking to interpret its intention. Despite these shortcomings, it can be observed that the courts have proved to be a key element in the shift of the balance of power between the levels of each federation, but it ought to be emphasized that they have mostly been forced into this situation because of the inability or unwillingness of the political system to resolve the questions of intergovernmental rivalry, which are resolved eventually through litigation.

In both countries there exists a variegated pattern of institutions for the allocation of power and resources throughout the federal system. Without question the most apparent of these in both federations has been the so-called Premiers Conferences in Australia and its Canadian equivalent, the Conference of First Ministers. It is this device through which most of the vertical fiscal imbalance is rectified, largely by means of negotiations around formulae on revenue sharing, and longer term agreements on public sector spending in the aggregate, and by major programme categories. Ironically, these conferences in both countries are without constitutional foundation, and widespread controversy exists over their effectiveness as a process for the intergovernmental allocation of resources, but there can be no doubt that they are the single most important political device in intergovernmental relations, and they come in for close scrutiny in later chapters. The Australian Premiers Conference is closely associated with another institution, the Loan Council. (See later chapters for a full description of the Loan Council's operations.) In effect, it coordinates all loan raising for the public sector as a whole and therefore virtually determines the size and distribution of government capital expenditure for the three levels of government. (This does not apply in general to the distribution between projects; rather the distribution between states.) The coordination is formal, and all levels must adhere to the Loan Council's decision, and it is for this reason that one can say that there is no Canadian equivalent (indeed there is no equivalent in any other federation), although it is true that in Canada there exists an unwritten agreement that a higher level of government would always guarantee the loans of a lower level. Consequently it can be said that in Australia, and to a lesser extent in Canada, there exists a high degree of coordination of government capital raisings, and the Premiers Conferences provide a looser and more haphazard coordination of revenue sharing and responsibility sharing. These governmental institutions are mirrored in turn by a collection of other political institutions and processes, including political parties, pressure groups, and in particular, the media. It is important to note that, in both countries, all of these institutions are structured and operate on a federated basis themselves so that they serve to reinforce the federal character of the society and its governments. For example, all of the major political parties are organized on a strong state/provincial base as are the pressure groups. More importantly, all of the major newspaper chains, and television and radio networks, in both Australia and Canada, operate very much on the principle of editorial autonomy at the state/provincial level. Thus it is the practice for the media to reinforce spatial loyalties, or at least present most political bargaining from a spatial perspective.

This leads to a consideration of yet another important aspect of these federal systems and one in which there is a wider difference in cultural and geographical features within the nation. There is no true Australian equivalent of Quebec. Nor does the geographical concentration of non-Anglo-Saxon immigrants in Australia have the same political significance as it does in Canada. In short there is more cultural homogeneity in Australia and more diversity in Canada. These, of course, are generalizations based solely on race, and it can be argued convincingly that on other cultural grounds there is more heterogeneity in Australia than appears to be the case at first glance. This is caused primarily by the sheer geographical size and diversity of the country, whereby those who live large distances from the main Sydney/Melbourne/Canberra axis have come to regard their interests as alien to those of other Australians, in the same way that those in the west regard their needs, aspirations and life styles, as different from those who live in the east, or those in the tropics view with some suspicion those who live in cool temperate parts of the nation. Canada, too, experiences exactly the same phenomena which are the product of a large country spanning many latitudes and meridians with their associated time zones. When it is politics which is being considered, the question is not so much whether people are culturally different throughout the nation, but whether they perceive themselves to be so. The larger the distances, the weaker the processes of nationwide communication, and the more likely these perceptions are to take hold, as they undoubtedly have in Australia and Canada.

As mentioned in the previous section, all dynamic federations are characterized by a balance of power between the sovereign units, and various means for the alteration of that power balance. In Australia and Canada there certainly exists such a power relationship between the national and subnational units of government, and there has been an oscillation around and about that balance, especially in the period since World War II. Various methods exist in both federations for alteration of the political relationship of the sovereign units, and we shall consider some of the more apparent ones. Both federations make provisions for formal amendment of their constitutions, but the Australian amending process involves a direct vote by the population at large, whereas the Canadian constitution prior to the patriation of the constitution in the early 1980s has not contained a general amending clause or procedure for amendment — the parliament of the United Kingdom was the amending agency although it did so only on Canadian initiative. Technicalities aside, the result is that there have been more amendments to the Australian constitution than to the Canadian, which have significantly affected the power balance between levels, although considering Australian experience one could not consider eight referendum proposals passed out of thirty-eight put, as being particularly significant either. (Technically there have been more total Canadian amendments than Australian amendments but very few Canadian amendments have involved a substantial shift of power between levels of government.) Moreover, only three of the eight Australian amendments really qualify under this criterion. They are the 1946 social services powers for the national government; the 1927 amendments instituting the national takeover of state debts and providing for the operation of the Loan Council; and the 1967 amendment giving the national government control over racial groups, specifically Aborigines, which has turned out to be a damp squib because the national government has only been prepared to accept partial responsibility for Aboriginal policy. Interestingly, neither in Australia nor Canada have the state or provincial governments been accorded a formal role in the actual launching of referendum proposals, although amendments in both countries are contained in legislation which generally must pass the respective Senates, and in Australia in the 1970s, a number of amendments originated out of constitutional conventions at which the states were strongly represented. The Canadian situation will change markedly now that the new provisions allow the provinces a formal role in dissenting from certain amendments, as well as a role for the legislative assembly in each province in having to approve certain kinds of amendments. Also, in both countries, there is often an informal practice of consulting the state or provincial governments before a decision is made to introduce the requisite legislation into the national parliament. Generally speaking it can be said that the constitutional amending process has not proved to be of great significance in altering the federal power balance in either country.

In the Australian and Canadian federations there was little attempt by the founding fathers to give the subnational units a voice in decision making by the national government, except for the creation of national upper houses to represent state/provincial viewpoints. If one examines all the key institutions in both countries which determine resource and value allocation, one will find very little formal provisions for the membership of those institutions to be appointed or at least approved by the state or provincial governments, and that includes membership of the bench of the High Courts which are the supreme legal determinants of the power balance between levels. Admittedly there are, once again, informal consultations which take place in this respect, but suffice to say that the founding fathers saw the Senates as the main avenue through which a subnational voice would be heard on decisions made at the national government level. There are, of course, significant differences in the composition and operation of the two Senates, the most notable being the direct election of the Australian Senate compared with the appointment (by the national government in effect) of the Canadian Senate. There are rarely any Canadian national ministers drawn from the Senate, a practice which is common in Australia. Indeed, attempts are made by most Australian Prime Ministers to ensure a geographical balance in their Cabinet of Ministers in the Senate as well as with their ministers in the House of Representatives. Modern Canadian Prime Ministers would have had great difficulty introducing such a measure to any significant extent because it would be rare to have even lower house members from every province represented in the governing party. In a formal sense, both Senates have similar powers, or more correctly, similar curbs placed on their powers and it seems probable, for example, that both the Australian and Canadian Senates can block supply; they can certainly delay it. What is of most interest to us here is whether these upper houses of the national parliament do in fact serve to represent regional interests. It has become popular sport to decry this aspect of the Australian Senate and to argue that party politics have turned the Senate into a duplicate of the lower house, solely because there are hardly any actual divisions along state lines in the upper chamber when it comes to formal voting. But as I have argued elsewhere,[1] this is a superficial approach, and it overlooks a vast array of informal and tangential Senate activity, such as the lobbying which takes place on a spatial basis in the caucus of each major political party, the reluctance of national governments to bring in legislation which overtly or covertly discriminates against particular geographical parts of the country for fear of reprisals in the Senate, and the power of state political figures, within their party machine, over endorsement of Senate candidates, not to mention the actual formal requirement for state governors to issue writs for a Senate election advised, of course, by their state governments. There are few Canadian parallels to these habits simply because Canadian senators are appointed, but it should be noted that the appointment process nowadays incorporates much informal consultation with provincial authorities. There have also been many suggestions in recent years for reform of the Canadian Senate, and it seems inevitable that Canada will soon have a reformed Senate which will be more geographically representative, and whose membership will probably be partially determined by provincial parliaments, if not the electorate directly. (Some of these suggestions came from the major political parties, and many reforms of this kind were suggested by the Trudeau government immediately prior to its defeat by the Progressive Conservative Clark government in 1979. At the time of writing no changes of this kind had been introduced.) In effect it will be a Senate which will be *seen* to be a house for the provinces. This will affect the power balance even if only in the informal manner which occurs in relation to the Australian Senate. It ought also to be noted that the Australian Senate is seen just as much as an institution for the protection of states against each other (especially small states against large states), as for the protection of all states against the national government, as reflected most explicitly in the electoral weightage which is a result of equal, or near equal, regional representation for sovereign units. It can safely be said that the Senates of both countries will loom in importance as power brokers between the levels of government in these federations in the near future.

There can be no doubt that in both federations it has been the area of fiscal relationships that has been the most dynamic aspect of the intergovernmental power balance. To some extent this has been due to national economic events which have sometimes produced demands for the services of one level of government at a much faster pace than demands for the services of the other, and at other times economic conditions have favoured the revenue-raising mechanisms of one level of government more than those available to the other level. For example, the growth of population attendant upon economic growth in the postwar period has caused enormous pressures on infrastructure, most of which had to be provided by state/provincial governments, whereas the energy crisis of the late 1970s has produced a demand for resources the royalties and taxes on which tend to belong mostly to the states/provinces. The constitutions of both Australia and Canada allow for a somewhat flexible pattern of financial relations. In Australia the states at present have no *direct* access to a reasonably stable percentage of income tax, despite the fact that that percentage has varied from quinquennium to quinquennium.[2] Under the very latest arrangements the states are given a fixed percentage share of a basket of taxes (see chapter 7), but various *ad hoc* arrangements concluded at the 1983 Premiers Conference have demonstrated once again the interference of politics in any rational allocation by formula. The Australian states have no current claim to company tax which is solely the preserve of the national government. The constitution does allow the states access to company tax, and the power was used by the states up to 1942. The states are also precluded from the bulk of indirect taxes because the Australian Constitution allocates "customs and excise duties" to the national government, and the High Court, in its wisdom or otherwise has tended to brand most wholesale taxes as an excise duty. Arising out of a little horse-trading early in the 1970s, the states gained payroll taxes and have been making great use of them ever since. The other major sources of revenue for states are royalties on minerals; stamp duties on business transactions; and taxes on motor vehicles, gambling and drinking. The Canadian situation as a whole is different in that the provinces do levy their own income and corporate taxes, and so are much less dependent on transfers from the national government than are the Australian states. The *British North America Act* allows the national government to raise money by "any mode or system of taxation", whereas the provinces are restricted to "direct taxation within the province in order to the raising of a revenue for provincial purposes". This latter provision results in a pattern of taxation for the provinces which, apart from income and corporate taxes already mentioned, is not greatly different from that of the Australian states. The Canadian provinces do have a more extensive power to tax mineral resources than do the Australian states because of the legal situation in Canada whereby provinces have sovereignty over below-surface territory in a different manner from that which the Australian states possess. Also, under Canada's new constitutional arrangements the jurisdiction of the provinces over the exploration, development, and management of nonrenewable natural resources is confirmed, and the provinces are given concurrent jurisdiction in interprovincial trade in nonrenewable resources. The provinces are also vested with the right to levy indirect taxes on nonrenewable resources. However, it is not the allocation of revenue-raising powers which has been the main source of a shifting power balance in federal financial relations in the two countries. Rather, it has been the mechanisms for transfer of finances between levels. The Canadian Constitution is virtually silent on this aspect, and so fiscal transfers are simply the product of political negotiation between the national and provincial governments. By contrast, the Australian Constitution, under section 96, allows the national government to make "grants" to the states on "such terms and conditions as it sees fit":

> During a period of ten years after the establishment of the Commonwealth and thereafter until the parliament otherwise provides, the parliament may grant financial assistance to any state on such terms and conditions as the parliament thinks fit.

It was a clause inserted at a Premiers Conference merely as a safety valve to allow periodic ad hoc allocations from the commonwealth to any state with special circumstances.

This provision, and other factors as well, make the transfer of finance from national government to state governments a political bargaining process with the odds stacked more heavily on the national government than in Canada. Nonetheless it is true to say, that in respect of the shifting power balance in the all important area of federal finance, it is the sphere of fiscal transfers between levels which is the focal point for examination, and this area is explored in depth in a later chapter. In both countries these transfers are negotiated through intergovernmental forums which have evolved for the purpose, the key ones being the Australia Premiers Conference and the Canadian Conference of First Ministers, which have already been mentioned.

Apart from the fiscal considerations, there are other formal aspects of the constitutional structure which provide explicitly for a shifting power balance between the levels. Australia, for example, has a constitutional provision for the interchange of powers between the levels of government, with the duration of the interchange being decided by the donor government.[3] This facility has been used very sparingly, although there has recently been a serious revival of interest in this concept to the extent of legislation, and a referendum proposal which failed to pass, arising out of the deliberations of the Constitutional Convention. There is no formal provision for the interchange of powers in the Canadian Constitution. Both Australian and Canadian constitutions make provision for the incorporation of new territory into the federation and for the creation of new subnational units by the fragmentation of existing ones; these are of course difficult and time-consuming processes and such events have rarely occurred, except, of course, for the creation of new Canadian provinces in the twentieth century and recent talk in both countries about the movement of certain territories towards sovereignty as states or provinces. By the same token it needs to be emphasized that there is no formal provision in the constitution of either Australia or Canada for any unit to leave the federation. Western Australia voted to secede in 1933 but this did not eventuate.

(Following the Western Australian vote the matter was referred to the Imperial Parliament in London which decided it had no jurisdiction and that the constitution made no provision for secession.) Also, the considerable debate which has surrounded Quebec's threatened secession has cast little light on how it might technically be achieved.

It was mentioned previously that there is present in some federations a desire to ensure equality of access to government services throughout the country, as well as a desire to protect the interests of minority groups. Both traits are evident in Australia and Canada, and in respect of public finances, both countries have devised fairly elaborate horizontal equalization schemes in an "attempt" to ensure that the standard of government services provided by any state or province does not fall below (owing to factors beyond the control of that state or province) that provided elsewhere in the federation. Australia's equalization scheme for state governments has involved a state having to apply for a special grant before it can be considered to be truly a "claimant state", and its claim is assessed by an independent statutory body, the Commonwealth Grants Commission, which compares that state's revenue-raising capacity *and* expenditure needs with those of the two "standard" states (New South Wales and Victoria), and finally recommends to the national government the amount of the special grant needed to make it possible for the claimant state to match the average fiscal standard of the standard states. (The claimant state procedure was placed in suspension following the government's reaction to the relativities exercises of 1981 and 1982. Each state agreed to forego the right to claimancy during the period of the new formula which was to last until 1985 — this is discussed in more detail later in the chapter.)

The Canadian equalization scheme has the same objective but completely different methodology, whence a formula is used to compare the revenue-earning capacity of all provinces (based on twenty-nine selected taxes) with the average for all provinces. The result is the so called "have" and "have not" provinces. The national government makes payments to the "have not" provinces. Thus it can be seen that the Canadian system does not explicitly take account of expenditure differentials, only revenue-raising potential, thereby presumably assuming that following revenue equalization, comparable standards of service may be achieved by equal per capital expenditures. Other Canadian fiscal transfers do not necessarily contain equalization elements at all, and in some cases are counter-equalizing. These, of course, are not the only elements of horizontal equalization in the two countries. There is a component of horizontal equalization in some of the fiscal transfers between levels, although it needs to be realized that each intergovernmental programme contains its own (inevitably different) formula for such "equalization". However, despite the fact that the amounts of money involved in the formal equalization scheme are dwarfed by the amounts involved in other intergovernmental fiscal transfers, it is the equalization schemes which are the most visible and therefore the most political. They brand a state as "claimant", or a province as "have" or "have not", which then becomes part of that state or province's advantage or handicap in the processes of political negotiation between that government and the national government, and also its counterpart units of government at the subnational level. The political perception may thus be quite contrary to the economic reality. For example, claimant states in Australia are not necessarily states with the lowest fiscal capacity, but may be claimant simply because of an inequitable share of tax-sharing and specific purpose grants.

There has, in recent years, been some questioning in both countries of the very worth of horizontal equalization schemes, and especially of the methods being used to achieve this objective. In Canada this has been exacerbated by the energy crisis whereby certain energy resource-rich provinces have become so disparate in their public finance performance as to skew the whole equalization formula. For example, it was clear by the early 1980s that unless the formula were modified, Alberta would be the only "have" province and all of the other nine provinces, including Ontario, would become "have not" provinces.

Nonetheless, in the new constitutional package, a commitment has been made for both levels of government to promote equal opportunities for all Canadians, the furthering of economic development to reduce regional disparities, and the provision of essential public services at a reasonable level to all Canadians.

A complete review of the full picture of relativities between all Australian states being conducted by the Commonwealth Grants Commission through 1978 to 1980, as part of the national government's new federalism policy, promised to overcome the Australian problems to some extent.[4] However, when the Grants Commission completed its review of relativity, the commonwealth government, perhaps predictably, refused to implement the recommendations in full because that would have meant favouring some states at the expense of others, the ones to be favoured being the larger states. Even after the Commission conducted a second more comprehensive review the government refused to bite the bullet. Giving everyone a little more cake is politically easy but cutting some slices thicker and others thinner is political suicide. In the event, a new tax-sharing formula was determined to keep all states happy, to last until 1985.

There are, of course, other dimensions to the fiscal equality question than the ones we have considered. Section 99 of the Australian Constitution, together with Section 51, subsections (ii) and (iii), effectively preclude the national government in any of its taxation from discriminating between states or parts of states. Section 99 says:

> The Commonwealth shall not, by any law or regulation of trade or commerce, or revenue, give preference to one State or any part thereof over another State or any part thereof.

Section 51, speaking of the powers to be given to the national government, among other things, says:

(ii)   Taxation; but so as not to discriminate between States or parts of States;
(iii) Bounties on the production or export of goods, but so that such bounties shall be uniform throughout the Commonwealth.

There is no Canadian equivalent of this requirement, but it would be a brave Canadian national government which levied its taxes at a differential rate from province to province. Perhaps the strongest protest related to horizontal equalization in both countries in recent times has been the argument that the horizontal equalization processes do not take full account of the effect of the uneven geographical impact of tariff and subsidy policy, transport freight and passenger rates, monetary policy and national government spending; nor does it take account of the uneven contribution of different geographical regions to export earnings. Cries of this sort are heard most frequently from states like Queensland and Western Australia, and provinces like British Columbia, Alberta, and Saskatchewan, who argue that they contribute heavily to exports, and therefore foreign exchange earnings, but are highly disadvantaged by tariff and national transport policies which concentrate industry in Sydney/Melbourne or Torontreal, and by monetary policy which is applied uniformly across the nation but formulated on the basis of conditions prevailing in the two largest capital cities which is often not appropriate for the rest of the country. This sort of attitude is, of course, based on a confused view of fiscal equalization and economic equalization, which are different issues, but it has nonetheless a superficial political appeal and has led to states and provinces making attempts to protect their own spatial interests. To this end Australian states and Canadian provinces have dabbled with tapered freight rates, preference for government tendering to "local" suppliers, tax concessions of various kinds, etc.; all of which provide something of a hindrance to the mobility of resources around the nation.

The equalization issue is also reflected, as indicated, in the protection of minority groups. Here the Australian experience can in no way match that of Canada with its constitutional language, religious, and racial safeguards, and its new Charter of Rights and Freedoms, incorporating aboriginal rights. Australia has none of these devices, indeed, national government attempts to enforce equality of treatment of any kind are dependent on the goodwill and cooperation of the states, which is not always forthcoming. In relation to Aborigines, the national government has, since a referendum in 1967, had the power to oversee their welfare but has been unable, unwilling, or both, to take full account of that responsibility.

The factors which have been outlined to date represent some of the key characteristics of the two federations we are examining which hold significance for attempts by any of the subnational units of those federations to engage in public sector planning. They are characteristics closely related to the divisive and fragmented nature of these federal systems and so it might be anticipated, as noted previously, that they will provide hindrances to any planning attempts. There are, of course, other features which differ between the Australian states themselves, and the Canadian provinces too are not identical in all respects. For example, the very machinery of government often differs markedly in structure and functioning. In Australia no state has the same cabinet portfolio groupings as another, the composition and operation of parliament and its committees are different, and the extent of the use of statutory corporations differs significantly, as does the relationship between state and local governments. The public service structure and the departmental profiles are also different from state to state. One state, Queensland, is unicameral, and in the other five states the franchise for election of upper houses differs, and their role in parliamentary activity also differs. One state, Tasmania, uses a completely different method of voting for its parliament compared with that used for the lower houses of the other five states. Some states have seen fit to alter the constitutional position of their governor in a bid to entrench their sovereignty. The point need not be laboured here because the consequences of these fundamental differences will be explored in later chapters. The Canadian provinces also are quite different in many of these aspects. Provincial parliaments are all elected to five year terms compared with mostly three year terms in Australia, despite an evident tendency for them to go to the polls after only four years. In respect of other aspects of the machinery of government the Canadian provinces also differ quite markedly.

So much then for the differences. It will be recalled that in the literature there are characteristics common to most federations which serve to bind them together, and in so doing, provide a measure of coordination and hierarchy which serves to offset the other divisive aspects. One of these is the guarantee of a mobility of resources within the whole federation, preventing any subnational unit from erecting economic or social barriers around its territory. This was uppermost in the minds of both the Australian and Canadian founding fathers, who feared the continuation of customs duties being levied by some states/provinces on goods entering their territory, and at different rates too, which opened the prospect of goods entering the country in the state or province with the lowest rate of duty. Three basic moves were made in both countries when federating to solve this problem. Firstly, customs duties were abolished between states and between provinces; secondly, the national government was given power over customs duties to ensure equal rates of duty on goods entering the country at any point; and thirdly, and most importantly, a clause was added to the constitution guaranteeing freedom of trade and movement around the federation. Section 92 of the Australian Constitution says:

> On the imposition of uniform duties of customs, trade, commerce, and intercourse among the States, whether by means of internal carriage or ocean navigation, shall be absolutely free.

Section 121 of the *British North America Act* says:

> All Articles of the growth, produce or manufacture of any one of the provinces shall, from and after the union, be admitted free into each of the other provinces.

In Australia, further strength was added to this intention by providing for the establishment of an Interstate Commission which would ensure that no state discriminated against another by means of its transport or other laws. But when that body started to show its teeth the true politics of federalism came into play, and by 1920 it was no longer in existence, despite the fact that the appropriate clauses in the Australian Constitution (Sections 101-103) to this day proclaim that "there shall be an Interstate Commission".[5] These provisions, of course, are not the only ones which serve to protect the mobility of resources. In both Australia and Canada control over immigration, currency, coinage, weights and measures, post and telecommunications, census and statistics, defence, external affairs, patents, copyrights, and marriage and divorce, etc., is also a guarantee of the mobility of resources, people, and ideas around the federation if only because it prevents subnational units gaining control of these powers which could be used to thwart the ideal.

Needless to say, this aspect of the practice of federalism in both countries has proved to be extremely contentious, striking, as it does, right at the heart of the sovereignty of the subnational units. There has been an enormous amount of litigation brought before the courts over the question of interstate/interprovincial trade, some of it resulting in puzzling and inconsistent decisions. Generally speaking the protection of mobility has been preserved, although the Australian states and the Canadian provinces have found many legal ways to defeat the objective. Some of their methods come about quite naturally and as a result of the division of powers. For example, in Australia the fact that the state governments have power over railways, education, health, industrial relations, and law and order, has led to quite different systems in each of these fields with quite different standards, so that mobility of both people, commodities, and concepts, is made difficult although not impossible. A parent will be reluctant to move to another state to take up employment if it means that children will have to face a quite different education system with different standards and emphases. A labourer may find a shift elsewhere difficult if the award wages and conditions are of a lower standard in the new location. The price and availability of hospital beds varies from state to state and may give cause for concern to the sick or elderly contemplating an interstate move.

However, not all state actions to defeat the idea of national mobility arise from purely natural aspects of the federal division of powers. Australian states (and Canadian provinces) have from time to time employed numerous other devices, including preferences to companies "resident" in that state for state government tendering; company law provisions, including takeover law; taxation concessions including, for example, concessional charges or even the complete abolition of payroll tax; stamp duty; road tax; rail freight charges; death duties; and the availability of housing or low interest capital with repayment holidays. These devices are often used to protect already existing residents of a state, to discourage them from leaving the state, and if possible to encourage new residents to enter from other states. The controls or incentives need not be monetary alone, and all Australian states, for example, compete for capital and migrants through the offices of the Agents General overseas by offering information and service. The laws governing portability of pension and leave entitlement rights of state public servants can, and do, have a profound effect on the mobility of public servants from state to state and from commonwealth to state.

There have been attempts by states to use other forms of legislation to protect local inhabitants and industry, including in more recent times, consumer protection legislation, but usually the High Court has been firm in negating other state laws when they serve to interfere with the mobility of resources across state boundaries. It must also be realized that the constitutional provisions which protect interstate mobility have another important effect in that they place limits on the degree of government intervention into the private sector by both national and state governments. For example, no national government in Australia would be able to nationalize any industry completely if that move interfered with the freedom of interstate trade and commerce, as the Chifley government found in relation to banking in 1947. By the same token, state governments can regulate industries only to the extent of their intrastate activity, as is demonstrated by the failure of various state marketing boards to control the sale of produce interstate.

It can be observed that the mobility question is not a settled one, giving rise to much uncertainty in both federations under review; and uncertainty is the antithesis of planning. The point being made here is that when mobility is regarded as an essential ingredient of federalism it creates a variety of centripetal forces, with accompanying coordination and hierarchical decision making and regulating patterns, placing the subnational units in a subordinate relationship to a national power, but not necessarily that of the national government.

As we have already noticed, most federations also contain other means of providing a hierarchical relationship between the national and subnational level. Australia has no parallel to the definite superior/subordinate dichotomy of the Canadian Governor General and the provincial Lieutenant Governors, including the formal power of reserving legislation. However, both federations do make provision for the dominance of the national level in cases of emergency, guarantees to prevent any unit from destroying other units or the whole system, and the granting of a residual power to one level. In respect of the last mentioned, the Australian Constitution gives defined powers to the national government and residual powers to the states, whereas the Canadian Constitution gives residual power to the national government. We shall examine later what difference, if any, these provisions have made to the actual functioning of the two federations; what we are doing here is noting that a hierarchical relationship exists, epitomized best of all by the provisions in both constitutions for national law to prevail in the event of a clash.

Another and most important element of coordination and hierarchy in the two federations comes via the existence of one umpire over disputes between the two levels. That umpire, the High Court, thereby assumes a decisive and authoritative role in distributing power throughout the federation. With respect to Australia, this point must be qualified by noting that, as a result of aggressive legal action, the states kept open an avenue of appeal to the Privy Council from their own Supreme Courts, and there existed until recently a slight possibility of an appeal from the High Court to the Privy Council on specific matters; but to all intents and purposes, the Australian and Canadian High Courts have assumed the role of an arbiter in the power struggle between the units of the federation. As long as it remains an authoritative arbiter that provides quite a degree of centralization and coordination in a fragmented system.

When it comes to considering aspects of these federations which are unifying in principle and practice one can, of course, point to various factors which led to federation in the first place, and most of these are common to both Australia and Canada. They include geographical proximity of the subnational units, fear of external aggression, benefits of economic integration, and national identity, especially with relation to the United Kingdom. There is also the concept which we have already examined, common to both countries, of a desire for equal treatment by, and access to, government activity. Because spatial areas, like human beings, are basically unequal in their resources and potential, such desired equality must, of necessity, be forced equality. It is an axiom that enforced equality leads to centralization of decision making because individual units of the federation have neither the capacity, nor knowledge, nor the altruistic stance required to consider all components of the nation equally. Thus, the task invariably falls to a central agency, once again, an arbiter, usually at the national level although not necessarily part of the national government. The process of equalizing resources, values, and opportunity in both Australia and Canada has produced a variety of centralized institutions which stand in a superior relationship to the subnational units. In Australia this facet is more clearly symbolized in bodies like the Commonwealth Grants Commission, the national film and literature censorship boards, and various other statutory commissions in particular sectors. Naturally the decisions of all of these bodies are not regarded as authoritative by all of the states all of the time, but they have become entrenched, by and large, as the agents of "equalization" of government activity, with a good deal of accompanying formal or informal power over the states. Other manifestations of this attempt at equality of treatment for various spatial units include the exactly (in the Australian case) and attempted (in the Canadian case) equal representation in the Senate, as well as the attempt by Australian and Canadian Prime Ministers to regionalize their cabinets so as to include all or most states/provinces. It is a task easier to accomplish in Australia than in Canada.

This chapter has provided an overview of those features of the Australian and Canadian federations of relevance to our efforts to determine the amenability of the two systems to public sector planning. It has not dwelt on many other characteristics of the two systems not considered relevant to this task. However, enough has been said to demonstrate a basic similarity in the structure and functioning of these federal systems. In the next chapter we proceed to identify more narrowly the specific aspects of both systems which appear to present the severest hindrances to the introduction of the various components of our planning system.

Division of Powers

It is obvious why the division of powers in a federation is such a fundamental hindrance to the attainment of public sector planning on a national basis. It is the hallmark of all federal systems, and more to the point, it is the most visible (and therefore symbolic) evidence of a division of sovereignty; an indication that the jurisdiction of government over a geographical entity (nation) is split between different governments, all of which are legitimate, and all of which are held to be supreme in relation to the powers that are specifically assigned to them under the federal compact. Such an arrangement is right at the margin or interface of intergovernmental relations, and is bound to present obstacles to such notions as harmonization of priorities, allocation of resources, forecasting, and coordination, and all the other components of our planning system. However, as it is divided sovereignty, one might expect each unit of the federation to have autonomy over at least the functions which come within its ambit, and so possess the ability to plan for each of those functions, and across the range of them. As will be observed, this depends on how discrete each of the assigned functions of government is, and more especially, how watertight the unit of government can be made in its relations with other units. In any event the point to be confronted here is that the division of powers in a federal system immediately creates a chasm, or at least a border; a functional dividing line as well as the familiar spatial dividing line. The question is — can planning in all its dimensions be achieved across this line, this border, this chasm? That would be a hard enough question to answer if the line were a static one as it has long been assumed to be; it is much harder still if the division of powers or allocation of functions is dynamic. It must be realized from the outset, that the concept of a neat division of powers stems in turn from the belief that there is some sort of fixed and proper relationship between levels of government. This is itself a product of what is known as coordinate federalism which was discussed earlier.

The idea that there can be fixed criteria for allocation of functions between levels of government stems primarily from those who view federalism from a functional perspective in the first place, and who believe that a federal system ought to be one where each level is compartmentalized in the sense that it is given a clearly defined package of tasks to perform. Those functions are to be mutually exclusive so that there should be no direct interpenetration between levels. This is not to deny that any one level will have a political influence over the activities of another level; indeed all federations make institutional allowances for this to happen. But the overwhelming desire is to make it perfectly clear to citizens which level of government is responsible for a particular function so that accountability of that level can be direct and unequivocal. Under such a coordinate system it is essential that the administration of any level of government concern itself solely with the assigned functions of that level, and not enter in any direct way the functions of another level. It is not unlike the process which takes place within each level of government in an attempt to maintain a clear separation of activity between the legislature, executive, and judiciary. Thus it is held to be democratic, efficient, and rational government.

Now it is clear from the literature that this is the sort of federal system envisaged by the Australian founding fathers, and which they attempted to lay down in specific terms in the Australian Constitution as witnessed by Section 51. (It is exemplified even more clearly in the *British North America Act* in Sections 91 and 92.) Consequently, it is not surprising that this notion continues to pervade popular belief about Australian federalism, especially given the mystique which has been built up about the wisdom of the founding fathers. It continues its grip in a large amount of current literature, especially that emanating from parliamentary and other political sources; and it is in many ways the basis of Australian Constitutional Law, since the courts are forced to assign functions on the basis of legal interpretation because the political process has negated its responsibility in this regard.

Thus it is essential to understand what the criteria of coordinate federalism are, despite the fact that, it will be argued, this form of federalism is no longer a reality or even a possibility in Australia.

Although it may sound trite, coordinate federalism seeks to give to national government functions which are national in character, to state level things which are appropriate to the state level, and to local government the things which are local. Obviously the whole question would be answered then and there if some easy way could be found of defining what the characteristics of national, state, and local functions were. In political terms, that is where the rub comes, since there must be room for value judgment in ascribing such characteristics.

It only remains to make an observation which is tautological but fundamental to an understanding of this problem, namely, that one's conception of the proper allocation of functions between levels in a federal system cannot help but be predisposed by one's conception of federalism itself. And the key element here regarding conceptions of federalism is the nature of the relationships between the national and subnational spatial units. For example, the very notion that there is some sort of fixed and proper relationship between levels of government is itself a product of what is known as coordinate federalism, as defined by Kenneth Wheare:

By the federal principle, I mean the method of dividing powers so that the general and regional governments are each, within a sphere, co-ordinate and independent.[1]

William Riker asserts that the notion that each government has the authority to make some decisions independently of the other, still admits a great many actual constitutional arrangements, and in fact, federal constitutions can be arranged in a continuum according to the degree of independence one kind of the pair of governments has from the other kind.[2]

Geoffrey Sawer prefers to speak of a federal situation:

that is a situation where geographical distribution of the power to govern is desired or has been achieved in a way giving the several government units of the system some degree of security — some guarantee of continued existence as organisations and as holders of power.[3]

Daniel Elazar claims that no single definition of federalism has proved satisfactory because of the difficulties of relating theoretical formulations to the evidence gathered from observing the actual operation of federal systems. He adds this highly pertinent statement:

As a political device, federalism can be viewed more narrowly as a kind of political order animated by political principles that emphasize the primacy of bargaining and negotiated co-ordination among several power centres as a prelude to the exercise of power within a single political system and stress the virtues of dispersed power centres as a means for safe-guarding individual and local liberties.[4]

We don't need to exhaust all the definitions and theories in order to make a single point which is evident from those quoted. Neither the coordinate concept of federalism, a static legal concept, nor the modern and dynamic political concepts, envisage an actual division of discrete and complete functions between levels of government. They speak instead of the allocation of power, and this in turn implies that there has to be some kind of coordination of those powers if a democratic federal system is to remain a system. This is in itself a political process, or a bargaining or negotiating process. In the words of Rufus Davis:

The exclusive hallmark of every constitutional system which purports to be federal, however, is the presence of an explicit "division" of legislative power in the constitution.

A "division of power", however, is an artificial, an imperfect, a generalized, a linguistic, a skeletal thing. Political life simply cannot be perfectly or permanently compartmentalized. Players, resources, beliefs, issues, the language of politics, the name and the dimension of things, the ways of persuasion and coercion all change, sometimes dramatically, but more often as imperceptibly as the changing voice of address and communication between aging parents and growing children. However ingenious constitutional draftsmen may be in composing a "division of power" that will work for and beyond their time, their words can rarely be more than approximate, crude, and temporary guides to the ongoing or permissible political activity in any federal system.[5]

Identifying Problems Caused by the Division of Powers

The main aim of this chapter is to pinpoint the problems for planning caused by the federal division of powers. This involves a review of the literature on the subject from both Australian and Canadian sources, together with the results of the interviews conducted in both federations. However, to set such a discussion in its proper context, we shall first examine the historical background to the divisions of powers, and the actual wording of the constitutions.

To conduct this exercise we shall be heavily dependent on the actual words of various authors who have analysed this problem, because one of the key issues involved in relation to a federal division of powers, is the very language which is used to describe that division. For the framers of any constitutional document, such language is difficult to conceive, moreover, its meaning tends to alter with the passage of time. In the words of Bailey:

> The satisfactoriness (or otherwise) of the division of powers in any federal con-
> stitution will therefore probably depend a good deal on circumstances which
> may have been difficult, or even impossible to foresee when the Constitution
> was being framed. I mean the extent to which the needs of the community will
> demand common action (e.g. uniform regulation) in matters left to the states,
> and the degree of readiness for such common action which the states will
> exhibit at any given time. The same problem arises where powers with respect
> to a given subject matter are divided between commonwealth and states — as
> for example in trade and commerce, including shipping and navigation, where
> the division takes place, as it were, at the state boundary, the Commonwealth
> having power with respect only to interstate operations. Opinions differ widely
> as to the success of the Australian division of powers, largely because opinions
> differ as to the extent to which unified action and direction are desirable in the
> matters concerned.[6]

In relation to Canadian experience the same problem was confronted by the Rowell-Sirois Royal Commission on Dominion-Provincial Relations, probably the most far-reaching federal review ever conducted. The commission expressed it this way:

> The vital core of a federal constitution is the division of legislative powers
> between the central authority and the component states or provinces. This divi-
> sion represents the compromise between the forces which make union possible
> and those which inhibit the formation of a close union. It marks the limits of
> what can be done by common agreement and the extent to which the separate
> states must be permitted to differ and work out their own destinies . . . the
> amount of care in phrasing the division of powers in a federal scheme will pre-
> vent difficulty when the division comes to be applied to the variety and com-
> plexity of social relationships. The different aspects of life in a society are not
> insulated from one another in such a way as to make possible mechanical ap-
> plication of the division of powers. There is nothing in human affairs which cor-
> responds to the neat logical divisions found in the constitution. Therefore, at-

tempts to exercise the powers allotted by the constitution frequently raise questions as to its meaning in relation to particular circumstances.[7]

Finally, to emphasize the problems caused for planning by the division of powers, the words of Else-Mitchell are most relevant:

> Central to the constitutional and legal problems of national planning and intergovernmental relations is the division of powers under our federal system. This denies the full legislative authority to the Commonwealth in fields in which it may consider national planning and development to be warranted and at the same time deprives the states of the requisite funds to undertake those tasks themselves.[8]

The Background to the Australian Division of Powers

Australia is a federation and like most, if not all, federations, it operates on the basis of a division of powers between three levels of government. As it has a written constitution, that division of powers is specified in a constitution, at least as far as the allocation of functions between the commonwealth and state governments is concerned. The constitutions of the states themselves, which consist for the most part of legislation enacted in the nineteenth century at the time each colony gained self-government, and amended since then from time to time, contain no written specific allocation of powers between state and local government, but rather simply assert the sovereignty of state government over local government.

The Australian Constitution, whilst delineating the powers of the commonwealth and state governments, contains in its wording virtually no accompanying criteria to illustrate the division of powers which is made there. The founding fathers of the Australian federation did not bother to leave to posterity the reasoning behind the way they allocated the powers of government in the federation they created. Very few of the historical works or biographical material relating to the period to 1901 make reference to the actual division of governmental powers between the levels of government. Sir John Quick, writing in 1919, makes this important observation:

> In deciding upon the distribution of powers, the Australian Federal Convention was guided, not only by the model of the United States Constitution, but by special considerations. It was thought that there should be reserved to the States all powers affecting private rights, municipal functions, local interests, resources, and trade; that they should control the administration of justice and local governing communities, and have free opportunity for internal development and local option, and choice in internal affairs. To the Commonwealth were ceded such powers as are of a truly national Australian character, whether relating to commerce, industry, finance, economics, defence or external affairs. It would have been a great calamity had the Convention drawn up an instrument of government intended to last as the citadel of national life for all time merely in a haphazard manner, without reference to fundamental and guiding principles . . .

. . . The success of the Commonwealth as a whole depends, not so much on the legislation and activity of the Federal Parliament as upon the legislation and activity of the state parliaments. They have reserved to them the right of controlling all domestic institutions, the home life, the education, the land and primary resources of Australia, from which are derived the springs of our national life, domestic, social, industrial and commercial . . .

. . . The powers left to the states are of a purely local, domestic and provincial character, and were left to them because it was believed that the Parliaments of the states, having special knowledge of local conditions, could be better trusted to solve local problems.

To the Federal Parliament were assigned powers permitting legislation of a uniform character, operative throughout the length and breadth of Australia. It was not intended that this Parliament should pass laws applicable to parts of Australia only. The power of dealing with local questions and the making of local differentiations, in accordance with territorial differences and conditions, was left to the states. The text of a federal power is this: will its exercise yield laws of general application, suitable to every part of the Commonwealth, and capable of application throughout the States? Where there must be a variety of laws or regulations, differing with parallels of latitude, or according to local conditions, their enactment is best left to the states. The fundamental distinction between a federal law and a state law is that the first must be universal and general in its application, and the second applicable to local circumstances. A power that must be exercised differentially is not a federal power, and should be left to the states.[9]

Quick illustrates his principles by the trade and commerce power which, he believed, would operate quite simply in that trade and commerce conducted within a state would be regulated by that state government, and only when it transgressed a state boundary would it become subject to commonwealth jurisdiction.

Norris, in his work *The Emergent Commonwealth*, traces some thoughts of the founding fathers pertinent to allocation criteria. Barton in 1897 had modified the resolutions of the 1891 convention for brevity and simplicity. He stated that the first of the principal conditions of federation was:

That powers privileges and territories of the several existing colonies shall remain intact, except in respect of such surrenders as may be agreed upon to secure uniformity of law and administration in matters of common concern.[10]

Norris then makes the following observation, which is extremely pertinent to an understanding of the difficulties of discerning the origin of the criteria for power allocation in Australia:

While the method of dividing the powers was never in doubt, members said little about the specific powers the central parliament should actually receive. Many delegates were well read in Constitutional history and thoroughly versed in the precedents of existing federal constitutions. In 1890 Griffith submitted the first list of legislative powers (derived largely from the American Constitutions, and the British, North American and Federal Council Acts) and comparatively few substantive additions or alterations were made later. Delegates apparently assumed that federal constitutions necessarily contained such powers, and most were content to leave questions of this nature to the experts. They seldom challenged the desirability of the presence of the great majority of Commonwealth legislative powers (or the absence of others) which eventually found their way mainly into sections 51 and 52 of the Australian Constitution. The handful of powers that delegates debated tended, therefore, to be those which they considered the most important, the more contentious, the new additions, and the obscure.[11]

Griffith continued to defend his list of commonwealth powers. Not one of them, he said, had caused a colonial government to fall, and none of them was specifically concerned with the domestic affairs of the states. State functions included almost all matters which had a direct bearing upon the social and material welfare of the people.

Quick and Garran give an excellent account of how the original colonies acquired more power regarding the Queen's representative, and they provide a résumé of imperial legislation which had enhanced the power of the colonies before 1850. This reminds us that the later proposals for federation or union were related to developments leading to colonial self-government in this period. It is worth noting their comment that, apart from provisions allowing New South Wales to set electoral machinery for Victoria, the new Victorian colony was given the same powers and restrictions as applied in New South Wales. In other words, from the moment of the creation of the second colony in Australia, there was no hierarchy between them, although the new position of the Governor-General in New South Wales is not elaborated upon.

The first formal moves towards Australian federation came of course in the form of schemes suggested to the colonies by the British Secretary of State for Colonies, Earl Grey, in his famous dispatch of 31 July 1847. In it he included, among other things, the idea previously raised by Governor Fitzroy, of a General Assembly to deal with matters of common Australian interest. This was the key passage:

> The principle of local self-government (like every other political principle) must, when reduced to practice, be qualified by many other principles which must operate simultaneously with it . . . For example, it is necessary that, while providing for the local management of local interests we should not omit to provide for a central management of all such interests as are not local. Thus, questions co-extensive in their bearing with the interests of the Empire at large and the appropriate province of Parliament.
>
> But there are questions which, local as it respects the British possessions in Australia collectively, are not merely local as it respects any of those possessions. Considered as members of the same Empire, those colonies have many common interests, the regulation of which, in some uniform manner and by some single authority, may be essential to the welfare of them all. Yet in some cases such interests may be more promptly, effectively, and satisfactorily decided by some authority within Australia itself than by the more remote, the less accessible, and in truth less competent authority of Parliament.[12]

Grey then went on in his dispatch to name some of the interests he thought would be common to all the colonies, including import and export duties, conveyance of letters, roads, railways, and other internal communications traversing two or more colonies.

The reception to Grey's suggestions was hostile, and William Charles Wentworth spearheaded resolutions to oppose them on the grounds that Grey's suggestions for a central legislature would jeopardize the position of New South Wales.

The next development of relevance was the 1849 Committee of the Privy Council which suggested, inter alia, that one Australian Governor should be Governor-General, there should be a uniform tariff, and a General Assembly with powers over ten topics which they specified. However, no grounds were given for the powers which had been selected. This however had little impact, especially after the departure of Governor Fitzroy.

In 1853, Wentworth's Constitutional Committee in New South Wales came up with a recommendation for a General Assembly for "intercolonial questions", and listed eight specific heads of power for that body. Again, no rationale is given, but Quick and Garran do note that Wentworth only had in mind a means of securing "uniform legislation on a few matters of common interest". A committee appointed in Victoria in 1853 to draft a new constitution for that colony also touched on the question, and said that there were questions of such vital intercolonial interest that provision should be made for occasional invoking of a General Assembly. But rather than list powers for that General Assembly, they proposed instead that it only have power to legislate on matters submitted to it by the colonies.

From 1834 to 1863 there were sporadic moves which produced some attention to the division of powers. Dean-Thomson said in Britain in 1856 that there were "seven great questions" that should be submitted to a representative federal assembly, and he named them. Wentworth, now living in England, drew up a draft bill in 1857 which expanded on the Dean-Thomson list. Duffy in 1857 in Victoria had a select committee look at the possibility of union, and suggested a conference be called of delegates from the colonies to delineate powers, whilst in New South Wales in the same year, a select committee suggested that a new General Assembly could have power to legislate on "all intercolonial subjects which might be submitted to it by the legislatures of two or more colonies interested in no other subject". A South Australian select committee in 1857 thought a federal legislature would be premature, but felt that there were many topics where the colonies had a common interest and where uniform legislation would be desirable. They added a few more powers to the list.

Between 1863 and 1880 there were debates on the tariff, and intercolonial conferences. These conferences, say Quick and Garran, were not adequate, but provided the only means of securing "uniform legislation and concerted administration on the subjects of common concern". One such conference on postal services led to suggestions of the establishment of a federal council. At an intercolonial conference in 1880–1881, Parkes submitted a basis for uniform duties of customs and excise, which was later expanded into broader recommendations, including a Federal Council to deal with all intercolonial matters.

It was the fear of external attack that prompted colonies to think of defence as a common function, and it was Griffith who pressed in 1883 for a Federal Australasian Council to deal with defence, pacific relations, the influx of criminals, regulation of quarantine, and any other matters referred by the Queen or any of the colonies. But the council was to have limited membership, and although it had some legislative powers, it had no effective financial or executive powers. The Colonial Conference of 1887 suggested an Imperial Officer be appointed to report on defences of the Australian colonies. Major General Edwards reported in 1889 and suggested federation of the forces by many means, and added "a uniform gauge for railways" to his list of defence reorganization.

On October 1889 Parkes was to use this defence report to urge federation in his famous Tenterfield Speech, in which he proposed a convention of delegates, and clearly envisaged creation of a central government modelled closely on that existing in Canada, but no powers were mentioned. There followed, of course, in 1891, Parkes's famous resolutions which served as the basis for the debates of the convention. They really ought to be repeated here:

1. That the powers and privileges and territorial rights of the several existing colonies shall remain intact, except in respect to such surrenders as may be agreed upon as necessary and incidental to the power and authority of the National Federal Government.
2. That the trade and intercourse between the federated colonies, whether by means of land carriage or coastal navigation, shall be absolutely free.
3. That the power and authority to impose custom duties shall be exclusively lodged in the federal government and parliament, subject to such disposal of the revenues thence derived as shall be agreed upon.
4. That the military and naval defence of Australia shall be entrusted to federal forces, under one command.

Quick and Garran comment on these resolutions: "The fundamental principles of union thus laid down were — intercolonial free trade, a federal tariff, federal defence, and the reservation of provincial rights in provincial matters . . . They were based, beyond all doubt, on a comparative study of the Constitutions of the United States and Canada."[13]

Unfortunately, the proceedings of the subcommittees of this convention were private, so it is not possible to delve directly into the minds of the founding fathers, especially those who drew up the actual constitutional document, including the delineation of powers. Again, the reaction from the colonies to the draft constitution which was produced reveals some disagreement about certain items of power, but no explicit rationale for determining which level of government should have that power.

The so-called "popular movement" had approached the question of assigning powers between levels of government but with little evidence of any overarching criteria in mind. The 1892 financial panic, it is claimed, had shown plainly that the prosperity of each colony was bound up with that of the others. Perhaps the leading force in the profederation movement was the Australian Natives Association, and in January 1890 just before the Conference convened by Parkes, the Association passed resolutions which included a specific list of fifteen powers that should be given to a new federal legislature, including defence, federal court of appeal, pacific relations, naturalization, uniform customs duties, railways, post and telegraph, public debt, federal revenue, division of any colony, marriage and divorce laws, insolvency, quarantine, coinage, and patents, copyrights and trade marks. It added that all legislation "affecting provincial affairs" should be left to each colony, but apart from that it gave no rationale for any or all of the powers so enumerated.

Dibbs, the Premier of NSW, drew up a unification alternative in 1894 and proposed, inter alia, federal control over debts, railways, and land revenues, as well as a list of other powers. His concepts were rejected completely and Quick and Garran reveal no surprise. They say: "The immense area of the different colonies and their climatic and industrial condition make the preservation of their individuality highly important; whilst they also offered a strong argument against entrusting unlimited powers to a central government which, in the nature of things, cannot have complete knowledge of, nor complete sympathy with all the different local requirements of the different colonies".[14]

At the Adelaide session of the convention in 1897 the legislative power of the proposed commonwealth parliament was extended, but the railway power was confined to defence purposes only. No clear explanation of the related reasoning is given. It was suggested that only by giving power over the River Murray could the problem of the conflict of riparian rights between the neighbouring states be resolved. Reaction from the colonies centred mostly on debates on narrow areas which affected that colony alone.

At the Melbourne Convention in 1898 an interesting debate ensued over whether the Murray River system was "national" in character, and whether both navigation and irrigation involving that river were a national matter. There was disagreement here. As Quick and Garran note:

> The debate proceeded mainly, however, on the recognised assumption that navigation — at least inter-state navigation — was a federal power, incident to the control of trade and commerce, whilst irrigation and conservation were state powers incident to the control and management of the land. The difficulty remained, that the two powers might possibly conflict. Irrigation and conservation works in the states if uncontrolled by the Commonwealth, might destroy the navigability of the rivers; whilst navigation regulations of the Commonwealth, and more especially works for maintaining or improving the navigability of the rivers, might seriously interfere with irrigation and conservation.[15]

In relation to railways, an opinion was expressed that it was disastrous to federalize the control of railway rates unless the financial responsibility of management was also federalized, and profound disagreement over control of railway rates led to increased powers for the proposed federal interstate commission. After substantial debate the commonwealth was given power over invalid and old age pensions. This is not analysed in any depth.

The remaining steps towards ratification of the constitution reveal little else in terms of argument relevant to division of powers. At the last minute Sir John Forrest, for Western Australia, agreed to join the federation, but he wanted the federal government to have powers to construct a transcontinental railway so he wouldn't require the permission of South Australia for its construction and its route in that colony. The few objections which Westminster did raise, and some of which were accommodated, had only marginal relevance to the division of powers between the commonwealth and the states, except perhaps the retention of appeals to the Privy Council where a dispute over such allocation should arise.

The Australian Constitution

In the words of Sir John Quick:

> One of the fundamental features of the Federal Constitution and the one which has been the subject of most controversy and most judicial decisions is the system of distribution of legislative powers between the Parliament of the Commonwealth and the state parliament. To effect such a distribution under a Federal Constitution it is necessary to divide the possible field of legislation by description of the various subject matters.
>
> Generally speaking the Australian Constitution, following the model of the Constitution of the United States, has given specific subject matters to the Federal Parliament and the residue of possible subject matters to the state Parliaments. This method of distribution leaves the states a mass of exclusive powers which cannot be invoked or interfered with by the Federal Authority and it also leaves to the states, in addition to their exclusive powers, certain concurrent powers as to matters within federal sphere to pass laws not inconsistent with federal laws.[16]

There are two things worth noting about this statement: firstly, it proceeds from the assumption that it is necessary to divide legislative competence by actually apportioning *subject matters*, by which of course is meant discrete government functions; and secondly, it gives no clue whatever as to how that division is to proceed. Quick does add that one of the key methods of deciding which powers the states would retain was that it was assumed they would retain most of the powers they had had as colonies. That was expressed in Section 107, which provided that "Every power of the Parliament of a Colony which has become or becomes a state shall unless it is by this Constitution exclusively vested in the Parliament of the Commonwealth, or withdrawn from the Parliament of the state continue as at the establishment of the Commonwealth".

This might be construed as a postfederation guarantee of state's rights and so, in a sense, a division of power in their favour. It is not the only such provision. There are other provisions which retain for each state the right to have direct communication with the Queen on state matters; which continue the state constitutions, in effect, except so far as they are inconsistent with the constitution of the commonwealth; which continue state laws in force until inconsistent provisions are legally made by the commonwealth parliament; which guarantee equal representation in the Senate and minimum representation in the House of Representatives; which allow state governors to issue writs for Senate elections; and which require the governor of a state concerned to be notified of vacancies in the Senate.

In relation to the judicial system, the national elements were determined by making the laws of the commonwealth binding, by allowing the High Court to determine appeals from state courts on questions of state laws, through the original jurisdiction of the High Court in some matters, and as far as the Federal Parliament has the power to nationalize state courts by investing them with federal jurisdiction. But there are elements reserved for the states here too. The constitution preserves state laws which are not inconsistent with commonwealth laws, it gives state courts exclusively original and primary jurisdiction over matters involving state laws, and it provides that the trial, or indictment, of an offence against any law of the commonwealth shall be held in the state where the offence was committed.

The powers of the federal government are most clearly enunciated in Section 51, and to a lesser extent Section 52, of the constitution. Quick and Garran make the important observations that:

> Looking down the sub-sections of Section 51, we find that in many of them the principle of duality is expressly recognized, and the trade and commerce power is confined to inter-state and foreign trade and commerce, and it is hedged in (Chap. IV) with a number of minute restrictions to prevent injustice or discrimination between states. The federal power of imposing taxation and granting bounties is similarly hedged about with conditions for the protection of the states. In sub-section X, the power over fisheries is confined to waters beyond territorial limits . . . In sub-sections xiii and xiv, the powers as the Banking and Insurance also contain a reservation of states rights. In sub-section XX-XV power to deal with conciliation and arbitration is only given to the case of interstate industrial disputes and so on. In all these cases, the duality of interests is recognized in the very gift of the power of the federal parliament, and the distribution of power is thus essentially federal. But in most of the sub-sections this nice analysis is not found. The advantages of uniform legislation, especially in matters relating to commerce, have prevailed, over the sentiment of local independence; and we find that if a subject has, on the whole, a national aspect, it is handed over unconditionally to the national legislature. Thus posts and telegraphs, defences, quarantine, currency, weights and measures, bills of exchange and promissory notes, bankruptcy and insolvency, copyright, patents and trade marks, naturalization and aliens, trading and financial corporations,

marriage and divorce, and other subjects are made unconditionally national. No state reserves any rights with respect to its internal posts and telegraphs, or of marriages between its own citizens, all these subjects are not federalized but nationalized — or at least, the power to nationalize them is given to the federal parliament.[17]

Of course Quick and Garran also annotate the individual subsections of Section 51, and it becomes quite apparent that there is considerable room for difference of opinion for what each subhead actually means, though they might appear quite self-evident to the layman. There are numerous examples of this, but for illustration we might look at one of Deakin's letters to the *Morning Post*, where he expresses a belief that the power over post and telegraphs means the Barton government could "put down" a state running lotteries, and also become master of the state railways by obliging them to carry the mail and then submit their charges for doing so to arbitration in the event of any dispute. As he added in a later letter: "One cannot have an omelette without breaking eggs nor a federal union without sacrifice of state independence".[18] Another perspective on the same question occurs in respect of social policies with the commonwealth government not long after federation interpreting the social welfare powers listed much more widely than had the conventions of the 1890s. Norris comments on this aspect:

> The sharpest contrast between the Convention delegates, who framed the Constitution, and the Commonwealth politicians who came to implement it, was the presence in parliament of a Labor party, which, as it happened, held the balance between Free Trade and Protection . . . The two specific social powers — arbitration and pensions — became part of the Constitution only after persistent attempts on the part of their sponsors . . . Yet federal legislation soon strained the Constitution for its limits . . . Therefore Labor, committed to a definite platform of social reform directly and indirectly influenced the orientation and course of legislation by "auctioning" its votes to obtain measures close to its interests. Social issues came to the fore.[19]

Another even more remarkable aspect arose in relation to the power over industrial relations, because the new commonwealth politicians quickly realized that it was not much good having power over the tariff, and free interstate trade, when different factory standards could exist in each state. Higgins introduced the first ever motion by a private member in 1901, for the commonwealth to acquire, subject to the concurrence of the states, "full power to make laws for Australia as to wages and hours and conditions of labour". Quite a lot of commonwealth politicians (including Prime Minister Barton) who at the constitutional debates of the 1890s had argued vehemently that industrial relations was a state matter, now warmly supported Higgins. Said Barton: "The effects of internal free trade and the uniform tariff would be 'crippled' unless the national parliament also had power to deal uniformly with the conditions of employment throughout Australia". Another member marvelled at the "miraculous conversion that had taken place".

Section 52 of the constitution began with the preamble that: "The Parliament shall, subject to this Constitution have exclusive power to make laws for the peace, order, and good government of the Commonwealth with respect to . . .". Whilst in some federations this phraseology "peace, order and good government" has been regarded as itself conferring very wide scope on the level of government to which it is ascribed, in the Australian case it was regarded just as common verbiage, and the three areas that followed were considered the vital portion of the section.

Space does not permit a complete examination of every one of the powers specifically allocated in the original constitution exclusively to the commonwealth, concurrently between the two levels, or exclusively to the states. Also, we have not examined the way powers of raising revenue were allocated. Suffice to reemphasize that in this document:

1. There was, even in 1901, some ambiguity about the meaning and extent of various government functions.
2. In the event of inconsistencies in laws between the two levels, commonwealth law would prevail to the extent of the inconsistency.
3. There was little provision for the interpenetration of the two levels and less for the states to oversee the commonwealth than vice versa.
4. There was already some suspicion that some of the powers at one level were inconsistent with other powers given to the same level, and more importantly, that there were important linkages between functions assigned one level and those assigned to a different level. These promised to cause practical difficulties.
5. There was no specific mention of local government.
6. Very few words indicative of anything resembling criteria for allocation of functions appear in the actual wording of the constitution.

Thus it becomes clear that even from the moment of its proclamation, the constitution was bound to become a document establishing rules for a dynamic relationship between levels of government, and not a static one. This is extremely important for the question of the division of powers. No better, or more prophetic statement of the situation could be given than that of Quick and Garran themselves:

> Whilst the life of the Commonwealth will begin with a clear differentiation of function and status, as between it and its corporate units, the states, it does not follow that the outlines and objects of that differentiation will be distinctly and permanently preserved. There will be, at the outset, a clear demarcation of spheres, a clear delimitation of powers separating the central government from the state governments, but the initial law must not be regarded as expressing a relationship as unchanging as the laws of the Medes and the Persians.[20]

Comparable Canadian Experience

The distribution of powers between the three levels of government in the Canadian federation differs in two basic respects from the Australian situation. Firstly, the *British North America Act*, specifies the powers of the provinces and grants residual powers to the Central or Dominion Government. Secondly, the founding fathers of the Canadian Constitution saw fit to enumerate a list of powers for the dominion government as well, although originally for illustrative purposes only. But the complications of having two lists of delineated powers in the one constitution has caused enormous difficulties for many reasons, not the least of which is the fact that the functions are not mutually exclusive and have become progressively less so with the passage of the years. Another difficulty which arises is caused by the fact that the preamble to the list of Dominion powers in Section 91 of the *British North America Act* states that the national parliament shall make laws for the "peace, order and good government" of Canada, and also adds that the central government powers cannot concern themselves "with matters of a local or private nature". Interpretation of these phrases has bedevilled many a legal, political and administrative effort to determine which level of government should possess a particular power, because it is strikingly obvious that a vast array of matters can affect the peace, order and good government of a country, and very few actions of any government do not in some way or other impinge on local and private affairs. The exclusive powers of the provinces are listed in Section 92 of the *British North America Act*. Education is treated as a special case in Section 93, and old age pensions and agriculture also come in for special treatment.

Founding Fathers

There is really no Canadian equivalent of Quick and Garran to guide us through the events leading to Canadian Confederation, so one is forced to rely on a scattering of historical works. It seems clear however that, as in Australia, there was no profound attempt to conceptualize criteria for the allocation of specific powers between the levels. Rather, the Canadians were keen to place the weight of legislative potential with the central government, as they interpreted the civil strife in neighbouring America to have been largely an outcome of the undue power possessed by the subnational units in that federation.

Creighton attributes the formal distribution of powers to Brown, and to him also the fact that two sets of powers were presented.[21] However, Macdonald had a model which he had sought to follow and which strongly favoured the proposed central government. Macdonald declared that "we have given the General Legislature all the great subjects of legislation", and Galt remarked of the central government's powers that "amongst them would be found all that could in any way be considered of a public and general character". When introducing the *British North America Act* into the House of Lords, Lord Carnarvon stated: "The real object which we have in view is to give the central government those high functions and almost sovereign powers by which general principles and uniformity of legislation may be secured in those questions that are of common impact to all the provinces". The attitude of the founding fathers to the powers of the provinces was that they should include "generally all matters of a merely local or private nature in the province".[22] It also seems that the costs of federation were a significant issue, and the founding fathers were influenced by a desire to ensure that the cost of the local (that is, provincial and municipal) governments would be small because, said Galt, "it would not do to affront the intelligence of the people and tell them we had devised an expensive kind of machinery to do a very insignificant amount of work". G.P. Browne points out that the Canadian founding fathers had another basic difficulty in delineating powers, and that was to ensure that the provinces kept control over cultural matters.[23]

Stanley credits Tache with having conceived the first basis for the distribution of powers, and says that Tache allocated to the federal parliament most powers which finally emerged, and everything relating to "family life" to the provinces. He also reveals that many of the founders could see the fault of enumerating a list for both levels of government. Says Stanley:

> From the evidence offered by Joseph Pope, it would appear that the delegates at no time seriously attempted to define the scope of the enumerated items or their possible overlapping, beyond George Brown's suggestions that the courts of each province should decide what is Local and what General Government jurisdiction, with Appeal to the Appeal or Superior Court.[24]

Stanley adds that "the colonial delegates had believed the enumerated powers to be mutually exclusive; only agriculture and immigration, which had been included among the powers assigned to both federal and provincial legislatures seemed to provide any real problems, and these were deviated by giving federal legislation in respect to these matters precedence over that of the provinces".[25]

It is Smiley who gives the most lucid account of the original distribution of powers in Canada. Some of the key criteria he observes from the relevant literature include the concern of the fathers in economic matters to make an implicit distinction between activities associated with land and activities associated with commerce, and on the basis of this distinction, they allocated powers to the provinces and the Dominion respectively. Smiley states that there has never been a satisfactory explanation of why the framers of the Act resorted to such an enumeration. It seems that the provinces were given matters in which the traditions of the English-speaking and French-speaking groups were significantly different, while the Dominion received matters with little cultural significance. The other broad class of subjects which the founders gave the provinces were those matters which had been the responsibility of local governments. As to the national powers, Smiley says:

> The powers conferred on the Dominion were deemed necessary to secure military defence, the eventual inclusion of all remaining British territories in

North America within Canada, and the establishment of an integrated national economy.[26]

These were, says Smiley, the "nation-building and nation-maintaining powers", and together with others they were also the costly functions of government, and the allocation of revenue powers had to be adjusted accordingly. With respect to the judicial system, which was to be a single one for both levels, it seems that the founders believed that, although the two levels would legislate and administer independently, the judicial system would operate through cooperation.

The Canadian Constitution

Apart from some of the factors which have emerged, there are a few other portions of the wording of the *British North America Act* which reveal some criteria regarding the role of levels of government. Although education was assigned to the provinces, the central government was made the protector of educational rights of denominational minorities against provincial encroachments. Law enforcement was divided, giving criminal law enforcement only to the central government, thus respecting longstanding guarantees to Quebec from 1774 onwards, so that the provinces were given exclusive power over "property and civil rights in the province", that is, civil law. The provinces could not amend legislation affecting the status and position of their Lieutenant Governor. In fact, the viceregal representatives in the province were in a hierarchical and subordinate relationship in many ways to the Governor General of Canada. Section 92 says provinces can levy direct taxes, but it is in order to raise revenue for "provincial purposes", and they can borrow money, but on the "sole credit of the province". They can establish and run hospitals and like institutions but not "Marine Hospitals". They have control over "Municipal Institutions". Their public works power cannot apply to communications and transport mediums connecting the province to another province or country or extending beyond the limits of the province, and also "such works as, although wholly situate within the province, are before or after their execution declared by the parliament of Canada to be for the general advantage of Canada or for the advantage of two or more of the provinces". Other powers mentioned, such as marriage, property and civil rights, and administration of justice are to be carried out solely "in the province" and the incorporation of companies is restricted to those with "provincial objects". Section 92 actually concludes with the powers of the provinces over "generally all matters of a merely local or private nature in the province".

The federal government was empowered by Section 94 to make provision for uniformity of all or any laws relative to property and civil rights in three of the provinces and also for court procedure in those provinces. In old age pensions the federal power was not allowed to affect any provincial legislation "on old age pensions" (later changed to prevent interference with provincial laws in "any such matter"). In Agriculture and Immigration, the powers are concurrent with federal legislation (superior), but it should be noted that the national government can legislate in these areas, and indeed in any of the areas of its power *in all or any one of the provinces*. The federal government can acquire provincial public property for defence purposes. Under the new constitutional package, provinces have concurrent jurisdiction over interprovincial trade in nonrenewable resources.

Lessons from the Literature

As mentioned earlier, there has been a wealth of both Australian and Canadian literature dealing with various aspects of the division of powers. Any comprehensive review, would include a résumé of the deliberations of such Australian sources as the 1929 Royal Commission on the Constitution, the 1959 Parliamentary Joint Committee on Constitutional Review, various Constitutional Conventions, and major academic treatises, symposiums, and textbooks. Canadian sources to discuss would include the 1950 Rowell-Sirois Royal Commission on Dominion-Provincial Relations and its copious commissioned studies, academic treatises, and texts, and some of the material related to the constitutional review process of the late 1970s. That literature appears to present the following *basic* problems as arising from the existence of the division of powers in the two federations.

1. Difficulties in achieving uniformity in the provision of government services. Examples arising from the literature include company law, marriage and divorce law, health, roads, aviation, transport, navigation and shipping.[27]
2. Problems in ensuring the equitable provision of government services throughout the whole nation.[28]
3. Confusion for the clients of government, difficulties in fulfilling community expectations (especially in the welfare area), distortion of political accountability to citizens, and undue increases in the cost of litigation for citizens against governments.[29]
4. Legal confusion in functions designated as concurrent under the constitution, and especially in relation to High Court interpretations in such cases. This problem is particularly evident in Canadian literature because of the effect of the existence of two sets of enumerated powers in Sections 91 and 92 of the *British North America Act*, alluded to earlier.[30]
5. In various forms the concept of "spillovers" appears frequently in the literature together with the problems of coping with such spillovers because of various forms of divided jurisdiction. The somewhat related problem of coping with mobile resources is also raised.[31]
6. A wide variety of concerns about the smooth functioning of the

economy have arisen because of the federal division of powers. These include many viewpoints, such as the general fear of overgovernment, the growth of the whole public sector, the complexity of the economy, and general control of the economy.[32]

7. A number of authors have highlighted the fact that because of the division of powers, taxing powers are separated from spending powers, inducing all levels of government to be politically irresponsible and engage in "buck passing".[33]

8. The inducement to public servants to build up a parochial power base behind their share of the division of powers has been noted, especially in the Canadian literature.[34]

9. The division of powers, it is claimed, can also lead to gaps in government powers overall, and even, in the words of one author, to "zones of anarchy".[35]

10. There is a good deal of concern expressed in the literature over the actual wording used in the constitution to describe the division of powers. The concern is as to its vagueness, and hence ambiguity, leaving considerable potential for conflicting interpretation. One particular aspect of this general concern relates to the way in which the wording of the constitution has resulted in fiscal powers being able to be used to override the actual explicit division of government functions between the levels, as stipulated elsewhere in the constitution.[36]

These then are some of the basic difficulties caused by the division of powers which appear to be relevant to our consideration of the hindrances to public sector planning in federations. The specific public functions which are most often mentioned in the literature as[37] being bedevilled by the division of powers include trade and commerce, navigation and shipping, industrial relations, health, roads, aviation, company law, aborigines, restrictive trade practices, family law, defamation, transport, education, and offshore resources.

Some other tangential aspects of the division of powers which were raised in the literature include the potential for dividing powers between levels on a legislative/administrative basis within functions (often known as a horizontal power division); the need for a division of powers as a defence against centralization and totalitarianism; the relationship between the size of the units of government and the division of powers (so that a power is not devolved to a unit incapable of coping with it); the role of local government and its potential role; and the confusion to the traditional division of powers caused by regionalism.

The Contribution of the Empirical Analysis

Virtually all these points which have been made in the literature were confirmed by the interviews which were conducted for this study. In particular, a very large number of functional fields of government activity were identified in which the division of powers posed basic problems for coordination. There seems little point in simply recounting yet further examples of the same points made in the literature. In any event, it will be observed that the bulk of the literature we have surveyed has been contributed by "practitioners" in the two federal systems, and hence it gives empirical viewpoints.

However, the interviews which were conducted stressed a number of extremely important points, relating to the division of powers, which appear only sporadically in the most recent Australian and Canadian literature, for the very good reason that these aspects are a product of only relatively recent developments and emphasis in intergovernmental relationships in the two countries. Let us now consider them, beginning with the most basic recent phenomenon.

1. The Dynamic Nature of Federalism and the Move towards Organic Federalism

It became clear from the interviews conducted that the Australian and Canadian federations are no longer coordinate, for various reasons, most of which are related to the growing interdependence of parts of the economy and society, and the need for substantially increased government intervention in general. The actions of each level of government have significant effects on other levels, and there are, moreover, a considerable number of government functions which are now performed by more than one level. Virtually all respondents believed that coordinate federalism in the old style was no longer a possibility because of the very interdependence of all spatial and functional elements within the nation.

This notion has also, of course, been identified in the literature, and more so in Canadian writing than Australian. For example, Smiley says that "Canada like other federations has moved away from 'classical federalism' in which each level of government performed the responsibilities assigned to it by the constitution in relative isolation from the other. In the contemporary world, both the citizens and constituent governments of federations have become so interdependent that if some matter within the sphere of public decision is of concern only to particular state or provincial communities, it is not crucial even to those communities."[38] Various other Canadian writers have elaborated on this aspect, confirming the trend with examples. They include, for example, Simeon, Black and Cairns, Corry, Johnson, Trudeau, Pearson, Pepin, Johnson, Hodgetts, and a variety of official inquiries.[39]

In relation to Australia, Mathews, speaking of developments in the 1970s, says:

> To those outside the political conflict, it had long been apparent that the growth and complexity of the public sector, the interdependence of decisions taken by the different planes of government, differences in the availability of information, and in the degree of political responsiveness, and the need to accommodate a varying mixture of national, regional, and local interests, were all com-

bining to give decision making in the public sector an intergovernmental or multiplane dimension. This made it inappropriate for governments to base their actions on premises of coordinate or coercive federalism, or even on cooperative federalism where cooperation was regarded as an option for autonomous governments affecting only the policy fringes.[40]

Reid expresses it this way:

> Nowadays the scale of governmental intervention in our everyday lives, and the scale of federal functions vis-a-vis state and local functions, make the theories of strict governmental independence patently false.[41]

These observations have been supported and verified by writers such as Sawer, Menzies, Crisp, Spann, Knight, Anderson, Mackintosh, Hawker, and Giblin.[42]

The weight of all these comments is to suggest that both Australia and Canada have left a situation of coordinate federalism (if they ever really occupied it in the first place), and have moved into a situation of what has been described as organic federalism. The era of coordinate federalism, with its emphasis on a division of discrete governmental powers between two levels, is held to have been applicable only in a situation of minimum government activity in general, and simple activity at that, in a society without the modern methods of resource mobility.

In any event, the respondents in this survey saw a rapidly increasing number of public sector activities, once the preserve of one level of government only, now becoming intergovernmental through methods of shared funding and/or shared responsibilities. Moreover, there were other by-products of this changed intergovernmental relationship, including what I have termed "linkages" and "overrides". (Those were not terms used by any respondent; they are concepts I have derived from the accounts of activity described by respondents.)

2. Linkages

It has become very evident in Australia and Canada that there are links between functions of government; some of them so strong that alterations to any aspect of the conduct of one function induce immediate and direct reaction to others. This may have been covertly recognized at the time of confederation but subsequent events have clarified it. These aspects emerged out of the interviews conducted for this study.

In the first place, the general health of the economy in its broadest sense affects a multitude of functions of government, irrespective of whatever level of government performs them. The rate of inflation, level of employment, economic growth, interest rates, volume of money in circulation, exchange rates, etc., all affect the performance of many government functions. It makes no sense to say simply that the national government should have responsibility for economic management, and then assume that "economic management" is a discrete government function exclusive to the highest level of government. By way of illustration, some other more direct linkages include the following:

(a) Navigation, irrigation, and conservation. It is impossible to control the navigability of streams without affecting the availability of water for irrigation, and consequently the conservation of water and other resources, and possibly the ecology. Yet in most federations, including Australia, different functions in this linkage are allocated to different levels of government.

(b) Trade and commerce, and industrial relations: The control of interstate trade and commerce is profoundly affected by differing levels of wastes, and different factory or industry standards in each state. But these functions are also split between levels.

(c) The linkages of land: Controls over land will have an automatic commensurate impact on property matters, town planning, pollution, food supply, ethnic groups with any land rights, public and private transport, peace and order, mineral royalties, etc. Land is such a basic resource that the government which controls it is in a powerful position to influence other functions of government even if it does not control them.

(d) Police linkages: Obviously the control of the police force gives any government a superior advantage when the question of allocating other functions arises. Take the control of flora and fauna, road safety, and even (as claimed in some of the literature) the control of aboriginal reserves.

(e) The linkages of education: These linkages are almost limitless. Education is connected with libraries, television, radio, language, investment in building and equipment, building up of national expertise, research, defence, and so on. Then there are the educational, exhortative, or extension aspects of almost all functions of government. Obviously it makes little sense to assume that any one level of government in a federation has complete control over the education function.

(f) Linkages of marriage and families: It will be singularly frustrating for any level of government which controls marriage and divorce if it does not also control in some degree, adoption, fostering, property settlements, illegitimacy, maintenance, succession, and most matters connected with the family, including the courts to hear the disputes on these subjects. The family is so basic and interconnected a unit that it almost has to be legislated for as a unit so that the linkages of each of its parts can be taken into account when dealing with any one component.

(g) Immigration linkages: The government controlling the nature and level of immigration will overtly or covertly influence the provision of all the social infrastructure throughout the nation, especially in Australia, as immigration has been such a large element of our population increase. That means that immigration is linked to employment, schools, hospitals, housing, utilities, welfare functions, and so on. Conversely, the rate of development of a region will in turn affect the demand for immigrants.

(h) Industry and employees: Dislocation will be caused if one level of government controls the fortunes of the industry (capital and ownership) and another controls the employees. Consider the present situation in Australia where the national government seeks to relocate employees to factories, and state governments endeavour to shift factories to employees. Or the effects of the commonwealth government in negating attempts by states to decentralize industries through payroll tax concessions. Industries are inextricably linked to their employees, especially, of course, if they are labour intensive.

We could go on for a long time looking for linkages. The ones outlined have caused most trouble in the Australian federation. Other more recent ones include the question of whether to control civil aviation properly the national government should control the whole manufacturing process for aeroplanes; the use of powers over radio and television in controlling cigarette smoking (a health function), and also the conduct of elections; the effect of income tax and company tax in breaking up properties; the use of control over post and telecommunications to control lotteries or racing or pornography; the question of whether the level of government which controls defamation should also have those matters heard in its courts or those of another level of government; the impact of a state, not conforming to daylight saving, on interstate travel timetables, national radio and television broadcasting, and national elections; the power of customs officials over the actual final use to which goods will be put; the overarching importance of health controls in relation to other functions like sanitation, garbage, irrigation, water, and sewerage; the importance of the control of shipping, bridges over rivers, motorboat behaviour, overhead cables, pollution, obstruction by hulks, and moorings; river lighthouses and ocean lighthouses; the link between the control of areas offshore and land-based jetties, which raises the point that vessels that explore or fish in commonwealth waters will probably have to ultimately tie up on state land, or the question of whether states can build jetties below the low water mark; the profound effect in the past of railways, and now motor cars, on land settlement; the question of whether preschools are a health function or one related to education and sport; the many facets of care of the aged, including the real connection betwen domicilary care and institutional care, each of which is often given to different levels of government; the question of whether a casino or hotel or ground transport company is so closely linked to the operations of airlines as to be regarded as part of the airline function.[43]

The list is probably endless because we live in a social system which is, by definition, linked throughout its parts. Some of the linkages are stronger than others. The difficulty can also come in applying any geographical or spatial dimension to the same government functions, such as having one level of government control interstate shipping and ocean lighthouses, and another controlling intrastate shipping and river lighthouses. That is another linkage.

There is no need to labour the point. It has been mentioned because it has bedevilled any attempts by the courts or governments to maintain a perfect coordinate system of federalism, and because it must be kept firmly in mind when playing about with reallocation of functions, especially in relation to those functions which are basic and have so many linkages spreading from them.

It is small wonder that the Rowell-Sirois Commission thought it best, in Canada, to speak of a primary role and a secondary role in so many public functions, thereby recognizing that many levels may have some interest in each function.

The concept of linkages is not well defined in the literature of Australian or Canadian federalism probably because such linkages are for the most part intangible, and their effects are most apparent to practitioners working in any of the three levels of government. They do arise in an oblique manner in some writings, including those of Davies, Peachment, Reid, Baxter, Heydon, Else-Mitchell, Giblin, and McGregor-Dawson.[44]

3. Overrides

It became apparent, through the interviews, that all aspects of the division of powers and the working arrangements of intergovernmental relations brought about by the organic state and its linkages, have in some periods been thrown into disarray by events, or goals, or even concepts which assumed special importance to the whole of the nation. To illustrate, many respondents stated that the energy crisis of the late 1970s had transformed the debate about, and practical operation of, the proper function of the levels of government, because that crisis was regarded by all as so dominant as to require that the interaction of levels of government should occur in the manner best suited to coping with the situation. Those respondents with long memories recalled exactly the same attitude about the war, of course, and then postwar reconstruction. What actually happens then is that these events or concepts *subsume* all other considerations. For example, to say that a function of government is "vital" is almost the same as saying it must supersede all normal deliberations about intergovernmental relations, and to describe a problem as being "of national importance" virtually precludes even considering which level of government should perform it. These were some of the examples which came out of the interviews:
*   War: The question thar arises in wartime is where should a function of government be placed to best aid the war effort, and in that sense all the other criteria become forgotten (although not completely, as the wrangling between levels of government over the Australian transfer of powers proposals in World War II reveals).

* Postwar reconstruction: A single goal or task, it usually means a gravitation of power and coordination to the national government even if actual functions are not transferred. Thus housing and education are no longer housing and education — they are postwar reconstruction.

* Development, and northern development: If this objective is desired keenly enough the question becomes which level of government can achieve it as quickly as possible.

* Free enterprise: If the overriding aim throughout the nation is to stimulate free enterprise, it becomes a question of which government has the greatest potential to do this, and also probably an argument for greater diffusion of functions through all the levels.

* Controlling the economy: If it should be thought that economic management were the dominant need of the moment, or the period, subordinate levels of government might acquiesce in transferring some or all of their functions to a higher national level, if only for a stipulated period.

* Planning: Since planning requires coordination and allocation of resources across the whole public sector, it is inevitably regarded as appropriate to a higher level of government.

* Energy crisis: To the extent that a sudden shortage in energy sources, coupled with uncertainty about future sources, dominates concerns of all levels of government, it will also assume, for the duration of the "crisis", an overbearing influence on intergovernmental discussions.

* Quality of life, civil liberties, national image, national self-sufficiency in oil or food or some other resource, and democracy: They are all further examples of "override" criteria which have been raised in the literature and indeed, in the course of events. Those who argue for their primacy are arguing for them to be the sole, or at least dominant and embracing, criteria to be used in determining the allocation of functions. Obviously they are "override" criteria because of their nature, being causes or ideologies or aims which span a vast array of government functions.

The reason that override criteria have been mentioned here is that they are a criterion, a super-criterion, for use in the allocation of functions, and in that sense it is probably best to deal with them first, where they do exist, because they will be such a magnetic reference point that they will swamp all attempts to consider functions of government in the light of the normal criteria. It is better to be aware of them and consider their nature at the outset of the reallocation process.

4.   Roles not Functions

The Rowell-Sirois Commission, some forty years ago, thought it best in Canada to speak of a primary role and a secondary role in many public functions, thereby recognizing that many levels have some interest in each function. As indicated, most respondents interviewed believed it was no longer practicable to secure levels of government into watertight compartments together with their electors and clients. It does not necessarily mean that all functions of government will be shared by two or three levels, but it is likely that the most expansive (and probably the most expensive) ones which touch the most people, will be shared, along with many other related functions as well. Thus it seems to have become accepted, in both federations, that the emphasis will have to shift from attempts at allocation of discrete government functions between levels of government to the *allocation of roles that each level of government will perform in their shared responsibilities.* The question now becomes that of how to define such "roles", and indeed the thorny question of what the concept "role" means in this context. None of the respondents could cast much light on these aspects but there have, in recent years, been a number of suggestions emanating out of various reviews of elements of the federal systems. We shall consider them in more detail in the conclusion, but three outstanding examples from Australian experience which can be mentioned here are the report of the Bailey Task Force on Coordination in Welfare and Health, the Holmes Report on Care of the Aged and the Infirm, and the Report of the Bland Inquiry in 1976.[45] The Bailey report spelt out roles for the three levels of government in welfare and health, adding that it was not realistic to set out clearly, and in a way that would be operative in all instances, the precise roles which the commonwealth, the states, and local bodies should exercise in the welfare/health field. Their objective was not so much constitutional "purity" as a sensible allocation of functions, given the present situation, and an ordered reallocation where change was desired. The Bland Report is worthy of close consideration also, because it represents the only attempt ever made in the Australian federation to obtain the view of the states about the role of the various levels of government. We shall encounter elements of the Bland report in later chapters. Interestingly enough, in no instance did a state suggest that any function then undertaken solely by the commonwealth should be transferred in whole or in part to the states, and no state functions were suggested for a transfer to the commonwealth — not even railways. Also, the states did see a number of areas where the commonwealth role should be expanded.

5. The View of the People

A number of respondents were concerned about the public confusion caused by the division of powers. Many saw this confusion being intensified, not reduced, by the shift to consideration of the roles of levels in shared functional areas. None made any serious suggestions as to how this problem could be overcome, but we consider the problem in more depth in a later chapter. Of course the literature of Australian and Canadian federalism confirms substantial confusion and a commensurate lack of accountability brought about by the division of powers. This is probably more evident in the case of Australia, which has the device of the referendum to help test public perceptions. Writers such as Parker, Partridge, Harris, Whitlam, Crisp, Davis, Menzies, Peachment and Reid, and Smiley, have all addressed themselves to this question. It was also one of the key preoccupations of the most recent proposals for constitutional change put forward by the Trudeau government just before its downfall in 1979. That review noted as fact that the overlapping of responsibilities and jurisdictions had made it difficult for citizens, and indeed governments, to know which government was responsible for dealing with a particular problem area of public concern. For Australians, Parker only adds to the confusion by the following expression of his opinion:

> I submit for discussion the view that the people as such, have no fixed or even long-term views about the Federal Constitution or about the distribution of legislative powers under it, because federalism and its legal implications are a mystery to the bulk of them.[46]

In Conclusion

It has been demonstrated, that both conceptually and in practical terms, the division of powers in a federal system is a fundamental impediment to the attainment of the coordination and harmonization necessary to achieve an environment in which priority determination based on forecasting, and leading to allocation of resources, implementation of that allocation, and a review of the process, could be achieved. That is to say, the division of powers is the first and primary hindrance or obstacle that must be overcome to achieve the sort of planning we envisage. These hindrances are made the more complex because of the shift we have observed in the dynamic federations of Australia and Canada towards organic federalism, and it becomes clear that to make our planning system work, some mechanism will be required to determine the role of each level of government in various components, as well as the totality of each federal system. That is attempted in our conclusion. Also, in the remaining chapters, some specific by-products of the division of powers, for example, fiscal transfer and intergovernmental agreements, are examined in depth to gain a more practical view of the hindrances already touched on, as are others which have arisen in the attempts through these devices to span the chasm presented by the division of powers, and to reconcile the sovereignty of the participating units in each federation.

In the meantime, and as a prelude to what is to follow, we can recapitulate some of the more significant points made in this chapter, and also raise a few pertinent questions.

Virtually all of the current political science and public administration literature in Australia and Canada declare it to be a futile exercise to attempt to identify rigid criteria by which allocations of complete functions of government can be permanently assigned to a particular level of government. That sort of exercise is deemed to belong to an era of the past century, the age of coordinate federalism when government itself was small, unobtrusive, and uncomplicated, and nations and their parts were undeveloped.

There is no literature available to us which reveals the actual criteria used by the founding fathers of the two federations in concocting their allocation of powers, generally or specifically.

The literature and the interviews reveal that even if criteria are formulated, people will then disagree about the meaning of those criteria.

There is considerable dispute as to whether a review of the allocation of functions in a federation can proceed prior to, or separate from, a review of the revenue arrangements. (This line of argument is rarely encountered in the literature, and did not arise in the interviews, but it does represent a legitimate alternate view of the process of federal power division.) It is generally seen as being easier, in practice, to adjust revenue sharing because little in the way of legislation or constitutional amendment is involved, compared with such difficulties in shifting functions around. Also, many government functions are, in themselves, revenue producing, so the relocation of those functions automatically rearranges the pattern of revenue sharing. Then again, some functions are considerably more expensive than others, and that must bring the question of revenue capacity into play for the level of government which will be the recipient of the function. There is also the question of the potential expense, gross or net, of each function, which may be of crucial importance with respect to funding. Finally, in this regard, Section 96 of the Australian Constitution, and the provisions for a reference of powers between levels, can be seen as direct alternatives, and the question of whether to realign revenue sharing or responsibility sharing must become fundamental and explicit.

There are some other fundamental questions which arise and should be answered before any attempt is made to be definitive about criteria for allocation of functions:

1. Can the same criteria be employed when discussing allocations between commonwealth and state levels, as between state and local, or, if practically possible, between commonwealth and local?

2. If there do happen to be any immutable perfect criteria available, why is it that the same function is often performed at different levels in different federations? The answer has to be that different cultural settings may alter the criteria, which cannot therefore be internationally, or comparatively, immutable or perfect.

3. Should criteria be concerned with actual functions of government or the objectives of those functions? Generally speaking, it has been found necessary to look at the functions, i.e., processes of government, themselves, rather than their objectives, if only because the former are more precise. But it must be acknowledged that the objectives of the functions are very important, and they lead to what I have

called "linkage" criteria and "override" criteria which have appeared in the practical experience of the Australian and other federations.

4. Should criteria be directed towards complete functions of government or subelements of particular functions? The founding fathers, of course, attempted in the main to allocate complete functions, although exceptions were made in Australia where, for example, trade and commerce was divided according to whether it was intrastate or interstate, as were industrial disputes; fisheries were divided according to territorial limits; and in Canada some elements of education were hived off to protect minorities.

5. Some functions unquestionably have a fuller meaning than others when they have to be translated into laws, as compared with the simple mention of their title in a constitution. There is thus no complete symmetry between individual functions because of the sheer problem of language, which in some cases can express a single government activity in a single word, but in other cases has to express a range of government activities in a single word.

6. Should functions be considered before spatial elements in a federation? To put it simply, what should you get right first, the geographical or numerical size of the unit of governments, or the sharing of functions? The obvious problem is that to tackle function allocation first may well mean allocation of government activity to a unit of government whose size is completely inappropriate to fulfil that function. On the other hand, to tackle size first preempts the allocation of the functions. The literature of regionalism, new states, and local government is bedevilled by this problem.

7. Should the allocation of functions be regarded as a zero sum game? That is to say, is the allocation of a function to a level of government a win for that level and a loss for another? This may be so in many cases, especially in political terms, but the viewpoint adopted here is that this ought not to be always the case.

8. Should you start from some broad notion of the sovereignty of each level of government rather than seek to allocate each function piecemeal? Much of the debate in the Australian literature seems to seek to regard a level of government as sacrosanct, or sovereign, or untouchable; and if this attitude pervades the process of drawing up criteria, it will become quickly clear that none of the three levels of government will sanction any loss of functions, although each will welcome a gain of any function.

9. Perhaps the most important point to make, and it is one which is overlooked in most of the literature itself, is that there must ultimately be a trade-off between criteria themselves. Most people who approach the question of the allocation of functions assume that each of the criteria will provide a total answer pointing the one way. As the Rowell-Sirois report in Canada was at pains to point out, some of the criteria will suggest allocations of functions to a higher level of

government, and some to a lower level. Or, in the words of F.A. Bland, it may be necessary to make a choice between low standards and autonomy, or high standards and unification. Maybe this is the greatest contribution which the literature of political science can make to this exercise, namely, to emphasize ever so strongly that the process of delineating criteria, together with the ultimate trade-off between them, is in itself a political process. If that is recognized and accepted at the outset it may save a lot of blood, sweat, and tears. A compromise is easier to make when it is accepted that there must be a compromise.

It only remains to repeat that one's view of the allocation of functions between levels of government in any federation will be basically and fundamentally influenced by how one defines and views federalism as a concept itself. It has been said that there are over 110 defined types of federalism, but we have distinguished between only two, namely, coordinate (also meaning static) federalism, and organic (meaning dynamic federalism, and literally anything that is not coordinate federalism, including cooperative, coercive, or coordinative federalism). The reason for using this distinction is that the very notion that there are criteria for allocation of functions came out of the concept of coordinate federalism, and as coordinate federalism means, by and large, static, or fixed relationships, it seems appropriate to regard that as the basic departure point for every other brand of federalism. This implies a more dynamic relationship, and one may assume, dynamic or at least flexible criteria. In the words of Mathews:

At the time the American, Canadian and Australian federal constitutions were devised good government was weak government . .·. In such a situation it was relatively simple to devise a constitution in which powers were divided vertically along functional lines . . . There was very little overlap in the allocation of expenditure functions; such overlap as occurred in the Australian Constitution may be traced to the fact that by the 1890's governments were at last beginning to take an interest in social and economic questions . . . our federal constitutions were thus based very clearly on the concept of divided responsibility of independent levels of government each exercising authority and providing services in functional fields that were designated by drawing vertical boundaries between jurisdictions. What has happened during recent years to change this situation? The main factors have been the extension of the range of government activities and the growth of the size of the public sector. These in turn have been occasioned by the growing strength and complexity of the economy and by community acceptance of the need for governments to provide greatly expanded services and economic controls.[47]

6

Intergovernmental Agreements

It is a seemingly paradoxical truth that the need for intergovernmental agreements arises basically because of problems caused by the division of powers and split sovereignty; yet these agreements are one of the key methods used in both federations to broach that division of powers, and harness that divided sovereignty. It is logical to assume that intergovernmental agreements, being the major tangible evidence of linkages between national and subnational levels of government, could be a prime vehicle for the introduction of planning into a federation. After all, in such agreements we have the most visible and practical form of coordination between the two levels of government, and so, it might be assumed, a ready vehicle for the introduction of processes of joint priority determination and its accompanying resource allocation.

Unfortunately, there is very little by way of literature on intergovernmental agreements to allow lessons of experience to be deduced. The reason is basically that such agreements have taken place on an ad hoc basis in particular narrow segments of the public sector, over the past fifty years or so, and it has only been comparatively recently that even governments have come to realise the scale of their involvement with other units of government through this device. This particular aspect of the nature of intergovernmental agreements also makes our task of researching them so much more difficult, because it is so hard to form an overview of them. In essence, it requires that we visit a large number of them individually in an attempt to form a consolidated picture.

As a consequence, this chapter will be heavily dependent on straight-out primary sources, and especially the interviews which have been conducted. This in turn is appropriate, because this particular aspect of federalism is one in which there has been a pronounced administrative input for reasons which will shortly be explained. We shall proceed by examining, first of all, the reason for agreements coming into being, and then inquire into the nature and purpose of agreements, followed by an analysis of the various methods used in making these agreements operative. Finally, we shall endeavour to locate the problems which have arisen in the implementation of agreements, and this ought to present us with a total perspective of the hindrances and/or achievements of this particular entity which is so typical of federalism at the operational level. In particular, of course, we shall be interested throughout to determine the potential of introducing public sector planning in view of the experience and opinion which is confronted.

The Reasons for Agreements

Intergovernmental agreements come into being because of a number of factors, but the basic reason, as intimated earlier, is because the coordinate, or layer cake federalism envisaged by the Australian and Canadian founding fathers can no longer exist, despite their attempts to lay down specific powers for each level of government (as we have already witnessed in section 51 of the Australian Constitution and sections 91 and 92 of the *British North America Act*). The federal systems of Australia and Canada are no longer coordinate as the actions of each level of government have significant effects on other units, and moreover, there are many government functions which are nowadays performed by more than one level. It is this latter area which has spawned the device of the intergovernmental agreement.

Quite apart from natural developments which render any division of power less relevant, the key fact to be borne in mind is that when it is government functions being considered, political influences are paramount. But underpinning the politics of the power division are a number of less obvious factors, including the vast improvement in twentieth century communications, whereupon citizens can now more easily compare the performance of their local or provincial government with that of others, which makes it harder for any single unit of government to stand apart from its counterpart units at the same level. Added to this is the fact that citizens in both Australia and Canada no longer "vote with their feet" as much as they used to. People will not travel far in search of employment or better living conditions these days, and demand that both these commodities be brought to them, as evidenced by progressively declining distances required for travel to work by authorities issuing unemployment benefit payments.

As we observed in an earlier chapter, these difficulties are compounded by the tendency for national and subnational units of government to promote their sovereignty to an increasing extent. They are also affected by the observable phenomenon, also mentioned earlier, that spatial loyalties are stronger than ideological loyalties, which goes part of the way towards explaining why a national government would desire, or be forced into, formal intergovernmental agreements with subnational units, even when those subnational units are governed by the same political party.

For whatever reasons, intergovernmental agreements now symbolize the symbiotic relationship which exists between the component parts of the two federations, and it is this symbolism which is politically as important as their substance. They have, in popular and academic writing, now come to be seen as (1) a method of altering the balance of power in the federations without resorting to any formal constitutional amendments; (2) part of the expression "cooperative federalism" which apparently is regarded as applying whenever elected or appointed officials from the various governments put their heads (or their swords) together. In other words, even if they are fighting they are still in some strange way cooperating; (3) responsibility sharing — a newer term which implies more than mere power balancing or cooperation. It should be noted that a pure form of responsibility sharing would mean that all levels of government would jointly take responsibility for government action or inaction; (4) part of the federal *culture*. If there is such a thing, then administrative or executive federalism is certainly a real part of it, and the intergovernmental agreements form a tangible part of that federal culture; and (5) more evidence of the props and supports necessary to preserve a tottering structure. Those who take this view regard federalism as the worst of all worlds, and they consider each agreement to be another piece of sticking plaster to cover over a crack in the facade and patch up yet another deficiency in the creaking federal system. Each agreement is thus a piece in the jigsaw puzzle of intergovernmental relations.

The Nature and Purpose of Agreements

The Canadian Federal-Provincial Relations Office lists over three hundred agreements in its descriptive inventory of "Federal-Provincial Programs and Activities", and acknowledges that the list is not exhaustive. Most of them have some fiscal implication, and as the publication states:

> Most of the programs and activities entail a transfer of funds between the federal government and another government: some involve other kinds of financial compensation such as loan guarantees, preferential prices, transfer of property, etc; under others, each government pays its share direct to contractors.[1]

The report then proceeds to give a ninefold classification typology related mainly to the method of funding involved in an agreement. For each agreement details are given of the body/bodies administering the agreement, its purpose, the legal authority under which it is conducted, the time frame involved, and the financing and operative details.

In Australia there is no equivalent of the Canadian Federal-Provincial Relations office and hence no official inventory of intergovernmental agreements. (The only official attempt ever made was in May 1975 when the Australian Department of the Prime Minister and Cabinet published a document entitled "Australian-State Government Cooperative Arrangements, Joint Consultative and Planning Arrangements". The publication was, however, far from comprehensive, and quite inaccurate in many details. In itself it demonstrates the difficulty of coming to grips with the whole area of intergovernmental agreements.) Neither has any Australian state attempted to make an inventory of all of the agreements in which it is involved, as has been attempted, for example, by Alberta, Quebec, and Ontario. The research conducted for this book revealed over 325 intergovernmental "arrangements" in Australia, and it is estimated that this would involve at least as many agreements, however formal and informal, although only two-thirds of them would involve financing.[2] Perhaps the very fact that there is no complete inventory of all intergovernmental agreements in either country is one of the most telling factors.

Richard Simeon suggests that patterns of decision making in federations result from the interaction or interplay of three levels of factors, namely, the social and cultural setting; the institutional and constitutional framework; and the particular goals, attitudes and behaviour of incumbent leaders, and the demands and problems facing the system.[3] These factors influence the frequency of the interaction, he asserts, but they also affect the specific form of intergovernmental relations, although in this case the institutional variables are the most important:

> Thus in Canadian and Australian parliamentary government with strict party discipline, together with centralization within both levels of government, appears to have been a sufficient condition to inhibit the effectiveness of national legislative bodies as arenas for adjustment and so to facilitate the development of a new set of institutional arrangements, the federal provincial conferences. This contrasts with the United States, where lack of party discipline and decentralization within governments has meant that the Congress has served as an important arena for adjustments. Moreover the larger number of units and the fact that senior executives cannot easily authoritatively commit each other in the United States would make federal-state Conferences on the Canadian model difficult if not impossible.[4]

These points are extremely significant in understanding the nature and forms of the agreements which exist in both Canada and Australia because, in both countries, an understanding of the nature of the conferences which spawned them is a useful guide to the agreements themselves. In fact, one could go so far as to say that the agreements, and the associated conferences, are often inseparable as objects for analysis of political and administrative behaviour. In describing the growth of intergovernmental conferences and agreements in Canada in the period post–World War II, Smiley makes the interesting observation that the more limited the scope of the interaction the more likely there is to be agreement, usually agreement based on the professional norms of engineers, foresters, social workers, or public health specialists.[5] He adds:

> In the past decade there has been a generalized trend toward subsuming federal-provincial relations at the middle and lower levels of the public services where under most circumstances professional and technical considerations are important to machinery where ministers and their deputies are participants. The concerns of these latter officials are of course more directly related to broader policies and to partisan politics.[6]

Smiley adds that sophistication in staff work is a significant element in the influence of particular governments in federal-provincial relations. The Australian experience has been similar, although intergovernmental agreements in Australia have come into existence in a more ad hoc fashion. An Australian inquiry into care of the aged and the infirm concluded that the consequences of programmes having been launched in an ad hoc fashion over the years included the absence of any satisfactory machinery for determining priorities between programmes, especially when they are administered by different levels of government, a lack of coordination between services supplied by different levels of government, and incentives towards the misallocation of resources.[7] They are formulated in a less formal manner and are perceived to be less binding than those in Canada. They also tend to apply for shorter periods which is only partly explained by the shorter statutory life of Australian parliaments. (See Canadian figures on length of agreements later in this chapter.)

Thus it is extremely difficult to generalize about intergovernmental agreements and the forms they take. In Canada, the Federal-Provincial Relations Office each year publishes an inventory of intergovernmental agreements from which the figures in table 2 have been derived. (The list is meant to be purely illustrative of the different forms of agreement, and too much should not be read into the actual figures themselves. Obviously, the Federal-Provincial Relations Office itself is dependent on departments and agencies to supply the requisite data, and it can be assumed that there must be a lack of uniformity in the formats supplied, if only because of the very real differences in the agreements themselves.)

Table 2   Canada: intergovernmental agreements (1979 to 1983)

Authority for agreements	Number of agreements
Federal Act	54
Agreement	41
Federal Act and agreement	21
Federal Act and regulations or Order-in-Council	8
Federal Act and complementary provincial legislation	3
Federal Act and departmental mandate	2
Federal Act and regulations and agreement	2
Federal Act and Treasury Board approval	1
Federal cabinet decision	8
Federal cabinet decision and agreement	1
Federal cabinet decision and Treasury Board approval	2
Departmental mandate and agreement	1
Order-in-council and agreement	5
Order-in-council alone	12
Departmental mandate alone	4
Federal/Provincial departmental agreement	2
Accord	1
Interministerial conference	3
Arrangements approved by Governor-General in council	3
Exchange of letters	3
International agreements	4
Treasury Board minute alone	6
Nothing	1

Source: Derived from Federal-Provincial Relations Office, *Federal-Provincial Programs and Activities* (Ottawa: 1978, 1979, 1980–81, 1981–82, and 1982–83).

Note: DREE (Department of Regional Economic Expansion) agreements are taken to be one agreement with each province.

The data published by the Canadian Federal-Provincial Relations Office also reveals indirectly that there is quite a different mixture of participating provinces involved in the various intergovernmental agreements. Table 3 indicates this.

Table 3   Canada: intergovernmental agreements (1979 to 1983)

Number of provinces involved	Number of agreements
10	76
9	15
8	3
7	2
6	9
5	10
4	11
3	10
2	6
1	48
n.a.*	4

Source: Derived from Federal-Provincial Relations Office, *Federal-Provincial Programs and Activities* (Ottawa: 1979–1983).
* Not available.

An Australian analysis[8] (which took seven years) of about two hundred and fifty intergovernmental agreements, conducted with the cooperation of state governments, revealed that the basis for such agreements ranged from formal contracts between governments through to the most informal mechanisms, namely:

1.   Contracts signed by legal entities, such as statutory corporations, and including commercial contracts.
2.   Formal written agreements for joint action signed by *either*:
     (a)   the Governor-General and/or Governor;
     (b)   the Prime Minister and/or Premier;
     (c)   the relevant national and/or state minister; or
     (d)   permanent heads of relevant national and/or state administrative organizations.
     (There seems to be no consistent rationale to determine at which level signatories are involved.)
3.   Memoranda of understanding signed by any of the previous combinations of signatories.
4.   Constitutions of joint ministerial or administrative bodies, which clearly specify the composition of the body, its terms of reference, etc. (However there appear to be more of these bodies that do not possess a constitution than there are that do.)
5.   Charters for joint bodies that have their origin in other intergovernmental arrangements. For example, many bodies have been established on the basis of formal minutes and proceedings of Premiers Conferences or similar institutions, such as the Australian

Agricultural Council or the Australian Transport Advisory Committee.

6. The wording and occasionally the accompanying schedules of national or state bills, and the expansion of aims contained in second-reading speeches in one or more parliaments.

7. Simple exchanges of correspondence (this is a frequently used device).

8. Informal discussions with no documented evidence of arrangements; occasionally no more than a telephone call.

9. Official manuals and other reports of joint action taken at the discretion of the administrators involved.

It can be seen that in both countries there is no semblance of any uniform pattern, nor are there clearly defined models which are followed in identical situations. Indeed, the actual origins of many of the agreements have been lost in antiquity. Moreover, it is difficult to speculate on which areas have witnessed most intergovernmental cooperation at the administrative level. Although in some cases the existence of a formal agreement can be construed as evidence of a desire to cooperate, in other instances real cooperation takes place more smoothly because of the absence of any written agreement.

However, the key question to ask in order to understand the nature of intergovernmental agreements is — what is the purpose of them? Very little has been written in either Canada or Australia in this respect. Most studies have been confined to a few of the better known and more controversial agreements and to that extent there is a public impression that agreements symbolize conflict, whereas the majority of agreements reflect a basic desire for cooperation and ease of administration. In the Australian research just mentioned it was discovered that Australian agreements tend to have been brought into being for one or more of the following purposes:

1. to achieve uniformity in the administration of a common functional area;

2. to avoid overlapping in the provision of administrative services;

3. to respond to vertical imbalance; that is, to distribute surplus commonwealth funds to needy areas of state government activity;

4. to disseminate information nationally;

5. to pool resources of governments for more effective administration;

6. to apply laws to mobile resources (i.e., ones which transgress state boundaries);

7. to achieve national solidarity;

8. to promote research;

9. to exhort the community on a vital issue;

10. to achieve complementary action between governments;

11. to review national priorities;

12. to provide a solution to an otherwise insoluble or unconstitutional problem;

13. to spy on other governments or to avoid being left out.

It is instructive also to look at the meetings or conferences which occur to discuss these agreements. An official study in the mid-1970s by the Australian Prime Minister's Department[9] found that:

* Just over half of all meetings had been established jointly.
* The big increases in officer level contact had been in the areas of education, health, housing, labour, social security, transport, and urban and regional development.
* Approximately two-thirds of the formally constituted ministerial meetings included representation from all states.
* Quite often officials concerned with areas of formalized consultation met as a servicing group for the various ministers' conferences and were responsible for the initiation of follow-up action from these meetings.
* Whilst the frequency of meetings varied considerably, most ministerial meetings were held annually but officials' meetings were either biannual or quarterly.
* More than one-third of all meetings held involved ongoing action in the form of subcommittees and/or working parties. Approximately seventy per cent of all formal ministerial meetings were serviced by officials' committees, subcommittees and working parties, often involving a wide range of both governmental and nongovernmental members.
* The extent of the distribution of material arising out of these meetings, either in the form of minutes, papers or press statements, presented a varied picture. Most ministers' meetings issued press statements, and, increasingly, tabled proceedings of the meetings in the Australian Parliament.
* Ministers and officials, in general, did not attend meetings with state officials outside their own portfolio areas. The major exceptions were the ministers for Northern Australia, Science, and Consumer Affairs who attended a number of formal council meetings.

Problems with Agreements

Many of the problems which arise when working with agreements are the same as those produced by conditional grants. This is not surprising as the vast majority of intergovernmental agreements are centred on conditional funding from national to subnational government. Thus the Canadian provinces and Australian states complain about actions by the federal government to seduce the provinces or states into an agreement, and then, after a short while, to terminate the agreement and force (in a political sense) the province/state to continue the agreements from its own funding. Another widely made assertion is that the existence of intergovernmental agreements interferes with the priorities of the province or state by forcing it to devote a proportion of its own resources to programmes which it may well have assigned to a lower degree of priority, or none at all. However, this is not the place to begin an analysis of the merits of conditional and unconditional funding. (That is attempted later.)

Other broader difficulties experienced in both Canada and Australia include ambiguity about the legal powers of each level of government, because of the wording of the constitutions, with the consequence of uncertainty about High Court interpretation. Legal interpretations have made significant differences in both federations to the powers of the various levels of government to collect revenue and carry out functions, and there is a small number of examples of intergovernmental agreements being rendered void by the High Courts on this basis.

Then there is the difficulty of coping with the ideologies of changing governments. Very often an agreement will be framed in a broad way allowing for choice of delivery mechanisms. A change of government may well produce a desire for a different mix of those delivery procedures. This has happened in both federations, for example, in the housing area where conservative governments stress sale of public housing to tenants, whereas socialist governments stress public ownership; or the problem encountered with roads agreements where national determination of the allocation of resources to each type of road might place limits on the pork-barrelling which can be done by a subnational government. Consider the spectacle of the federal government in Australia which was committed ideologically to a new federalism policy (dispersal of power from Canberra), which abrogated the results of a 1967 referendum giving the national government power over Aboriginal affairs by allowing state control to continue; or the events of June 1979 when almost at the same moment the federal government established joint control with one state over the Great Barrier Reef (clearly a national resource), and in the next breath initiated discussions for the states to hand over all their industrial powers to the federal government to prevent national strikes. The same government maintained control over legal aid in all but one state where it bowed to political pressure and allowed all national legal aid offices to be transferred to that state. This leads also to the more fundamental difficulty of coping with different degrees of commitment by different governments to intergovernmental agreements, which affects the time span of the agreement and the certainty with which public servants can implement it. (In the same week, for example, two Australian states had opted for stricter environmental controls over motor vehicle emission, thereby forcing the other four states to follow suit. One of those two states then refused to sign an agreement for companies legislation, thereby inhibiting national regulation of company law.) It is a slightly more prevalent problem in Australia where all governments are elected for a maximum three year term of office, and hence there are more frequently changing political outlooks and thus shorter intergovernmental agreements than is typical in Canada. In both federations, however, this also raises the difficulty of coping with the recalcitrant state or province, that is, the ones which will either not join in an agreement, or having signed the agreement, refuse to implement it.

These problems seem to be common in both federations, and they pose great difficulties for the public servant intimately involved with agreements at the working level, mainly because of the uncertainty they create. In the Canadian interviews, in summary, these were respondents' views about intergovernmental agreements:

1. Too many agreements stress uniformity in delivery across the nation and do not take account of the particular circumstances of each province. This was especially true, it was claimed, of social programmes where the provinces could not devise their own schemes to suit the local environment, and often had to invest artificial administrative devices, like means tests, to qualify. It was also demonstrated by federal government-devised eligibility requirements, residential requirements, national standards, universality, and portability which locked the province into a quality of service that might not be appropriate to that province and might need to be varied from period to period.

2. The fear of the federal government pulling out of an agreement, which in the latter part of the 1970s tended to induce the provinces not to enter some agreements at all.

3. The main area of freedom which agreements left to the provinces was in relation to wage and salary levels (and professional fees) because of provincial power to enter collective bargaining for public sector wage rates. The provinces seemed to relish this freedom.

4. Provinces preferred an agreement to be negotiated around lump sum or block funding, whereas the federal government favoured earmarking of all components of the amounts flowing to the provinces. The provinces preferred to have the power under an agreement to reallocate the funding between sectors and programmes, and there was a distinct impression that provinces would prefer that the federal government not publish too widely the breakdown of its grants to the provinces, so the local pressure groups would not come "a-lobbying" for what they would then regard as "their" share of federal money.

5. The timing of an agreement is all important in that it must be common for all provinces or it may tend to favour one province rather than another. This could also encourage provinces to become late participants, especially as the terms of federal finance assistance have often become more generous in the twilight of the agreement's lifetime. However, provincial public servants seem unanimous in desiring long term fixed agreements, compared with provincial ministers, who welcome shorter agreements to allow for greater bargaining and less fixed commitments.

6. Welfare agreements can be turned off easily technically but not politically.

7. The disproportionately severe consequences of termination or alteration of an agreement on small provinces, compared with that for larger ones, because of the greater impact on smaller budgets.
8. Agreements which are labour-intensive are much more severely affected by alteration or termination.
9. The amount of information required by the federal government under various agreements produces much too heavy a burden on provincial and local bureaucracies, and the provinces doubt whether all the required information is really necessary. In the words of one provincial Deputy-Minister: "The federal government keeps wanting crazy statistical data on a national accounts basis and jazzy presentations".
10. Some provinces argue that the "region", or some other subprovincial level, is the appropriate spatial area for the conferring of benefits arising out of intergovernmental agreements. This is especially so with welfare and infrastructure agreements. The irony is, of course, that the provinces still claim it should be they, and not local or regional government, to negotiate such agreements. Indeed, in those agreements (especially DREE ones) where the federal government looks directly at regions, the provinces often claim that their sovereignty is being maligned.
11. Agreements can unduly interfere with the administrative structure of a province. This often depends on how programmes are classified and defined, but there seemed, for example, to be a lot of consternation about mental health and whether it is a health or a welfare function. If it is defined in a certain way under an intergovernmental agreement, the province may well have to rearrange the whole of its administrative machinery to suit, although it disagrees with the way the function has been defined in the agreement. (There has been a similar problem in Australia in relation to preschools, which some governments see as a welfare or health function, and some as an education function.)
12. Insufficient attention has been paid to the basic differences between agreements involving capital costs and those involving current or ongoing costs. There arises a serious problem if the federal government negotiates only a capital agreement and doesn't provide ongoing funds as well, or terminates the agreement in a way that the province or local government is left with the ongoing costs to bear.
13. Canada has cities which are heterogeneous, and yet so many intergovernmental agreements for urban programmes are drawn up on the fundamental assumption of homogeneity. Thus it has been claimed, for example, that there might be more poor people in Toronto than in the whole of the Atlantic provinces.
14. The tardiness of updating agreements to modern social needs, including demographic changes, which leads to the claim that because of the rigidity of past agreements there are too many bassinets in Canadian hospitals and not enough beds for geriatrics.

15. The practice of negotiating individual agreements for particular functions and segregating them in relation to the powers of levels of government can make for problems where they meet at the margin. Who, for example, should install and pay for railway level crossings?

16. There was a strong suspicion amongst most provinces that funding for a particular function in a province could be sabotaged by a federal department also responsible for that function. This concern was exposed most strongly in relation to DREE agreements, where it was assumed by the provinces, that a province's claims were submitted by DREE to the particular federal department for comment. That federal department would be reluctant to recommend that too much federal money go to the province for that function, because it might mean a commensurate decline in that federal department's own budgetary allocations. Fisheries was an area which figured prominently in this respect.

Now these arguments are not exhaustive and they do not canvass opposing viewpoints. For example, do the provinces really have priorities of their own to be distorted; isn't there some need for national supervision; does the federal government abruptly terminate an agreement or is it that the agreement has simply run its full course and the provinces wrongly assumed it would be continued; doesn't the federal government enter a lot of agreements precisely because the provinces accuse it of being too remote from the people; and couldn't many of these difficulties be overcome if the provinces got together for preliminary discussions before entering into dialogue with the federal government? These questions remain unanswered here, but they are also part of the framework which leads to the practical difficulties of working with agreements.

Problems of Accountability

Some years ago Donald Smiley asked these questions about federal-provincial conferences. They are, nowadays, equally pertinent questions to ask in relation to intergovernmental agreements:

> Who has the authority to cause a conference to be called? How is the agenda determined? Are Conferences to be open or closed? Should final communiqués contain references to disagreements among the participating governments? Is it reasonable to expect that First Ministers commit their administrations at conferences or are there circumstances where such commitment can be withheld? Is it appropriate for governments to introduce new proposals into conferences without prior consultation with other governments? To what extent, if at all, is an incoming government bound by its predecessor? What are reasonable conditions of secrecy in federal-provincial relations?"[10]

When analysing the matter of accountability for intergovernmental agreements it is natural that we should turn first to the control devices prevalent at each level of government purporting to control administrative discretion. Consider first the question of the legality of intergovernmental agreements. A senior official of the Canadian Federal-Provincial Relations Office expressed the opinion in interview that most of the so-called agreements are not agreements at all; they are federal legislation which is mostly not signed by the provinces. If this is the case, then they are binding only on the federal government, and, even then, only as long as the Act is not changed. The Medicare "agreement" was not a signed agreement but rather a basis of principles, and no fixed time was stipulated. There *were* signed agreements under the Canada Assistance Plan. Under the Hospital Insurance Plan there were signed agreements and a mandatory notice of five years to quit. In postsecondary education there was no agreement, just an audited statement from the province. The Established Programmes Financing arrangements do require formal notice from governments before changes are made. It also seems that there is a real possibility that agreements could be taken to the national arbitration authorities, but this too is unclear. The legal standing of intergovernmental agreements is just as uncertain in Australia. There have certainly been challenges mounted in the High Court to determine the validity of the federal government entering into a particular agreement in the first place. The court has rarely proscribed such action because of the far-reaching powers it assumes, attributed under Section 96 of the Australian Constitution, which allows the national parliament to "make grants to the states on such terms and conditions as it sees fit". But there has been little litigation which has sought to determine whether the national government is either escaping its responsibility or exceeding it under any particular agreement. There have been cases, as with the establishment of growth centres and the operation of national instrumentalities to operate in the spatial area of a state government, where complementary legislation had to pass the national parliament and the parliament of one or more states. Thus for the Albury-Wodonga growth centre at the border of New South Wales and Victoria, requisite complementary legislation had to pass the national parliament and that of those two states. The Snowy Mountains Authority, a national statutory corporation which engages in engineering consultancy to government, requires legislation to be passed in a state before it can serve as a consultant to that government.

The situation is made even cloudier, as in Canada, because of the uncertain constitutional status of local government in relation to agreements. A well-known High Court decision in Australia established that the national government could not enter into agreements directly with local government *per se*, but if a local government cared to register as a charitable organisation or under some other "hat" and "handle" provided for in the requisite national legislation, such agreements could be made and money could flow direct, thus bypassing the states. (The case arose out of a state challenge to the Australian Assistance Plan, a welfare programme where money trickled from the national government directly to regional welfare bodies elected/established for the purpose. Some of those bodies were local governments.) It would seem that the same is true for Canada. The legislation which a few Canadian provinces have passed, forbidding any direct dialogue or funding between national and local government, is thus effectively circumvented. Suffice to say that it is not possible to look to the courts for the means of enforcing complete accountability; and the usual processes of administrative law would not be suitable for this purpose either.

The other immediate line of accountability in a Westminster system is to parliament. However, very few intergovernmental agreements are debated in either federal or state/provincial parliaments before or after they are negotiated. On the few occasions when they are debated, the appropriate minister issues a plea that there be no changes to the arrangements contained therein because of the daunting logistics involved in getting eleven (Canadian) or seven (Australian) governments to agree. The situation is worse when it is a province or state which is *refusing* to join in some intergovernmental agreement. Then the opposition in that parliament would be reliant on its colleagues in another parliament to furnish details of the agreement in question. As regards continuing debate on any agreement, in Australia, a backbencher would spend most of his or her time (1) ascertaining that there was an agreement, (2) obtaining a copy of it, and (3) trying to determine which minister was responsible for it. Having followed this tortuous process, he or she would ask a question only to find that the minister could shift blame to the other level of government, or even refuse to answer the question without falling at all foul of the Speaker. It must be admitted that there is an extremely poor degree and level of debate about intergovernmental matters in both Australian and Canadian parliaments, largely because there are few votes to be won or lost by it; but then there is a poor standard of debate on all broad policy matters anyway. Research has revealed that there is no formal requirement in either country that all intergovernmental agreements must be tabled in any parliament within that country. To compound the issue, the executive of the national, provincial/state, or local government have a vested interest in blurring the degree of responsibility they have under any agreement, and in this they are aided and abetted by an electorate which is largely unaware of even the broad allocation of government functions in the constitution, although Australians are worse in this respect than Canadians. Apart from sporadic forays into particular policy areas, there are no standing committees in national, provincial/state, or local assemblies which constantly scrutinize intergovernmental agreements.

What of some of the other external checks on the accountability of public servants? The Auditor-Generals are effective in this area only to a limited extent because they are precluded from investigating affairs of another level of government. Unlike the situation in the USA, in both Australia and Canada, the national Auditor-General cannot monitor the final destination of funds given to states/provinces under intergovernmental agreements, and must accept a certificate from the state/provincial auditor certifying that the funds were spent in the manner designated in the agreement. Since few state/provincial auditors are conducting efficiency audits as yet, the most scrutiny that state and provincial public servants operating the agreements receive is the traditional compliance audit whose inadequacies are well known and needn't be canvassed here. Similarly the powers of national and state/provincial ombudsmen are hamstrung in relation to intergovernmental agreements. Whilst they may ensure there is no maladministration in the delivery of the government programmes contained in the agreement, they cannot judge the arrangements provided for in the agreement as a whole, or the wisdom of the legislation itself. It would be extremely interesting to know where an ombudsman would apportion the blame if the tests, of say eligibility or portability, contained in an agreement were found to be defective, especially if those tests had been drawn up and ratified at a federal-state or federal-provincial conference.

The media is not a very effective watchdog over public servants at the best of times for a variety of reasons.[11] In the area of intergovernmental agreements, newspapers, radio, and television seem too busy at their wits' end endeavouring to understand the process and report the political wrangling, to question the role of public servants in the process. Moreover, the federalization of the media, mentioned earlier, usually results in all matters of intergovernmental negotiation being repeated and criticized from a spatial perspective, which only tends to reinforce the parochialism of the politicians and public servants involved.

There are also, of course, internal controls on the accountability of public servants, and that includes Departments of Finance, Treasury Boards, Public Service Commissions, Premier's Offices and the like, not to mention the hierarchical control patterns within particular departments. Until the early 1970s there was very little involvement by this sort of central coordinating agency, and intergovernmental agreements, both in Australia and Canada, were negotiated between functional departments at the state/provincial level and their counterparts at the national level. The arrangement was usually that the state/province had the constitutional power and the federal government had the finance, but the central fiscal institutions were not involved much because the funding often came from within a national department's own budget allocation and involved quite a deal of technical expertise (hospitals, schools, roads, etc.), which central agencies didn't possess. The situation changed in both countries in the early 1970s. In both countries it was partly because the national governments became more centralist (more noticeable in Australia with the advent of the socialist party in 1972), which forced the subnational governments to obtain a better view across the whole of their own public sectors to defend them more adequately. The appearance of the cry about interference in state/provincial priorities can be linked to the beginning of some overview by central institutions of those governments in intergovernmental affairs in the states of Australia and the provinces of Canada. In Canada those offices flexed their muscles quite strongly so

that, for example, Alberta quickly grasped the total dimension of its dealings with Ottawa, and in Quebec all intergovernmental agreements had to
be vetted by the Ministry of Intergovernmental Affairs and also signed by
that minister. In Australia the counterpart state bodies were usually set up
as small branches of the premier's own department and they played a
much more low key role, often confined solely to briefing the premier and
cabinet with a second opinion on some, but not all, intergovernmental
agreements. (The role of those central agencies is examined later.) From
the mid-1970s to the present, national governments in both countries have
fought stagflation largely by way of public expenditure cutbacks thus forcing provinces and states to curtail spending under intergovernmental
agreements. So this central scrutiny has continued, and in some cases has
been strengthened, although it is more the treasuries who now have the
upper hand.

One should not overlook the informal behaviour of public servants in
this environment. The Westminster model tells us that public servants are
to be silent, permanent, anonymous, and neutral. It implies a code of
ethics which would have a public servant loyal to the government of the
day on the assumption that the government is acting in the public interest.
But when it is intergovernmental agreements we are considering, the
dilemma, confronting the public servant at the drafting table, or the one
negotiating with his counterpart from the other level of government, or
the one implementing or overseeing the agreement, is: which is the
government of the day, and whose is the correct public interest? If he or
she is a provincial public servant, should his or her behaviour be conditioned by an endeavour to draft or negotiate or implement an agreement in
the interests solely of the government and people of that province (bearing
in mind the difficulty we met before of defining who the people of a
province are), or is there a loyalty on the part of all public servants to the
citizens of the nation? Consider the extreme case of a provincial public
servant whose salary under the agreement being negotiated will be paid
out of national funds.

Part of the problem is that the nature of public services in both countries has changed. Up until the 1970s both federal and state/provincial
senior public servants were postwar products, with an altruistic outlook of
endeavouring to speed economic recovery and growth, and generally
discover pragmatic solutions which were in the best interests of the nation
as a whole. In Australia, and to a lesser extent in Canada, most of the thinking function fell to the national bureaucracy, and the subnational levels
supplied the action. In the 1970s, however, public servants themselves
became caught in the politicking and assertion of tub-thumping sovereignty. Astute young provincial/state public servants (and municipal
employees) these days are as concerned, if not more concerned, with the
interests of their government alone, partly because it is forced on them, and
one suspects, partly with an eye to their own career prospects. The situation is more accentuated in Australia where there was not the equality of

bargaining ability and intellect between federal and state public servants as exists between federal and provincial public servants in Canada, mainly because there is very little movement of federal public servants to the state public services, and even less movement from state to federal public service, or indeed between the states themselves. An extremely perceptive analysis in Australia by a recent task force on coordination in welfare and health[12] pointed out, that for public servants engaging in consultative arrangements, the three major pitfalls to be avoided were the generation of unrealistic expectations at the inception of discussions, using tokenism in claiming that others who were consulted have agreed with whatever line was now being taken, and politicking by means of excessive "barrow pushing" by participants.

This leads us, of course, back to where we started, namely, the difficulty of public servants defining their own role, and particularly nowadays, that of their level of government in the agreement business.

The problem of accountability can be seen in its truest perspective if one assumes for a moment the place of an aggrieved citizen or a pressure group. Assuming such a person or group were dissatisfied with the education system, or the hospital services, where would the lobbying be directed? Who is responsible? Each level of government would be able effectively to pass the buck quite legitimately to another level. Because all are responsible; no one is responsible. In that sense, Reid's generalisation is correct, that all of the institutions of "cooperative federalism" are undemocratic because they diminish ministerial responsibility to the electorate and parliament, in direct relationship to the binding power of their decisions.[13] This is true of intergovernmental agreements, and we might conclude that the answer to the question — "to whom is the public servant accountable" — is that such public servants are accountable to their own minister in theory, and to nothing but their own consciences in practice.

The Planning Potential of Intergovernmental Agreements

At first glance, across the vista of executive federalism manifested by intergovernmental agreements, in both Australia and Canada, the prospect of introduction of public sector planning might well seem to be slight indeed. As we have already noticed, these agreements contain a varied mixture of terms and a plethora of authority devices. Some of them are concerned with functional areas in which both the levels of government are interested, whilst others are purely spatial and involve the federal government dealing with a geographic entity or area. There is also a vast array of review processes built into the various agreements, and in some cases, no review process at all. The duration of agreements varies considerably, and it can confidently be stated that not every state or province is involved in every agreement (indeed the Canadian statistics show that one-quarter of the intergovernmental agreements involve only one province). Most importantly, there is quite a variegated pattern of the type of funding, some agreements involving only capital expenditure or revenue, some current expenditure and revenue, and a few containing a mixture. Indeed, a great many agreements in both countries are for a particular project, and the duration of the agreement is the construction time for that public project, or an agreed estimate of its natural life. The involvement of ministers in each agreement is usually different. This also emphasizes that the agreements differ in the nature and degree of their public accountability, although as we have seen, all are low on accountability. At least in Canada the very publication of an inventory of agreements on a reasonably uniform basis by the Federal-Provincial Relations Office, and similar attempts by some of the provinces, provides a guide for interest groups to gain access into these systems of executive or administrative federalism. It is also important to note, in this respect, that both levels of government are generally able to reopen negotiations on each agreement, although this is more true in Canada than Australia.

However, taking a broad picture of intergovernmental agreements as an entity in themselves, it is an inescapable conclusion that they represent a major and important link between national and subnational components of both the Australian and Canadian federations. More particularly, most of the individual agreements show very promising potential for the application of a complete planning system, such as the one we are endeavouring to apply. Already the bulk of these intergovernmental agreements are negotiated for a fixed term longer than one year; there are objectives spelt out within the arrangement; the mechanisms which are devised to implement each agreement provide for allocation of responsibility between levels or units, and the sharing or transfer of resources; and often a provision for review of the agreement close to its termination. Each of them is thus already close to the ideal type of planning system envisaged. This point applies with greatest force to the fact that experience with terms of longer than one year is fairly common in respect of intergovernmental agreements, even in Australia, which is not renowned for forward commitments beyond one year in the public sector.

Data are not available to illustrate the extent of forward thinking in Australian intergovernmental agreements, but for Canada it is possible to construct a rough guide from the inventory of the Federal-Provincial Relations Office. (See table 4.)

Using the figures in table 4 as even a rough guide, it becomes apparent that a longer term perspective has now become commonplace in this field of intergovernmental agreements. However, it is just as apparent that there is *no common time frame* for them, *nor is there a common originating or terminating year*. This means, in effect, that the forecasting, implementation, and review processes are conducted individually for each agreement and not across all agreements, or even across groups of them in the same field. (Exceptions, to a certain extent, are presented by the Established Programmes Financing, and Regional Economic Expansion arrangements, but these

Table 4   Canada: intergovernmental agreements (1979 to 1983–1984)

Time frame	Number of agreements
1 year	2
2 years	6
3 years	10
4 years	4
5 years	25
6 years	2
8 years	1
9 years	2
10 years	11
10 years +	2
Indefinite or continuous	117
To a particular year	4
Ad hoc or no time frame	8
Length of life of the project	16

Source: Derived from Federal-Provincial Relations Office, *Federal-Provincial Programs and Activities* (Ottawa: 1978, 1979, 1980–81, 1981–82, 1982–83, and 1983–84).

Notes:

1. Some agreements specify a maximum duration and where this is so the maximum term has been used.
2. For the umbrella agreement over a long time frame the individual agreement within the overall time frame has been used.
3. There is a whole range of conditions attached to longer time frame agreements, including a specific period for either level giving notice to quit, the necessity of a review of an agreement after a fixed period, the necessity for provincial legislation to remain in force, and so on.
4. Where the length of life of the project is specified there are often other accompanying conditions as well.
5. Where an agreement is classified as "indefinite or continuous" there is nearly always an assumed review process carried out by an annual or biennial meeting of appropriate ministers or public servants. There is also, in such instances, the provision for consultations to occur between levels of government at any time (such consultation can be requested by any of the parties).

could be regarded as clusters of agreements, and they represent only a portion of the public sector.) In other words, whilst these factors and processes are characteristic of single agreements, they do not occur *across* all the agreements. That being the case, our attention is shifted to the process for, and machinery of, coordination of intergovernmental relations *between and within* each level of government in the two federations.

Coordinating Intergovernmental Agreements

In both Australia and Canada serious concern over the coordination of intergovernmental relations has arisen only in the past ten to fifteen years. Prior to this time intergovernmental agreements, like most other aspects of intergovernmental relations, took place directly between corresponding ministers, and for their public servants at the different levels in the federation. In the 1960s and 1970s such "executive federalism" (to borrow Smiley's term), became an "industry" in itself (to borrow Stevenson's term), and led to the so-called machinery of intergovernmental relations. Smiley's observations about Canada in the decade following World War II are equally applicable to Australia:

> Institutionalized federal-provincial interaction was for the most part limited to two kinds of matters — the periodic renegotiation of the tax arrangements and cooperation in respect to specific services and facilities, the latter often within the framework of shared cost programs. There was relatively little integration of these two kinds of matters and the sharing of taxes and revenues was determined by finance and treasury departments in relative isolation from collaboration between officials and agencies of the two levels with concerns limited to specific programs. Neither . . . was there institutionalized collaboration in fiscal policy as an instrument of economic stabilization.[14]

In Canada, the 1955 Continuing Committee of Fiscal and Economic Matters is seen as the turning point in the formal institutionalization of federal-provincial relations, in the sense that it provided for the continuation of particular overview machinery. However, the situation in Canada has not differed greatly from that in Australia, in that the intergovernmental conferences which meet to consider revenue-sharing matters are quite distinct from those that are concerned with responsibility sharing, and in the case of the latter, there tends to be a multitude of conferences each dealing with a particular sector. In other words, there is really no single intergovernmental conference which considers the whole sweep of intergovernmental revenue and expenditure or programme matters. The cynic would say that nowadays such a conference would be a technical impossibility; that it could never consider the whole gambit of intergovernmental interaction because of the sheer scope, complexity, and scale of such relationships. Others might say that the Australian Premiers Conference, or the Canadian Conference of First Ministers, would be the appropriate vehicle for such an exchange, but the sheer logistics of conducting conferences with seven participants (Australia) or eleven participants (Canada) has precluded discussion on all but the most pressing intergovernmental issues. The only occasion when these conferences take on something of the posture being suggested is in relation to periodic renegotiations of the broad intergovernmental revenue-sharing agreements and associated formulae, but even here revenue tends to be discussed quite apart from expenditure, and there is no consideration of priorities across all expenditure programmes but merely an analysis of subnational expenditure in total.[15] (A more detailed analysis of intergovernmental fiscal negotiations is given in the next chapter.)

Apart from the Premiers or First Ministers Conferences there is, of course, a plethora of intergovernmental conferences held in both countries in particular fields. These are well documented and reasonably well understood in Canada,[16] and in a relatively recent paper, Veilleux produced the information in table 5 from the calendars of meetings prepared by the Federal-Provincial Relations Office.

Table 5   Canada: number of federal-provincial bodies and frequency of their meetings

	1957	1967	1973	1977
Ministerial	5/-*	14/17	20/30	31/39
Administration	59/-	105/142	62/121	127/296
Total	64/-	119/159	82/151	158/335

Source: Gerard Veilleux, "L'évolution des Mécanismes de Liaison Intergovernmentale", in *Confrontation and Collaboration — Intergovernmental Relations in Canada Today*, ed. Richard Simeon (Toronto: IPAC, 1979).
* Number/frequency.

The growth in the number and frequency of such meetings is obvious from table 5. Veilleux also noted that his figures were incomplete, and in a footnote he acknowledged some data supplied by the Department of Intergovernmental Affairs in Alberta which showed that there had been 782 federal-provincial meetings in 1975. (We should not lose sight of the significance of the fact that the Alberta government kept such detailed statistics.)

It is not possible to reproduce similar data for Australia. I have presented elsewhere such details as are available.[17] It is a safe generalization to say that the number and frequency of such Australian conferences would not be much fewer than is the case in Canada.

Some data of particular interest, supplied once again by Veilleux, relate to interprovincial bodies and the frequency of their meetings. (See table 6.)

Table 6   Canada: number of inter-provincial bodies and frequency of their meetings

	1975	1977
Ministerial	16/19*	17/22
Administrative	19/23	13/15
Total	35/42	30/37

Source: Gerard Veilleux, "L'évolution des Méchanismes de Liaison Intergovernmentale" in *Confrontation and Collaboration — Intergovernmental Relations in Canada Today*, ed. Richard Simeon (Toronto: IPAC, 1979).
* Number/frequency.

From table 6, it can be seen that the number of bodies is considerably smaller than that for federal-provincial bodies, and the bulk of them were created in the 1970s. Comparable data are not available for Australia, and indeed, from the time of Richard Leach's analysis in 1965,[18] the comment has frequently been made that formal interstate collaboration in Australia is a rarity.[19] On this subject Veilleux makes an observation with particular significance for the coordination potential of intergovernmental matters in both countries: "Their importance in purely quantitative terms seems to confirm the hypothesis often expressed during the sixties that the provinces might find it to their advantage to reach a consensus among themselves before negotiating certain agreements with the federal government".[20] There is now a reasonably large body of Canadian literature (and a much smaller collection of Australian literature) which has analysed the reasons for the evolution of this intergovernmental machinery, its nature and its role; and we could spend a good deal of time in this field. However, our prime concern in this chapter is to assess the potential of such machinery for the coordination of intergovernmental agreements.

The research associated with this study has revealed that the associated intergovernmental machinery in both countries now comprises the following catalogue:

1. conferences of ministers from the national and subnational levels;
2. conferences of administrators associated with (1) or meeting quite independently of their ministerial counterparts;
3. a national cabinet minister appointed as minister for federal-state/federal-provincial relations;
4. a national department or division charged with responsibility for intergovernmental liaison;
5. a consultative or advisory body comprising representation from the different levels of government;
6. particular national cabinet ministers nominated as a liaison point for a particular state/province;
7. national ministers and their ministries responsible for regional activity (in substate/subprovincial regions);
8. state/provincial ministers appointed as ministers for intergovernmental affairs in each state/province;
9. state/provincial departments or divisions responsible for intergovernmental liaison);
10. conferences of ministers and officials solely from the states/provinces.

Let us examine each of these briefly in turn.

1.   Conferences of Ministers from the National and Subnational Levels of Government

It is these meetings at which intergovernmental agreements are usually formulated, although there is something of a pattern in both Australia and Canada whereby the need for an agreement is originated at the Premiers Conference/Conference of First Ministers, and then referred to a subsequent interministerial conference in that particular government function. As we have noted earlier, there has been considerably more research on ministerial conferences in Canada than is the case in Australia. Taylor documented them in 1957,[21] but only briefly analysed them. Gallant, in 1965, made an astute observation about this machinery by comparing it with the pattern of international relations. He expressed the comparison this way:

In our federal-provincial relations our machinery has evolved in a reverse order. We have first developed numerous committees and conferences at a specialist level. We have not had a comparable network of intelligence concerned with the total picture of intergovernmental relations.[22]

Gallant remarked of the Conference of Premiers and Prime Ministers that it was concerned more with specific policy issues than with the continuous overview of federal-provincial matters, and the same was true of the other ministerial conferences. The basic thrust of his remarks at that time was that, although such consultation in individual programme areas had proved to be very effective, there was inadequate provision for coordination of the whole process, thereby running the risk of the left hand not knowing what the right hand was doing. He concluded:

The various federal, provincial, and joint programs may be proceeding satisfactorily, taken individually, but how do we assess their combined effect on the economy, or determine which area should receive emphasis relative to another at a particular time.[23]

Commenting in the same symposium, Burns observed that a broad policy coordination role might be difficult to expect of such conferences, given that one was trying to "bring into regular consultation a group of ministers of divergent political views, all with their own responsibilities in an area where policy determinations are most difficult to reconcile".[24] Burns suggested a four-tiered approach to such ministerial conferences with the apex consisting of regular Prime Minister–Premier Conferences with a limited agenda dealing with broad matters of policy which would overlap what he called "jurisdictional bounds". Below that would be the Federal-Provincial Plenary Conference to consider what he called "the larger problems of policy", and where necessary, matters could be hived off to subconferences of ministers concerned with the particular problem. Under this structure would be the conference of ministers in the same programme area, and in turn, below that would be the meeting of supporting officials.

Writing in 1978 Gordon Robertson, Secretary to the Federal Cabinet for Federal-Provincial Relations, indicated that the decade from 1968–78 had seen twenty meetings at the level of First Ministers, whereas federal and provincial ministers and senior officials had come together at formal meetings an average of five hundred times a year. He acknowledged that interministerial conferences were an adjunct of executive, not parliamentary, power and hence were the "centrepiece" of executive federalism. The subjects for discussion at such conferences were usually the operation of the federal government, not of the provincial governments. He also made the interesting observation that "the effect on the federal government of initiatives of individual provinces tends to be dealt with in bilateral exchanges".[25] Writing in the same forum, Stevenson outlined what he saw as three roles for intergovernmental conferences: information exchange, programme and policy harmonization, and policy determination.

However, in relation to the second and third category, he was referring to policy between levels, but in individual sectors rather than across sectors.[26]

2. Intergovernmental Conferences of Administrators

There has been relatively little written about this aspect of the intergovernmental machinery of both Australia and Canada, largely because it is regarded as an integral part of the interministerial conferences. As such it forms part of the overall connotation about the role of public servants so prevalent in Westminster systems, which seeks to portray them as passive and subservient actors acting merely as advisers to their political masters. However, longstanding observers of Premiers Conferences and ministerial conferences are well aware of the process which occurs, whereby meetings of the equivalent public servants occur before the political conferences, to identify areas where there are differences of opinion and invariably to devise a solution, formula, or trade-off, which can serve as a basic discussion point for the ministers concerned. This role is particularly pronounced for intergovernmental agreements, and it is the public servants from the different levels of government who engage in the drafting of the argument. This role is conducted predominantly by the public servants from the relevant programme area, or in the case of tax measures, by the fiscal central departments, and there is little of an overview of all the agreements from the centre except for some involvement by the central agencies, old and new. (See following discussions.)

3. A National Cabinet Minister Appointed as Minister for Intergovernmental Relations

This experiment has been tried in both Australia and Canada, and in both countries experience has shown that such a minister looms as little more than a figurehead, and when the crunch comes, is completely subservient to the prime minister. There has certainly been no substantive role for such a person in relation to the overview of intergovernmental agreements, although the minister tends to be a focal point for lobbying by the state/provincial and local governments. The role may be circumscribed even further if there is a national cabinet committee specializing in intergovernmental relations, as has been the case in Canada in recent years.

4. A National Department or Division Charged with Responsibility for Intergovernmental Liaison

This pattern is considerably more entrenched in Canada through the Federal-Provincial Relations Office, which has no true Australian equivalent, although the Department of Prime Minister and Cabinet has a section which handles intergovernmental liaison and some briefing of both the prime minister, and the minister mentioned in (3), for the major inter-ministerial conferences. In the mid 1970s, there were some signs that the Australian Prime Minister's Department was attempting to follow the example of the Canadian Federal-Provincial Relations Office, and the most tangible evidence of this was its first and only attempt to produce an inventory of intergovernmental agreements.[27] The foreword to that publication had this to say:

> At the Premiers' Conference in Canberra on 19 June 1975, the Prime Minister initiated discussion on aspects of Australian-State Government co-operative planning. In his address to the Premiers he said: "The Australian government will be seeking in the longer term a more rational and coordinated system of assessing needs, setting priorities and allocating resources in the public sector — one based on cooperation between governments. It may take years to develop a new approach of the kind we have in mind, of the kind discussed among our officials. But we believe a start should be made, now. Joint-planning and consultative arrangements are necessarily an integral part of this approach."

Virtually no progress was made towards this aim, mostly because of the change of government in 1975. Today the Department of Prime Minister and Cabinet does provide significant professional briefings to the Prime Minister and the Minister for Federal-State relations on individual items as they arise, together with briefings from the Treasury, but there has been no impetus towards a coordinating role across all the intergovernmental machinery. Relations between the Australian national government and local government have also been handled partly by the Department of Prime Minister and Cabinet, but predominantly by separate departments, such as the Department of Urban and Regional Development, and at present the Department of National Development through its small office of local government.

Consequently our attention must shift to the Canadian Federal-Provincial Relations Office which, strange to say, has rarely been the subject of detailed academic investigation. The fact that the FPRO publishes a comprehensive list of intergovernmental agreements each year might lead one to assume a heavy *coordinating* role for the office in the substance of such agreements, but this is not really so. However, the office has many programme experts and professional staff with a broad knowledge and expertise, and they provide substantial briefings on individual intergovernmental fires as they ignite from time to time. They are involved heavily in the renegotiation of particular major intergovernmental agreements as they fall due for renewal or reform. The office also acts as the central point for the sifting of federal bureaucratic advice on intergovernmental agreements which transgress the boundaries of public sector agencies. Veilleux argues that the FPRO provides for an effective consideration of provincial viewpoints by the federal government. He describes its operations thus: "The Federal-Provincial Relations Office is structured along both regional and operational lines; there is a desk for each province and for each sector of government activity. Any document submitted to cabinet is examined or analysed by the person responsible for the relevant desk".[28] Clearly this process of operation represents a micro, rather than a macro approach. However, Kernaghan presents quite a different view of the operations of the FPRO: "The office is structured so that its senior officials can take a comprehensive view of federal-provincial interaction. Officials of this Office assess the implications for federal-provincial relations of documents requiring Cabinet consideration. Operating departments have the primary responsibility for answering such questions as what consultations have been held with the provinces, what is the likely degree of support or opposition among the provinces, what are the implications for provincial-municipal relations in financial, administrative and jurisdictional terms, and what tactics should be adopted if it is necessary to take up the matter with the provinces." Kernaghan then quotes from an official cabinet directive on the handling of cabinet information to say that "the Federal-Provincial Relations Office is usually able to contribute to these answers based on its overview of the interaction between federal and provincial activity".[29] Despite the fact that Kernaghan claims a "comprehensive view" for the FPRO he provides no evidence that it applies such a view to the whole range of intergovernmental relations at the one time. Rather it is a "comprehensive view" on particular issues or negotiations which arise.

The latest and perhaps most interesting study of the FPRO, by Campbell and Szablowski, as part of their review of federal central agencies, paints a picture of the FPRO as just another central agency vying with other central agencies to dominate advice to cabinet on federal-provincial relations. They do, however, acknowledge it to be the "primary authority" in the field (that is, compared with Finance, Treasury Board, Prime Minister's Office and the Privy Council Office).[30] My own interviews with senior officials of the FPRO confirm all these views about the organization (specifically in relation to intergovernmental agreements), and it is clear that, whilst the FPRO does review each agreement in the light of the prevailing mood and prospect of federal-provincial relations in general in that period, it nonetheless reviews each agreement seriatim. Apart from occasional attempts at the consolidation of a number of agreements, as occurred with the Established Programmes Financing arrangements, there is no attempt to engage in a regular or periodic review of all the major intergovernmental agreements and their attendant resource allocation.

5. A Consultative Advisory Body Comprising Representation from the Different Levels of Government

Australia has such a body though Canada does not. The Australian Advisory Council for Inter-government Relations (ACIR) was established (partly on the American model) after 1975 as part of the Fraser government's new federalism policy. It is comprised of five representatives from the national government, six from the states, six from local government, and five citizens. Its terms of reference confine it to operating on the basis of references from the Premiers Conference. Although it has before it very broad references on the relationships which should exist between the three levels of government, it has as yet made no attempt to gain an overview of intergovernmental agreements.

6. *Particular National Cabinet Ministers Nominated as a Liaison Point for a Particular State or Province*

Both Australia and Canada have experimented with this technique, although it is made more difficult in Canada when the party governing at the national level has no elected representatives, let alone ministers, in a particular province. In both countries the national governments have used this device mainly as part of an intelligence network to feed reaction from the states and provinces back to the national capital, and also to keep national officials in that state or province aware of national government policy decisions affecting that state or province; something akin to a low-key, ambassadorial-cum-espionage function. To this extent such ministers become slightly involved in intergovernmental agreements by conveying viewpoints to Canberra or Ottawa and displaying a symbolic presence in the state or province when the agreement is announced or ratified.

7. *National Ministers and their Ministries Responsible for Regional Activity (in Substate or Subprovincial Regions)*

This has been a development of the 1970s in both countries. In Australia the impetus came from the election, in 1972, of the Labor government, which was committed to public spending on the cities and a disrespect for the states as social or economic entities. A minister and department of urban and regional development quickly began formulation of policies with accompanying specific purpose grants for existing cities, particularly capital cities, as well as growth centres, and particular regions. In conjunction, the Commonwealth Grants Commission was given a brief to introduce horizontal equalization for local governments. The bulk of such contact had to be through the states because of their constitutional responsibility for local government, but there was also some direct dealing. These actions did involve intergovernmental agreements, including the negotiation of previous agreements, such as housing, roads, and education, as well as some particularly interesting new ones, for example, the growth centre concept (which on one occasion required legislation to be passed in the commonwealth and two state parliaments because the centre concerned, Albury/Wodonga, straddled an interstate border). These developments came to an abrupt end in 1975 with the dismissal of the Whitlam government. In Canada this process is more firmly established and certainly more sophisticated. The Regional Economic Expansion programmes administered by the national Department of Regional and

Economic Expansion (DREE) are now well known. Their significance in the total scenario of intergovernmental arrangements has now diminished and their basic orientation has also changed, but they do represent, as did the brief Australian experiments, the only real attempt to consolidate a number of intergovernmental agreements at once, and look at resource allocation in a wider perspective than one programme or one project or one sector. The very manner of the negotiation of the DREE agreements, with a master framework agreement between the federal and provincial governments, and various subsidiary agreements for particular projects within that master agreement, represents a small step towards the type of coordination which we are seeking; so does the manner in which the DREE agreements managed to merge capital and recurrent funding, although admittedly, they often had a heavy capital emphasis.

8. *State/Provincial Ministers Appointed as Ministers for Intergovernmental Relations in each State/Province*

This phenomenon exists in both Canada and Australia, having begun earlier in the former than the latter. (In fact the process was begun by Quebec in the early 1960s and followed by Ontario and Alberta and then other provinces. In Australia the move was unquestionably prompted by the election of the Whitlam Labor government in 1972.) In some provinces/states a separate minister has been designated as responsible for intergovernmental affairs but in the majority of cases the role has fallen to the premier. The more interesting fact of this development is the bureaucratic structure which supports these ministers, and we shall examine that shortly. The role of the ministers has been an ambivalent one, and has tended to fluctuate in importance according to the condition of intergovernmental relations. However, such ministers have become powerful at certain times and in certain cases. For example, the Quebec Minister for Intergovernmental Affairs, as well as the sector minister, has been required to approve intergovernmental agreements before cabinet will consider the agreement in question. Alberta and Ontario have followed this model, but it should be emphasized that the coordination which is being spoken of here is simply the centralized scrutiny of intergovernmental agreements one after another in a manner not too different from that performed by a Minister of Finance or Treasury Board or Attorney-General. Admittedly the newly fledged Ministers of Intergovernmental Relations and their supporting ministries are fully aware of, and completely sensitive to, their state/province's overall attitude to intergovernmental relations, and they bring that perspective to bear on the intergovernmental agreements which they scrutinize, and that is a fresh perspective. But they rarely review all of the intergovernmental agreements as a total package.

9. *State/Provincial Departments or Divisions Responsible for Intergovernmental Affairs*

Until very recently there has been little research conducted into this aspect of intergovernmental machinery in both Australia and Canada. Quebec introduced the concept with its Department of Federal-Provincial Relations in 1961, and it has been reorganized since into a stronger position. Ontario originally established a composite department of Treasury, Economics and Intergovernmental Affairs, obviously by means of tacking on intergovernmental affairs to the fiscal function, but late in the 1970s a separate Department for Intergovernmental affairs was formed which also oversees provincial-municipal liaison. Alberta's Department of Federal and Intergovernmental Affairs was founded early in the 1970s and it has also assumed responsibility for the international relations of the province. Newfoundland also set up a separate department devoted entirely to intergovernmental affairs, as has Saskatchewan, but the other provinces generally established an intergovernmental branch within an existing department. It has also been noticeable in Canada that several functional departments in provincial governments have added small sections to their structure to examine the intergovernmental aspects of their activity.

The comparable situation in Australia has not been publicly documented or analysed. Largely in response to the election and subsequent initiatives of the Whitlam Labor government (1972-75), all state governments created central bureaucratic structures to cope with intergovernmental affairs. There was no common practice followed, and at the time of writing the situation is thus: Western Australia has a Minister for Federal Affairs who is also the Attorney-General, and a Federal Affairs Office, comprising only a couple of officials, operates in the Crown Law Office; in South Australia there is no Minister for Federal Affairs as these matters are handled directly by the Premier and a small staff totalling four people operates out of the Premier's Department and must report through the permanent head of that department; the Premier of Tasmania handles federal affairs and he is advised *directly* by the Director of the Cabinet Office; Victoria has a Federal Affairs Division in the Premier's Department numbering seven people but that Division reports through the permanent head of the Premier's Department; whilst New South Wales had a large federal affairs contingent in the Whitlam era, Premier Wran disbanded most of it and the remnants now form part of the normal staff of the Premier's Department on a much smaller scale; in Queensland there is a Federal Affairs Division of four people in the Premier's Department which reports through the permanent head of that department to the Premier on most intergovernmental matters, although it does also service the Attorney-General on a few aspects, such as his involvement as the state's representative on the Australian Advisory Council for Inter-government Relations.

Some aspects of the growth of this administrative machinery are worth noting. Veilleux, in analysing the growth of all intergovernmental machinery in Canada, puts forward some causal factors under what he calls the "political thesis" and the "administrative thesis". The former is virtually the interdependence of the levels of government which has accelerated in the postwar period. The second is more interesting for our present purposes, and it has to do with the practical difficulties raised by the management of intergovernmental relations. The first impinges upon the second and "the increase in the interventions of governments, as well as their efforts to rationalize these interventions, have produced a network of intergovernmental ties which have become so numerous and so complex that governments have been forced to set up internal administrative structures and bodies whose function it is to coordinate those ties". This, according to Veilleux, accounts for the existence of both federal and provincial departments or divisions devoted exclusively to intergovernmental relations. Of the officials in these bodies he is critical for not always taking the interests of the whole nation into consideration, but rather viewing intergovernmental relations as a game and trying to maximize advantages or concessions from the other level. He continues:

> In my view, as a result of this attitude, more importance is often attached to the process of intergovernmental relations than to their substance, that is the *manner* rather than the *matter* that counts.[31]

Simeon argues that provincial governments have sought to achieve greater control over their spending priorities and so have increased central coordination of their activities: "Governments have sought to ensure that official relationships will be subordinate to overall political strategy". He adds that:

> The development of new techniques for policy analysis and political control within government has, perhaps ironically, had the effect of sharpening intergovernmental conflict and rendering policy coordination more difficult.[32]

Simeon agrees with Veilleux on the aspect of substance becoming subservient to process, because of the rise of the central agencies, and uses the Pension plan to demonstrate that, because of the dominance of the central bodies, it came to be viewed as a fiscal problem rather than a welfare problem. It was a similar sentiment that caused Stevenson, himself the head of the Ontario Department of Intergovernmental Affairs, to argue that central bureaucracies such as his own should be kept small in size.[33]

The most recent and perhaps comprehensive analysis of the intergovernmental officials of whom we are speaking has come from Kernaghan, who begins by stressing the difficulty of identifying all public servants who are involved in intergovernmental relations. They certainly do not all reside in the central agencies but are also scattered throughout programme departments. He observes that the normal indicators of bureaucratic power (financial and human resources, discretionary authority, influence with political actors, knowledge and experience) are not as important to intergovernmental officials, who rely more on diplomatic and bargaining skills, as well as their position in the hierarchy and the scope of their perspective on intergovernmental relations.[34] He puts forward three models of the role and power of intergovernmental officials: (a) the *cooperation model* typified by programme specialists with a great deal of autonomy and concerned with technical rather than political matters (we have already encountered this earlier with Smiley's descriptions of intergovernmental relations in the postwar period); (b) the *bargaining model* involving ministers and senior administrators from each order of government and focusing on specific policy matters (typified by Simeon's analysis of a number of specific intergovernmental policy negotiations);[35] and (c) the *bureaucratic politics model* which refers to "bargaining over intergovernmental matters among ministers and officials in departments and agencies *within* each order of government". In other words, it involves intragovernmental bargaining which, it is argued, impacts upon intergovernmental bargaining.

Now this third model is a quite neglected aspect in both Australian and Canadian literature. Those who have dabbled in it tend to suggest that past studies have been wrong in regarding "governments" as a single unit in the intergovernmental relations process, because of the contact between officials of the different levels of government, and because of the conflicts between the provincial departments and their central agencies.[36] Kernaghan concludes:

> Thus, on the basis of studies of Canadian federalism conducted to this date, it is risky to correlate too closely the power of officials in intergovernmental relations with their level, position and departmental or agency affiliation in government. Available case studies suggest that the exercise of power in the intergovernmental policy process, both by officials and other political actors, depends very much on the issue under consideration.[37]

Kernaghan adds that, despite all the sophistication of the machinery of intergovernmental relations, including the central agencies, a great deal of informal contact between officials still underpins the whole process including in particular telephone contact. This is certainly also true in Australia.

In the light of this discussion it has become reasonably clear that it is difficult to pronounce what role the new central agencies have in relation to intergovernmental agreements. No analyst in Canada or Australia has yet suggested a complete coordinating role of the kind that our planning system would envisage. My own interviews show that the situations which come closest to this model in either country are in the provinces of Quebec, to a slightly lesser extent Alberta, and to a slight extent Ontario, where there is a formal requirement for intergovernmental agreements to pass the sanction of the ministry responsible for intergovernmental affairs, but the sanction is applied basically within the perspective of the agreement under consideration rather than any attempt at macro resource allocation. (My interviews reveal that in Quebec there is a rigid adherence to the rule that the Department of Federal-Provincial Relations should monitor and even veto particular intergovernmental agreements, and this requirement is applied less severely in Alberta and Ontario. As no interviews were conducted in Saskatchewan or Newfoundland, I am unable to comment on the extent to which this aspect prevails in those provinces.) Nonetheless, such central agencies in these and other Canadian provinces, and even in the much more weakly coordinated Australian states, do attempt to place the deliberation over an intergovernmental agreement in the perspective of a perceived attitude to intergovernmental relations in general.

10. Conferences of Ministers and Officials Solely from the States/Provinces

As mentioned earlier, it has been rare in Australian experience for the states to manage liaison between themselves, let alone the capacity to enter into binding relationships. This is, of course, related to the fact that at any one time there will usually be at least two of the six states governed by parties different from the other four states, and that situation is further complicated by the fact that some of the states will be governed by the same party as is governing at the national level and those states will be less willing to be seen to be conniving with the other states against their "friends" in Canberra. There have been some singular and notable attempts by the states to form a more permanent front, such as their compilation of a proposal for new federal arrangements, which was submitted at a Premiers Conference in 1970.[38] This is analysed later, but it only took a firm stand by the prime minister and a weak stand by the premier of New South Wales, to see the states divided again. In the mid-1970s it looked as if there was a distinct possibility of the establishment of a Council of States in Canberra as a lobby group, and information and liaison secretariat. However, the Labor states baulked at the proposal and even the major advocates in the non-Labor states lost enthusiasm. In the late 1970s the state premiers in Australia met without the presence of the commonwealth to review the tax-sharing arrangements of "New Federalism", which were due for renegotiation, but the outcome was a relatively soft approach to be put to the Commonwealth Government which would not disadvantage any particular state. It has been known for state ministers and officials to gather together immediately prior to an intergovernmental conference to seek some common ground before confronting the national government, but such actions are loosely structured and are usually well overridden by the happenings of the actual intergovernmental conference itself. Unlike the situation in Canada it has been unusual for particular states, even contiguous ones, to form solid alliances. Even the recent attempts of Western Australia, Northern Territory, and Queensland to form a solid bloc for lobbying for northern development have been riven by jealousies between these entities. (For example, the chief minister of the Northern Territory disagreed with the Queensland Premier over the remote area allowance that should apply for concessions on national income tax.)

In Canada interprovincial liaison is more common and in the 1970s there were a number of such conferences. However, Canadian experience has not demonstrated lasting solidarity in those circumstances where all provinces have been involved, due no doubt to the differing needs and perspectives of various provinces.[39] What has proved to be more durable in Canada is liaison and commitment between contiguous provinces with common regional interests; specifically the Council of Western Premiers and the Council of Maritime Premiers. (It should also be noted that these bodies have formed a loose alliance with counterpart state groupings from American states just across the border.) Research indicates that this development has led to a "regional perspective" on the subject matter of some intergovernmental agreements, such as postsecondary education; but there is, as yet, no common interprovincial coordination or even viewpoint across all intergovernmental agreements, and it is, naturally, doubtful that will occur. The historic Western Economic Opportunities conference in the early 1970s did demonstrate, however, the ability of provinces to get together and analyse all the areas of intergovernmental arrangements which had a bearing on their common grievances against the federal government, namely, spatial discrimination against the west. This has something of a counterpart in Australia when the resource-rich, export-oriented, lesser populated states link up (in rhetoric at least) against the national policies on tariffs, transport, monetary policy, etc., which, they claim, are framed to suit the denser populated importing states located in the south-east of the continent.

Clearly then, this regionalism suggests some capacity for a superstate, or superprovincial, level of resource allocation in relation to one or several public functions. However, the scope for such a reallocation across the whole public sector of all participating regional units of government seems very limited, if only because its occurrence would ultimately lead to a questioning of the viability of the participating individual politics and the possibility of their merging more formally and more permanently. In any event, it is bound to be more of a phenomenon in an east-west federation rather than a north-south one, and particularly where the former abuts the units of yet another political federation (the USA).

Accountability

So we have now examined the bulk of the intergovernmental coordination machinery in these two federations, and must conclude that there is no comprehensive coordination of intergovernmental agreements which would comply with the prerequisites of our planning model, although several elements offer some potential in this direction. Within each level of government, in both federations, the coordination process is weak, and each level of government is not yet in a position to achieve coordinated planning across the whole field of its intergovernmental relations, although the Canadians are a little closer to this situation than are the Australians. To put it another way, the planning which does take place is sectoral and vertical planning within particular agreements, and not horizontal planning across all agreements and then between levels.

Another severe problem, as we have noted, is that the planning which is achieved per medium of intergovernmental agreements is largely in secret. The central problem relates to the question of who is to be held accountable for the creation and implementation of these agreements, to whom, and in what manner. They are largely drawn up by their architects away from public scrutiny within the confines of executive policy, and when completed, they are implemented for a fixed period of time through methods which escape any searching analysis or debate in civic, state, or national parliaments. Public servants are intimately involved in this whole process from birth to delivery to maturation (and occasionally abortion). This has to be so, not only because of their expertise, but also because in the divisive politics of intergovernmental relations in Canada and Australia, it is often the public servants who have to keep the federation hanging together. A key method they have to achieve this is the introduction and maintenance of intergovernmental agreements of one kind or other. In the performance of these roles, however, two fundamental questions arise: (1) to whom are such public servants responsible, and (2) to whom do public servants perceive themselves to be responsible? Accountability to each level of government and to the public is quite blurred. Most of the writers we have already considered are perfectly willing to concede that intergovernmental agreements are part of Smiley's "executive federalism", and in some ways the most intractable part of it. There is the question of the lack of accountability to national and subnational parliaments, already touched upon earlier. There is the very difficult problem for pressure groups and citizens who cannot pinpoint responsibility within agreements. (One of Australia's largest pressure groups, the Australian Medical Association, came to grips with this problem by recommending that full responsibility for hospitals be transferred to the national government so that pressure groups and the community in general could pinpoint accountability. See submission by the AMA to the National Inquiry into Hospitals, 1979.) There are many other problems of accountability already touched upon. The difficulty is especially pronounced in relation to the role of public servants. As Kernaghan says: "It is clear that the participation of officials in formal intergovernmental meetings is only the top of a sizeable iceberg. Below the water line is a complex network of formal and informal interactions which affect significantly the outcome of intergovernmental negotiations".[40]

Gordon Robertson has made a spirited defence of the closed nature of interministerial conferences, and since it is those conferences which spawn most of the interdepartmental agreements of which we have been speaking, his points are worth noting. He argues quite forcefully that "the foremost purpose of federal-provincial ministerial conferences remains to secure agreements, understandings and sometimes binding, precisely-defined decisions, affecting intergovernmental business, to arrive cooperatively at solutions to practical problems posed by the acknowledged interdependency of governmental activities".[41] Robertson believes that for the achievement of these objectives, conferences cannot be entirely open. The following is a summary of his reasons:

* Open conferences hamper the process of reaching decisions, because of reluctance on the part of the participants to make concessions that might cause problems with the audience back home. If this forces the necessary bargaining "underground", the role of officials may be magnified.

* For bargaining to begin, political and partisan rhetoric must give way to straight talk. This usually requires closed doors, since the public stance of contests between leaders of opposing parties is essential to the political process.

* Openness can be a divisive influence in that the debate, under the compulsion of the confrontational quality of the bargaining process, can highlight differences of opinion and viewpoint rather than the common ground.

* Individual, practical problems can become hostages to a public relations exercise that may be necessary for broader political or other purposes.

If one accepts these arguments it becomes clear that secrecy is likely to remain a feature of intergovernmental conferences as long as they remain so political. After all, the sheer existence of intergovernmental conferences is a monument to the domination by the executive over the legislature, which has been a feature common to the national and subnational governments of both Australia and Canada, all of which profess to operate Westminster systems. One wonders whether the level of secrecy in intergovernmental relations is any higher than it is in relation to the executive activities in the affairs within either of the national governments, or those of the states/provinces. This, however, does not overcome the objections raised, ironically by Stevenson, when he describes agreements hammered out at federal-provincial conferences as "virtual faits accomplis which tend to erode the legitimacy of both Parliament and the provincial legislatures".[42]

Thus, although there are some strong elements of planning already apparent in the functioning of intergovernmental agreements in Australia and Canada, it is not the totally comprehensive or democratic planning we are seeking, nor is it in any way fully accountable.

Accountability and coordination are the two fundamental difficulties we have encountered in this examination of intergovernmental agreements; others which have arisen are of a more technical nature and should be able to be overcome much more easily. Of course the two basic aspects can be overcome too, the first by means of a different kind of coordination from the centre of each level, and the second by opening up the processes, although this will automatically make the very processes of the operation of intergovernmental agreements more political and more tardy. Specific suggestions for resolution of these difficulties will be proposed and discussed in our concluding chapter.

Federal Finance: Basic Dilemmas

There is no more obvious element of the consequences of a federal division of power than the fiscal arrangements, and none more political either.
All federations are characterized by revenue sharing and/or responsibility
sharing between levels, and the dimension and nature of that sharing is
made manifest in fiscal terms. Moreover, the conflicts which occur across
the line of the division of powers because of divided sovereignty are
usually about the ownership of resources, or access to and use of them.
Any compromise which is derived is expressed, in most cases, in financial
terms.

Consequently we might well expect to find that the area of federal financial relationships will be the most fruitful field for an assessment of the
potential for public sector planning. This is so for a number of reasons:
(1) fiscal transfers of all kinds are relatively easy to identify and isolate;
(2) financial relations are so often symbolic of political relationships;
(3) more has been written about the fiscal side of federalism than any other
aspect, so that we have more literature to guide us; and (4) in the interviews conducted for this project, respondents were more than willing to
speak of fiscal matters, and were often able to conceptualize the problems
of federalism most easily by resorting to fiscal example, analogy, or
metaphor. In other words, financial aspects have so pervaded the literature
and discussion of federalism that a great deal of the debate about broad
issues and viewpoints takes place within the confines of fiscal terminology.

We are going to explore that terminology and its supporting concepts in
our endeavour to identify the hindrances posed by federalism to planning,
and once again our attention will be focused not so much on the internal
aspects of the fiscal administration of each level of government, but rather
upon the *intergovernmental* fiscal relationships, that is, the processes which
take place across the division of powers by the players in this game — the
sovereign government entities.

As we observed in earlier chapters, it is impossible to create a division of
powers which will perennially secure the levels of government into watertight compartments, with a fixed list of functions, and a commensurate
array of revenue sources to finance them. This is particularly true of
Australia and Canada which, like all federations, experience what has been
termed "vertical" imbalance. Vertical imbalance refers to the fact that
there is not a neat or complete matching of expenditure responsibilities
and revenue potential for each level, so that one level inevitably has more

expenditure responsibilities than it can finance adequately from its own sources, and the other level is in the obverse situation with more revenue potential available to it than it needs to discharge its constitutional obligations effectively. In both Australia and Canada the situation since the second world war has been that the national governments have found that the arsenal of taxing powers which accrue to them under the division of powers is more than adequate to finance the functions of government they have been allocated. On the other hand, the states and provinces are in a situation where their expenditure responsibilities, as allocated under the constitution, require more finance than can effectively be raised using the taxing powers they have been allocated. This results in the overt manifestation of vertical imbalance being sizeable fiscal transfers of one kind or another from the national government to the states or provinces. We needn't go into the cause of this dilemma here — it has to do with the inability of the founding fathers of both countries to foresee the growth of the public sector, as well as the strange way in which the supreme courts in both countries have interpreted spending and taxing powers under the constitution, and certainly in ways that the founding fathers never intended. It should also be emphasized that the magnitude of vertical imbalance increased significantly during the second world war in both countries, so that its impact has been felt most heavily since that time. As will be demonstrated, both the Australian and Canadian national governments took over the main state/provincial revenue sources as a wartime expediency, and never really handed them back after hostilities had ended, preferring instead to engage in a process of huge transfers of "national" funds to the lower levels in return for continuing to occupy the taxation fields. Now there are some important divergences in practice between the two countries in the period since the second world war, and they are differences which are quite instructive for our purposes here. We shall be analysing these different approaches. It is sufficient to note, at this point, that in both Australia and Canada, the second world war marks the beginning of a period of profound vertical fiscal imbalance between the levels of government.

There are really only a limited number of ways to rectify vertical imbalance. Firstly, functions could be transferred between the levels of government. Secondly, taxation powers could be so transferred. Thirdly, there could be sharing of functions (responsibility sharing), and fourthly, there could be revenue sharing. All of these methods have been tried in both countries, as we shall see. Looking at the four basic options it becomes readily apparent that vertical fiscal imbalance can generate a number of difficulties for the introduction of a planning system, such as the one we are envisaging, particularly if its solution involves sharing revenues or responsibilities rather than discrete shifts of taxing or spending powers between levels. Since it is the "sharing" concept which has pervaded Australian and Canadian experience (because attempts to move taxing and spending powers between levels have been fairly unsuccessful),[1] we can be forewarned.

Another form of fiscal imbalance in federations is termed "horizontal" imbalance, and refers to the fact that each of the units of a federation *at the same level* of government will not be equally endowed in terms of resources and the potential to exploit them. Thus, in both Australia and Canada, the states/provinces display marked variations in numerous characteristics of their terrain and their populations, which means differences in the capacity of those state/provincial governments to raise revenue, and different pressures upon them to spend that revenue. It can most forcefully be expressed by saying that some states/provinces are richer and some poorer, but that conveys only a picture of absolutes rather than emphasizing the different potential which also exists. In both countries there is a popular feeling that such horizontal imbalances should be eliminated, or at least minimized, and to the extent that a rigid conviction is held on this point it does not, superficially at least, seem to pose difficulties for the superimposition of planning across the intergovernmental interface. However these are questions of the methodology to be employed to restore horizontal balance, as well as the fact that horizontal imbalance is intimately related to vertical imbalance, in that each of the subnational units of the federation will, in truth, have a different degree of vertical imbalance with the national level. Thus, attempts to rectify vertical imbalance will affect horizontal imbalance, and vice versa. We shall explore this aspect also in terms of the experience of the two countries.

So, to recapitulate, we shall examine federal fiscal relations mainly from the aspect of the intergovernmental transfer of funds and attempts at revenue sharing, in an endeavour to understand how such relationships operate, and whether, within those relations, there is potential for the injection of a planning system. The very conceptual basis of federal financial relationships, especially the notions of vertical and horizontal imbalance, warn us that there are a number of fundamental difficulties to be overcome. This analysis will for the most part involve assessment of the copious polemic which already exists in this subject matter area both in the literature and arising out of the interviews. But beforehand, it is imperative to give at least a brief description of federal finance in the two countries, to provide a frame of reference for the many points of dispute which will follow, especially those contained in the next chapter which deals exclusively with the conditional funding debate.

Federal Finance in Australia

For the national government in Australia, taxes, fees, and fines comprise the bulk of funds available, and at the latest count represented over eighty-five per cent of all funds available to that level of government. The nature of these taxes can be seen from table 7.

Table 7 Australia: commonwealth government finance

Levies[a]			Percentage of total				
	1970–1971	1974–1975	1978–1979	1979–1980	1980–1981	1981–1982	1982–1983[p]
Income taxes on individuals[b]	44.2	54.2	54.4	54.6	53.7	55.9	56.2
Income taxes on companies	19.2	16.5	12.8	12.3	14.3	13.3	11.8
Other income taxes	0.7	0.6	0.5	0.5	0.5	0.6	0.7
Excise duties	14.7	12.2	16.3	19.0	18.7	16.4	17.2
Sales tax	8.8	8.1	7.5	6.8	6.4	7.5	8.5
Customs duties on imports	6.5	5.9	5.8	5.6	5.5	5.4	5.0
Other	5.9	2.5	2.7	1.2	0.9	0.9	0.6
Total	100.0	100.0	100.0	100.0	100.0	100.0	100.0

Source: *Commonwealth Government Finance Australia.*
a Excludes taxes collected by Northern Territory Government authorities.
b Includes Medibank levy payable from 1 October 1976 to 31 October 1978.
p Preliminary figures.

Table 7 demonstrates some features of great importance for federal financial relations. In summary, the observation can be made that income tax on individuals and companies, excise duties, sales tax, and import duties are the lifeblood of the national government, reflecting the Australian situation whereby each of those taxes is now the sole preserve of that level government, whereas most other federations are characterized by a sharing of one or more of these significant tax sources.

In relation to income tax, the situation arises from the fact that the national government, during the second world war occupied the income tax field exclusively, thereby taking from the states their most lucrative revenue source, and reimbursing them at first according to the revenue each of them would have collected had they retained this taxing power. Those arrangements (the uniform tax scheme) have persisted since that time, despite two High Court challenges by the states in which the court upheld the commonwealth's power under Section 96 of the Australian Constitution to make grants to the states on such terms and conditions as it sees fit, although legal opinion is that the states could re-enter the field of income tax at any moment, if they were united in this desire.[2]

The main transformation which has occurred in these arrangements relates to the manner in which a share of the resultant funds from income taxes have been transferred back to the states. As has been explained, during wartime and immediately after they were called "taxation reimbursement grants", but later became "financial assistance grants", being calculated on a formula which took account of population distribution among the states, age distribution of that population, and a betterment factor to make some recognition of each state's potential. The change of name and method of distribution was of considerable political significance, because it symbolized a situation where the states were no longer automatically entitled to any predetermined share of income tax, as had been the case when the resulting grants from the commonwealth to the states had carried the nomenclature and substance of being for taxation reimbursement.[3] The new financial assistance grants' formulae were renegotiated each five years, until the advent of the Fraser government in 1975 and its "new federalism" policy, which as phase one, provided for the financial assistance grants to be replaced by a fixed percentage share of personal income tax to be returned to the states, distributed amongst them according to pre-existing relativities, in a five year agreement, and with a floor guarantee that no state should receive less than it would have under the old arrangements. (The guarantee applied only for the first four years of the new arrangements.) The legislation provided for a complete review of the relative distribution of the grants among the states to be undertaken by 1981 in time for their renegotiation. Other elements of the Fraser government's new federalism will be analysed later, but it has to be pointed out at this stage that it also provided for a second phase whereby any state would be able to authorize a national government surcharge, or grant a personal income tax rebate to resident taxpayers of that state. No state passed the requisite legislation for the implementation of this second phase (a proposal reached the notice paper stage in Western Australia but was subsequently withdrawn), although the national government did not contemplate moving out of the income tax field to allow the states room for the imposition of such an income tax surcharge. Consequently, it can be seen that the sole occupation of income tax powers by the national government produces two major effects in the Australian federation: (1) it ensures that all income taxes, both individual and corporate, are levied at a uniform rate across the nation, unlike the situation pre–World War II when state income taxes varied significantly in their incidence and severity (all commonwealth taxes and levies must always be uniform between states according to the Australian Constitution); and (2) it results in the necessity for a massive transfer of revenue gained from income taxes by the national government to the states. There have been a few occasions in postwar history in Australia when the states have had explicit opportunities to regain their income taxing powers, but, in the final analysis, they have preferred a situation where the commonwealth government incurs the political odium of levying all the income taxes. This does, of course, produce a situation of constant political argument between the levels of government, with the states forever claiming a larger grant than is being offered by the commonwealth, despite the existence of a quinquennial formula for these fiscal transfers for most of the postwar period. In 1982 the formula was changed to allow the states a fixed percentage share of a basket of taxes including income tax.

In relation to indirect taxes (excise duties, sales tax, and import duties) a different situation prevails. The Australian constitution does specify customs and excise duties as a power of the national government but offers no definition of what constitutes such a tax. Thus it has fallen to the High Court to make judgment on this matter, and despite substantial prevarication from time to time, the view has emerged from the court that all taxes levied at the point of wholesale are the preserve of the national government. This is not the place to enter into an argument about the merits of such a judgment, but we can note that its practical effect is to give the commonwealth government a monopoly over excise duties, import duties, and sales tax, despite some recent successful attempts by various Australian states to impose similar sorts of taxes at the point of retail, such as the taxes on tobacco and petrol.

So it is that the national government in Australia dominates taxation collection. This in turn creates a situation of considerable vertical fiscal imbalance in the federation, with a consequent necessity for the transfer of funds from the national government to the subnational levels. It is that transfer which will occupy most of our subsequent attention, and we can begin by examining its significance for the outlays of the national government, as in table 8.

From table 8 it can be seen that something over a third of the commonwealth government's outlay goes on the transfer of funds, in one form

Table 8 Australia: commonwealth government finance

Outlays	Percentage of total outlay			
	1970–1971	1974–1975	1978–1979	1982–1983p
Grants to the states:				
for current purposes	21.5	21.5	27.1	24.6
for capital purposes	7.1	8.1	5.1	4.1
Grants to Northern Territory[a]	—	—	1.0	1.2
Net advances to the states[b] and local government authorities:*				
for loan works	4.7	3.4	2.7	1.9
other	2.0	3.6	1.2	n.a.†

Source: Commonwealth Government Finance Australia.
a   The Northern Territory became self-governing on 1 July 1978.
b   This terminology is used because it appears thus in official publications. However it is of course misleading to treat Loan Council allocations to the states as commonwealth loans or advances. They are, strictly speaking, a state entitlement.
p   Preliminary figures.
*   Separate local government data not available.
†   Not available.

or another, to the states, and the latest figures are indicative of the trend under the Fraser government towards a mixture of funding with more emphasis on funding for recurrent rather than capital purposes. Table 9 presents a somewhat similar analysis in more detail, and it is significant, that in the seventies the percentage growth rate of commonwealth grants to the states and local authorities was nearly twice that of total commonwealth outlays, the major boosts having come in 1970–71 and 1974–75.

Table 9 Australia: outlays of commonwealth budget

Time period	Percentage of total outlay	
	Grants to states and local authorities	Net advances to states and local authorities
1967–1968	21.0	10.1
1968–1969	21.4	9.4
1969–1970	22.1	9.1
1970–1971	27.2	6.4
1971–1972	26.5	6.5
1972–1973	27.3	6.6
1973–1974	28.1	6.1
1974–1975	29.0	6.9
1975–1976	32.4	6.3
1976–1977	31.8	5.3
1977–1978	32.8	4.7
1978–1979	33.2	3.9
1979–1980	33.7	2.8
1980–1981	33.0	2.6
1981–1982E	32.1	2.1

Source: Derived from Commonwealth Year Book.
Note: All figures include Northern Territory.
E Estimated.

What is of more significance from the point of view of this study is the proportion of state revenue which is comprised of transfers from the commonwealth government. It is not possible to obtain a measurement of this using state government budgetary data, because there is a distinct lack of uniformity in the presentation of state budgets in Australia. Instead, we have to look to other sources which can provide a consistent, uniform presentation of state public finance; and there are only two such sources — the Australian Bureau of Statistics and the Commonwealth Grants Commission. Table 10 presents data from the Bureau of Statistics public finance series on state authorities. It can be seen immediately that, taking all of the Australian states together, grants from the commonwealth government in 1981–82 comprised almost 60 per cent of total state receipts and almost 50 per cent of total funds available to the states from all sources. Net advances from the commonwealth provide a further 3.2 per cent of the funds available to the states, and so in all, 52 per cent of all the funds available to the states comes from commonwealth funding.

Table 10 also highlights a number of significant trends. Most significantly, there has been an unmistakable tendency for the states. taken as a whole, to become more dependent on commonwealth grants. (Later analysis suggests that these generalizations do not necessarily apply to

Table 10   Australia: intergovernmental transfers in relation to state revenue

Year	Grants from commonwealth government			Net advances from commonwealth government		Total commonwealth funds	
	Percentage of total receipts	Percentage of total funds available	Percentage increase	Percentage of total funds available	Percentage increase	Percentage of total funds available	Percentage increase
1964–1965	50.9	35.0	6.9	18.9	7.2	53.9	7.0
1965–1966	52.5	35.8	12.5	18.3	6.3	54.1	10.3
1966–1967	52.0	37.0	9.7	18.0	5.0	54.7	8.1
1967–1968	51.9	37.4	10.8	18.0	9.1	55.4	10.2
1968–1969	51.1	37.0	8.2	16.5	0.2	53.5	5.6
1969–1970	51.5	37.9	14.0	15.7	6.3	53.6	11.7
1970–1971	58.1	45.4	36.1	10.7	-23.1	56.1	18.7
1971–1972	53.8	42.4	7.6	10.4	12.9	52.7	8.6
1972–1973	53.7	44.1	16.2	10.6	13.1	54.7	15.6
1973–1974	54.9	45.5	23.4	9.9	12.1	55.4	21.2
1974–1975	60.1	48.1	49.9	11.4	63.7	59.5	52.4
1975–1976	62.3	53.5	35.8	10.5	12.0	64.0	31.2
1976–1977	61.0	51.0	9.5	8.5	-6.9	59.5	31.2
1977–1978	61.7	51.0	27.2	7.4	-1.3	58.4	11.9
1978–1979	62.0	51.6	10.3	6.0	-10.6	57.6	7.6
1979–1980	60.5	51.2	10.6	4.3	-20.5	55.5	7.4
1980–1981	60.6	49.5	12.3	3.9	4.5	53.3	11.7
1981–1982	58.7	48.7	10.0	3.2	-7.9	51.9	8.7

Source: Derived from Australian Bureau of Statistics, Public Authority Finance: State and Local Authorities.

each state, nor is there always a continuous trend of commonwealth dependence for those states which have become more dependent. It is not possible to be definitive on this matter because of the totally different basis on which the figures are compiled by the Bureau of Statistics, on the one hand, and the Commonwealth Grants Commission on the other.)

It can be seen from table 10 that in 1964–65, grants from the commonwealth government represented 50.9 per cent of total state receipts. (The use of the term "receipts" is somewhat misleading. It is used here because that is the way the statistician employs the term. Strictly speaking, what is being referred to here is receipts on current account.) But in 1981–82 they represented 58.7 per cent. By comparison, net advances from the commonwealth, although recording an absolute increase, have come to represent a declining proportion of the total funds available to the states (3.2 per cent in 1981–82 compared with 18.9 per cent in 1964–65). In terms of the funds available to states, total commonwealth government transfers (i.e., grants and net advances) have remained stable. ("Total funds available" is another term used by the statistician which does not have a strict equivalent meaning in terminology used in presentation of Treasury data. Here it means recurrent plus loan funding, that is, funds from all sources. In 1981–82 some 51.9 per cent of all funds available to the states came from commonwealth transfers of some kind or other compared with 53.9 per cent in 1964–65. We can safely conclude that well over half of all the funds available to the Australian states have come from commonwealth transfers, mainly in the form of grants, and the proportion has approached 60 per cent. One other important feature revealed in table 10 should not be overlooked, and that is the marked annual fluctuations in commonwealth funds for the states. In the table, this is recorded as the percentage increase each year and, especially in relation to grants from the commonwealth government, it can be seen that a small increase one year can be followed by an extremely large one in the next year. Indeed, the grants to the states from the commonwealth government have shown annual increases ranging from 6.9 per cent to 49.9 per cent. The pattern in respect of the net advances from the commonwealth is slightly smoother overall, although annual movements here have still ranged from a decrease of 23.1 per cent to an increase of 63.7 per cent. Perhaps the most significant statistics in this respect are those for total commonwealth funding, and table 10 shows once again the annual variability factor with annual increases ranging from 5.6 per cent to 52.4 per cent, although the annual increases in total commonwealth funding are more cyclical than for commonwealth grants alone. Of course it has to be borne in mind that in interpreting the fluctuations in the figures in table 10, there were several changes during this period in the division of powers and functions between the commonwealth and the states. This forms part of the explanation for the wide fluctuations in some years and serves to reinforce the point regarding the unpredictability of dependence upon the commonwealth.

Of course the total picture for all states combined is of only limited significance for our exercise in this study. Our concern is more with the impact of commonwealth funding on each state individually. A detailed statistical study was carried out, with the aid of state public finance data from the Australian Bureau of Statistics and the Commonwealth Grants Commission of each Australian state, for a fifteen year period to the end of the 1970s, to assess the trends in the dependence of each state on intergovernmental transfers. The data arising from that study is simply too unwieldy to reproduce here but a summary is provided in table 11.

Table 11   Australia: impact of commonwealth transfers on state revenue

| State | 1981–1982 | |
	Total commonwealth grants as percentage of total state receipts	Total commonwealth funding as percentage of total funds available to state
New South Wales	56.0	51.0
Victoria	52.5	43.4
Queensland	59.9	52.4
South Australia	64.9	60.8
Western Australia	63.7	58.2
Tasmania	66.4	59.8
Six states	53.5	47.0

Source: Derived from Australian Bureau of Statistics, State and Local Government Finance.

The data in table 11 demonstrate that each Australian state has a different level of dependence on commonwealth funding, and, generally speaking, the level of dependence increases as the size of the state (by population) decreases. (This generalization does not hold for the relative positions of New South Wales and Victoria but it is widely acknowledged that the latter has a greater tax base than the former even though its population is smaller.) The trend analysis reveals that this pattern has always been evident with Tasmania being the state almost always most heavily dependent on commonwealth funding. This is not the place for an examination of the reasons for the disparate levels of state dependence on commonwealth funding, but it would seem to be due to a combination of the fact that most commonwealth funding is distributed to the states on the basis of formulae whose components produced an increased weighting the smaller the state, together with the existence of some level of correlation between the size of a state and its tax base for the sorts of taxes the states themselves levy.

The trend analysis also revealed a number of other pertinent factors: (1) all states have experienced a steady overall trend towards greater fiscal dependence on commonwealth funding; (2) there have been pronounced annual fluctuations in all elements of commonwealth funding in every state, that is, grants for current purposes, grants for capital purposes, and advances (but grants for current purposes have exhibited a somewhat smoother pattern than either grants for capital purposes or advances, both of which have been quite erratic); and (3) these generalizations held also for the impact on the state government's budget subsector, which is especially significant since state governments have regarded their budget subsector as reflecting their options, constraints, and preferences, because that is the only segment of each state's public finance which comes into view coherently and regularly.

All states' budgets are now considerably more dependent on state taxation than they were fifteen years ago, the general pattern being for state taxes nowadays to comprise double the share of budget revenue that they represented in the mid 1960s. The difference between the states in the contribution of state taxes to budget revenue is quite marked, with New South Wales, and particularly Victoria, recording a much higher level than other states, due mainly to their commensurately lower level of dependence on commonwealth funding and the different machinery of government arrangements, referred to earlier, which create a different budget make-up.

Another relevant factor revealed by the trend analysis is that, with the exception of two or three particular years common to all states, the level of dependence on both commonwealth payments and state taxation has not fluctuated widely from one year to another. The exceptions to this generalization are 1965–66, 1970–71 and 1977–78, years in which all states received a boost in commonwealth funding. To say this is to reveal the basic pattern of state budget formulation on the revenue side where Australian state governments tend to see what sort of funding they are going to receive from the commonwealth government before determining levels of state taxation. In effect, our analysis has shown us that there is a relatively smooth pattern of state budget revenue dependence on commonwealth payments for general purposes, and the relationship of such commonwealth payments to state taxation. We cannot make any observations about such a pattern with respect to commonwealth payments for specific purposes because we don't have the data available on a segregated basis.

We have examined the impact of Australian intergovernmental transfers on the outlays of the commonwealth government and the revenue of the state governments. The next logical step is to analyse the nature of the funds being transferred between levels. Table 12 provides a broad functional breakdown of all the commonwealth payments to state and local authorities. Inconsistencies in tabulation prevent the extrapolation of this data before 1973–74. The table is of limited usefulness because of the large proportion of intergovernmental funding which has not been allocated to any function. (We examine the split between general and specific purpose funding later.) But this merely serves to illustrate the fact that the bulk of intergovernmental transfers in Australia are general purpose, that is, unconditional. The largest single functional category has always been "general revenue funds" which is, in reality, income tax sharing (formerly

Table 12 Australia: functional classification of payments to or for the states, state government Loan Council programmes, Northern Territory and payments made direct to local government authorities

Function	1973–1974		1974–1975		1975–1976[a]		1976–1977		1977–1978		1978–1979		1979–1980		1980–1981		1981–1982[b]		1982–1983		1983–1984[c]	
	% total	% inc.	% total	% inc.	% total	% inc.	% total	% inc.	% total	% inc.	% total	% inc.	% total	% inc.	% total	% inc.	% total	% inc.	% total	% inc.	% total	% inc.
Defence	*		0.4	247.4	0.4	30.8	0.4	5.9	0.2	-36.1	*	-45.9	*	-81.2	*	5.2	*	82.9	*	131.1	*	-31.4
Education	14.3		20.1	112.8	16.6	9.1	18.7	18.8	18.1	8.7	17.9	6.1	18.1	7.2	18.1	10.7	19.5	15.4	18.9	13.4	17.9	8.6
Health	1.2		1.6	107.7	12.8	902.3	9.5	-21.2	11.0	29.8	10.5	2.3	10.7	11.0	11.0	13.3	1.5	-85.2	1.5	24.2	2.3	71.0
Social Security & Welfare	0.7		1.1	133.3	2.8	51.6	1.2	-56.2	1.1	11.7	0.9	-12.2	0.6	2.3	0.5	-11.6	0.4	-14.9	0.6	54.6	0.6	17.3
Housing	5.5		6.1	70.8	4.3	-7.2	4.1	1.7	3.8	2.4	2.9	-16.7	2.2	-18.1	2.1	5.9	1.6	-13.1	2.7	91.5	3.7	55.3
Urban & Regional Development & Environment	1.3		3.7	319.6	3.1	11.9	1.4	-52.5	0.5	-57.6	0.4	-22.6	0.4	5.5	0.4	5.9	0.1	-66.3	0.3	270.0	0.3	14.8
Cultural & Recreation	*		0.2	550.0	0.1	-7.7	0.1	-16.7	*	-40.0	*	—	*	-6.2	*	-2.5	*	43.1	*	33.6	0.1	71.9
Transport	7.5		6.5	29.2	5.8	18.1	5.7	3.4	5.4	5.3	5.3	2.4	5.4	11.7	5.5	14.8	5.4	9.3	6.1	29.9	6.6	24.7
Water Supply & Electricity	0.6		0.6	44.4	0.5	24.3	0.4	-26.1	*	-9.1	0.2	-91.8	0.2	b	0.3	50.9	0.3	10.2	0.5	84.7	0.4	-4.9
Industry Assistance & Development	1.7		1.3	15.8	1.3	29.4	0.9	-25.5	0.7	-12.2	0.6	15.3	0.8	-11.8	0.3	-38.7	0.4	64.9	1.3	254.1	0.4	-61.7
Labour & Employment	*		0.1	33.3	0.1	50.0	0.1	100.0	0.1	16.7	0.1	—	0.1	-11.5	0.1	-1.5	*	-6.1	1.0	100.8	2.2	145.9
General Public Services	0.2		0.1	6.2	0.1	-11.1	0.1	62.5	0.1	-15.4	0.1	9.1	0.1	6.2	*	-96.7	*	30.7	*	100.8	*	-13.8
Outlays not allocated to function:																						
General revenue funds	44.1		38.3	30.7	36.8	24.3	41.5	19.3	43.1	16.6	46.9	10.6	46.8	13.3	47.0	11.1	56.2	31.0	53.6	11.6	52.7	12.4
State government Loan Council	13.5		11.3	26.0	8.4	19.8	8.3	5.1	7.8	5.4	5.5	-1.8	5.5	-17.6	5.2	5.2	71.8		6.1	-8.3	5.4	0.6
Capital grants	6.4		5.4	24.5	5.1	24.3	5.1	5.1	4.8	5.8	3.6	-13.2	3.6	7.4	3.4	5.0	3.4	5.0	0.4		0.3	
States debts assistance	2.1		1.6	14.3	0.6	-54.8	0.5	—	0.5	4.3	0.5	4.1	0.5	7.4	0.5	19.7	0.4	3.5	0.4	3.3	0.3	3.1
Payments to Northern Territory	—		—		—		—		*		1.9	428.3	2.9	20.0	3.2	20.4	3.6	18.3	3.5	14.4	3.4	13.2
Assistance to local government	—		0.9		0.9	40.4	1.6	75.0	1.6	17.9	1.9	103.8	1.9	8.5	2.4	24.2	2.5	16.6	2.6	21.0	2.5	8.2
National disaster relief	0.6		0.7	88.7	0.3		0.3		0.5		0.1	-54.7	*	-56.1	*	-76.0	*	-70.3	0.8		0.7	-7.1
Grand total (Percentage increase)			50.6		31.8		5.6		12.5		7.1		7.4		10.9		8.7		16.9		14.2	

Source: Derived from *Payments to or for the States*, Budget Paper No. 7.

a Health figure affected by early payment of assistance for hospital running costs.
Social Security and Welfare figure affected by unemployment relief grants.
b Commencing 1981–1982 general revenue payments include identified Health Grants that in previous years were classified under "Health".
c A special amount of $62.9 m was also set aside in 1983–1984 as special assistance for S.W. Tasmania.
† Substantial increase.
* Insignificant or irrelevant.

financial assistance grants), which have come to represent an increasing proportion of intergovernmental transfers during the past decade.

However, it is clear from table 12 that the largest functional areas of commonwealth payments to other levels of government have long been education, health, transport, and housing. Education has become progressively more important, health has fluctuated but now represents a similar proportion of intergovernmental funding to what it represented six years ago, transport (mainly road funding) has gradually lessened in importance, as has housing. The only other significant single element of intergovernmental payments has been the capital funding component represented by Loan Council borrowing, and capital grants from the commonwealth, but this sector has become noticeably less of a feature in the picture of the intergovernmental flow of funds in recent years.

Table 13   Australia: commonwealth payments to states

Time period	Total funds for recurrent purposes		Total funds for capital purposes		Total funds
	Percentage of total	Percentage increase	Percentage of total	Percentage increase	Percentage increase
1972–1973	57.8		42.2		
1973–1974	58.1	21.2	41.9	19.9	20.6
1974–1975	56.9	47.4	43.1	55.3	50.6
1975–1976	63.4	45.3	36.6	10.4	30.3
1976–1977	66.8	12.6	33.2	-2.9	6.9
1977–1978	70.6	18.1	29.4	-0.9	11.8
1978–1979	73.2	8.8	26.8	-4.6	4.8
1979–1980	77.2	12.0	22.8	-9.8	6.6
1980–1981	78.2	11.3	21.8	6.4	11.2
1981–1982	79.7	10.4	20.3	1.1	8.4
1982–1983	80.0	16.9	20.0	24.3	16.9
1983–1984	79.7	13.8	20.3	16.0	14.2

Source: Derived from *Payments to or for the States*, Budget Paper No. 7.

Table 13 presents the basic split between funds for recurrent purposes and funds for capital purposes. Here the trend is unmistakable. Since 1972–73 there has been a marked increase in commonwealth payments to the states for recurrent purposes and a commensurate decrease in capital purpose funding. Whereas in 1972–73 funds for capital purposes represented 42.2 per cent of all commonwealth funds transferred to the states, in 1983–84 they represented only 20.3 per cent of the total. The hospital cost-sharing arrangements have played a significant role, but this switch in funding came predominantly in the period of the Fraser government, that is, since 1975–76, and partly represented definite elimination of various Whitlam government programmes which were capital intensive (growth centres, land acquisition, sewerage, area improvement, etc.). It is also partly due to the general Liberal philosophy of public sector cutbacks as part of economic management, which have fallen most heavily on capital forms of expenditure. As can be noted from the table, both forms of funding have been the subject of marked fluctuations from year to year. The pattern of annual fluctuations is only partially due to changes in the inflation rate.

Table 14 is a useful picture of a longer period which reveals the mixture of recurrent and capital funds going to each state. Clearly the overall trend in every state has been towards recurrent funds rather than capital funds. But the mixture does vary between states. New South Wales has received more from the commonwealth for recurrent purposes than for capital purposes, and that trend has become pronounced in a fairly smooth and gradual manner, except for the common flattening off in the period 1971–72 to 1974–75. Victoria has had pretty well the same mixture of funding as has New South Wales and the same comments apply. Queensland has varied marginally from the two larger states, occasionally having a slightly higher component of one form of funding, and at other times a lower component. In recent years there has been a slightly heavier emphasis on recurrent funding for Queensland than has been true of New South Wales and Victoria. The South Australian pattern is much more at variance, and this state has consistently received a significantly lower proportion of recurrent funds that has been true of most of the other states. Indeed, during the 1970s South Australia received more commonwealth funds for recurrent purposes than for capital purposes. There is a clear demarcation point in Western Australia's history in these matters because, until 1972–73, Western Australia was proportionally lower on recurrent funding than most other states, but since that time the situation has been reversed and except for isolated exceptions Western Australia has consistently recorded a higher component of recurrent funding than any other state. Four-fifths of the commonwealth payments to Western Australia are now for recurrent purposes and only one-fifth for capital purposes, whereas in the mid to late 1960s Western Australia received more in capital than recurrent payments. By contrast, after 1971 Tasmania has had a heavier emphasis on commonwealth funding for capital purposes than any other states, and the difference in the mixture for Tasmania has varied significantly from that of other states. Tasmania now receives a noticeably higher percentage of its commonwealth payments for capital purposes than does any other state.

Table 15 casts further light on Australian intergovernmental fund transfers firstly by revealing the overall split between general and specific purpose funding (which we shall examine in depth later). It also shows that funding to the states for recurrent purposes has always been predominantly in the form of general purpose funds, whereas funds for capital purposes have usually contained a much more even mixture of general purpose and specific purpose funding, especially in recent years. The only type of funding which has experienced reasonably smooth increases year to year has been recurrent funding for general purposes, whereas recurrent funding for specific purposes has been quite erratic, as has been all forms of

Table 14 Australia: total commonwealth payments to or for the states and states government Loan Council programmes[a]

Recipient state	Percentage of total																		
	1965–66	1966–67	1967–68	1968–69	1969–70	1970–71	1971–72	1972–73	1973–74	1974–75	1975–76	1976–77	1977–78	1978–79	1979–80	1980–81	1981–82	1982–83	1983–84
New South Wales:																			
Recurrent purposes	52.3	53.8	53.8	55.2	55.8	59.4	58.4	58.7	58.3	56.7	63.7	66.8	70.9	73.2	77.4	77.9	79.5	79.5	78.3
Capital purposes	47.7	46.2	46.2	44.8	44.2	40.6	41.6	41.3	41.7	43.3	36.3	33.2	29.1	26.8	22.6	22.1	20.5	20.5	21.7
Victoria:																			
Recurrent purposes	52.3	52.8	53.9	54.9	56.4	58.8	57.7	58.1	59.1	56.3	63.4	66.9	70.9	73.4	77.5	78.4	79.4	79.3	79.9
Capital purposes	47.7	47.2	46.1	45.1	43.6	41.2	42.3	41.9	40.9	43.7	36.6	33.1	29.1	26.6	22.5	21.6	20.6	20.7	20.1
Queensland:																			
Recurrent purposes	51.9	52.5	50.1	54.8	55.9	58.5	57.1	58.8	58.1	57.7	64.5	67.7	72.1	74.8	77.5	79.9	81.6	77.9	77.5
Capital purposes	48.1	47.5	49.9	45.2	44.1	41.5	42.9	41.2	41.9	42.3	35.5	32.3	27.9	25.2	22.5	20.1	18.4	22.1	22.5
South Australia:																			
Recurrent purposes	46.4	47.0	48.2	47.2	48.6	53.6	54.0	56.2	55.3	55.3	61.6	65.2	67.8	71.3	76.0	77.4	79.1	77.6	78.4
capital purposes	53.6	53.0	52.8	52.8	51.4	46.4	46.0	43.8	44.7	43.7	38.4	34.8	32.2	28.7	24.0	22.6	20.9	22.4	21.6
Western Australia:																			
Recurrent purposes	50.2	49.7	49.2	52.1	53.7	56.5	56.7	57.6	59.9	59.3	66.2	69.7	72.6	74.9	79.3	79.8	81.1	79.9	79.3
Capital purposes	49.8	50.3	50.7	47.9	46.3	43.5	43.3	42.4	40.1	40.7	33.8	30.3	27.4	25.1	20.7	20.2	18.9	20.1	20.7
Tasmania:																			
Recurrent purposes	50.3	51.3	46.6	48.9	50.2	54.3	51.5	53.2	54.7	54.3	57.0	60.2	63.4	67.1	71.7	72.2	72.8	72.1	69.0
Capital purposes	49.7	48.7	53.4	51.1	49.8	45.7	48.5	46.8	45.3	45.7	43.0	39.8	36.6	32.9	28.3	27.8	27.2	27.9	31.0
Six states total:																			
Recurrent purposes	51.2	51.9	51.6	53.3	54.5	57.8	56.9	57.8	58.1	56.9	63.4	66.8	70.6	73.2	77.2	78.2	79.7	78.7	78.3
Capital purposes	48.8	48.1	48.4	46.7	45.5	42.2	43.1	42.2	41.9	43.1	36.6	33.2	29.4	26.8	22.8	21.8	20.3	21.3	21.7

Source: Derived from *Payments to or for the States,* Budget Paper No. 7.

[a] Funds for capital purpose are on a gross basis, i.e., before deducting repayments of commonwealth advances to the states and sinking fund payments on state Loan Council borrowings.

Table 15 Australia: nature of intergovernmental transfers

Year	Funds to states for recurrent purposes				Funds to states for capital purposes				Total general purpose		Total specific purpose		Total funds to states
	General revenue funds		Specific purpose payments		General purpose		Specific purpose						
	% inc.	% total	% inc.	% total	% inc.	% total	% inc.	% total	% inc.	% total	% inc.	% total	% inc.
1972–1973		47.1		10.8		27.2		15.0		74.2		25.8	
1973–1974	13.1	44.1	56.4	14.0	-11.7	19.9	77.3	22.0	4.0	64.0	68.6	36.0	20.6
1974–1975	30.7	38.3	98.6	18.4	25.4	16.6	81.8	26.6	29.0	54.8	89.0	45.2	50.6
1975–1976	23.8	36.4	91.2	27.1	18.7	15.1	5.2	21.5	22.3	51.5	39.9	48.5	30.3
1976–1977	19.6	40.7	3.1	26.1	5.0	14.8	-8.5	18.4	15.4	55.5	-2.0	44.5	6.9
1977–1978	16.5	42.5	20.4	28.1	5.7	14.0	-6.3	15.4	13.7	56.5	9.4	43.5	11.8
1978–1979	10.6	44.8	6.1	28.4	—	13.4	-8.7	13.4	7.9	58.2	0.8	41.8	4.8
1979–1980	13.1	47.7	10.3	29.5	-13.2	10.9	-6.4	11.8	7.0	58.6	4.9	41.4	5.2
1980–1981	11.0	48.0	13.1	30.2	5.0	10.4	6.1	11.4	9.9	58.4	11.1	41.6	10.8
1981–1982	31.0	57.5	-21.5	22.2	—	9.5	2.1	10.8	25.5	67.0	-15.1	33.0	8.4
1982–1983	11.6	55.1	23.7	23.6	5.0	8.6	36.8	12.7	10.7	63.7	28.0	36.3	16.4
1983–1984	12.4	54.2	16.4	24.1	7.0	8.0	23.0	13.7	11.7	62.2	18.7	37.8	14.2

Source: Derived from *Payments to or for the States*, Budget Paper No. 7.
* Commencing 1981–1982 general revenue payments include identified health grants that in previous years were classified as a specific purpose health payment.

capital funding. Of course it must be remembered that the unconditional recurrent funding represents nearly half of all Australian intergovernmental transfers, the bulk of it comprising the income tax–sharing arrangements which are determined by a stable formula. In 1983–84 it is worth re-emphasizing that the intergovernmental transfer of funds is made up of 54.2 per cent recurrent funding for general purposes, 24.1 per cent recurrent funding for specific purposes, 8.0 per cent capital funding for general purposes, and 13.7 per cent capital funding for specific purposes. In the years of large increases in overall funding for the states, it has been specific purpose payments of both recurrent and capital funds which have been boosted (more so for recurrent purposes), and in years when the states have been squeezed for federal funds it has been capital funds which have been pruned the most, particularly specific purpose capital funds.

A trend analysis was also performed on a functional breakdown of grants and advances from the commonwealth to the states. The grants for current purposes are mostly taken up with tax sharing, and education was the only other dominant area of current purpose grant funding until 1975–76 when changes to Medibank funding methods made health the only other significant area. All components of grants for current purposes have fluctuated markedly from year to year. In the spread of these current purpose grants among the states distinct variations do occur. The dominant category comprises mainly the tax-sharing/financial assistance grants which, it has already been noted, are distributed by formula amongst the states. Apart from this category, education and health are the dominant areas in this form of funding. In education, it is Victoria which has by far the highest component in its mix, and Tasmania well and truly the lowest, although Queensland and South Australia are quite low too. In such health funds, New South Wales is dominant but Western Australia prominent too, with Queensland and Tasmania quite low. The analysis also revealed that the proportion of current purpose grants to the states devoted to particular functions has varied significantly over the past decade. The mixture of funding is different for each state, but, when that mixture tends to change its composition, it does so in the same direction for every state.

In respect of commonwealth grants to the states for capital purposes, the only dominant functions are roads and education, with a much smaller emphasis on health and welfare, urban public transport, and agricultural activities. Such grant funding has also shown severe annual fluctuations within the overall framework of a reduction of all capital funding over the past few years, which we have already observed. In terms of interstate distribution, the road function has a high emphasis in the mixture of funding for Queensland and Western Australia and, for a while, Tasmania, and a low profile in Victoria and South Australia. In education it is once again Victoria which is dominant and Tasmania which is very low in emphasis, with Western Australia and South Australia also a little lighter in emphasis. Again, the mixture of funding here is different for each state, and shifts in the mixture usually occur in similar directions in all states.

The Commonwealth Advances (loans) to the states are mostly for the states' works programmes under the Loan Council arrangements described elsewhere. Apart from this, housing stands out as the only other noticeable single functional area to be a recipient of such advances, with a small emphasis on the support of agricultural and pastoral industries. Once again there have been marked fluctuations in this form of intergovernmental funding.

Summary

We are now in a position to summarize the main features of Australian intergovernmental transfers. Taken together they represent a very large component of national government outlays, current around 37 per cent and they are progressively increasing in importance. The state governments (and local governments too for that matter) are heavily dependent on intergovernmental transfers as sources of revenue; the degree of vertical imbalance being higher the less populous the state. Moreover, the states are gradually becoming more dependent on intergovernmental funding, although this dependence is now more upon grants than upon advances. The intergovernmental funding in Australia varies markedly from year to year in its magnitude, and annual increases have ranged from 6 per cent to 52 per cent. Commonwealth payments to the states for current purposes tend to change more smoothly than those for capital purposes, and the trend is rapidly towards recurrent rather than capital funding. Indeed, only about one-fifth of intergovernmental transfers in Australia are now for capital purposes. Different states vary in the mixture of recurrent to capital funding but the overall trends are the same in all states. The degree of dependence of state *budget* revenue varies from state to state but there have been no pronounced fluctuations in this factor for all states from year to year. Any changes in commonwealth funding are, of course, accompanied by a commensurate rise and fall in the degree of each state's dependence on its own taxation. The majority (58 per cent) of intergovernmental transfers in Australia are unconditional (that is, general purpose), and income tax sharing dominates the inventory of intergovernmental payments. The other dominant sectors for intergovernmental funding in Australia are education, health, transport (especially roads), and housing. Although the absolute amounts devoted to particular functions have varied widely from year to year, the proportion going to each function has remained fairly constant. In years when there have been substantial boosts in overall intergovernmental funding it has been mainly specific purpose payments which have expanded, predominantly in the form of recurrent payments; and when overall contractions have occurred it has been capital funds which have been squeezed, especially those for specific purposes.

Federal Finance in Canada

No attempt will be made to elaborate upon the history of federal fiscal relations in Canada because that has been handled competently elsewhere.[4] Our concern is primarily to analyse the contemporary features of fiscal federalism in Canada, especially to the extent that they provide useful comparisons with Australian experience.

It must be said immediately that there is a considerably lesser degree of vertical fiscal imbalance in Canada than obtains in the Australian federation. This is not because of any influences in the division of public functions between the levels of government; indeed we have already seen the similarity of the division of powers. Rather it is because of a higher degree of revenue sharing in the Canadian situation, in particular the capacity for the provinces to levy personal and corporate income taxes with the national government, income tax being (as in Australia) the largest single source of government revenue. Since 1977, when arrangements were modified for financing established shared-cost programmes (Established Programmes Financing), an enlarged personal income tax field has been available to the provinces equivalent to about 44 per cent of basic federal tax. However, provincial governments are free to specify rates above or below that level and in the late 1970s the rates were: Newfoundland 58 per cent (i.e., 58 per cent of the basic national tax, which is the national government's income tax after a dividend tax credit but before any foreign tax credit or special national tax reduction), Prince Edward Island 50 per cent, Nova Scotia 52.5 per cent, New Brunswick 55.5 per cent, Ontario 44 per cent, Manitoba 56 per cent, Saskatchewan 58.5 per cent, Alberta 38.5 per cent, and British Columbia 46 per cent. In Quebec provincial income tax is not related to basic federal tax, but is levied at graduated rates which accommodate a national government tax abatement, granted to that province after it "contracted out" its shared-cost programmes in 1964. The national tax abatement now granted to Quebec taxpayers represented 16.5 per cent.

In respect of company tax, in provinces other than Ontario and Quebec, the provincial corporation income tax is imposed on the same bases as that of the national government's corporation income tax. Corporate taxable income earned in a province has been eligible for the 10 per cent national abatement to compensate corporations for provincial taxes payable. In Ontario and Quebec the determination of corporation taxable income followed closely, but not exactly, the national scheme but these provinces collect their own levy. The rates that applied were: Newfoundland 14 per cent (i.e., 14 per cent of the company's income), Nova Scotia 12 per cent, Prince Edward Island 10 per cent, Quebec 12 per cent, and Alberta 11 per cent. Five provinces introduced a preferential low tax rate for small business income. The dual corporate rates for these provinces were: New Brunswick 12 per cent and 9 per cent, Ontario 12 per cent and 9 per cent,

Manitoba 15 per cent and 13 per cent, Saskatchewan 14 per cent and 12 per cent, and British Columbia 15 per cent and 12 per cent.

In 1980–81, the latest years for which figures were available, the gross revenue of the Canadian national government came from the sources outlined in table 16.

Table 16 Canada: national government sources of revenue

Revenue	Percentage of total
Personal income tax	36.5
Corporation income tax	13.9
General sales tax	9.3
Unemployment insurance contributions	5.7
Customs duties	5.5
Universal pension plan levies	4.5
Tobacco and alcoholic beverages tax	2.6
Petroleum levy	2.4
Oil export charge	0.1
Motive fuel taxes	0.8
Other taxes	4.0
Total taxes	85.3
Return on investments	7.4
Sales of goods and services	5.6
Other revenue	1.7
Gross general revenue	100.0

Source: Federal Government Finance (Ottawa: Statistics Canada).

In relation to expenditure of the Canadian national government, transfers to provincial, territory, and local governments have comprised between a fifth and a quarter of the national government's gross general expenditure in the 1970s, as shown in table 17.

Table 17 Canada: federal government transfers

| Time period | Percentage of gross federal expenditure | |
	General purpose transfers to other levels	Total transfers to other levels
1971–1972	8.5	24.1
1974–1975	8.7	21.7
1977–1978	7.6	21.6
1978–1979	6.6	22.1
1980–1981	6.5	19.3

Source: Federal Government Finance (Ottawa: Statistics Canada).

As the figures in table 17 indicate, the bulk of the intergovernmental transfers in Canada (unlike Australia) are for specific purposes rather than for general purposes, and this has been the case for all of the decade of the 1970s. (See table 18.)

Table 18   Canada: transfers to provincial governments, territories, and local governments

Transfers	Percentage of transfers				
	1971–1972	1974–1975	1977–1978	1978–1979	1980–1981
General purpose	35.2	40.2	35.1	30.1	33.1
Specific purpose	64.8	59.8	64.9	69.9	66.9

Source: Federal Government Finance (Ottawa: Statistics Canada).

However, this data conceals the extremely important fact that the mixture of general purpose and specific purpose transfers varies considerably from province to province. Consider table 19 and it is readily apparent that there is an enormous variation, with Newfoundland, Nova Scotia, New Brunswick, and Prince Edward Island receiving a slight majority of transfers in the general purpose form; Quebec having a slight majority in the specific purpose form; and the other provinces receiving the vast majority of their transfers in the specific purpose form. The reasons for this will be examined later but one of the key factors is the equalization payment, which is a general purpose payment of considerable magnitude, and which, naturally, varies between provinces and can vary significantly for the same province from one year to the next. The equalization formulae which have been used in Canada are usually referred to as a "representative tax system", which consists of a broad range of the various taxes and revenues that the ten provinces actually levy. These are classified in such a way as to give separate recognition to the relative provincial capacities to derive funds from taxes and revenues which are distributed in a unique or distinctive way. In calculating equalization, the yield of the representative tax system, namely, twenty-nine individual provincial tax sources, is estimated for each province. This is done by calculating what each tax in the system would yield in each province if applied on the basis of uniform rates and structures to the province's tax bases. The resulting yields of all the taxes in each province are then compared. Since some provinces have richer tax bases than others, the yields vary. Those provinces for which the total yield of the representative tax system is below some prescribed standard are entitled to equalization to bring them up to that standard.[5]

Table 20 throws more light on the nature of Canadian intergovernmental transfers. We have already examined the extent to which total transfers absorb national government expenditure. This table reveals that apart from general purpose transfers, the main functional areas in which large intergovernmental transfers take place are health, social welfare, and education (again very similar to the Australian situation). Another area becoming slightly more prominent is "agriculture, trade and industry and tourism", but most of this funding is taken up in the encouragement of industry. Development of regions, once a fairly significant recipient of intergovernmental funding, has diminished in importance. An Australian observer would be surprised at the low proportion of such funding to be directed to roads, but the road construction and maintenance function is

Table 19 Canada: transfers to provincial governments and territories and local governments

Transfers	Nfld	P.E.I.	N.S.	N.B.	Que.	Ont.	Man.	Sask.	Alta	B.C.	Yuk.	N.W.T.	Total
1971–1972													
General purpose transfers: Percentage of total	54.5	45.8	45.3	45.5	62.7	58.7	29.0	47.3	7.1	2.8	85.4	92.2	35.2
Specific purpose transfers: Percentage of total	45.5	54.2	54.7	54.5	37.3	41.3	71.0	52.7	92.9	97.2	14.6	7.8	64.8
1974–1975													
General purpose transfers: Percentage of total	55.1	52.0	58.4	52.6	67.0	14.9	42.2	35.7	12.5	7.3	80.4	86.1	40.2
Specific purpose transfers: Percentage of total	44.9	48.0	41.6	47.4	33.0	85.1	57.8	64.3	87.5	92.7	19.6	13.9	59.8
1977–1978													
General purpose transfers: Percentage of total	58.2	52.8	60.9	55.0	44.2	13.1	44.3	9.4	18.2	10.0	86.7	90.6	35.1
Specific purpose transfers: Percentage of total	41.8	47.2	39.1	45.0	55.8	86.9	55.7	90.6	81.8	90.0	13.3	9.4	64.9
1978–1979													
General purpose transfers: Percentage of total	58.7	48.5	55.3	52.0	39.6	4.4	39.6	18.8	12.1	5.1	75.0	83.5	30.1
Specific purpose transfers: Percentage of total	41.3	51.5	44.7	48.0	60.4	95.6	60.4	81.2	87.9	94.9	25.0	16.5	69.9
1980–81													
General purpose transfers: Percentage of total	61.1	54.0	58.1	50.1	48.1	4.4	48.8	14.8	7.9	1.3	77.1	86.9	33.1
Specific purpose transfers: Percentage of total	38.9	46.0	41.9	49.9	51.9	95.6	51.2	85.2	92.1	98.7	22.9	13.1	66.9

Source: Derived from *Federal Government Finance* (Ottawa: Statistics Canada).

Table 20   Canada: major federal government transfer payments to provincial governments, territories, and local governments

Major transfers	1972–1973		1974–1975		1977–1978		1978–1979		1980–1981	
	% of transfers	% of gen. exp.	% of transfers	% of gen. exp.	% of transfers	% of gen. exp.	% of transfers	% of gen. exp.	% of transfers	% of gen. exp.
General government	—	—	—	—	*	*	—	—	*	*
Protection of persons and property	0.1	*	0.2	*	0.2	*	0.2	*	*	*
Transport and Communication	1.0	0.2	0.7	0.1	1.4	0.3	1.7	0.4	0.9	0.2
Health	33.5	8.1	31.5	6.9	28.8	6.2	31.8	7.0	30.6	5.9
Social Welfare	10.8	2.6	11.3	2.4	14.9	3.2	15.7	3.5	15.8	3.1
Education	14.0	3.4	9.1	2.0	13.5	2.9	14.3	3.1	13.7	2.6
Natural Resources	0.2	*	1.2	0.4	0.3	*	0.3	0.1	0.4	0.1
Agriculture, Trade, Industry and Tourism	1.7	0.4	3.3	0.7	4.4	0.9	3.9	0.9		
General purpose transfers	35.2	8.5	40.2	8.7	35.1	7.6	30.1	6.6	34.0	6.6
Total transfers†	100.0	24.1	100.0	21.7	100.0	21.6	100.0	22.1	100.0	19.3

Source: Derived from *Federal Government Finance* (Ottawa: Statistics Canada).

* Insignificant or irrelevant.

† Insignificant transfers not tabulated.

more evenly spread in Canada with the provinces having most of the direct responsibility. It should also be noted from this table, and from all other data which follows, that Canadians do not distinguish between funding for capital and recurrent purposes, at least in the tabulation of statistics, and these figures include both types of spending.

Having gained some idea of the dimensions and the nature of Canadian intergovernmental fiscal transfers, the question arises as to what impact they have upon the provinces. To begin with, the figures in table 21 give some idea of the average sources of provincial revenue.

Table 21   Canada: provincial revenue sources

Revenue source	Percentage of estimated gross general revenue	
	1977–1978	1978–1979
Provincial taxes	56.8	53.0
National resource revenue	8.5	10.3
Privileges, licences and permits	2.7	3.0
Sales of goods and services	2.0	2.0
Return on investments	8.5	9.3
Other revenue from own sources	0.9	1.0
Total gross general revenue from own sources	79.5	78.6
General purpose transfers from federal government	6.2	5.8
Specific purpose transfers from other levels	14.3	14.6
Total transfers*	20.5	20.5

Source: Provincial Government Finance (Ottawa: Statistics Canada).
* Insignificant transfers not tabulated.

The key feature of these figures is that, as a whole, Canadian provinces raise nearly eighty per cent of their own revenue requirements, or to put it the other way, they receive only one-fifth of revenue from intergovernmental transfers, a situation of much less dependence, on average, than we noted for the Australian states. However it is equally clear that within that one-fifth of revenue which comes from transfers, specific purpose transfers are double those for general purposes. Another especially interesting facet of these figures, for an Australian comparison at least, is the composition of the provincial tax list. This is elaborated in the following figures in table 22. It can be appreciated from the figures in table 22 that the provinces' own income taxes comprise about half their taxation revenue, and when added to the various "sales" taxes, the figure is swelled to over three-quarters of their tax revenue. The significance of this for Australian comparison is, of course, that none of these taxes is directly available to the Australian states under present arrangements. Overall then, the situation is that Canadian provinces are considerably more autonomous fiscally than are the Australian states in the senses of a lesser general revenue dependence. As we have already observed, about one-fifth of average provincial revenue

Table 22 Canada: provincial taxes revenue

Tax source	Percentage of total	
	1977–1978	1978–1979
Personal income tax	40.8	43.0
Corporation income taxes	9.5	9.8
General sales taxes	21.8	17.4
Motive fuel taxes	7.0	6.2
Tobacco taxes	2.1	2.5
Taxes on successions and gifts	0.7	0.4
Health insurance premiums	4.4	5.5
Social insurance levies	4.8	5.8
Universal pension plan levies	2.8	2.6
Other taxes	6.0	6.6
Total taxes	100.0	100.0

Source: Provincial Government Finance (Ottawa: Statistics Canada).
* Insignificant tax sources not tabulated.

comes by way of intergovernmental transfers. However, table 23 illustrates that the degree of vertical imbalance is far from symmetrical across the whole federation. The level of fiscal autonomy ranges from the highly autonomous provinces of Alberta, British Columbia, Ontario, Saskatchewan, and Quebec, which receive only a relatively small share of their gross revenue from intergovernmental transfers (10.0 per cent, 15.6 per cent, 16.5 per cent, 18.3 per cent, and 21.9 per cent respectively), through to the highly dependent provinces of Prince Edward Island (55.1 per cent), Newfoundland (49.2 per cent), New Brunswick (48.7 per cent), and Nova Scotia (48.2 per cent). Manitoba is at the centre of the range (34.6 per cent), and the fact that it is also geographically at the centre of Canada's east-west string of provinces highlights the fact, revealed in table 23, that it is the western and central provinces which are more independent of fiscal transfers and the eastern provinces which are particularly dependent, largely though not completely attributable to the foundation and application of the horizontal equalization process. Table 23 also reveals that whilst the provinces which have traditionally been more fiscally autonomous have become progressively more so during the past decade, those provinces which have been fiscally dependent have maintained the same degree of dependence on intergovernmental transfers.

Table 23, in addition, reveals the mixture of general and specific purpose funding which was analysed in Table 19. However, table 23 gives a more graphic portrayal because it reveals, for example, that some provinces, namely, Ontario, British Columbia, Alberta, and Saskatchewan, are not at all dependent on general purpose transfers. In 1978–79 general purpose transfers comprised only about 1 per cent or 2 per cent of the revenue of these provinces. Two other provinces, Quebec and Manitoba, have only a minor degree of dependence on general purpose transfers (9.3 per cent and 13.9 per cent of gross revenue respectively). Clearly the

Table 23 Canada: provincial governments and territories revenue sources

Revenue Sources	Percentage of estimated gross general revenue												
Item	Nfld	P.E.I.	N.S.	N.B.	Que.	Ont.	Man.	Sask.	Alta	B.C.	Yuk.	N.W.T.	Total
1971–1972													
Gross revenue from own sources	42.7	47.4	54.5	54.4	74.8	80.5	65.8	60.8	77.1	81.2	34.2	17.0	74.0
General purpose transfers from other levels	30.1	23.5	24.0	22.0	15.9	0.7	9.3	17.6	1.3	0.2	28.7	63.6	9.0
Specific purpose transfers from other levels	27.2	29.1	21.6	23.6	9.3	18.7	24.9	21.7	21.6	18.6	36.6	19.5	17.0
Total transfers	57.3	52.6	45.5	45.6	25.2	19.5	34.2	39.2	22.9	18.8	65.8	83.0	26.0
1974–1975													
Gross revenue from own sources	48.0	45.7	54.9	54.3	77.7	82.9	67.3	72.1	82.9	82.7	29.2	17.1	77.2
General purpose transfers from other levels	28.5	29.2	26.1	24.1	10.3	0.8	14.9	13.3	6.6	1.2	25.3	62.2	7.9
Specific purpose transfers from other levels	23.5	25.1	19.0	21.6	11.9	16.3	18.7	14.6	10.5	16.1	45.5	20.7	14.9
Total transfers	52.0	54.3	45.1	45.7	22.3	17.1	32.7	27.9	17.1	17.3	70.8	82.9	22.8
1977–1978													
Gross revenue from own sources	51.6	43.6	54.1	56.2	78.4	83.8	68.3	87.8	88.8	83.4	22.9	11.4	79.0
General purpose transfers from other levels	27.6	28.4	27.3	22.1	9.8	1.0	13.4	-4.2	1.1	1.0	36.2	57.3	6.5
Specific purpose transfers from other levels	20.8	28.0	18.6	21.7	11.8	15.2	18.3	16.4	10.1	15.6	40.9	31.3	14.4
Total transfers	48.4	56.4	45.9	43.8	21.6	16.2	31.7	12.2	11.2	16.6	77.1	88.6	21.0
1978–79													
Gross revenue from own sources	50.8	44.9	51.8	51.3	78.1	83.5	65.4	81.7	90.0	84.4	18.9	17.5	78.9
General purpose transfers from other levels	28.7	29.7	28.3	25.9	9.3	-0.1	13.9	1.9	0.7	0.4	34.0	50.0	6.2
Specific purpose transfers from other levels	20.5	25.4	19.9	22.8	12.6	16.6	20.7	16.4	9.3	15.1	47.1	32.5	14.9
Total transfers	49.2	55.1	48.2	48.7	21.9	16.5	34.6	18.3	10.0	15.6	81.1	82.5	21.1

Source: Derived from *Provincial Government Finance: Revenue and Expenditure Estimates* (Ottawa: Statistics Canada).

Canadian situation is that those provinces which have a very low degree of dependence on intergovernmental transfers have the transfers they do receive in the specific purpose form. Those provinces which are highly dependent on intergovernmental transfers receive their transfers in a fairly even mix but with a majority in the general purpose form. (This is because equalization is by way of general purpose transfers and is only up to a national average standard.) In other words, the heavier the degree of dependence on intergovernmental transfers, the greater the general purpose component of the transfers, and conversely, the lower the degree of dependence on intergovernmental transfers, the greater the specific purpose content. Nonetheless, the most telling generalization of this table is the simple fact that about half of the provinces in Canada raise four-fifths or more of their income and the other half raise around one-half of their own revenue. This can be compared with the Australian situation where, as we have already noted, no state raises as much as half of its own receipts and most raise only about one-third of their own receipts. In 1978-79 the percentage of total state receipts raised from own sources were Victoria 44 per cent, New South Wales 41 per cent, Queensland 34 per cent, South Australia and Western Australia 33 per cent, and Tasmania 31 per cent.[6] Quite evidently there is a lesser degree of vertical fiscal imbalance in the Canadian federation than in the Australian federation, although the incidence of vertical imbalance in Canada is much less symmetrical than it is in Australia. Maybe this is just another way of saying that Australia has a greater degree of vertical imbalance but a lesser degree of horizontal imbalance.

A trend analysis for individual Canadian provinces of provincial government revenue sources and their annual fluctuations shows that overall there has been an absence of any marked fluctuations in gross general revenue, and that has been true for all provinces. A couple of provinces have experienced wider fluctuations than others, namely, Manitoba, Saskatchewan, Alberta, and British Columbia, with particularly large changes in certain years. Interestingly, different sources of revenue present a picture which differs by province. Provincial personal income tax has grown fairly smoothly in total and in most provinces. Corporation income tax revenue in the provinces has displayed substantial annual fluctuations and that pattern is characteristic of every province. Sales taxes have produced provincial revenue which has fluctuated substantially in all provinces, while annual changes in revenue from motive fuel taxes have been remarkably smooth in all but two provinces (Alberta and Saskatchewan). The picture for revenue from all other forms of provincial taxation is one of considerable fluctuation year to year in all provinces, whilst non-tax revenue from the provinces' own sources has displayed even growth in the vast majority of provinces. Our particular interest is in revenue coming to the provinces from intergovernmental transfers and here the overall provincial pattern has been one of annual variations, but not perhaps as marked as for other sources of provincial revenue, though significant nonetheless.

In some provinces, namely, Newfoundland, Prince Edward Island, Nova Scotia, Quebec, and to a lesser extent New Brunswick, there has been a smooth pattern of annual increases, but in all the other provinces there has been a pattern of pronounced annual variations (both increases and decreases), particularly in the case of Ontario, British Columbia, Alberta, and Saskatchewan. Once again it is a geographical pattern with the eastern provinces recording the smooth flow of intergovernmental transfers, and the central and western provinces experiencing rises and falls in the revenue they gain from such transfers. This is of course, as we have seen, another way of saying that the provinces most dependent on fiscal transfers receive those transfers in a pattern of smooth annual growth, but those provinces which are less dependent on fiscal transfers receive their transfers more in fits and starts. We shall examine this phenomenon further when we consider Canadian conditional funding in more detail.

The Hindrances to Planning

What is it about federal financial relationships which could frustrate attempts at forecasting, priority determination, allocation of resources, implementation of that resource allocation, and a review of these processes? The literature has been scoured to cast light on each of these points, and in addition, every interviewee was asked at length to consider each element, and the system as a whole, in the light of his experience with federal financial dealings. What has resulted is a vast array of polemic — not always supported by tangible evidence, and often contradictory between literature source and respondent. We shall now examine all of these arguments in turn seeking to determine their veracity and significance. It is worth recalling that it is politics which lies behind most federal fiscal relationships, and thus it is natural that those authors or respondents associated with a particular level of government should stress the hindrances which they claim another level causes for them, but downplay the hindrances which their actions produce for others. We shall examine first the more general arguments relating to the federal fiscal process, and then move to a separate analysis of the debate surrounding conditional funding which lies at the hub of the controversy over fiscal transfers.

General Perspectives

We have seen that the Australian federal system, and to a lesser extent the Canadian, is typified by sizeable transfers of finance from the national to the subnational level. Commensurately the level of tax sharing in Australia is much less than it is in Canada. In view of this situation, it is not surprising that national governments should argue that they are hindered in the determination of their own priorities because of the need to allocate a substantial share of the revenue they raise back to the states/provinces in the form of transfers, especially if it is difficult for the national government to control the size of those transfers. This is somewhat linked to the argument, also often advanced at the national level, that if too large a proportion of national government expenditure is transferred away to other levels, or if too large a proportion of taxation space is shared with other levels, that will hinder the national government's attempts to regulate the economy using fiscal policy and thereby set overall goals for the whole economy. (It should be noted that no government and no other source has yet come up with a definitive statement on just how much national control is necessary for economic management purposes.)

Some other arguments which are advanced in favour of greater fiscal centralization have already been encountered when we were speaking of intergovernmental agreements. They include the need to cope with spillovers, mobility of resources, and horizontal equalization. There is also an argument advanced that greater fiscal centralization allows citizens to deal primarily with one level of government in relation to taxation and that makes administration simple, uniform, and, it is claimed, more efficient. It is often pointed out as well that by assuming responsibility for the bulk of taxation, the national government is insulating the subnational levels from the vagaries of fluctuations in economic activity reflected in jolts to public revenue collections, especially if firm long term agreements have been signed between the national and subnational governments for a guaranteed transfer of funds. In view of all these arguments, and others, the national governments in both Australia and Canada see the processes of fiscal transfers as an extra burden for them to carry and an additional complicating factor in the determination of how funds in the central coffers are to be allocated.

The states and provinces, on the other hand, see the large degree of vertical fiscal imbalance as a result of their legitimate revenue entitlements having been raided by the national government, so that the fiscal transfers which occur are nothing less than their just deserts. In other words, they tend to view the national government simply as their collection agency, and regard it as axiomatic that they should be entitled to an automatic guaranteed share of national government spending.[7] Of course they are dissatisfied about their level of dependence on the national government which, as we noted, is much higher for Australian states than for Canadian provinces and, of course, much higher for some states than others, and much higher for some provinces than others. There has been an added concern, as the years have rolled by since the second world war, that the national government has come to regard payments to the states/provinces as just another national programme which should compete with other national programmes during budget deliberations. (In Australia this is symbolized, in the view of the states, in the change of name of the tax-sharing arrangements from "Taxation Reimbursement Grants" to "Financial Assistance Grants" in 1959–60.) Thus, in times of public sector cutbacks the national government will apply the same outlook to the fiscal inter-level transfer payments that it does to other programmes in its budget, most of which are its own constitutional responsibility under the division of powers. It is also the claim of the subnational units that this situation of vertical imbalance makes it quite difficult for them to predict the volume of funds they will receive each year both in total and by individual compo-nent. Because of their dependence on the transfers, and because of the in-tricacies of timing, they claim this makes it very difficult to forecast ahead on the revenue side and hence make long term commitments on their own expenditure side.

Invariably these arguments quickly move to a debate over the manner in which the vertical imbalance should be rectified. It might be expected at first glance that subnational units of government would prefer to be given increased forms of taxes, or a bigger share of joint taxation to serve this end. That has certainly been the case in Canada, although even there the view has not been unanimous at that level for the simple reason that some provinces have a worse tax base than others, and they know that to accept greater tax room in return for reduced vertical transfers is to penalize them in relation to richer provinces. Only the promise of horizontal equaliza-tion has allayed their fears. In Australia the reasons are more pragmatic. The states have long complained that they no longer levy their own income taxes (despite the fact that they could re-enter that field at any time). And yet on a couple of occasions when the national government has encouraged states to resume taxation of incomes they have politely declined the offer, realizing the odium which goes with taxation, and preferring instead to be able to blame Canberra for their economic ills. It is exemplified to some extent also in the refusal of the Australian states to adopt phase two of the Fraser government's new federalism arrangements and impose their own income tax surcharges or grant rebates, although it must be emphasized that the national government did not withdraw from part of the tax field to let the states in, in the way that the Canadian na-tional government has always reduced its own tax burden by an amount equal to that which it arranges for the provinces to occupy. Perhaps part of the explanation for the different attitude in Canada lies in the existence of Quebec which, more for philosophical reasons, has always favoured transfer of taxes rather than funds, but it also owes something to Ontario's attitude of willingness to share responsibility with the national government for national fiscal policy across the whole nation.

These arguments serve to highlight a point often made in the literature,[8] that the separation of taxation from expenditure is inherently dangerous because it promotes irresponsibility in public expenditure to the extent that the spending government is not required to raise the necessary revenue, and by the same token the taxing government cannot be fully held to account for the final destination of those taxes. A somewhat related point is that to separate taxation from spending leads to less rational appraisal of expenditure priorities for both levels of government, especially as the expenditure decision is thus made in isolation from political demands.

It is those sorts of arguments which lie at the heart of the debate over the means to be used to rectify the inevitable fiscal imbalance in these federations. The attitude of the Australian states, and to a slightly lesser extent the Canadian provinces, is conditioned to a large extent by a number of what they claim to be basic factors relating to the nature of their fiscal activity:

1. The sorts of taxes available to them in their own right, under the respective constitutions, are, they claim, mostly not growth taxes. (This use of the word "growth" is very misleading. When Australian states and Canadian provinces use the term they regard only personal income and company income tax as well as excise duties as being "growth" taxes, losing sight of the fact that their payroll tax, liquor, racing, tobacco, and lottery taxes are also "growth" taxes, not to mention some major stamp duties such as those on conveyances.) Also, many of the taxes are regressive. Therefore it is difficult for them to make a quick response from their own resources to any changes in the level of federal funding.

2. It follows that it is unlikely that their own revenue sources will provide sufficient funds to keep pace with expenditure needs, if only because the division of functions under the constitution has left the states and provinces with the sorts of public functions increasingly in demand, especially those related to welfare and the provision of economic infrastructure.

3. A very large proportion of the expenditure of each Australian state and each Canadian province is already uncontrollable in the sense that it is devoted to wages and salaries and interest on debts. (The increasing level of indebtedness is itself a by-product of the vertical fiscal imbalance in the two federations.) As these subnational units are not completely autonomous in their own revenue raising they are left, they claim, with little room to shift priorities in their expenditure allocations. The addition of revenue dependence on another level of government simply complicates the whole matter and, so the states and provinces argue, adds yet another major constraint on their ability to be able to determine their own priorities.

Against these factors must be weighed a number of counter-arguments:

1. Fluctuations in economic activity, especially as they affect the subnational level, are such that a state or province would find it much easier to forecast their revenue from formulae-determined grants from the national government than it would be to forecast revenue from their own direct and indirect taxes. This is especially true in Australia and Canada because the major pattern of fiscal transfer has usually been by means of formulae, whose components, whilst not being

stable, are less prone to fluctuation than the return from direct and indirect taxes, and especially as the national governments of both countries have inevitably inserted a guarantee into such formulae to provide a floor or minimum level of transfer to the subnational units.

2. The states and provinces have often artificially constrained their own internal fiscal priority determination process by establishing earmarking of certain taxes for trust funds, and erecting artificial division of spending into capital and current accounts, and other accounting divisions such as "economic" and "social". (This division has applied for example in the province of New Brunswick where the government has seen fit to view government spending as being for "economic" or for "social" purposes, loosely translated as being for future or present purposes, on the basis of the argument that welfare expenditure is a once only item but spending geared to the promotion of economic development provides a basis for the generation of future government revenue.)

3. They have also underexploited modes of taxation legally available to them under the constitution.[9]

4. These factors have been compounded by the attitude of state and provincial governments to local government, whereby they have locked themselves into various support schemes, and encouraged local government towards a degree of dependence on them which is reminiscent of their dependence on the national government.

5. With respect to the overriding problem of wage costs the states and provinces have not taken a tough enough stance on wage negotiations, especially where (as in Canada) they have devolved or decentralized the power of wage negotiation in relation to wages which must ultimately be paid out of their coffers. These arguments arise most often in relation to the salaries in the education and health system.

6. A similar argument applies to the general pattern of fragmentation of government activity at the state/provincial level whereby their own funds, and particularly those which come from intergovernmental transfers, are dispersed through a multitude of departments, agencies, public enterprises, crown corporations, marketing boards, banks, utilities, and other semigovernment bodies and qangos, all of which have varying degrees of autonomy and therefore preclude any sort of centralized rational priority determination within any individual state or province. In other words, it is wrong to blame national government impingement on the subnational level for distorting the latter's planning potential when their own structure and processes are largely at fault, and would be even without revenue or responsibility sharing with the national government.

7. It is also relevant that states and provinces have seen fit, for social and political reasons, to subsidize many of their own government activities (especially public transportation and other utilities), usually by

way of concessional charges, so that the full scale and extent of the subsidization is hidden, and has been so for decades. That also means that it would be extremely difficult for such subnational units to engage in any rational reallocation of resources irrespective of the source of the revenue.

These arguments do, of course, assume a relatively stable relationship between the levels of government in their fiscal dealings, as the mention of formulae would imply. But of course that has not been true of either country, and the major elements of the transfer of funds have been subject to constant political negotiation, even though the formulae provide a starting point. We can note here that, broadly speaking, intergovernmental fiscal transfers in Australia and Canada are constantly open to political manoeuvring, and to that extent an element of uncertainty is projected at all times across the fiscal processes we are describing and debating.

So far we have been speaking in an extremely broad way about the fiscal imbalance in these federations, which stems from the division of powers. However, the real issues are to be found more in terms of the nature of the means used to alleviate that imbalance, and in Australia and Canada that means a discussion of the merits of general and specific purpose funding or, in Canadian terms, unconditional or conditional funding.

Federal Finance: The Conditional Funding Debate

In Australia the preference of all the states is undoubtedly for unconditional fiscal transfers from the national government, and it goes without saying that they prefer these transfers to be as large as possible. Nonetheless they have usually been more concerned with the share of funding each state would receive, and have rarely focused their attention on the size of the *total* national payout to the states. On a few occasions when it seemed the states would press for a radical restructuring of the system and a larger share for all, the national government was able effectively to call their bluff. (One notable exception occurred in 1970 when the national (Gorton) government took over $1,000 million of state debts over five years. This occurred in response to an approach by all states for a radical restructuring of the system.)

The net result is that the size of the total fiscal transfer from national to state level in Australia has remained relatively stable, being affected only on those very rare occasions when a shift in taxation powers has taken place, as with receipts duty and payroll tax, or when a function has been transferred, as with the handover by some states of their railway systems. However even on these isolated occasions, the fiscal transfer from national to state level has been adjusted by an amount equal to, or close to, the amount of the tax being handed over or the cost of the function being acquired. (Adjustments for Tertiary Education have provided equal reimbursement, but in the cases of railway takeover and transfer of payroll tax the states gained some bonuses.) Under what was termed phase three of the new federalism arrangements of the Fraser government, the national government even spoke of handing over a few national functions to the states but without adjusting the fiscal transfer to accommodate the accompanying expenditure. Also, the Australian states all adhere rigidly to the balanced budget doctrine, believing that they have no role, or an extremely limited role, in economic management. Consequently it is not surprising that their attention is riveted too intensely on the formula which governs the transfer of funds from the national government to the states, and it must be pointed out that the components of past formulae, for example, population movements, wage rises, and the betterment factor, are such that forecasting revenue from the national government has not been particularly difficult. The situation under the Fraser federalism arrangements was slightly different in that the states were guaranteed a fixed share of income tax, as well as a guaranteed minimum, and for some reason the national treasury in Australia found it difficult to forecast income tax receipts and indirect taxation receipts with much accuracy. The states have also not been impressed in recent years when the national government has unilaterally imposed taxation surcharges which it claims to be outside the tax-sharing federal arrangements. Nor has it helped when the national government has vacillated on tax indexation, so that in one year the growth of income tax revenue has been capped, whereas in other years it has been left prone to the vagaries of inflation. This argument also applies when there is uncertainty about the national government's determination to proceed with taxation changes announced in its budget, as with taxation on dependants' incomes, family trusts, and capital gains. It is again relevant when the national government has appeared to give serious consideration to a shift of emphasis from direct to indirect taxation, or in more recent times, for allocative as well as revenue reasons to impose an oil and natural gas levy, and use burgeoning revenue from excise duty on energy sources to lower the severity of income taxation as well as refusing to allow the states a direct share of energy taxes. All of these aspects, claim the states, create considerable uncertainty as to the size of the revenue they can anticipate from the major fiscal transfers from the national government, and that, in turn, affects their ability to forecast and engage in priority determination.

In Canada the preference of the provinces has been far from uniform. As indicated earlier, Quebec has always favoured the national government handing over taxation powers rather than fiscal transfers, and because the Canadian arrangements operate on the basis mainly of income tax sharing this has inevitably meant granting of tax points to the province. In recent years the larger, more affluent provinces have favoured this method of rectifying imbalance also. The middle and smaller sized provinces do not favour this method because of their more limited tax bases, and they will only accept such a solution if it is accompanied by a strong equalization element. However, all Canadian provinces (including probably Quebec) would agree that there is some limit to the degree of tax sharing that can take place, and they face the inevitable consequence of there having to be fiscal transfers from the national to subnational level. It is at this point that they adopt the same stance as their Australian counterparts and plead for those transfers to be unconditional, for basically the same reasons.

It is most significant that the interviews found no serious complaints from the Canadian provinces about the revenue-sharing arrangements. Whilst the timing of the receipt of the revenue had occasionally caused concern, the actual forecasting of such revenue occasioned no alarm, and the provinces seem to have a very harmonious relationship with the national ministry of finance which, in turn, seemed far more competent than its Australian counterpart at predicting income tax receipts and far more willing to share that intelligence with the provinces. There are also a number of other avenues of economic forecasting available to the Canadian provinces which would not be available to the Australian states.

The arguments which were advanced about the attitude of the Australian states to the size of the fiscal transfers to them from the national government, apply with equal force to the Canadian provinces which have also usually had difficulty "getting their act together", although it is not as serious a matter in Canada since the degree of dependence on these transfers is not as great. There have been difficulties with elements of the transfer, as with the equalization programme where inordinate delays have occurred in receipt of funds by the "have not" provinces, and miscalculations have occasionally resulted in the national government having to ask a recipient government to return a portion of the money it received in an earlier year — a politically pregnant action. Because of the construction and operation of the Canadian horizontal equalization formula there is always the distinct possibility (and in recent years reality) that taxation decisions in the largest provinces will affect equalization receipts in the poorer provinces, as occurred with sales tax cuts in Ontario and Alberta. In other words, the amount of revenue received out of equalization by a "have not" province can be significantly affected by a policy decision in another province. (It would appear that the same thing could occur in Australia if a standard state alters its taxation policy.)

This discussion has related to the total size of the fiscal transfer between the levels of government. It has been orientated towards unconditional funding within that transfer, which is especially appropriate to Australia because the bulk of the fiscal transfer in that federation is unconditional. Some of the aspects which were canvassed identified possible hindrances to the attainment of public sector planning at the subnational level, although the Canadian experience would seem to demonstrate that these difficulties need not loom so large. These arguments, however, pale into insignificance when compared with the passions aroused over the other type of funding not yet discussed, namely, conditional or specific purpose funding. We shall examine these arguments at length for the very reason that national governments believe such funding to be necessary to achieve their priorities, whereas state/provincial governments claim such funding to be the single most significant aspect of interference with their own priority determination. Over the past decade there has been more written and spoken about conditional funding than any other single aspect of federal financial relationships, and most of it is misleading in the extreme.

The Reasons for Conditional Funding[1]

Conditional transfers are initiated by national governments because of what they perceive to be national needs for government action. Thus they apply in situations that we have already encountered, such as when there is a need to ensure a minimum standard of government service or to capture spillovers, cope with resource mobility and to equalize. The national government may also wish to ensure that the money is spent in the designated way because it wishes to be seen to be responsible for the programme, especially if the particular programme formed a clear part of its election mandate. There is also the frequent political consideration that the national government wishes to receive the credit for the particular programme which is being funded, through the means of a conditional grant, implying that it will also accept the blame if things go wrong.

It can also be the case that the national government wishes to see a greater accent given to government services already provided by states/provinces. In this case it is a deliberate superimposition of national emphasis on subnational activity, and is very often accompanied by fiscal and administrative measures to make sure that the subnational units do not withdraw their level of support to that activity by merely substituting national funds for their own. If the national government were to give money for a particular purpose but did not attach conditions of minimum accompanying expenditure, there would be little point in specifying the purpose in the first place, because the recipient governments would merely substitute those funds for others. This can lead additionally to the attachment of even further conditions to prevent national expenditure from going out of control at the behest of a state or province as, for example, when a conditional grant is negotiated solely on the basis of so much money from the national government for each dollar spent by a subnational government — the method used in this case would be to impose a ceiling on national expenditure.

There are many other reasons advanced by national governments for the use of conditional funding. Once a decision has been made that a national need exists for a particular type of government service it may be desired to ensure that the programme is characterized by uniformity in provision, portability in entitlement, universality in coverage, and accessibility to all. The easiest way to achieve these aims is seen to be the attachment of conditions to the grants given to the subnational governments for the purpose. Conditional grants can also be used to prod or stimulate subnational governments in particular fields of activity perceived at the national level as having been neglected or requiring quick and vigorous action in the short term, as for example with unemployment relief.

Conditional grants are often devised and offered by national governments who perceive that there are gaps in the programmes already being offered by states/provinces. This can occur for example in welfare programmes, and was part of the reason for the Canada Assistance Plan. This example also reminds us that it has not been uncommon for provincial governments themselves to request the national funding in the first place, and some conditional grants have begun this way. Whilst on the subject of welfare, the conditional grant programmes in the welfare area have often been designed in a way that ensures unification of administration of welfare measures, experimentation by the recipient governments including research and development, and the special consideration of certain groups, such as Eskimos or Aborigines, or groups for whom the national government feels particularly responsible.

This is by no means an exhaustive inventory of the origins of conditional funding[2] but it does point to the basic reason for their use, namely, to identify, establish, and monitor the priorities of the national government, and to overcome the major weakness of unconditional funding which divorces taxation decisions from expenditure decisions and so breaks down political sensitivity and accountability. In both Australia and Canada the question of horizontal equalization always lurks behind the scene and exerts a strong influence on conditional funding, either by means of injecting some sort of equalization process into each conditional programme, or by means of the argument, often advanced at the national level in Canada, that any reduction in conditional funding would make provinces even more dependent on the formal equalization programme itself and so be more vulnerable to changes in it. Conditional grants, argues the national government, represent a fixed commitment from the national government, with the conditions inevitably determined only after detailed analysis of provincial conditions and consultations with provincial governments. It helps achieve the implementation of national priorities through the subnational governments as delivery mechanisms and spending agencies. The question of how these conditional grants affect priorities of the subnational governments will be examined soon, but for the moment we can accept Lane's analysis that specific purpose grants in Australia are used for four basic purposes: (1) correction for vertical imbalance; (2) correction for horizontal imbalance; (3) promotion and/or control of expenditure on specific functions or projects; and (4) particularly pressing problems like unemployment relief or natural disaster relief.[3] This analysis is also pertinent to Canada although the Canadian constitution, on the face of it, does not give anything like the carte blanche approach available to the Australian national government under the High Court's interpretation of the wording of Section 96, which in effect, allows the national government to attach whatever conditions it wishes to grants made to the states. In this respect Smiley makes the observation that in Canada there are four main limitations on the national government's spending power:

1. provinces and local governments have the right to participate or not;
2. the national government cannot oust a province from what is a provincial constitutional activity — it must use the province;
3. conditional grants have little relevance to the sharing of power with respect to regulatory functions; and
4. under the *British North America Act* the national parliament cannot contribute to a particular provincial activity from the proceeds of a national levy made for that purpose.

The practice, if not the constitutional theory of these conditions, would apply to the Australian situation as well.[4]

The Nature of Conditional Funding in Australia

The following figures, in table 24, show the break-up of intergovernment fiscal transfers in Australia as between funds for general purposes and specific purposes.

Table 24   Australia: commonwealth payments to the states and Loan Council borrowings

Time period	For general purposes			For specific purposes			Total
	Amount $M	% of total	% increase	Amount $M	% of total	% increase	% increase
1972–1973	2682.9	74.2		931.5	25.8		
1973–1974	2790.5	64.0	4.0	1570.1	36.0	68.6	20.6
1974–1975	3600.9	54.8	29.0	2967.0	45.2	89.0	50.6
1975–1976	4402.6	51.5	22.3	4152.3	48.5	39.9	30.3
1976–1977	5078.6	55.5	15.4	4068.5	44.5	-2.0	6.9
1977–1978	577.2	56.5	13.7	4449.1	43.5	9.4	11.8
1978–1979	6234.2	58.2	7.9	4485.6	41.8	0.8	4.8
1979–1980	6673.3	58.6	7.0	4706.0	41.4	4.9	6.2
1980–1981	7325.3	57.9	9.8	5334.9	42.1	13.4	11.3
1981–1982	9192.7	67.0	*	4529.6	33.0	*	8.4

Source: *Payments to or for the States, The Northern Territory and Local Government Authorities*, Budget Paper No. 7 (Canberra: AGPS).
* Not applicable because of different definition of health funding.

It is evident from table 24 that the bulk of intergovernmental transfers in Australia (since 1942) have been in the form of general purpose payments, although it is true that the proportion of general to specific purpose funding became almost equal in the mid 1970s as a result of the Whitlam government's policy of using conditional funding. The relationship, by 1981–82, seemed to have flattened out with around 58 per cent of transfers being general purpose and 42 per cent for specific purposes, as contrasted with the beginning of the 1970s when only one-quarter of intergovernmental transfers were for specific purposes. (Unfortunately, inconsistency in the compilation of these statistics prevents us from extending the table further backwards in time.) In the years of very large increases in overall intergovernmental funding it has been specific purpose payments which have expanded most significantly. Similarly, when a sharp contraction has occurred it has been mostly in specific purpose funding, although figures for the latest year available would tend to suggest that the two forms of payments are now in something of a fixed relationship. Nonetheless, the important point remains that specific purpose payments have changed in fits and starts compared with a much smoother pattern of annual variation in general purpose funding.

Table 25 gives a further breakdown of specific purpose intergovernmental payments in Australia between those for recurrent and those for capital purposes.

Table 25   Australia: specific purpose payments

Time period	For recurrent purposes			For capital purposes			Total	
	Amount $M	% of total	% increase	Amount $M	% of total	% increase	% increase	
1972–1973	390.0	41.9		54.15	58.1			
1973–1974	609.9	38.8	56.4	960.2	61.2	77.3	68.6	
1974–1975	1211.5	40.8	98.6	1745.5	58.8	81.8	89.0	
1975–1976	2315.9	55.8	91.2	1836.3	44.2	5.2	39.9	
1976–1977	2387.6	58.7	3.1	1680.9	41.3	-8.5	-2.0	
1977–1978	2873.9	64.6	20.4	1575.2	35.4	-6.3	9.4	
1978–1979	3047.8	67.9	6.1	1437.8	32.1	-8.7	0.8	
1979–1980	3360.3	71.4	10.3	1345.8	28.6	-6.4	4.9	
1980–1981	3885.8	72.8	15.6	1449.2	27.2	7.7	13.4	
1981–1982	3049.4	67.3	-21.5	1480.2	32.7	2.1	-15.1	
1982–1983E	3516.0	65.1	15.3	1883.0	34.9	27.2	19.2	

Source: Payments to or for the States, The Northern Territory and Local Government Authorities, Budget Paper No. 7 (Canberra: AGPS).
E Estimate.

Table 25 reveals an unmistakable trend of the 1970s for a shift in the mixture of specific purpose payments from capital to recurrent funding. By the end of the decade, recurrent purposes claimed 73 per cent of all specific purpose payments compared with 42 per cent in 1972–73. In this respect the turning point, clearly, was 1975–76 when there was a most significant decline in the growth of specific purpose payments for capital purposes. From that time, each year witnessed an actual reduction in specific purpose capital payments until 1980–81, when a flattening out occurred. On the other hand, specific purpose payments for recurrent purposes have seen a small amount of growth in real terms. The annual movements in both forms of specific purpose funding display quite an erratic pattern.

Having identified the relevance of specific purpose payments in the total dimension of Australian intergovernmental transfers, we now turn to the pattern that applies for individual states, as revealed in table 26. As can be seen every state in Australia has, during this period, almost always received a higher proportion of commonwealth government funding in the general purpose form, the only exceptions being New South Wales and Victoria in 1975–76, but the mixture varies significantly from state to state. The two most populous states, New South Wales and Victoria, have received a significantly lower proportion of their funding in the general purpose form than have the other four states, but this has only been the case since 1974–75. Queensland has generally received a slightly above average proportion of general purpose funding but once again this has only been since 1974–75, and before that year Queensland was slightly below the average for the general purpose component of the mixture. A similar situation existed for Western Australia. South Australia has, for most of the past fifteen years, had a higher mixture of general purpose

Table 26 Australia: total commonwealth payments and Loan Council borrowings

Recipient state	1965–66	1966–67	1967–68	1968–69	1969–70	1970–71	1971–72	1972–73	1973–74	1974–75	1975–76	1976–77	1977–78	1978–79	1979–80	1980–81	1981–82	1982–83	1983–84
New South Wales:																			
General purposes	74.2	74.2	74.2	75.5	75.0	75.2	77.9	74.1	63.1	52.5	49.1	53.2	54.2	55.6	55.9	54.8	66.6	63.8	61.2
Specific purposes	25.8	25.8	25.8	24.5	25.0	24.8	22.1	25.9	36.9	47.5	50.9	46.8	45.8	44.4	44.1	45.2	33.4	36.2	38.8
Victoria:																			
General purposes	77.6	77.4	75.4	75.9	76.6	76.0	78.9	74.8	63.2	51.4	48.2	52.4	53.9	55.2	55.8	54.9	64.3	61.6	60.6
Specific purposes	22.4	22.6	24.6	24.1	23.4	24.0	21.1	25.2	36.8	48.6	51.8	47.6	46.1	44.8	44.2	45.1	35.7	38.4	39.4
Queensland:																			
General purposes	73.0	73.2	68.9	74.8	71.6	72.1	72.3	70.4	62.4	56.6	55.1	57.9	59.4	60.9	60.6	60.8	70.5	64.9	63.1
Specific purposes	27.0	26.8	31.1	25.2	28.4	27.9	27.7	29.6	37.6	43.4	44.9	42.1	40.6	39.1	39.4	39.2	29.5	35.1	36.9
South Australia:																			
General purposes	72.6	73.5	73.5	71.4	72.6	74.5	81.2	78.7	65.4	59.2	54.8	59.1	58.9	61.9	63.0	62.7	64.1	60.3	63.7
Specific purposes	27.4	26.5	26.5	28.6	27.4	25.5	18.8	21.3	34.6	40.8	45.2	40.9	41.1	38.1	37.0	37.3	35.9	39.7	36.3
Western Australia:																			
General purposes	69.6	69.4	67.9	70.0	70.5	72.5	74.4	71.7	64.7	57.0	53.8	57.8	58.1	59.9	61.5	60.3	71.1	68.6	65.9
Specific purposes	30.4	30.6	32.1	30.0	29.5	27.5	25.6	28.3	35.3	43.0	46.2	42.2	41.9	40.1	38.5	39.7	28.9	31.4	34.1
Tasmania:																			
General purposes	80.2	79.1	74.1	77.9	77.0	79.6	81.1	79.3	73.2	65.4	59.5	65.4	65.7	68.6	68.7	67.3	67.4	65.5	63.4
Specific purposes	19.8	20.9	25.9	22.1	23.0	20.4	18.9	20.7	26.8	34.6	40.5	34.6	34.3	31.4	31.3	32.7	32.6	34.5	36.6
Six states total																			
General purposes	73.9	74.5	72.9	74.5	74.2	74.8	77.4	74.2	64.0	54.8	51.5	55.5	56.5	58.2	58.6	57.9	67.0	63.7	62.2
Specific purposes	26.1	25.5	27.1	25.5	25.8	25.2	22.6	25.8	36.0	45.2	48.5	44.5	43.5	41.8	41.4	42.1	33.0	36.3	37.8

Percentage of total

Source: Derived from *Payments to or for the States*, Budget Paper No. 7.

funding than the average and reached a record 81.2 per cent of funding in this form in 1971–72. Tasmania was substantially above the Australian average in relation to the mix of general purpose funding, and has been so throughout most of the period under review.

But perhaps the most basic point to be made is that, since the mid 1960s, specific purpose payments have never exceeded general purpose payments in the four less populous states — never exceeding 45 per cent of the total intergovernmental transfers. In the two most populous states there has been only one (common) year when they have exceeded general purpose funding, and even then it was only by one or two per cent and in a year of large overall intergovernmental funding. Whilst it is year-by-year funding which is of greatest concern to us here, it is of interest that the average of the annual specific purpose mixtures for the various states since 1965–66 is 35 per cent for New South Wales, 35 per cent for Victoria, 34 per cent for Queensland, 32 per cent for South Australia, 35 per cent for Western Australia, and 27 per cent for Tasmania, compared with an average for the six states of 34 per cent. In other words, the average pattern in Australian states has been for around one-third of all intergovernmental fiscal transfers to be in the specific purpose form. There have been some individual years when the mixture of general to specific purpose funding has altered sharply, especially in 1973–4 to 1976–7 (reflecting two changes of national government, and 1981–82 (reflecting changes in the treatment of health grants), but for the most part the change in the mixture has been fairly gradual in all states. It appears to have settled down into a stable relationship in the past few years in all states, although the less populous states are now receiving a significantly smaller proportion of their funding in specific purpose payments than are New South Wales and Victoria.

We now turn to an examination of the functions of government to which intergovernmental conditional funding is directed in Australia. Table 27 presents the distribution of specific purpose grants for recurrent purposes during most of the 1970s. Without question the dominant functional area until 1980–81 was the running costs of public hospitals, with tertiary education a close second, and schools also very prominent. Local government tax sharing is also significant, though this is a somewhat dubious category to list as a specific purpose grant, since the only real condition which attaches to it is that it must be forwarded on to local government. In terms of trends one can only really look to the period since 1975–76 because that saw the introduction of the running costs of public hospitals as a specific purpose payment, and that category very much dominated the whole picture. The distribution of these grants has remained quite constant, but in recent years, there have been significant annual fluctuations in the largest functional areas, and the changes in amounts devoted annually to smaller functional areas like community health, school dental schemes, preschools, and assistance for deserted wives, have been quite marked.

Table 28 gives a similar breakdown for the specific purpose payments

Table 27 Australia: commonwealth specific purpose payments to the states for recurrent purposes

Major items	1972-1973 % total	1972-1973 % inc.	1973-1974 % total	1973-1974 % inc.	1974-1975 % total	1974-1975 % inc.	1975-1976 % total	1975-1976 % inc.	1976-1977 % total	1976-1977 % inc.	1977-1978 % total	1977-1978 % inc.	1978-1979 % total	1978-1979 % inc.	1979-1980 % total	1979-1980 % inc.	1980-1981 % total	1980-1981 % inc.	1981-1982 % total	1981-1982 % inc.	1982-1983 % total	1982-1983 % inc.	1983-1984 % total	1983-1984 % inc.
Universities	20.7	19.6	32.8	147.5	30.9	89.0	18.4	12.8	21.4	20.0	20.0	12.3	19.5	3.5	19.4	9.8	18.8	12.2	27.7	15.4	24.3	8.7	22.1	5.6
Colleges of Advanced Education	6.8	45.1	20.5	368.2	19.6	91.7	12.4	19.9	15.5	28.6	13.8	7.2	13.6	4.6	13.5	9.4	13.1	12.4	17.7	6.3	15.8	10.6	15.1	11.0
Technical & Further Education	—	*	1.7	*	2.0	139.8	1.7	63.0	1.9	10.1	1.6	3.2	1.7	13.5	1.8	16.0	1.9	20.8	2.8	16.4	2.6	17.4	2.6	17.2
Schools	10.5	38.5	14.0	109.0	19.2	173.8	14.3	41.5	17.7	27.1	15.9	8.0	16.1	7.9	16.4	12.3	17.0	19.4	26.5	22.9	26.1	21.6	24.6	9.8
Public hospitals — running costs	—	—	—	—	—	—	37.6	*	26.4	-27.5	32.9	50.1	33.8	8.9	33.3	8.6	32.8	13.8	5.6	*	5.8	28.3	2.9b	-42.2
Community Health Programme	—	*	0.9	*	1.3	207.2	1.5	120.0	2.1	41.6	2.0	12.8	1.4	-27.0	1.3	8.8	1.5	26.7	*	*	*	*	*	*
School Dental Scheme	—	*	0.6	*	0.5	65.4	0.5	69.8	0.6	39.5	0.5	4.8	0.5	-10.1	0.6	46.5	0.5	-1.9	*	*	*	*	—	—
Assistance for deserted wives	2.5	65.9	1.3	-21.5	0.6	-9.4	0.4	40.2	0.6	37.3	0.7	50.5	0.9	29.8	0.7	-5.4	0.4	-42.8	*	*	—	—	—	a
Preschools and child care	—	—	0.7	*	1.7	-50.3	1.6	81.4	1.7	10.2	1.6	10.4	1.3	-9.0	1.3	4.6	1.1	1.3	1.5	5.0	a	a	a	a
Aboriginal advancement	1.7	299.3	1.1	0.3	1.1	97.0	0.7	29.0	0.7	3.5	0.7	11.6	0.7	3.5	0.7	10.1	0.7	15.5	0.9	1.3	0.8	11.3	0.7	4.3
Local government tax sharing assistance	—	—	—	—	4.6	*	3.5	41.8	5.9	75.2	5.8	18.1	5.9	8.5	6.6	23.6	7.7	35.6	11.5	16.6	11.2	21.0	10.5	8.2
Employment grants	26.6	284.5	2.0	-88.4	3.3	233.3	1.3	-25.0	*	*	*	*	—	—	—	—	—	—	—	—	—	—	—	—
Housing	1.8	66.0	1.1	-0.3	0.6	1.7	0.3	-0.2	0.2	-14.9	0.2	-6.4	0.2	-1.0	0.2	0.0	—	—	—	—	—	—	*	*
Total		56.6		56.4		100.3		89.6		3.1		20.4		6.0		10.3		15.6		-21.5		23.7		

Source: Derived from Payments to or for the States, Budget Paper No. 7.
a No longer recorded under this category.
b Does not include medical funding which comprises a further 6.2 per cent.
* Insignificant or irrelevant.

Table 28 Australia: commonwealth specific purpose payments to the states for capital purposes

Major items	1972–1973 % total	1972–1973 % inc.	1973–1974 % total	1973–1974 % inc.	1974–1975 % total	1974–1975 % inc.	1975–1976 % total	1975–1976 % inc.	1976–1977 % total	1976–1977 % inc.	1977–1978 % total	1977–1978 % inc.	1978–1979 % total	1978–1979 % inc.	1979–1980 % total	1979–1980 % inc.	1980–1981 % total	1980–1981 % inc.	1981–1982 % total	1981–1982 % inc.	1982–1983 % total	1982–1983 % inc.	1983–1984 % total	1983–1984 % inc.
Housing for servicemen	1.1	-12.4	0.8	26.0	1.5	245.2	1.9	27.5	2.1	2.8	1.4	-35.9	0.8	-48.5	*	-87.5	2.9	-19.5	3.3	15.3	2.6	7.6	2.7	28.0
Universities	4.9	15.1	5.1	85.0	3.8	34.8	2.7	-26.0	3.4	16.7	3.3	-8.0	3.6	-2.4	3.9	2.1	2.7	-13.5	2.6	-1.7	2.0	3.8	1.8	16.5
Colleges of Advanced Education	5.8	14.5	4.2	27.8	6.3	174.0	4.7	-21.1	4.6	-10.6	3.4	-30.4	4.7	26.2	3.3	-34.2	6.7	23.2	7.3	11.9	6.1	14.6	4.6	-8.0
Technical and Further Education	2.4	75.1	1.9	41.7	1.2	10.8	1.3	20.7	2.0	37.0	2.9	37.7	4.5	39.9	5.9	21.3	6.7	21.3	7.3	17.1	7.6	14.6	7.6	5.4
Schools	5.1	21.1	7.9	130.1	11.4	162.4	7.8	-28.0	8.8	2.9	11.6	24.2	12.4	-2.5	10.8	-19.0	9.6	-4.4	10.9	18.9	8.9	9.6	9.6	*
Aboriginal Advancement	2.8	103.7	2.7	66.6	1.3	-5.5	1.2	-7.7	1.0	-23.5	0.8	-26.0	1.0	9.4	1.0	-3.6	0.7	-18.8	0.2	-66.1	0.2	31.9	0.2	29.9
Housing (including welfare housing)	1.2	*	22.8	*	22.1	76.3	19.9	-5.4	22.3	2.9	24.8	4.0	22.0	-19.0	17.1	-27.2	16.6	-3.6	12.5	*	12.4	*	15.9	*
Pensioner housing	1.2	-15.1	0.5	-22.7	0.3	20.9	0.7	116.9	0.6	-17.4	0.6	-7.7	1.0	40.0	2.2	114.3	2.1	3.3	2.1	1.6	1.5	*	1.3	11.4
Growth centres	—	*	0.7	*	3.5	831.3	3.8	13.0	2.6	-36.8	1.6	-41.3	1.7	-3.2	2.0	9.1	2.0	6.2	2.2	12.0	1.7	4.0	1.5	14.8
Land acquisition	—	*	1.2	*	2.4	256.4	3.0	32.3	1.4	-55.9	1.7	9.6	1.0	-44.5	1.2	7.7	1.2	1.7	0.4	-62.9	0.4	16.2	0.3	*
Roads	51.5	13.9	33.0	13.5	20.8	14.5	23.6	19.5	25.8	6.1	30.3	-12.7	35.3	6.3	40.6	7.5	41.9	11.1	44.6	9.1	34.9	9.1	30.1	6.0
Urban public transport	—	*	0.5	*	2.6	*	1.8	-24.7	3.5	61.7	3.2	12.7	2.9	-17.9	3.1	0.5	3.0	4.7	—	*	—	*	—	*
Water resources assessment	0.7	100.4	0.5	19.2	0.3	21.4	0.3	9.3	0.4	11.6	0.4	1.0	0.6	20.3	0.8	135.2	0.5	17.1	1.1	-1.7	0.9	7.1	1.7	149.8
Rural Adjustment Scheme	—	—	—	—	—	—	—	—	0.6	*	2.6	319.7	3.3	16.7	1.1	-67.8	1.1	8.7	1.1	-1.7	2.0	*	—	*
Rural reconstruction	9.4	27.0	3.7	-29.6	1.6	-19.5	1.6	4.2	1.2	-33.5	0.2	-85.3	—	*	—	*	—	*	—	—	—	—	—	—
Sugar industry	*	*	*	*	—	—	—	—	—	—	*	*	—	—	2.1	*	—	*	—	—	2.0	*	—	—
Natural disaster relief	—	*	2.5	*	3.0	118.8	1.6	-42.0	1.7	-5.7	3.5	93.5	1.7	-56.0	1.1	-41.6	3.8	292.2	1.4	-63.3	4.8	379.5	4.3	10.2
Hospitals — capital development	—	*	0.2	*	1.7	1181.0	5.8	253.6	6.4	-0.2	2.8	58.4	—	—	—	-5.0	—	—	—	—	—	—	—	—
Sewerage	—	*	2.9	*	6.7	318.8	6.1	-4.1	2.9	-56.9	—	—	—	—	—	—	—	—	—	—	—	—	—	—
Bicentennial road development	—	—	—	—	—	—	—	—	—	—	—	—	—	—	—	—	—	—	—	—	5.4	*	16.4	270.9
Total	18.0		77.3		81.8		5.2		-8.5		-6.3		-8.7		-6.4		7.7		2.4		36.8		23.0	

Source: Derived from *Payments to or for the States*, Budget Paper No. 7.
* Insignificant or irrelevant.

which are made to the Australian states for capital purposes. The largest function here is unquestionably roads (including the bicentennial road programme) which now make up 46.5 per cent of such payments. Roads have always been the major area of specific purpose capital funding for the states. Their share of all such funding has varied, and there have been significant annual variations in amounts of capital devoted to roads, despite the fact that road funding is allocated on a formula basis. Housing is the second largest function, although its prominence has been gradually declining and the amounts devoted to it annually have varied markedly. Capital funding for schools has always been a significant item and has maintained a constant share of the total despite quite remarkable fluctuations in the amount going to this function year to year. The proportion of specific purpose capital funding going to tertiary education has remained fairly constant but the mixture between the different forms of tertiary education has changed. Capital payments for Technical and Further Education are now more than twice those for either Universities or Colleges of Advanced Education. The annual shifts in capital grants for Universities, Colleges of Advanced Education, and Colleges of Technical and Further Education have been quite marked despite the existence of long term (three year) agreements in these areas. Table 28 also demonstrates the susceptibility of this form of intergovernmental transfer to a change of government, because functions such as growth centres, land acquisition, sewerage, pensioner housing, and aboriginal advancement have been scaled down or eliminated since the fall of the Whitlam government in 1975. This table on specific purpose payments for capital purposes also reflects a phenomenon we observed with respect to specific purpose payments for recurrent purposes, though to a much lesser extent, namely, that although there are often extremely marked variations in the absolute amount of money allocated to a function from year to year, the change in the proportion of the total payments represented by that function is usually less severe. This again tends to suggest a pronounced annual pattern of incrementalism in the determination of the composition of these payments although, as mentioned, the clear elimination of some of the payments within only one or two years demonstrates that governments can break an incremental pattern if the will is strong enough. Of course capital payments are easier to terminate than recurrent payments because of the generally greater human dependence on the latter than the former.

Some interesting features come to light if we compare Table 27 with Table 28. Firstly, although the running costs of public hospitals is the dominant payment for recurrent purposes, there have been only relatively minor commonwealth payments made for the capital component of hospitals. By contrast, although roads are clearly the largest area for capital payments they do not figure as a recurrent payment. And there are other functions which have dominated capital payments but not recurrent payments, and vice versa. We can quite simply conclude that there is no linkage or symmetry between the two forms of payment indicating, in the

Australian federation, a different form of the division of powers, where it is often the case that *within* a particular public function one level of government can be responsible for capital expenditure and another level responsible for recurrent expenditure, and vice versa. This lack of symmetry is also borne out by the fact that in *common* functional areas the growth of payments for capital purposes (i.e., both the annual and secular growth) in similar periods, can be quite different. This has been particularly true in the overall field of education.

A trend analysis was conducted for the composition of specific purpose payments, as between those for capital and recurrent purposes, for each of the Australian states. Aspects of individual states will be considered later but for the moment we shall confine our analysis to interstate comparisons.

In relation to specific purpose grants for recurrent purposes, there are differences in the profile of functions in the different states. In New South Wales the proportion of such funding going to universities has been higher than is the case in all the other states, much lower on colleges of advanced education, a little higher than most in technical and further education, higher than most for schools, and much higher than Victoria, Queensland, and South Australia for hospital running costs. Victoria, by contrast, has been stronger than most states in its mixture on colleges of advanced education and schools, but much lower than all states in respect of public hospitals. Queensland has been close to the interstate average in the distribution of these payments between functions. South Australia has been slightly lower than most states in the schools function. Western Australia has been below other states in the relative share of recurrent grants going to universities and also schools, but quite higher than the others in relation to hospital running costs, and a little higher in respect of colleges of advanced education. Tasmania has been significantly lower than other states in the prominence received by colleges of advanced education, a little below in respect of schools, and a little above for hospital running costs.

In all states there have been trends where certain functions have become more or less dominant in their share of specific purpose recurrent payments, but those changes in the profile of such payments have, at least since 1975–76, been quite gradual. Annual fluctuations in such payments have been much more pronounced, although more so for the smaller functional areas than the large ones.

With respect to specific purpose payments for capital purposes, there is again a different pattern of distribution for different states. New South Wales has been higher than the interstate average on universities, but about the average in most other functions. Victoria has been high on colleges of advanced education, a little higher in relation to technical and further education, a little higher for schools and housing, and quite a deal lower in its emphasis on roads. In Queensland there has usually been a slightly lower emphasis on universities and colleges of advanced education, whereas in relation to technical and further education this state has been above the average in some years and below in others; similarly in relation to school funding. Queensland has had a significantly lower emphasis on housing in its receipt of these specific purpose capital payments, but has usually been well above all other states in the dominance of road funding. South Australia has recorded a slightly greater emphasis on technical and further education, has been generally lower on schools, but significantly higher in the emphasis on housing funds, whilst roads have been much less dominant than in other states. Western Australia has had a slightly lower emphasis on university capital funding in its mixture of specific purpose funds (this is true also of colleges of advanced education), and has generally been lower than other states in relation to schools. It has been well below the average in housing, but higher than most states in the roads function, although lower for urban public transport. In Tasmania, university funding has been much less dominant than in any other state, and the same has generally been true for colleges of advanced education. Until recently the same pattern was true for technical and further education. But Tasmania has most noticeably been behind the other states in relation to the prominence given to school funding in these specific purpose capital funds from the commonwealth. By contrast, housing has had a much greater emphasis than in other states, and roads have been given an emphasis equal to the interstate average, although urban public transport is lower.

In all states it has been the case that there have been most pronounced annual variations in specific purpose capital payments, considerably more pronounced than those in recurrent payments. This has resulted in changing profiles of the distribution of specific purpose capital payments as between public functions, in each state, which are not marked variations but do portray a shift much more noticeable than was the case for recurrent payments. As was the case with the total picture analysed earlier there is little symmetry between the specific purpose capital and recurrent payments functional distribution in any state.

We will have recourse to this analysis again later in looking at each state separately but there is one element of the transfer of conditional funding which ought to be made immediately more explicit. The variations in profiles of the specific purpose payments which the national government passes to the Australian states suggests that there are quite significant differences in the relative distribution of various categories of payments as between states.

This factor is made quite apparent in table 29 which reveals the interstate distribution of the main basic forms of intergovernmental transfer for each of the past five years to 1978–79, the latest year for which such data is available. It becomes immediately apparent that there is quite a significant difference in the way in which each category of funding is distributed. New South Wales receives higher proportions of the total for specific purpose, recurring funds and less for general revenue funds, but overall it

Table 29 Australia: interstate distribution of commonwealth government payments to the states and Loan Council borrowings

Transfers	New South Wales			Victoria			Queensland			South Australia			Western Australia			Tasmania		
	1974–75	1976–77	1978–79	1974–75	1976–77	1978–79	1974–75	1976–77	1978–79	1974–75	1976–77	1978–79	1974–75	1976–77	1978–79	1974–75	1976–77	1978–79
General revenue funds	30.1	30.4	30.5	22.4	22.6	22.7	17.9	18.5	18.0	12.7	11.6	11.7	11.4	11.8	12.1	5.6	5.0	5.0
General purpose capital funds	30.7	31.8	32.3	25.0	25.3	25.1	14.1	13.4	13.3	13.4	13.1	13.0	9.2	9.3	9.3	7.4	7.1	7.0
Specific purpose: Recurring	34.6	34.8	35.3	28.9	28.1	27.4	13.5	13.7	14.2	10.1	10.1	9.8	9.5	10.2	10.2	3.5	3.1	3.1
Specific purpose: Capital	32.3	32.4	32.4	25.1	24.1	23.6	17.0	18.0	17.1	11.3	10.8	11.0	10.1	10.2	11.5	4.2	4.5	4.4
Total payments	31.8	32.2	32.4	24.7	24.7	24.4	16.4	16.7	16.5	11.8	11.1	11.1	10.5	10.9	11.3	4.9	4.5	4.4
Payments + borrowings:																		
General purpose	30.3	30.8	30.9	23.2	23.3	23.3	16.8	17.1	16.9	12.9	12.0	12.0	10.8	11.2	11.4	6.1	5.6	5.5
Specific purpose	33.2	33.8	34.4	26.6	26.5	26.2	15.6	15.5	15.1	10.8	10.4	10.2	9.9	10.2	10.6	3.9	3.7	3.5
Total	31.6	32.1	32.4	24.7	24.7	24.5	16.2	16.4	16.2	11.9	11.3	11.2	10.3	10.7	11.1	5.1	4.7	4.6

Source: Derived from Payments to or for the States, Budget Paper No. 7.

does better out of specific purpose payments than general purpose payments. (The words "better" and "worse" are only used here in a relative sense and imply no absolute disadvantage for that state overall.) Victoria's position is similar to that of New South Wales. Queensland does best out of general revenue funds and specific purpose capital payments, the reverse position to that of the two largest states. Overall Queensland does not differ markedly in the share of general purpose funding compared with specific purpose funding. South Australia clearly fares best in its share of general purpose capital funds and worst in terms of its share of specific purpose funds for recurrent purposes. Overall South Australia has a better share of general purpose than specific purpose funding. Western Australia, like Queensland, does best in its share of general revenue funds, and worst out of general purpose capital funds, and overall is slightly better off in the share gained from general purpose intergovernmental funding than that for specific purposes. Tasmania achieves a much higher proportion of its funding in general purpose capital funds and a much lower proportion in specific purpose funds for recurrent purposes, but overall does better out of general purpose than specific purpose funding. These figures seem to demonstrate convincingly the lack of symmetry in the distribution of all forms of intergovernmental funding in Australia. The fact that the patterns have been such for every year indicates that the resultant horizontal balance between states is different for each of the various major forms of intergovernmental funding, namely, general purpose revenue funds, general purpose capital funds, specific purpose funds for recurrent purposes, and specific purpose funds for capital purposes. This in turn means that the interstate relativities are different for the distribution of capital and recurrent funds in general, as well as those for general and specific purposes.

Summary

We are now in a position to summarize the main characteristics of conditional funding in Australia which has, since 1942, constituted less than the amount of unconditional funding. Even at the peak of the Whitlam government's centralism, conditional funding was barely equal to unconditional funding. Specific purpose payments have been the flexible aspect of Australian intergovernmental transfers; in years of very large increases overall in intergovernmental funding it has been specific purpose payments which have expanded most significantly, and similarly, when an overall sharp contraction has occurred, it has been specific purpose payments which have borne the brunt of that cut back. This and other factors have led to a trend in specific purpose payments with marked annual fluctuations. Trends also reveal an unmistakable shift in the mixture of specific purpose payments from capital to recurrent purposes, the latter now representing over seventy per cent of all conditional funding, mainly as a result of the Fraser government's new federalism which concentrated, among other things, on the elimination of certain capital intensive programmes funded by specific purpose payments to the states. However, annual movements of specific purpose payments for both recurrent and capital purposes have been quite erratic. The two most populous Australian states now receive a significantly higher proportion of their funding in the conditional form that do the other states but the mixture varies from state to state. Generally speaking, it has been the pattern that the less populous states have received lower proportions of their federal funding in the conditional form. The main functional areas which receive specific purpose payments in Australia are running costs of public hospitals, and education in its various stages, in terms of recurrent spending; and roads, housing, and education for capital purposes. Whilst there often have been pronounced annual variations in the amount of specific purpose funding going to a particular functional area (especially in payments for capital purposes), the proportion of the total allocated to each function (on average and in each state) has remained remarkably stable. There does, however, seem to be no linkage and a complete lack of symmetry between specific purpose capital payments for a functional area and specific purpose recurrent payments for the same function. It seems clear that the allocation of all forms of specific purpose funding proceeds on an ad hoc basis and it is also apparent that, sometimes, within the same functional area, one level of government can be responsible for capital expenditure and the other for recurrent expenditure. The profile of distribution between functions of specific purpose payments of both a recurrent and capital nature is different for each of the states; in some cases significantly different. In all states this functional mixture has changed only gradually, although annual fluctuations in absolute amounts have often been quite pronounced, more so for capital payments than recurrent payments. Finally, the evidence is clear that the relative distribution of intergovernmental transfers in Australia between states is different for each form of funding, and within the conditional payments component it is different for recurrent funding as compared with capital funding. This means that each state has a different profile of intergovernmental transfers received from the national government. In other words, the *methods* of distributing funds between states in Australia are different for each major form of funding, and also vary across functional areas which receive conditional funding. In conclusion it probably should be emphasized that conditional intergovernmental funding in Australia consists almost entirely of national government payments to the states for activities which *are clearly the constitutional responsibility of the states.* That is to say, the conditional funding is not of the form of national payments to states for the implementation of national government powers, which is true of some federations. Indeed the fact that it is state functions being conditionally funded, and the largest state functions at that (education, health, roads, etc.), points to the basic cause of the highly political nature of this element of the rectification of vertical imbalance in the Australian federal system.

The Nature of Conditional Funding in Canada

We have already observed a number of features about Canadian intergovernmental conditional funding which perhaps bear repeating in summary form. Specific purpose transfers represent, on average, only 15 per cent of provincial revenue — as much as 25 per cent for one province and as low as 9.3 per cent at the other extreme. However they are, overall, a more prominent part of intergovernmental transfers than are general purpose funds, and on average are now more than double them. But again this varies between provinces, and specific purpose transfers comprise as much as 96 per cent of one province's total intergovernmental transfers; yet as little as 41 per cent of another's. The more fiscally autonomous the province, the more likely that specific purpose transfers will be dominant in its receipt of funds from the national government. Finally, the major specific purpose transfers are directed to the functions of health, social welfare, and education; and to a much lesser extent, transport and communications. Table 30 demonstrates the functional breakdown of major specific purpose transfers more graphically.

The most interesting aspect of table 30 is that the distribution pattern of specific purpose transfers, taking all provinces as a whole, has not changed markedly over the decade. Health, social welfare, and education continue to be the dominant function recipients, and their shares of the total have remained little changed, although health is slightly less dominant and social welfare is slightly more prominent. For each province the distribution pattern is different to some extent, as we shall see later, but the important point to note here is that there have been a number of instances of particular provinces defying the trend for particular functions. For example transport and communications have become of lesser significance in Nova Scotia and New Brunswick, but of increased importance in Saskatchewan and Alberta. Social welfare has become a conditionally funded area of slightly lesser significance in Manitoba and Saskatchewan, when it has become of greater prominence in other provinces. Education has become much more dominant in British Columbia and in most provinces except Quebec, Prince Edward Island, and Alberta. The increase in significance of specific purpose transfers for industry has been extremely pronounced in the Maritime provinces.

A trend analysis of each province reveals annual fluctuations in the various major transfer payments to the provinces. Clearly there are severe changes year to year in a great many of the transfer payments going to each particular function in each particular province; there is little consistency in movements within a function as between provinces or within a province as between functions. Comparison of data also reveals a phenomenon which we noticed in relation to the Australian states, namely, that despite pronounced annual fluctuations in the amount of intergovernmental transfers going to a particular function, it is common for the proportion of all conditional funding devoted to that function to

Table 30   Canada: major specific purpose transfers from federal government to provincial governments

Function	Nfld	P.E.I.	N.S.	N.B.	Que.	Ont.	Man.	Sask.	Alta	B.C.	Total
1971–1972											
Transport and Communications	0.3	4.7	10.3	10.1	1.4	0.5	0.7	0.7	1.0	0.2	1.8
Health	37.0	29.1	54.7	43.4	38.0	62.4	50.2	60.1	56.8	54.7	53.3
Social Welfare	20.4	14.4	17.6	17.1	—	20.0	22.9	18.1	17.6	22.5	16.4
Education	10.0	12.4	14.5	11.5	39.6	16.5	20.7	18.6	22.5	9.3	19.7
1974–1975											
Transport and Communications	10.8	3.7	1.2	10.0	6.5	*	0.5	2.4	1.6	0.8	3.1
Health	40.2	29.3	54.5	45.9	26.9	65.6	57.2	56.4	60.6	60.2	51.8
Social Welfare	19.0	17.4	18.1	20.9	25.3	20.7	20.4	19.2	18.2	31.1	22.3
Education	8.4	13.3	18.6	8.9	34.2	11.9	12.7	8.7	16.1	3.8	16.3
1977–1978											
Transport and Communications	14.1	6.8	0.9	6.7	3.5	0.2	*	3.0	1.9	0.7	2.5
Health	33.9	20.5	42.7	36.3	40.3	53.8	45.2	46.9	48.8	43.1	45.3
Social Welfare	17.2	12.1	17.3	20.8	24.6	20.1	22.9	13.9	19.9	33.9	22.0
Education	13.9	8.9	19.7	19.9	21.3	22.9	24.4	20.1	19.7	17.7	20.6
1978–1979											
Transport and Communications	4.0	4.8	3.6	3.5	1.1	0.2	3.1	6.4	5.3	1.7	2.1
Health	37.2	26.5	45.3	39.3	40.8	55.4	48.9	43.5	47.6	48.0	47.1
Social Welfare	21.7	14.6	17.2	21.4	28.1	20.1	20.2	17.0	23.6	26.7	23.0
Education	15.0	11.6	18.3	19.6	22.7	22.9	21.2	18.4	16.3	20.2	21.0
1980–1981											
Transport and Communications	2.3	1.7	1.3	3.8	0.8	*	0.6	2.3	0.6	1.2	1.0
Health	42.5	31.1	47.6	34.2	40.7	54.4	46.6	42.4	48.3	44.3	36.8
Social Welfare	21.5	15.7	17.6	23.1	31.4	20.0	16.7	17.1	23.7	30.7	24.0
Education	17.5	12.6	20.3	19.4	21.2	23.5	20.3	17.8	17.2	19.3	20.8

Source: Derived from *Federal Government Finance* (Ottawa: Statistics Canada).

* Insignificant or irrelevant.

Table 31 Canada: distribution profile of major federal government transfers to provincial governments

Function	Nfld	P.E.I.	N.S.	N.B.	Que.	Ont.	Man.	Sask.	Alta	B.C.	Total
Equalization:											
1977–1978	53.2	49.5	57.3	50.9	39.2	—	37.7	-4.1	—	—	25.5
1980–1981	56.5	51.2	53.2	47.5	46.7	—	47.4	14.1	—	—	28.8
Total general purpose transfers:											
1977–1978	58.8	54.1	61.7	55.9	44.5	11.3	43.9	8.8	17.5	8.9	33.5
1980–1981	61.1	54.0	58.1	50.1	48.1	4.4	48.8	14.8	7.9	1.3	31.7
Transport and communications:											
1977–1978	—	0.3	0.8	0.2	0.4	*	2.6	3.4	4.3	5.4	1.2
1980–1981	0.1	0.8	0.5	1.9	0.4	*	0.3	2.0	0.5	1.1	0.6
Health:											
1977–1978	14.2	10.7	16.9	15.7	23.9	47.5	23.7	37.1	39.6	37.0	30.4
1980–1981	16.5	14.3	20.0	19.3	21.1	52.1	23.9	36.1	44.5	43.8	32.0
Social Welfare:											
1977–1978	9.1	6.0	7.8	10.1	11.7	20.1	12.7	19.4	21.4	27.3	15.3
1980–1981	8.4	7.2	7.4	11.5	16.3	19.1	8.6	14.5	21.8	30.3	16.4
Education:											
1977–1978	5.7	4.7	7.0	9.1	15.0	19.4	10.6	14.9	10.8	18.4	14.3
1980–1981	6.8	5.8	8.5	9.7	11.0	22.5	10.4	15.2	15.9	19.1	14.3
Agriculture:											
1977–1978	0.6	23.9	*	0.1	*	0.6	2.0	12.7	3.3	0.7	1.4
1980–1981	0.2	17.8	*	*	*	0.5	1.5	9.7	3.9	0.6	1.2
Trade and Industry:											
1977–1978	11.2	*	5.4	8.3	3.8	0.5	2.6	3.0	0.9	1.0	3.2
1980–1981	5.7	—	5.1	7.3	2.4	0.9	2.4	2.3	1.0	2.9	2.6
Total specific purpose transfers:											
1977–1978	41.2	45.9	38.3	44.1	55.5	88.7	56.1	91.2	82.5	91.1	66.5
1980–1981	38.9	46.0	41.9	49.9	51.9	95.6	51.2	85.2	92.1	98.7	68.3
Total transfers:											
1977–1978	100.0	100.0	100.0	100.0	100.0	100.0	100.0	100.0	100.0	100.0	100.0
1980–1981	100.0	100.0	100.0	100.0	100.0	100.0	100.0	100.0	100.0	100.0	100.0

Source: Derived from *Federal Government Finance* (Ottawa: Statistics Canada).
* Insignificant or irrelevant.

remain reasonably constant. The trend analysis also reveals some other interesting factors. In some provinces, notably Newfoundland, and to a lesser extent New Brunswick, Prince Edward Island, Manitoba, and Alberta, the annual changes in specific purpose transfers match those in total transfers; but in the other provinces there is very little correspondence, and at times a complete divergence of movement. There also seems to be no connection between movements in general purpose transfers and specific purpose transfers in any province except Newfoundland. It is of course also true that all annual fluctuations in both conditional and unconditional funding transfers are a great deal more pronounced than the changes in gross revenue of the provinces.

Table 31 takes up a theme which we referred to earlier, namely, the variation between provinces of the proportion of federal transfers which go to particular functions. Looking at transfers in total, in Newfoundland there is a higher than average emphasis on general purpose funding, including equalization, as well as a stronger emphasis on trade and industry but a much smaller emphasis on health, social welfare, and education; whereas, by contrast, the profile of distribution of transfers in Ontario gives strong emphasis to health and education, but very low emphasis to unconditional funding (with no equalization), and a lower than average emphasis on trade and industry, agriculture, and transport and communications. To put it simply, each province has a different profile of the functional distribution of total federal transfers of funds. Even provinces which have a basically similar mixture of unconditional and conditional funding, and a similar degree of overall fiscal dependence on transfers, find that the composition of the conditional element of their transfers does differ.

Table 32 provides a different perspective to reveal an aspect we considered in relation to Australian conditional funding. This table shows the distribution between the provinces of conditional transfers in each of the main functional categories. It demonstrates quite effectively that the distribution pattern of conditional funding differs from that for unconditional funding. Consider, at the extreme, Nova Scotia with 11.8 per cent of the unconditional transfers and 4.1 per cent of the conditional transfers, or Ontario with only 1.7 per cent of the unconditional funding but 32.0 per cent of the conditional funding, or Quebec with 42.3 per cent of the unconditional transfers but 27.3 per cent of the conditional ones. Our main interest is in the particular categories of conditional funding, and the distribution pattern of various specific purpose transfers shows quite clearly pronounced variations. Consider for example, Prince Edward Island and Saskatchewan, which both receive sizeable slabs of the money for agriculture (23.9 per cent and 29.8 per cent respectively), but hardly any of the funding for trade and industry (nil and 3.4 per cent). Admittedly this is a smaller conditional programme, and when one turns to consider the major areas of conditional funding (health, welfare, and education), the distribution pattern between provinces is quite consistent due, no doubt,

Table 32 Canada: major federal government transfers to provincial governments and territories

Function		Percentage of each function by province										Total[†]
	Nfld	P.E.I.	N.S.	N.B.	Que.	Ont.	Man.	Sask.	Alta	B.C.		
Equalization:												
1977–1978	11.0	2.6	15.3	11.1	51.5	—	9.0	-0.1	—	—		100.0
1978–1979	12.4	2.4	13.8	12.0	47.8	—	8.7	2.8	—	—		100.0
Total general purpose transfers:												
1977–1978	8.6	2.0	11.7	8.7	41.4	7.5	7.4	0.8	3.1	1.9		100.0
1978–1979	11.1	2.2	11.8	10.3	42.3	1.7	7.4	2.6	2.3	1.1		100.0
Transportation and communications:												
1977–1978	—	0.4	4.7	0.8	10.8	0.8	13.2	9.7	23.3	36.3		100.0
1978–1979	6.2	2.3	6.7	6.4	14.1	3.6	7.1	14.5	19.4	8.3		100.0
Health:												
1977–1978	2.5	0.5	3.8	2.9	26.2	37.2	4.7	4.1	8.2	9.6		100.0
1978–1979	2.6	0.5	3.9	3.3	23.6	37.7	5.1	4.4	7.9	10.4		100.0
Social Welfare:												
1977–1978	3.1	0.5	3.5	3.7	25.5	31.2	5.0	4.3	8.8	14.0		100.0
1978–1979	3.1	0.6	3.0	3.6	33.3	27.9	4.3	3.5	8.1	11.9		100.0
Education:												
1977–1978	2.1	0.4	3.3	3.6	35.0	32.4	4.5	3.5	4.8	10.1		100.0
1978–1979	2.4	0.5	3.5	3.7	29.6	35.0	4.9	4.2	6.1	9.9		100.0
Agriculture:												
1977–1978	2.2	23.0	0.1	0.5	5.7	10.4	8.8	30.6	14.9	3.9		100.0
1978–1979	0.4	23.9	0.1	*	2.2	13.2	9.0	29.8	17.7	3.5		100.0
Trade and Industry:												
1977–1978	18.5	—	11.4	14.5	39.3	3.7	4.9	3.1	1.9	2.5		100.0
1978–1979	16.4	—	14.5	14.6	41.0	1.9	3.3	3.4	2.4	2.4		100.0
Total specific purpose transfers:												
1977–1978	3.3	0.9	3.9	3.7	27.8	31.7	5.1	4.6	7.8	10.8		100.0
1978–1979	3.3	0.9	4.1	3.9	27.3	32.0	4.9	4.8	7.9	10.2		100.0
Total transfers:												
1977–1978	5.1	1.3	6.6	5.4	32.6	23.2	5.9	3.3	6.2	7.7		100.0
1978–1979	5.6	1.3	6.4	5.8	31.8	22.9	5.6	4.1	6.2	7.5		100.0
Population (as at June 1977)	2.4	0.5	3.6	2.9	27.0	36.0	4.4	4.0	8.2	10.7		100.0

Source: Derived from Federal Government Finance (Ottawa: Statistics Canada).
* Insignificant or irrelevant.

to the heavy emphasis on population distribution in the formulae for those transfers. (It can be seen from the table that the distribution of those conditional transfers matches the population distribution fairly closely.)

We had one other set of data for Canada which is not available in the same format for Australia. This is contained in table 33 and table 34, and it relates to the participation of provinces in conditional funding programmes. (Data published as part of the commonwealth budget presentation could be used as a rough basis for the compilation of similar Australian figures, although the specific purpose programmes are not broken down to

Table 33 Canada: conditional grants and shared-cost programmes

Participating provinces	1974		1976		1977	
	Number of programmes	Percentage of total	Number of programmes	Percentage of total	Number of programmes	Percentage of total
10	12	15.4	13	16.7	13	16.3
9	1	1.3	4	5.1	4	5.0
8	1	1.3	—		4	5.0
7	3	3.8	2	2.6	1	1.3
6	—		—		1	1.3
5	—		2	2.6	1	1.3
4	3	3.8	4	5.1	4	5.0
3	14	17.9	12	15.4	7	8.8
2	10	12.8	10	12.8	11	13.8
1	34	43.6	31	39.7	34	42.5
Total*	78	100.0	78	100.0	80	100.0

Source: Derived from Canada Year Book.
Note: All grants and programmes in Regional Economic Expansion regarded as one single programme.
* Figures rounded.

Table 34 Canada: conditional grants and shared-cost programmes

Participating provinces	Percentage of programmes participating		
	1974	1976	1977
Newfoundland	28.2	32.1	30.0
Prince Edward Island	27.0	24.4	26.3
Nova Scotia	28.2	26.9	32.5
New Brunswick	25.7	30.8	38.8
Quebec	34.6	39.7	38.8
Ontario	46.2	51.3	47.5
Manitoba	41.1	37.2	47.5
Saskatchewan	39.7	44.9	47.5
Alberta	33.3	38.5	37.5
British Columbia	32.1	32.1	36.3
Average to Provinces	33.6	35.8	38.3

Source: Derived from Canada Year Book.
Note: All grants and programmes in Regional Economic Expansion regarded as one single programme.

the extent that they are in Canadian data.) Care has to be exercised with these figures because they reflect only the number of programmes and not their financial significance. Thus, for example, it could be possible for a province to be a strong participant in conditionally-funded programmes, but those programmes might all be for small amounts of money. Or a province might choose to participate solely in those programmes that offered substantial funding. From table 33 we can deduce immediately that the bulk of conditional grants and shared-cost programmes are concluded between the national government and just one or two provinces. Indeed, the frequency with which more than half the provinces participate in these programmes is confined to only 30 per cent of them, and conditional programmes where every province participates represent only 16 per cent of the total. It can also be observed from table 33, although it is a generalization, that the tendency is for either all the provinces to be participating or just a few to be participating. From table 34 it is clear that there is some variation in degree of participation in conditional funding from province to province. The "lower" participators are Prince Edward Island (participation in 26 per cent of the programmes) Newfoundland (30 per cent), and Nova Scotia (32 per cent). The "higher" participants are Ontario, Manitoba, and Saskatchewan (all 47 per cent). But perhaps the most significant facet of this table is that no Canadian province participates in more than half of the conditionally-funded programmes, and most participate in only a little more than one-third of these programmes. This picture has not changed much in recent years.

The Reaction to Conditional Funding

To say that the introduction of conditional funding has produced a hostile reaction from the states of Australia and provinces of Canada would be an understatement. They have raised innumerable objections to the use of conditional funding by the respective national governments, and we shall attempt to do justice to all of those objections by means of the interview responses, supplemented by the voluminous amount available in the literature on this subject. If all the objections to conditional funding can be synthesized into one basic point it is that conditional funding, according to the states and provinces, distorts their own priorities and interferes in the very processes of their own priority determination. As can be readily appreciated, this argument, if valid, represents a very serious hindrance to the attainment of our planning system, requiring as it does harmonization of priorities and agreed allocation of resources despite the fact, which has already been observed, that where there are spillovers or externalities the logic of the situation identified under those headings requires some "overriding" of state or provincial priorities by a central government. We shall proceed eventually to this essential element of the debate about conditional funding, but it is also necessary to survey other objections raised by the Australian states and Canadian provinces to conditional funding. For the sake of convenience the various grievances have been grouped into broad categories and the interview responses have been supplemented by material from the literature. There is some degree of repetition of argument because the same point was often made by respondents in different contexts.

1. Arguments Related to Efficiency and Effectiveness of Government

Responses to the interviews produced a number of strong viewpoints including the following:

(a) Conditional grants are often made for capital purposes without due consideration being given to consequent and associated current expenditure requirements, and vice versa. The same argument is used for conditional "grants" given as loans which do not take account of subsequent debt repayment, so that an additional capital grant gives rise to future indebtedness whose realization diverts funds from other purposes. Depending on the level of funding it could follow that subnational governments are forced to pay greater attention to debt repayment than current community needs. In these senses conditional payments increase a state or province's obligations rather than decrease them.

(b) The uncertainties of future national government policies affect the discretion of the subnational governments mainly through the inability to predict commencement and/or termination of new programmes.

(c) States and provinces are tempted to spend in high, cost-shareable functions or programmes, when they often ought to be spending on lower cost but nonshareable areas. This, it is argued, is compounded by the political risk which a state or province takes if it departs from a high, cost-shareable area, and it could lead to a deterioration in standards in many areas not recognized by the national government for conditional funding. (The political risk referred to relates to the likely criticism of a provincial or state government which fails to avail itself of any substantial funding offered by the national government.)

(d) States and provinces are induced by conditional funding to keep programmes going solely to get "national" money, even when they know that the programmes should be scrapped. In other words, it discourages a true review of spending efficiency and efficacy. Also, in conducting any review of priorities there is a tendency to favour cost-shared areas over areas which are funded solely from state or provincial revenue, simply because there is more to be saved in cutting back in the latter than in the former. In other words cost-shared programmes tend to be given priority when they may not deserve it. (We examine this argument in more depth later.)

(e) Conditional funding, especially cost-shared arrangements, can lead to an undue emphasis on certain types of projects, for example in social infrastructure, which was claimed to be overabundant in Canada in the health and education areas, and which was inefficiently located and utilized in the health area in Australia.

(f) Because of the kudos which can be associated with conditional programmes, there is a tendency for national money to be offered more for glamour areas, and the "bread and butter" activities are left to the states/provinces.

(g) Many conditional programmes result in duplication and overlapping between national and subnational jurisdictions, brought about often by an excessive amount of detail laid down in the conditions of the funding.

Most of the arguments have been raised, if not analysed, in the literature. Mathews identifies concerns which have been expressed about the allocative or distributional effects of specific purpose grants:

> These are related to such matters as the proliferation of overlapping programs; uncertainties about eligibility and the growth of grant lobbies and "grantsmanship"; the duplication of bureaucracies at each level of government; the tendency to encourage unrestrained growth of the public sector; inadequate arrangements for consultation and policy coordination between units; unwarranted interference by granting governments in the detailed administration of grant programmes; failure to match grant programmes to policy objectives, inadequate accountability; lack of systematic analysis of expenditure needs; and failure to distribute grants on a basis which reflects relative needs and fiscal capacities.[5]

Elsewhere Mathews has made the observation that specific purpose grants, by their design, can distort the pattern of expenditure of recipient governments. In particular, matching requirements can make "recipient governments direct funds from one crisis area to another". Under these circumstances, says Mathews, general revenue grants without restrictions are more likely to achieve an efficient allocation of resources.[6] Gates also takes up this theme. He puts it this way:

> In fields in which both the Commonwealth and the State governments operate, it is often possible to document the contrast between relative lavishness on the one hand and relative parsimony on the other; and less precise observation suggests strongly that the duality extends to functions that are the exclusive province of one level or the other. An implication is that the transference of resources from the margin of expenditure at the Commonwealth level to the margin of expenditure at the State level would effect an increase in the real output of government services. This may well apply with equal force between State and local government administrations.[7]

This raises the "duplication" argument which is also well entrenched in the literature, a favourite cry of state premiers in particular, who stress that the states generally have an expertise in the area in question built up over many years, and conditional funding brings an unnecessary duplication of such expertise at the national government level, all at the taxpayer's expense. Hunter states quite categorically, of Australian experience, that detailed conditions being attached to specific purpose grants involved a duplication of effort and cost associated with numerous conferences of federal and state ministers and officials. The 1970 statement of the Australian premiers expressed concern about duplication of responsibility for pensioners with a resultant inconsistent cost impact on the states between programmes.[8] Trudeau, in his 1969 working paper on the constitution, referred to the welfare area as one where there could be overlapping and cautioned against the practice of having two levels of government transferring money to persons.[9] Smiley has a theory on the reason for the gradually increasing resistance by Canadian provinces to conditional funding, which he attributes to increasing administrative sophistication:

> The earlier arrangements came into effect when the provinces were on the whole little disposed to budgetary or program planning. Thus "50 cent dollars" were attractive and the restrictions on provincial autonomy in the range and standards of services not very onerous. These circumstances have now changed. Just as administrative rationality has made federal officials anxious that the conditional grant device leads to heavy and unpredictable financial burdens without any guarantees that national purposes are effectively and efficiently pursued, so increasing administrative sophistication in the provinces results in reactions to the uncertainties and controls inherent in federal participation.[10]

On this subject of uncertainty, Carter says of the Canadian EPF arrangements (which as we have seen involve a sharp reduction in conditional funding) that they have increased predictability of funding for both national and provincial governments, and opened the possibility of more efficient provincial spending in the health field.[11] And on the subject of administrative rationality Stevenson makes the interesting observation, in recalling Corry's work for the Rowell-Sirois Commission, that the "divided jurisdiction" inherent in shared-cost programmes prevents bureaucracy from "operating in the rational and orderly manner prescribed by Max Weber since there is no single hierarchical chain of command when more than one level of government is involved".[12]

Other authors have reinforced some of the arguments which emanated from the interviews. Thus Grewal says that aided programmes have often been selected hastily, and in many cases the objectives not spelled out clearly and precisely. He goes on:

> Ideally, specific purpose grants should be related to program output. But as measurement of output is not possible in many cases, actual grants are often related to input levels for example so many dollars per person. The result of this practice . . . is that recipient governments are almost solely concerned with spending the grant moneys, without regard to efficiency. Frequently, the national governments also do not have any effective means of evaluating the efficiency of grant programs. This results in overall loss of efficiency in the use of fiscal resources.[13]

Wade draws attention to the practice of attaching interest and repayment conditions to conditional grants, and warns against the concept of regarding conditional grants as some method of investing national government funds at interest. Rather, he says, the test should be related to whether the national government would or would not levy an interest charge if it were able to finance the programme directly.[14] Speaking of the Australian context, Hunter observes that about two-thirds of specific purpose payments are of a capital nature and in a sense therefore bypass the evaluation of the Loan Council.[15] Speaking in relation to education funding, Berkeley emphasizes that timing is an important component of efficiency and states need to be given sufficient time to spend the funds allocated under conditional funding. This can also be dependent on whether the conditional funding is simply aiming at supplying new initiatives or just more of the same, and that, in turn, may be affected by how run down the system is when the federal grant begins.[16] Auld supports this argument from Canadian experience and says that it may take two or three years before a conditionally funded programme is operating in an efficient and desirable manner. He goes on to question the conventional wisdom that the national government is always the appropriate level to deal with the redistributive function.[17]

2. Administrative and Technical Viewpoints

It is not surprising that interviews with public servants on this subject evoked a strong response regarding the administration of conditional funding. This was certainly the case, and the main points raised were as follows:

(a) The time span of different conditional grant programmes is different, as are the conditions, methods, and mixtures of funding, making it difficult for any single state or province to obtain an overview of the conditional programmes as a whole.

(b) Conditional grants weaken rather than strengthen the ability and desire of a state or province to innovate in both revenue raising and expenditure because of the stringent conditions attached to federal transfers.

(c) Frequent changes of government or even changes of outlook, especially on the part of the national government, can cause technical problems with the delivery of a programme, especially where those changes are ideologically based.

(d) Because conditional programmes are formulated and negotiated outside the ambit of the state or provincial government budget process, they are bound to lead a life of their own and thereby preempt any review in budget formulation and appraisal. In other words it becomes an "uncontrollable" or "locked in" area.

(e) The amount of detail required for reporting on conditional programmes leads to duplication and overlap between levels. Also there is often insufficient time allowed to the subnational governments to design and introduce the programmes in view of the administrative difficulties involved.

(f) The criteria are often too rigid, especially regarding eligibility (including means tests, etc.)

(g) After the programmes are finally running there can be inordinate delays in payment to the recipient government caused, at times, by the foolishness of some national ministers who insist that they should approve every project in the programme. Further complications will arise if the national government is not prepared to accept the audit of the state or provincial governments on the programme in question.

(h) Occasionally too much of the conditional funding process is conducted by means of verbal dialogue between national and subnational government officials, which poses various problems including subsequent disputes over what is acceptable if key personnel happen to shift. For this and other reasons there are also disagreements about exactly which items are cost shareable, because even the wording of an agreement accompanying a conditional programme cannot possibly cover all eventualities.

(i) A quite serious administrative objection, raised particularly by the provinces in Canada, is the manner in which conditional programmes interfere in their administrative structure. This can occur when the national government specifies the delivery mechanism to be used for the programme, which can well alter the location of the funding between different provincial government agencies. Provinces claim they have been forced to relocate programmes in their machinery of government when they believe that, on the basis of experience and local knowledge, the programme should be delivered through different administrative arrangements.

These points have all recurred throughout the literature on both Australian and Canadian federalism, although they have tended to be downplayed because of the scant regard with which administrative arguments are usually viewed by politicians, journalists, and even academics. Holmes and Sharman, however, point to the seriousness of administrative factors when they state quite explicitly that under the Whitlam government's centralist policies vertical imbalance was shifted from the political arena of the Premiers Conference to the administrative arena.[18] They go even further and assert that the states, especially Victoria and New South Wales, have progressively built up the expertise of their "advisory public services to counter central government 'know-how' ". Holmes and Sharman strongly imply that in adopting this strategy the Australian states are following the pattern established in Canada a decade earlier in the face of national government expansion.[19]

Many writers have been willing to acknowledge the administrative complexity in coordination of all the conditional programmes. Mathews expresses it this way:

The (grants) machinery problem is partly one of fitting the grant program into the budget priorities and processes of each of the governments concerned and partly one of co-ordinating the policies of granting and recipient governments. In the absence of constitutional provisions for responsibility sharing of the kind which exist in West Germany, policy co-ordination between governments involves legislatures as well as executive governments so that appropriate administration machinery (such as ministerial councils) for purposes of consultation and policy formulation is not a sufficient condition for responsibility sharing through specific purpose programs".[20]

Canadian writers, with perhaps the benefit of greater hindsight, see other basic elements of the administrative coordination problem in relation to conditional funding. Both Burns and Stevenson, for example, are agreed that in the Canadian provinces conditional funding has resulted in tension between central agencies and programme departments. Burns expresses it this way:

In recent years the thrust of (specific purpose) programme growth has been gradually eased, due in part to provincial opposition but more realistically to the fact that most of the expensive areas of co-operation seem now to have been covered. No suitable alternative to this form of transfer is yet readily available, for as the business of supplying public services becomes more complex and all-embracing, the extent of overlapping interests and responsibilities becomes even more evident. Except for Quebec, even the provinces which express their concerns most strongly appear to appreciate the realities of the situation and in few cases has resistance been maintained in the face of attached financial advantages. As always, an important factor is still the division of interests within the provincial governments themselves. The programme departments which have benefited from the availability of Federal funds continue to seek funds from their counterparts in Ottawa, while financial officers at both levels resist the weakening of their control.[21]

Stevenson sees the medicare programme as the one which crystallized provincial opposition to conditional grants, and regards Ontario's Ministry of Treasury, Economics, and Intergovernmental Affairs as the leader in expressing such sentiments. According to Stevenson, shared-cost programmes lessened the ability of this ministry to assert its authority over programme departments such as Health, Education, or Community and Social Services. Stevenson inclines to Corry's view that this tendency cannot go too far because of the "hierarchical and centralizing nature of parliamentary Cabinet government".[22] The increasing power of this ministry and other similar central agencies would reinforce this assertion, as we saw in the chapter on intergovernmental agreements. The Ontario Ministry, referred to by Stevenson, published in 1972 a critique of federal-provincial, shared-cost programmes in Ontario. That report made the following pertinent observations:

All provincial expenditures should properly be part of a central budgetary plan which reflects the policies and priorities of provincial Cabinets. Yet it has become evident that shared-cost programs tend to take on an autonomous life of their own, largely outside the provincial budget planning process. Sustained largely by the program departments responsible for the original initiative and rigidly fixed by federal-provincial agreement for an unstated duration, each program develops its own "clientele" inside and outside government. This makes flexible and independent provincial programming difficult and, in essence, preempts large portions of provincial budgetary funds from annual review and adjustment. In 1972, for example, $2.3 billion or 39 per cent of the Ontario budget was locked into shared-cost programs.[23]

This document also listed other specific administrative problems of shared-cost programmes. That list included delayed federal payments, auditing difficulties, differences about programme aims and eligible costs, abrupt changes in programme definition, and unsatisfactory procedures for programme review or renewal. It was the delayed payments which were regarded as the most serious and the paper observed that, whereas the provinces were obliged to meet a range of deadlines in various programmes, similar time constraints did not apply to the national government in the release of funds. It was also the case that definitions of eligible costs were established by national auditors rather than through intergovernmental negotiation.[24] Speaking of roughly the same period, a provincial minister of finance characterized shared-cost funding arrangements prior to EPF in the following terms:

> Rapid cost escalation, particularly in the early years, which led to the introduction of ceilings on federal contributions. Major restrictions on hospital insurance cost-sharing, which encouraged expansion of the most expensive services and facilities, which were shareable, over less expensive alternatives which were not. A complicated set of shareability rules under the postsecondary programs, which took years to work out and which, even today — twelve and a half years after the program started — are still being debated.[25]

He also claimed that, during the negotiations for the EPF arrangements, the national government argued that to ensure accountability it had to build in specific provisions requiring, on penalty of loss of payments, that provinces publicize federal payments in a specific way, for example, by issuing regular nationally prepared news releases. The provinces resisted those restrictions but agreed to less formal modes of publicity for national contributions.

There are, of course, similar examples of cumbersome administrative arrangements applying to Australian conditional funding. Wade gives examples in the three functional areas of schools, urban and regional development, and preschools during the Whitlam government's term of office. In the case of schools there were seven categories of grants available under twenty-five headings, and in a number of cases the national minister was required to approve individual projects being financed in individual schools; and even in the area of government schools a special group of payments to "disadvantaged schools" was dependent upon a declaration by the national minister that particular schools nominated by the state minister were disadvantaged schools. For preschools only two months were allowed for completion of purchase. In the field of urban and regional development Wade comments that the complexities of the attaching conditions provided a continuous series of "field days" for government legal offices. "In addition it has brought to light an extraordinary number of eminent 'bush lawyers' from officers who were otherwise economists, engineers, accountants or administrators. And it has produced an amazing number of conferences and interstate journeys for both Federal and State officials. It is by no means an exaggeration to visualize Federal and State officials locked in earnest negotiations, sometimes for hours on end and sometimes well into the night, debating the merits of the inclusion of a particular phrase in a clause of a draft agreement or what a series of words written in English really are intended to mean."[26]

Speaking of the administrative detail required in education conditional funding in respect of accountability requirements Berkeley observes:

> The mass of detail sought under the accountability requirements is not normally a feature of State accounting and reporting systems. While in some instances it may be justifiably argued that it should be, in a great many others the detail is of no use other than for the purposes of accountability. The fact that the required detail is not readily available has meant that staff have had to be diverted from other tasks to extract it. This is usually a tedious, time-consuming process in which the efficient use of manpower is difficult. Further, the staff diverted to these tasks are usually drawn from planning, financial management or management support personnel. Their services could be utilized far more advantageously elsewhere . . .[27]

The appointment by Australian Prime Minister Fraser of the Bland Administrative Review Committee provided an open opportunity for all the states to raise their objections to conditional funding, especially as it had been manifest under the Whitlam Labor government. As might be expected this process produced a catalogue of complaints, and the ones relating to administrative matters included a grievance that within each programme there was often a multitude of projects, but it was solely the national government which determined whether particular projects were compatible with the programme. The states also believed that they should retain tasks concerned with technical concepts and design, environmental impact, economic evaluation of alternative projects, financial management, and the allocation of funds among all projects that met the broad requirements of the programme. The states believed that such a division of authority would allow them to select and develop projects for funding, which were compatible with their own "planning" objectives, with respect to such matters as the quantity and quality of physical and social infrastructure and interregional development. Inflexibility and delay was another charge levelled by the Australian states over conditional funding. Harris expresses their feelings in these words:

> . . . given the inexperience in many functional areas of the Commonwealth administration, there was a considerable lack of appreciation in the administration

of the program lead times, of the time taken to conceive, generate, execute and review new programs. This led to serious problems for efficient planning and expenditure patterns by the States when funds were made available by the Federal Government on a fiscal year basis, but where delays in making approvals and notifying those approvals to the State meant that work could not actually begin until a significant part of the year had passed. The States claimed that they drew up proposals seeking an allocation of specific purpose funds to be expended over a full year, but that they sometimes received those funds as late as half-way through the year. As a result the States made hurried decisions, uneconomical design and excessive provisions on the project in an effort to secure commital of funds and to ensure expenditure. The States apparently accepted this inefficiency because not to have done so might have been to lose Commonwealth financial assistance, since there was no automatic approval by the Commonwealth to allow the States to transfer unexpended funds from one year to the next.[28]

The states also complained that the audit requirements of specific purpose funding delayed cash flow and were often inconsistent between programmes and departments.

However, the administrative aspect of Australian conditional funding, which has been the object of most attention in the literature, relates to the role of advisory commissions, a phenomenon which is not unique to intergovernmental relations in Australia, but which became a key component of the Whitlam government's decision-making process, especially in regard to conditional funding. These bodies are statutory entities of the national government set up in particular sectors, for example, schools, health, universities, welfare, etc., and required to advise on, and sometimes oversee, the distribution of conditional funding. Needless to say the states resented this para-bureaucratic intrusion in their line of communication with Canberra, especially as they were nearly always forced to appear before them as witnesses and protagonists rather than as equal partners. These commissions were an articulated component of Labor Party policy well before that party came to power nationally in 1972. Whitlam held hopes that they would become "planning" instrumentalities for each sector to overcome what he saw as fragmentation of decision making between the commonwealth and the states.[29] Said he: "Failing such commissions I see no way of determining the objective priorities for those Commonwealth grants without which neither schools or hospitals can improve".[30]

Mathews believes that the conditions under which these commissions operated tended to be destabilizing with respect to the economy and the commonwealth budget. This, he says, was because the recommendations of the commissions were largely formulated outside the normal budgeting processes of priority determination and financial appropriation. "Each Commission made its assessment of needs independently and without explicit regard to budget constraints". This meant that the assessment made by each commission was virtually open-ended in its budgetary implications. These recommendations cumulatively resulted, inter alia, in massive increases in specific purpose payments, and the failure to integrate their recommendations into the budget affected both vertical and horizontal balance.[31] Other problems with the use of advisory commissions identified by Mathews include duplication of the work of public service departments, the fact that the role of the commissions and their relationship with the executive government and parliament were not clearly defined, and the fact that they did not act as intergovernmental agencies despite the fact that they were recommending functions which were state responsibilities.[32] They were also supposedly concerned with achieving equalization in fiscal performance, but because of the difficulty of comparing outputs they usually resorted to equalization of expenditure inputs. Mathews adds that the commissions seldom took into account differences in the capacity of the states to provide services or their relative revenue-raising and expenditure efforts, but they "frequently recommended grants which had the effect of compensating particular states for deficiencies arising from their own past priorities or policies".[33] Else-Mitchell, too, draws attention to the effects of the advisory commissions on horizontal balance,[34] and Lane sees these bodies as part of a piecemeal approach to horizontal equalization in the Australian federation.[35] Weller and Smith believe that the state and local governments were simply incapable of providing the information required by the national government and its commissions, and because of variations in local conditions the commissions had difficulty in understanding some of that information.[36]

There have of course been kind words spoken about the advisory commissions. Even Mathews speaks well of the efforts of some of them to work towards rational (meaning developing specific purpose payments appropriate to their purpose) and objective criteria, especially in the case of roads and universities.[37] Cranston is enthusiastic about them for broadly similar reasons.[38]

On the subject of statutory bodies Hayes raises a Canadian problem which exists in Australia but only as a fairly minor intergovernmental issue. Hayes says that provincial governments in Canada are sometimes frustrated by the fact that certain decisions which impact on them are in the hands of statutory bodies independent of national ministers, and he cites freight rate regulation and energy transmission as examples. The problem is the old familiar one of the balance between control and autonomy for government statutory bodies, but in this case the grievance is that the provinces cannot influence those national entities in the same way as they might influence a national minister.[39] No doubt the same argument could be made in both countries about statutory bodies responsible for monetary policy and tariffs.

3. The Standards of Government Services

Respondents were concerned that:

(a) There can be a tendency for a duality of standards to arise where the national government chooses to fund only a certain narrow segment of a particular government sector, for example, a particular type of hospital or educational institution; or it can lead to marked differences of emphasis within bands of the one sector, for example, if conditional funds are given for tertiary education but not primary or secondary education or for some classes of roads but not others, or for support of existing facilities rather than the encouragement of providing new facilities more urgently needed (or vice versa).

(b) If states and provinces are tempted to spend in high, cost-shareable forms they will inevitably neglect lower cost but nonshareable areas, leading to a deterioration of overall standards.

(c) Because of the political nature of the funding, conditional programmes are often in glamour fields while "bread and butter" issues are left to a state or province's own more meagre resources. Some would argue that the reverse should be true.

Very little has been written on this aspect of conditional funding other than to list it in the catalogue of state/provincial grievances. Wade argues that there is a need to distinguish between existing programmes at a higher cost and standard, and new initiatives and new standards. The Australian states, he argues, should have an adequate tax base to cover the former situation with conditional grants restricted to the latter use.[40] The 1970 statement by the Australian premiers drew attention to the need for conditional funding to be escalated to take *full* account of inflation and particularly the associated labour costs of the programmes. They then made the following statement, the gist of which was encountered in the interviews:

> The trend to greater emphasis upon special purpose Commonwealth provisions rather than upon general purpose provisions has introduced a secondary disparity in standards of provisions within the States' own functioning, somewhat comparable with the disparity between standards of provision for the constitutional fields of the States and those of the Commonwealth. There is, for instance, a disparity in standards between the provisions for university education, in which the Commonwealth participates, and primary education in which it does not; between provisions for roads in which the Commonwealth participates, and provisions for ordinary rail transportation in which it does not; between provisions for science laboratories and libraries, in which the Commonwealth participates, and provisions for class-room accommodation in which it does not; and so on.[41]

Berkeley makes the point, in relation to education, that conditional funding raises expectations on the part of recipients that associated standards will always be maintained, whereas this may not be a realistic aspiration and may indeed be subject to the whims of the national government.[42] In the Canadian situation there have been fears expressed, that following the introduction of EPF with its attendant backing-off from heavy conditional funding, national standards in various areas may fall. This is because there will be less opportunity for the national government to redistribute funding between provinces. However, the fact that some of the payments are in the cash form does retain a potential for monitoring standards, but the variation in agreement conditions between sectors (for example, health is different from postsecondary education) affects the degree to which this can take place.[43] A study published by the Ontario Economic Council agreed that the EPF arrangements would take most of the heat out of the arguments about conditional funding. It was recognized that conditional grants to provinces had been justified on the ground that the national government had a duty to ensure that all Canadians enjoy common minimum standards of certain social services, health care, and education, even though these responsibilities fell within provincial jurisdiction. However the "common minimum services" argument, it was claimed, seemed to rest on at least one of several specific assumptions:

(i) The decisions of provincial governments do not reflect the wishes of their constituents.

(ii) The provincial governments are technically incompetent to take action in some fields constitutionally within their jurisdiction.

(iii) Although the decisions of provincial governments may express the wishes of their own constituents, the residents of other parts of Canada, acting through the federal government, should be able to impose expenditure programs the latter feel to be desirable.

When stated in this way, the proposition seems much less acceptable, provided one believes that the provincial governments are as legitimate an expression of the democratic process as the federal government.[44]

Perhaps the difficulty with the arguments about standards is that, as Robinson points out, it is extremely difficult to determine whether past conditional funding has improved the level or quality of the services provided. He asks "at the operational level, do the amounts spent represent increased or improved output or are the increased expenditures merely shifted backwards to become higher wages and profits for workers and supplying firms? Even more difficult to measure is the effectiveness of the increased expenditures. For example capital grants to hospitals may result in increased purchases of X-ray equipment, but does the additional equipment significantly improve hospital services as indicated by measures such as reductions in work time lost in industry from illness and injury or more lives saved? Would a hospital have purchased the equipment if the grants had been unconditional?"[45]

Of course the real point of this debate is, as Else-Mitchell says, that, particularly in Australia with its high degree of vertical imbalance:

it must be conceded that there are considerable difficulties, political and otherwise, in terminating specific purpose grants programmes or reducing the amounts voted annually under those programmes. Quite apart from the prospect of electoral backlash, continued Commonwealth involvement is regarded as essential to ensure reasonable uniformity from State to State in the standards of services provided by the States with the assistance of Commonwealth grants. This is especially the case with education, health, and hospital services, which are the subject of the largest grants to the States. Moreover, if the major specific purpose payments were phased out and the amounts saved added to the general tax entitlements of the States, there would be no assurance that the policy objectives of the Commonwealth government would be respected by those States which have differing political objectives or philosophies.[46]

4.   *The Potential for Discrimination against Particular States and Provinces*

The view of respondents on this matter related mainly to the *unintended* consequences of conditional funding resulting in regional discrimination:

(a)   The fact that the time span of different conditional grant programmes are different, as are the conditions, methods and mixtures of funding, gives rise to the possibility of discrimination against certain states or provinces.

(b)   The design of a programme may impinge upon the ideology of some state/provincial governments but not others.

(c)   The timing of the introduction of conditional programmes is held to be important because it may penalize states or provinces which have already spent a lot of money on the area in question, and benefit those who have lagged behind. This will be accentuated if the recipient governments are required to make matching contributions.

(d)   The more prosperous states and provinces, it is claimed, are induced by conditional grants to spend less from their nongrant sources, than they would otherwise do, and the poorer ones are induced to spend more.

(e)   Shared-cost arrangements associated with conditional funding result in some states/provinces entering programmes they cannot really afford. This might also be true if the programme is designed to provide a public service which turns out to be in greater demand in a particular state/province than in others, for example, historical sites, unemployment relief, or facilities for the aged.

(f)   Some conditional programmes are designed solely to benefit certain regions *within* states or provinces, which causes acute embarrassment for state or provincial governments because they believe other regions or their whole space should so benefit, or because it is political suicide for them to be seen putting any of their money into one region but not another. This does not rebound on the national government in the same way.

From the literature on this subject there seems little doubt that the potential exists in conditional funding for the sort of discrimination in distribution to which respondents referred. As we have already observed the effects of conditional funding on horizontal imbalance are already well known.[47] In relation to Australia, Holmes and Sharman say that the "developing imbalance in the rate of development between the various states in the 1950s resulted in the growth of Section 96 special purposes control grants".[48] This problem has become particularly evident in

Australia following the attempts under the Fraser government's new federalism to absorb specific purpose payments into general purpose payments to the states, one of the major stumbling blocks being that the incidence of horizontal imbalance between the specific purpose payments differs markedly from the general purpose payments and, just as important, the degree of horizontal imbalance varies significantly from one specific purpose programme to another.[49]

Canadians have been forced to come to grips with this aspect, perhaps in starker terms that Australians, because of the greater frequency of "opting out" of conditional programmes by particular provinces — especially Quebec. When this occurs the problem is made very explicit. As Trudeau put it in his constitutional paper, if a province doesn't participate in a programme the citizens of that province are still paying their national taxes and so they are seen to be propping up programmes for other provinces.[50] From another perspective Hayes points out that the complexities of various conditional programmes may disfavour small provinces who don't have the bureaucratic resources to cope with the details of the programme,[51] and Stevenson cites the Canadian medicare insurance programme as one which was fundamentally at odds with those provinces ideologically opposed to regulating the medical profession.[52] Young, in the Ontario Tax Council study, admitted that national conditional programmes could be effective means of preventing provinces from erecting barriers to national mobility by ensuring universality, accessibility, and hence mobility, in regard to government services, but he also argued that there should be a better option than the use of conditional programmes to achieve this objective.[53] Finally, Donald Smiley, in work for the Canadian Tax Foundation, has asserted that because of conditional funding provinces that have already established a programme qualifying for grants are given an unfair advantage over other provinces; poorer provinces must often reduce their spending in other fields of activity so as to match the federal grants; and provincial programmes will gradually tend to become more uniform even without federal pressure.

5. The Legality of Conditional Funding

It is not intended to enter into the many intricacies of the legality of federal financial relationships. However, two points made by respondents will be mentioned because they have a profound influence on the whole attitude of subnational units of government to conditional funding:

(a) Australian state governments and Canadian provincial governments argue that the use of conditional funding is a circumvention of the constitution when it involves national government intrusion by means of funding, and especially administration, in functions clearly allocated to the subnational level under the constitutional division of powers.

(b) Conditional funding, because of the nature of the activities for which it is given, restricts the ability of states and provinces to deal as they choose with the local authorities within their boundaries.

The first of these arguments is a very old one and it is natural that it should recur because the largest conditional payments in both countries are for the largest functional areas of the state and provincial governments, namely, education, health, and welfare. The legality of the national government entering these functional areas has been upheld by the courts in both countries, and the long and short of it is that the spending power of the national parliaments overrides the formal power division under the constitution.[54] In relation to the second point there are much tighter restrictions in both countries on the national government passing funds directly to local governments, although it does happen in various forms, more so in Canada than in Australia.

Holmes and Sharman believe that there are occasions when the state governments in Australia are not necessarily opposed to national policy which lies behind a conditional programme, but they feel forced to oppose it because it transgresses the division of powers.[55] The Administrative Review Committee found a unanimous reaction from the Australian states that the expansion of specific purpose programmes was an indirect way by which the national government was seeking to obtain control over functions within the area of state responsibility; control which it could not obtain through constitutional amendment.[56] The counter argument has already been touched on, and it must be repeated that we have no intention of entering the legal aspects of the issue. Suffice to use Cranston's succinct summary of the opposing viewpoint:

> But how can it be said that the Australian government has no constitutional right whatever in areas like housing, education, water conservation, and roads when Section 96 undoubtedly gives it a right to provide specific purpose grants for such matters? The argument must mean that certain parts of the Constitution, principally the limitations on Australian Government power contained in Section 51, are to be given precedence over another part, namely 96, or that section 96 is to be limited to some notion of federal balance which is to be divided in the Constitution. Over the last fifty years the High Court has been unimpressed with such propositions and has consistently held that limitations cannot be placed on the plain wording of the section.[57]

Cranston is also of the opinion that it is doubtful whether the national government could obtain judicial remedies requiring the states to observe any conditions anyway, although his opinion is not shared by all constitutional lawyers.[58]

Trudeau advances a quite different justification for national intrusion of this kind. The justification was, he believed, to be found in the very nature of the modern federal system: "in its economic and technological interdependence, in the interdependence of the policies of its several governments, and in the sense of community which moves its residents to contribute to the well-being of residents in other parts of the federation. To understand these characteristics of an industrialized, Twentieth Century federal state is to understand the rationale for the spending power of the Parliament of Canada."[59] According to Burns, the provincial concern about jurisdictional independence was generally subservient to the fiscal advantages of conditional funding, and it was only gradually that such resistance built up, outside Quebec at least.[60] As Stevenson points out, no provincial government has ever sought to challenge directly the legality of conditional programmes, and, in his view, any provincial government that objected to them on principle could protect its autonomy by refusing to accept them, as Quebec did on more than one occasion.[61] (We examine this argument later.) Nonetheless, in the round of constitutional discussions of 1979 between national and provincial ministers, the stage was reached of considering a draft constitutional amendment which would limit the use of the national government's spending power, at least in areas of provincial jurisdiction.

6 *National Priorities versus Subnational Priorities*

Here is the hub of the argument about conditional funding which is most relevant to our interest in the potential for public sector planning. The views of the Australian states and Canadian provinces were quite plain:

(a) The national government directs or seduces states/provinces into programmes which they do not want at all and would never have contemplated of their own accord.

(b) The national government enters programmes already operated by the states/provinces but by means of its funding mixture and other conditions induces or directs the recipient government to devote more of its own funds into that programme than it would have done. This is especially so, it is claimed, when matching conditions are used.

(c) Action of either of the two kinds just outlined diverts funds which a state or province would have used for other purposes.

(d) Having seduced states or provinces into particular programmes the national government pulls out after a time leaving the recipient government to finance that programme completely from its own resources.

(e) The stringent conditions attached to some programmes weaken rather than strengthen the ability and desire of a state or province to innovate both in revenue raising and expenditure.

(f) The mere existence of conditional funds acts to encourage subnational governments to pursue those funds rather than seriously contemplate increased taxation or aim at a greater share of unconditional funding.

(g) It is argued that the national government makes decisions about the level of conditional funding against a completely different spectrum from that which the states/provinces use, and this can only result in differing priorities being given by each level to the same programme. There may be a further complication if the programme in question is part of a functional area which applies at the two (or even three) levels (for example, primary industries, or fisheries, or transport), so that the national government will be tempted to allocate resources for that purpose to its own agency rather than pass them to the subnational level. This may also result in distortions in the appraisal of the state/provincial programme if the national government uses its own functional agency to perform such an appraisal, because that agency will, at best, see the conditional programme as a threat to its own share of national expenditure and, at worst, will be tempted to inject unduly stringent conditions on performance of the subnational unit.

(h) Differences of opinion arise between levels of government about the duration of programmes and agreements. For example, the Canadian national government favours long term agreements whereas some provinces, such as Quebec, have preferred them to be short for the sake of expediency.

(i) States and provinces are induced, by conditional funding, to keep programmes going solely to get national money even if they believe the programmes have outlived their usefulness. Then, in conducting any review of state/provincial priorities, there is a tendency to favour cost-shared areas over areas which are funded solely from state/provincial revenue, simply because there is more to be saved in cutting back in the latter than in the former. That is to say, cost-shared programmes may be given priority by subnational governments when they don't deserve it.

These arguments and the general contention behind them are difficult to deal with. We have encountered some of them in earlier discussion. It has become commonplace assertion and entrenched mythology, in Australia at least, that conditional funding always distorts state priorities. The literature is full of statements to this effect particularly from state politicians. The arguments advanced to support this line are seldom given but when they are they tend to fall into a number of categories.

Firstly, there are those who equate a straightforward increase in conditional funding, in the absolute, or more especially relative to unconditional funding, as an automatic reduction of state policy-making autonomy. Naturally this argument reached its peak in Australia in the years of the Whitlam Labor government when specific purpose payments increased to represent roughly half of all federal fiscal transfers.[62] Indeed, in their 1970 statement, the Australian state premiers had clearly identified this trend and claimed even then: "This has meant that more and more the Commonwealth has been able by indirect means to take out of the hands of the States the determination of priorities of expenditures over a widening area of functioning in which the States have clear constitutional responsibility".[63] Also contained within this statement is an astute implication, that if conditional funding were adequately escalated to take account of inflation by means of formulae built into the programmes, but unconditional funding were not so escalated, this too would result in a gradual shift from general purpose to specific purpose funding. One state under-treasurer expressed the fears of the states very vividly when he said that:

(a) the states saw the financial assistance grant as their entitlement for forgoing income taxing but the commonwealth government regarded it as just another item of expenditure from *its* tax revenues;

(b) the states were, generally speaking, starved for funds; but

(c) the commonwealth was pouring money into areas of state responsibility with conditional funding, thereby proving that the funds were available and that the areas of state need did exist;

(d) the financial assistance grant was not calculated on a true needs basis;

(e) because the financial assistance grant was so insufficient and the states were so short of money they accepted more readily the conditions attached to specific purpose payments.[64]

Secondly, there are those who see this question of priority conflict in terms of national government activity competing with that of subnational units. Prest, for example, berates the Australian national government for its actions in the postwar period in paying off the national debt when the states were in desperate need for additions to their schools, hospitals, and sewerage systems.[65] This is, to some extent, an admission that given the political nature of government spending, if the national government did not have the device of conditional funding available to it (whereby it retains the kudos), there would be an even greater tendency for national government functions to grow at the expense of those of the states, even though it could be demonstrated that the states' needs were more basic and urgent. As Holmes and Sharman say of the 1960s, grants to the states doubled but areas of direct responsibility quintupled.[66] To the extent that this trend increased the indebtedness of state governments and created pending frustration at the standard of state government services, it acted as a constraint on state policy making.

Thirdly, a number of writers have analysed the aspect, evident in the responses to the interviews, that the different backgrounds to decision making by the different levels of government is significant. Mathews and Jay, writing in 1972 about the need to restore vertical balance in the Australian federation, comment forcefully that "although Commonwealth grants to the States have increased significantly, they have often been based on decisions which the Commonwealth has made arbitrarily or by reference to information that would be regarded as inadequate if the Commonwealth was directly responsible for the functions in question".[67] Describing the Canadian tax abatement developments of the 1950s and 1960s, Hayes has this to say:

> There are major difficulties in the way of governments agreeing explicitly on overall national priorities. It is difficult enough for two levels of government to agree on their respective objectives and roles in one functional area . . . the problem is compounded when all functional areas are considered together. In such a case, the federal government has to make an assessment of, among other things, the relative priority of exclusive provincial responsibilities such as

primary and secondary education; and the provincial governments have to assess the relative priority of such federal responsibilities as defence expenditures. Ideally, too, individual legislators in the respective federal and provincial legislatures should be given the opportunity to make comparable assessments. It is small wonder that governments prefer to avoid such explicit assessments and to be guided instead by their own implicit judgements of the relative priority of the responsibilities of the two levels of government. The appropriateness of these implicit judgements are then — again implicitly — endorsed or rejected by the voters in federal and provincial elections.[68]

And Trudeau spells it out especially in relation to capital expenditure:

> ... the *terms of reference* by which a provincial government is guided differ necessarily from those which the Government of Canada must take into account. The criteria which was used by the provinces and their municipalities in determining the amount they will borrow each year, for example, are necessarily different than those employed by the Government of Canada. The provinces and municipalities are guided by their views as to the proportion of capital expenditures they think ought to be borne by present as opposed to future generations, their judgement as to the amount which can be borrowed in different capital markets, and the needs of their respective economies. The Government of Canada is guided, on the other hand, by its judgement as to the total demands which are likely to be placed upon the supply of resources and capital in the economy as a whole, including those by the provinces and municipalities, the desirable balance between fiscal and monetary policy, and other related considerations.[69]

Fourthly, and perhaps most importantly, there is the actual practical effect of conditional funding on subnational governments. Quite a number of authors have endeavoured to explain just how it is that the nature of conditional funding interferes with the priorities of subnational governments. Each one approaches the question in a slightly different way so we are forced to canvass their opinions in some depth. Mathews portrays methods of vertical cooperation as a spectrum of possible decision-making combinations and financing arrangements for any two levels of government, from the extreme of complete independence between levels, to the extreme of total dominance by the national government. The use of conditional funding can be midway along this spectrum or close to national dominance depending on the conditions imposed. In the block funding situation, he says, there can be a conflict between national and state priorities and a failure to achieve either. If the same information source can be used for the decisions of both levels there can also be duplication. However, such a two-tier allocation process can result in more effective decisions, by devolving responsibility upon levels of government which have superior information sources or are more likely to seek improvements in the quality of services through innovation or experimentation. But a different kind of conflict occurs, he argues, if national priorities are "superimposed on state priorities by means of either (i) specific purpose grants with matching conditions, or (ii) specific purpose grants subject to revenue-raising as well as expenditure conditions. In both cases there is the possibility of inconsistency between federal and state priorities, but where matching conditions are imposed the problem is compounded by the probability that state priorities in other fields of expenditure will also be distorted."[70] Unfortunately even this framework is too vague for our purposes because it doesn't explain the manner in which such priority distortion can occur. However Mathews elsewhere elaborates further:

> Because of the possibility that grants will not achieve their purposes if they simply result in recipient governments reducing their own tax efforts, governments making specific purpose grants frequently specify matching requirements or relate the grants to fiscal effort. But budget constraints often mean that matching requirements merely make the recipient governments divert funds from one crisis area to another, while other kinds of revenue constraints distort the pattern of choice available to the governments which are best placed to determine priorities.[71]

This is still quite a vague statement per se but a little later Mathews gives an example. The matching grants for universities and colleges of advanced education, he claims, distorted the pattern of state spending on education generally by forcing the states to divert funds from primary and secondary education to universities and colleges. In the case of roads the states had not been encouraged to construct interstate expressways (as would be a proper objective of conditional funding), but they had been forced to spend money on country roads whether they wanted to or not.

Wade gives some methods whereby conditional funding can cause priority distortion. One is where a state or local government may have given a high priority to a certain programme some time before a national decision is made to provide a specific purpose grant for that field. That state would then receive relatively less assistance from the conditional programme and no help whatever toward other areas of responsibility. He claims that this distortion is further accentuated if the state has to provide a matching grant or pay interest on the conditional transfer. Finally he asserts that continued emphasis on capital funding not only affects the capital expenditure state priorities, but also, unless appropriate adjustments are made in general revenue assistance, this can severely distort the current account section of a state budget.[72]

The only writer who has confronted this whole question in anything like a detailed way is Jay who has distinguished four types of conditional payments which do not affect state priorities and four other types which do. Those which do not affect state priorities are (a) grants which meet a proportion of the contractual obligations of the states for debt charges; (b) grants, mostly in the welfare field, which represent the expenditure of funds in areas which are the constitutional responsibility of the national government. Here the states are merely the disbursing agents; (c) grants made under arrangements or agreements based on cooperation between equals rather than the imposition of priorities by the national government; and (d) pure revenue-sharing grants for specific purposes (for example, pre-1959 road grants related to collections of customs and excise duties). The specific purpose grants which do affect state priorities are (a) grants necessary for a state to discharge its functions where the national government specifies how the grants are to be spent; (b) grants related to a national plan of expenditure on a state function, where the national government provides a substantial part of the funds but makes adherence to the national plan a condition of the grants; (c) grants provided in the form of specific purpose payments, where the states are required to make matching contributions as a condition of the grants; and (d) arrangements whereby the national government takes out the entire responsibility for financing a state government function and reduces general purpose grants and state Loan Council programmes by amounts which the state governments save.[73] It can be readily appreciated that even this classification is quite vague in parts and rather simplistic, for example, to the extent that it assumes that all grants with any kind of matching condition will distort state priorities. Unfortunately Jay does not attempt to measure the magnitude of each category, although he does say elsewhere that roads and education are the only fields where matching conditions apply, and he also makes the important statement that the source of the state's own contribution to the funding is important.[74] On the subject of matching grants, Prest offers the opinion that he doesn't think they are particularly appropriate to Australia except where a service could be partially financed by sources of income normally outside state budgets, such as university or hospital fees and some forms of road taxation. Otherwise, he says, matching funds can only be obtained by reducing expenditure in some other field, often equally important, or pressing the national government into increasing its general purpose grants, in which case it might as well have given the full grant in the first place.[75] We could go on citing authors[76] relevant to Australian experience but would not obtain any more precision to the argument. To date nobody really knows the extent to which subnational priorities have been distorted in Australia. Grewal probably sums it up best:

> The question that arises is whether the distortion of expenditure priorities is due to the instrument of specific purpose grants as such or the manner of their application? The answer to this depends partly on whether matching or other revenue conditions are attached to the grants and whether revenue and expenditure substitution takes place at the sub-national level. If there are no revenue conditions, sub-national expenditure priorities are not distorted but the national government's priorities are superimposed to the extent that sub-national governments do not switch their expenditures. If expenditure substitution is prevented by the attachment of matching or other revenue conditions to the grants, the principal effect of specific purpose grants is to stimulate total expenditure on the selected functions. But this may occur at the expense of a distortion of the sub-national governments' own priorities if the latter governments are required

to spend more on those functions than they would do in the absence of the grants. If this is accepted, the responsibility for distortion of sub-national expenditure priorities must lie with the decision making processes which select the aided functions and the form of the grants. Selection of aided function is the most crucial stage in the application of specific purpose grants. A . . . weakness has been that the aided programs are chosen unilaterally and arbitrarily by the national government(s). Inadequate attention has been paid to the consideration of the opportunity costs of these programs, in terms of other competing national and sub-national programs.[77]

This subject has also of course been raised in the Canadian context and views are basically similar to those voiced in the Australian literature. It is interesting to note, that prior to the introduction of the EPF arrangements, conditional funding was tending to distort the priorities of the *national* government to the extent that many programmes were open ended, and the provinces were able to escalate the national payout on them by increasing their own spending under the matching arrangements.[78] It also happened in Australia in the mid 1970s, rather more indirectly, that the continued payment by the national government of conditional and other funds to the states caused the national government to incur a higher level of indebtedness that had been experienced for a long time. Thus conditional payments unwittingly interfered with the priorities of the Australian national government.[79] Robinson concludes on the basis of the available evidence that intergovernmental grants do increase the expenditures of recipient governments, but it is still not clear how this occurs. He poses a number of questions which have not yet been satisfactorily answered: "Do grants stimulate the activities they are intended to stimulate and to the extent intended? Are the expenditures new expenditures or substitutions?" He then makes the pregnant statement that: "The exigencies of intergovernmental politics are such that, if there is a possibility of an intergovernmental grant, the potential recipient is not likely to show his hand in the bargaining process by announcing the amount that will be spent if a grant is not forthcoming. Alternatively, instead of diverting expenditures to another item, a recipient government may reduce its own taxes, or, even more elusively, hold off a tax increase that will otherwise have been imposed."[80]

This leads us then to another point in the "priority debate"; the fact that subnational governments can refuse to accept conditional funding if they find it is causing too much distortion of their own preferences. It is true that both the Australian states and Canadian provinces have refused some conditional funding especially where the programme was at odds with the ideology of the recipient government, as with land purchasing or home rental versus sale. However, with the exception of the Quebec case, the incidences of such refusal have always been for relatively small amounts in minor programmes. We have already encountered one of the main reasons, namely, that the taxpayers of all states/provinces are funding the national government, and if a conditional programme is not accepted they are seen to be not reaping the benefits from their taxes. The subnational position was put succinctly by a former premier of New South Wales:

> ... revenue has become regulation. The grant is offered to the State with strings attached. What else can a revenue-starved State do but accept the regulation that is imposed by the Commonwealth along with the grant? ... Assume the Commonwealth puts forward the suggestion of a $ for $ contribution to some project. The project may seem worthwhile to the public at large, at least as long as one puts aside priorities. But that is just the point. The State's understanding of its priorities, of what is in the best interest of the State, can be thwarted by the Federal grant which the State is almost obliged to accept.[81]

Mathews approaches the argument this way:

> The expansion of specific purpose programs was a direct consequence of the vertical financial imbalance which resulted from uniform income taxation and the other shifts in financial powers ... deprived of access to their own tax revenues and limited in the amounts they could borrow through the Loan Council, the States were forced to accept the specific purpose payments and with them the conditions which the Federal government attached to the payments. These were mainly spending conditions involving acceptance of the Federal government's priorities and policies, which were often formulated without adequate planning or consultation with the States.
>
> To the extent that revenue conditions were imposed, these generally took the form of a requirement that the States maintain their existing revenue effort and seldom involved burdensome matching requirements. Even the grants for up to 50 per cent of hospital operating costs did not impose onerous revenue conditions on the States, since they substantially relieved the States of existing expenditure responsibilities and enabled them to switch funds to other uses. Specific purpose payments for capital purposes usually took the form of advances rather than grants where the payments were to be used to acquire revenue-producing assets.[82]

This does of course lead us into the difficult question of inducement versus coercion. We have already canvassed the argument as to whether the actual conditions of conditional funding can be legally imposed, and there is a somewhat related point, though a moral rather than legal one, as to when the conditions (and amount) of a national programme are made so attractive that they cannot be refused by subnational governments. This problem is a familiar one and is not confined in its application to intergovernmental relations. Even Cranston, who strongly decries the arguments about the extent of interference caused by conditional funding and the claims that they place onerous burdens on the states, concedes that "in a political and economic sense the States have to accept specific purpose grants" (although he goes on immediately to list a number of examples where states refused them).[83]

7.   Political Considerations

Our analysis has already revealed much of the politics which surrounds conditional funding. It is a fertile field. The responses from interviewees brought some more to light:

(a) If the national government pulls out of a conditional programme this amounts to political blackmail because it is extremely difficult to terminate such programmes, especially those which are welfare oriented.

(b) The potential offered by conditional funding for the imposition of the ideology of the national government upon that of the subnational government negates the democratic process, and undermines the legitimacy of governments at both levels.

(c) It is political suicide for a state/provincial government to refuse a conditional grant because of the possibility that the opposition will use that fact as a weapon to attempt to convey a picture of neglect by one state/province as compared with another which has taken up the conditional funding.

(d) The method whereby the national government encourages potential clientele support groups for each programme builds up expectations prior to intergovernmental negotiations, and so circumscribes the present and later freedom of the state or province in relation to those programmes.

(e) Differences in party political outlook between the national government and a subnational government can result in conditional programmes being negotiated for very short periods of operation when the nature of the programme demands a longer term commitment on both sides.

(f) The political nature of conditional funding can lead to an overemphasis on glamour projects and a neglect of more urgent but basic government action.

(g) The politics of conditional funding also leads to attempts by national ministers to gain publicity from each phase of the project, leading to undue interference and an insistence that the national minister personally approve each phase.

A number of writers have attempted to probe the basic reasons for political conflict over conditional funding. Weller and Smith have this to say about the ideological conflict:

> This kind of conflict is caused not by arguments about State independence, but by debate about whether a particular program is acceptable. The States would naturally prefer a system of fiscal federalism, with a guaranteed and sufficient income; but since they must accept money by way of Section 96 grants, they then argue about the acceptability of the aims. Medibank and the provision of leasehold (rather than freehold) land are two well known examples. The offer to take over state railways is another. It is in these matters that the comment that two premiers, one Liberal one Labor, have more in common than two Labor men, one a state premier the other prime minister, has the least truth. On

grounds of status leading State Labor politicians may regret Federal incursions into state affairs, but on ideological grounds they accept the necessity for this action if a social policy considered important is to be implemented across the whole country.

In ideological disputes, the parties are opposed to one another. But it is difficult to dismantle well-established schemes. Once a program has become institutionalised and once states, local governments or other bodies have come to depend on that program, the ideological contest of last year tends to become the political fact of life of next year. In the arena of Federal-State relations, status conflicts are eternal, inevitable and often rhetorical, ideological conflicts are prone to change their ground and their colour.[84]

Holmes and Sharman suggest that states are willing to criticize national governments of the same political persuasion over conditional funding, because the national government leaders lack direct political support in state-based party machines even though they share a nominal label.[85] Mathews regards the disputes over conditional funding as being essentially about power, political and bureaucratic power, which diverts attention from policy goals and decision processes. He says "on the one hand, the States complained that programs and policies were formulated without adequate planning and consultation and without regard to legitimate State interests . . . on the other hand, the States were often loath to accept the fact that national interests, more adequate information sources at the Commonwealth level and the effects on other States of decisions taken by individual States often made it necessary for programs and policies to be formulated by the Commonwealth government".[86] Jay admits that specific purpose payments can be sheer political instruments to favour states of a like persuasion, and have been used in particular states in strategic areas at strategic times to win votes. He also sees some of the smaller programmes as having resulted from states demanding money for a project, however small, when there seems to be the chance of a handout. Jay argues that a very good reason should be given why such projects should not be financed by the state from its general purpose funds: "one of the criteria governing specific purpose grants, therefore, should be that if the amount is trivial it is suspect".[87] As something of a counter argument, the 1970 statement of the state premiers said that the proliferation of conditional programmes tends to make the public think that the states are being well treated by the national government.[88] In this respect Stevenson acknowledges the Canadian experience that provincial officials used to get largesse out of spending conditional health and welfare grants.[89] Else-Mitchell offers the opinion that, because specific purpose payments have been made in many areas for so long, they are taken for granted and the source of power and methods of verification of expenditure are not questioned.[90]

Both Hunter and Stevenson reveal another facet of the politics of conditional funding when they show that for both Australia and Canada there is a clear distinction between what Stevenson classifies as the government functions of "accumulation" and "legitimization", which roughly corresponds with Hunter's categories of "development" and "welfare". Stevenson's contention is that conditional funding of the former type does not come in for criticism but that of the latter type does. This is because accumulation expenditures "directly benefited the influential classes in the provinces — businessmen and in some cases farmers — persuading them that they received good value in return for their taxes. . . . another advantage . . . was that accumulation expenditures (public works, resource development, subsidies to business, and so forth) largely remained within the province; in other words there were few spillovers. On the other hand, the provinces showed little disposition to spend heavily on legitimization, by which is meant such areas as health, welfare, social insurance pensions, protection of the environment, or support of the arts, letters and the sciences. These activities did not directly, and in the short run, benefit the dominant classes; taxes levied to support them would be viewed as a burden disproportionate to the benefits received. Those residents of the province who would benefit directly were politically weak and poorly organized, usually without even a political party that reliably represented their interests. Ideology and tradition provided no impetus towards such expenditure. In addition, the mobility of the population ensured that the direct benefits of expenditure on legitimization might be largely reaped outside the province."[91] According to Stevenson's account, the provinces thus always had spent their own funds on accumulation rather than legitimization, always preferring a dam to a hospital, a railway to a university, and an industrial subsidy to a pension. So, Canadian conditional grants were formulated primarily as a means of overcoming this situation. He goes so far as to say that the provinces cannot be relied on to spend enough in this field of policy without substantial incentives and in some cases actual coercion. But the significant point is that conditional grants of the accumulation type do not come in for the criticism directed at conditional funding in general, and Stevenson thinks this fits neatly with North American rhetoric about the evils of government spending, which he sees as meaning really opposition to welfare spending; not spending to boost industry. The national government is slightly more attracted to the legitimization type of spending because it has more funds at its disposal, and spillovers don't worry it so much because welfare recipients rarely leave the country. But, according to Stevenson, the national government funds such programmes conditionally, rather than directly, because it too lacks full enthusiasm for them, and likes to be able to have the potential beneficiaries blame the provincial government if it refuses to accept the programme. There is also an age-old feeling in Canada that welfare is a provincial function. Now the complete details of this Canadian scenario do not completely match Australian experience but the analogy does sit reasonably squarely. In the Australian context, Hunter expresses the opinion that one can only guess at the amount of spending which specific purpose grants promote which the states would have undertaken on their own initiative, but he believes it would be a large amount "especially since the initiatives for many grants, especially those in the developmental as opposed to the welfare category, come from the states. Moreover, these initiatives are almost certainly related to the relative paucity of the states' financial resources. If this is true the states have an incentive to press for specific purpose grants (assuming they cannot receive general purpose grants and wish to avoid higher state taxes or charges), whatever the merits of the programmes in question. Indeed, one criticism is that the approach tends to be a pragmatic response to political pressures. It has been claimed, for example, that these pressures emanate from the states who regard specific purpose grants as the reward for successful bargaining power."[92] These factors, says Hunter, are less evident in countries without such a high degree of vertical fiscal imbalance. This pragmatism in conditional funding in Australia is further reflected by the fact that very few of the Australian conditional programmes are conducted on a long-term, formula basis; they are mostly of an ad hoc nature.[93]

There are innumerable other political aspects of conditional funding which could be analysed, and associated political ploys which can at times make for humorous reading if the situation were not so serious. (Consider the Australian water programme which was terminated when only one half of the city of Adelaide had been covered and the state government was forced politically to meet the cost of completing the other half of the city. Or the Canadian practice by provincial governments to erect signs on conditionally funded projects with mention of the name of the national government at the bottom of the sign so that it is covered in winter by the snow line.) But enough has been said to make the point. We can conclude with the perennial argument, so often appearing in the literature, that conditional payments distort accountability to the electorate. Stevenson has already shown us how a nationally devised programme like Medicare can interfere in the relationships a provincial government wants between the medical profession and its clients, or how an education programme can challenge a provincial government's view of the role of the church, or how a welfare grant can interfere in the provincial government's outlook on the family unit. He discounts the accountability distortion argument by simply saying that "since every Canadian citizen entitled to vote in a provincial election can also vote in a federal election, and vice versa, this argument does not seem exceptionally persuasive".[94] Nonetheless, in Australia, one of the largest and most influential pressure groups has recommended an end to cost sharing for hospitals and the placement of complete hospital funding with the states from boosted general purpose revenue funds from the commonwealth. Their main reason was the difficulty of determining just which level of government was really responsible for the standard of hospital services; fifty/fifty cost sharing had, they believed, resulted in a situation such that "what is everybody's responsibility is nobody's responsibility".[95]

The overwhelming impression to be gained from the literature on this subject, coupled with the interview responses, is that there are clearly arguments for and against conditional funding. The extent to which it poses a hindrance to planning will be considered in our concluding chapter. Politically the line-up is obvious — the national governments favour the device and the subnational governments oppose it. On this aspect we can leave the last word with Lane who says: "State and local governments often complain that the conditions attaching to specific purpose payments distort their priorities and prevent them from making the best use of the money they receive. It is worth noting that, to the extent that they view the situation in terms of their own particular interests, they would inevitably see it this way. Whether the intervention by the high-level government is desirable has to be judged from a broader viewpoint."[96]

We shall reserve judgment on the arguments surrounding conditional funding for the next, concluding chapter.

9

Conclusion

It is clear from the foregoing analysis that it is difficult to attain public sector planning in a federal form of government. We have defined planning as a system, and our application of that system to the theory and practice of federalism reveals a significant degree of incompatibility between the two concepts.

As observed earlier there are marked conceptual differences between planning and federalism. Planning, at least as we have defined it, is characterized by such notions as logic, rationality, symmetry, predictability, concentration of decision making, an unbroken pattern of control, and sequential linkages, all geared to the resource allocation process. Federalism, by contrast, is typified by fragmentation, asymmetry, bargaining and hence uncertainty, and the sharing of power or control, including control over resources.

Our analysis of federalism as a concept, and also as a practice in the two countries of Australia and Canada, has revealed that the aspect of federalism which poses the greatest hindrance to the introduction of the sort of planning we are envisaging is the fact that sovereignty is divided between a national government and subnational units of government; power is thus fragmented. The most tangible expression of this divided sovereignty is the actual division of functional powers in the two federations.

Split sovereignty and the division of powers does not affect all parts of our planning system with equal force. The planning system, it will be recalled, comprises forecasting, determination of priorities, allocation of resources, implementation, and review. For example, forecasting is a function which could adequately be handled by one level of government acting for itself and for the other levels as well. Similarly the review function could become the responsibility of just one of the levels of government. It is the determination of priorities and the actual allocation of resources which are the most political elements of our planning system, and hence it is in these functions that the involvement of different levels of government and a formal division of power between them causes most difficulty. To a lesser extent this is also true of the implementation function since it is rare for one sovereign level of government to be willing to allow another unit of government complete autonomy in the implementation of policies in whose formulation it participated. We shall return to this aspect later.

Our analysis of the division of powers in both Australia and Canada revealed a number of factors highly unconducive to smooth and efficient priority determination and resource allocation. By splitting sovereignty this also fragments legitimacy, leading to rival power-seeking by both politicians and administrators of the separate governments. Being rivals, their basic interest is often in conflict, rather than in cooperation or coordination, since each has its own electorate to appease. Contrary to the expectations of the founding fathers of both federations, the division of power has become a line across which a bargaining process is constantly taking place, and that line is a dynamic one so that the relationships between the units of government are constantly changing and are not the static, neat dichotomy portrayed in the wording of the Australian or Canadian constitutions.

The formal division of power in these federations has also become dated by the wording of the constitutions which tends to be in terms of subject matters whose meaning has changed over time. Moreover, in those few functions of government where power is deemed to be concurrent, the power relationship between the levels of government has become unsettled because of the absence of any mechanism, save the nominal supremacy of the national government, which is really politically unworkable.

This leads to another difficulty, namely, that the formal division of powers tends to terminate the geographical jurisdiction of governments simply because the units of government in a federation are constructed with spatial boundaries. Thus a two-dimensional political struggle takes place in these federations; over functions of government generally, and over the control of functions within a particular geographical territory. The founding fathers of both federations compounded this problem by actually affixing a spatial dimension to some public functions. Thus the industrial relations power in Australia is divided by the constitution in a manner which gives the national government jurisdiction only over industrial matters extending beyond the limits of one state; and the same effect is produced in Canada in regard to public works and company incorporations where it is the power of the provinces which is similarly circumscribed, or education where the power of the Canadian national government is limited, or the law function which in Canada is divided between the levels according to the nature of the law. In Australia the control of shipping is fragmented between the two levels of government by constitutional provisions which seek, very falsely at times, to distinguish between interstate and intrastate shipping. Indeed, the division of powers has been responsible for the fact that jurisdiction over many simple and identifiable government functions has been split between the levels of government. Take transport, for example, and there is a mixture of responsibility over the various transport modes, for example, roads, air, rail, sea, pipeline, cable, etc., where different levels of government are responsible for different modes, and within a particular mode it can happen that one unit of government's jurisdiction is spatially limited. Thus, in Australia, the national government controls most air transport but shares power with the states over intrastate transport; similarly for sea transport; rail transport is divided with both levels of government actually conducting railway operations; road jurisdiction is split to the extent that the commonwealth gives road funding and both state and local governments engage in road construction; bus and ferry transport are split between state and local governments, and so on. In the case of hospitals, in both Australia and Canada it is possible for national and subnational units (including local government in some circumstances) to construct hospitals.

The point of these examples is simply to demonstrate that the formal division of power in a federation serves to fragment control over individual public functions. This can only be a hindrance to planning because public sector planning proceeds by way of expressing priorities in terms of one public function against another, which, in turn, requires that each public function must be capable of being perceived and regulated as one discrete entity. How, for example, could an Australian or Canadian national public sector plan hope to cope with certainty, on a national basis, with the transport function or the hospital function? The spatial and functional breakages render the task particularly difficult.

The sheer existence of a division of powers creates another hindrance for any planning attempt because it creates the necessity for an umpire to arbitrate between the levels of government, and even between the units of government at the same level. This role is played in both the Australian and Canadian federations by the respective High (or Supreme) Courts. The decisions of those courts over the years have, as we have witnessed in earlier discussion, changed the very division of powers itself by virtue of their interpretations of the constitution, and more particularly because of differing interpretations of the same matters from time to time. The presence of an umpire itself presents an obstacle to planning because it provides yet another locus of decision making in a structure already complicated by the presence of more than one sovereign government. It also creates delays, and, most importantly, it introduces an element of uncertainty into the various deliberations associated with the planning process. This would be true of any federation and it is of course a necessary obstruction given the nature of federalism. (It is also true of a unitary system of government to the extent that the judiciary acts as a check on the executive and even, to a slight extent, on the legislature. However, the role of the court being emphasized here is its function of determining legitimacy of *levels* of government.) But the court, too, especially in Australia, proved to be an even greater hindrance because of the substance of some of its decisions which have tended to fragment power even further between the two main levels. Thus, for example, the liberal interpretation by the court of Section 92 relating to interstate trade has limited centripetal forces emanating from the national government, but has also placed limits on the extent of regulation of state governments over activities originating from within their boundaries but transgressing their borders.

It might be imagined that a satisfactory division of powers in a federation would at least enable each unit of government to plan its own activities in a satisfactory manner, even if it could not do so for its intergovernmental relations. Indeed our extensive review of the history and literature of Australian and Canadian federalism has revealed that this was the basic intention of the founding fathers of both federations. But the division of powers which was created in each country was undertaken at a time when the role of government in the community was a limited one. It was also a time when the Westminster model of political accountability had reached its highest point of refinement in Britain and her colonies. There was also limited mobility of resources between colonies and limited communication between them. This meant that clear lines of accountability had been established from the executive to the people through a parliament which was not inhibited by party divisions. Hence the founding fathers had reason to believe that the division of powers which they desired could be a discrete division encapsulating each unit of the federation into a watertight compartment.

Here then is the essence of the shortcomings of the division of powers in both federations. The role of government has been substantially extended and the nature of government activity has also changed. Resources are now highly mobile around the federation, and this, together with other factors, has led to a complexity of society, an interrelatedness which cannot be adequately regulated by a federal system which attempts to rest on a simplistic division of powers. Society has evolved at a much faster rate than the institutions of its government.

Our research has revealed a considerable number of linkages which exist within, and between, functions of government which have occurred in a natural manner as the economy and society in general have become more mobile, more communicative, more dependent, and so, more sophisticated. These natural linkages stand in stark contrast with the artificial divisions of government power in the respective constitutions, and it is this juxtaposition of natural connections with artificial breakages in government regulations which provides one of the most fundamental stumbling blocks to the introduction of a planning system such as the one envisaged.

Earlier we listed and examined many of the linkages between individual functions of government. It will be recalled that this list included, among other things, the connection between post and telegraph; the conduct of lotteries; the impact of rail and road transport on land settlement; the manner in which taxation laws can splinter family estates; the obvious linkage between navigation and irrigation on rivers; the impact of industrial matters on trade and commerce; the connection of education to broadcasting, literature, research, etc.; the clear relationship of powers over marriage and divorce with family matters; the influence of radio and television on cigarette smoking, and so on. That is one form of linkage which is not adequately catered for by the formal division of powers. If one were to take the trouble to construct a complete catalogue of such linkages, one would find that all the chains in the link will be controlled by different levels of government, for example, posts and telegraphs being a national function and lotteries a subnational function. These are reasonably specific linkages and tangible ones, even though we tend not to view them as such because the institutions of government at each level, as well as between levels, fragment them for purposes of government control. Thus, natural social and economic linkages are just as much a problem for the separation of powers as for the division of powers.

As well as those more tangible linkages between actual government functions, we have also identified a subtle form of linkage between the levels of government in a federation which occurs where the unilateral actions of one unit have consequences for other units, even though the active unit is acting completely within its formal power boundaries. As we have seen, this occurs mainly as a result of national actions which impact upon subnational governments, as with monetary policy, tariff protection policy, broadcasting, etc., where national policies affect subnational government activity. Immigration is another good example in the Australian context because the level of immigration has a real consequence for the provision of infrastructure by state and local governments. In a like manner, any fiddling by a national government with its criteria for various pension entitlements will create problems for state/provincial or local governments who offer various concessions on their normal charges for government services to pensioners. The reverse process can also occur, though less frequently, as when states tax resource utilization or change land utilization policies forcing reconsideration of national policies. In Australia, government control over Aboriginal affairs provides an interesting example because, although a referendum in 1967 gave the national government unequivocal powers over Aboriginal matters, the state governments retain all powers over land utilization. Since a great many aspects of legislation for Aboriginal affairs relate to land tenure, the division of powers is a significant hindrance to the implementation of national government policies for Aboriginal people. Again there are the spillover effects of the actions of a single government unit which have formed such a large part of our earlier analysis. The point about linkages of this type is that, once again, the institutions of federalism are not constructed to cope with them because the constitutional division of powers does not recognize them. More particularly, few provisions exist for one unit of government to participate in all those decisions which affect it.

These then are some of the hindrances which arose when we engaged in a contemplation of the division of powers. Our technique, it will be recalled, was to examine the two most prominent manifestations of the power division to determine the intractability or otherwise of those problems in a more practical context. Intergovernmental agreements and federal financial relationships were analysed as the areas where intergovernmental relations take on the most tangible form.

The examination of federal financial relationships in Australia revealed many problems facing the introduction of our planning system. The very existence of vertical fiscal imbalance is a major obstacle to the subnational units of government because, especially in Australia, it leads to a very high level of dependence for them on transfers from the national government. (Of course it follows that this vertical imbalance automatically makes it easier for the national government to plan its activities in accordance with "national priorities".) Moreover, the lack of uniformity between the states or provinces leads to asymmetry in both federations whereupon each state or province has a different level and nature of dependence on intergovernmental transfers. In other words, both federations also display a significant degree of horizontal imbalance made manifest in the overall incidence of dependence, together with differing mixtures of current and capital funding, and differing mixtures of unconditional and conditional funding. Offsetting this factor, to some extent, is the very existence of a systematic policy of rectifying horizontal imbalance through equalization payments which, if nothing else, should remove some degree of the uncertainty for a subnational unit in projecting its likely revenue.

Of particular importance is the pronounced variability in intergovernmental funding year to year, and the necessity for the annual variations to be offset by quick shifts in revenue-raising policies of the recipient governments. It must be recognized that this need not be an inherent problem of federalism per se, but could also at times reflect the way in which the national government uses its powers. All of this is compounded by the fact that, in both Australia and Canada, the largest blocks of conditional transfers from the national government are for functions which are constitutionally assigned to the state/provincial governments, thereby rendering the formal division of powers even more redundant. This situation is exacerbated by the processes of fiscal coordination *within* units of government which are not themselves conducive to priority determination because they are fragmented; for example, national, as well as state or provincial budgets, are uncomprehensive owing to the existence of public or crown corporations, other statutory bodies, and the use of trust funds and other accounting devices which fragment fiscal policy *within* the subnational level itslf. This lack of coordination within units of government naturally bodes ill for any attempt at intergovernmental coordination, which lies at the heart of our planning process. These, and other internal inadequacies of subnational governments in particular, figured prominently in our earlier discussions.

What was not so explicitly recognized earlier was a number of other factors which lie at the heart of the difficulty of achieving the elements of our planning system in federal financial relationships. These are, in effect, linkages which would have to exist within the pattern of federal financial relationships for democratic priority determination and resource allocation to take place effectively. The first is some sort of connection between taxation and expenditure decisions. What is needed is a linkage at the marginal level of decision. Thus, it is not so much a matter of the *degree* of vertical imbalance but rather a question of whether the level of the vertical fiscal transfers is subject to negotiation or argument at the margin, so that for each government a change in expenditure has to be considered in relation to a change in its own revenue raising. It is clear that in both federations this linkage is missing, especially in Australia with its high degree of vertical imbalance. The national government makes decisions about the level and nature of taxation to raise revenue which will be spent to a significant degree by the states/provinces. On the other hand, the states/provinces make choices about expenditure allocations against a background where the national government will supply a large component of that spending. In such a situation the national government is responsible to its electorate for raising revenue whose disbursement it will only partially control, whereas the subnational units are not responsible to their electorates for the raising of all the money that they spend. To oversimplify the problem we can say that with one sovereign government raising this money and a different sovereign government spending it, it is inevitable that they will find it difficult to coordinate their views in order to agree on priorities, and the attendant allocation of money to achieve those priorities. Moreover, the electorate of each of the two levels will find it singularly frustrating to place the credit or blame for government activity if it disagrees in any way with the priorities and allocations which emerge. In other words, it is politically irresponsible that the government which spends funds has little say in the raising of them and vice versa.

Secondly, there is, within the financial relationships of both federations, a very tenuous relationship between decisions about capital expenditure, and decisions about recurrent expenditure. Indeed there are separate institutional frameworks for the intergovernmental allocation of the two types of funding in both federations. Yet for the introduction of our notion of public sector planning it is essential to recognize the link between capital and recurrent spending. If this is not done it can result, in the extreme, in the provision of hospitals with no staff to run them, or a surplus of teachers with an inadequate number of schools, and so on. Our analysis has shown no connection between the movements in the intergovernmental transfers for capital purposes and recurrent purposes. The pattern in both Australia and Canada is for the two types of funding to be negotiated separately in different parts of the political and bureaucratic framework. Once again it needs to be stressed that this is not an inherent aspect of the federal form of government and could occur just as readily in a unitary system. However, the problem is exacerbated in a federation where sovereign units have some further power to reallocate funds between capital and recurrent purposes. In terms of the actual flow of funds, the usual pattern is for a relatively smooth trend in recurrent payments, but an erratic trend in capital payments, because the former are more concerned with "uncontrollable" elements of public expenditure, such as wages and salaries and interest on debt. From within recurrent and capital funding the intergovernmental allocation of expenditure and priority determination does not take place according to our concept of planning. Essentially this is because the spatial emphasis is stronger than the functional emphasis so that, for example, the Australian Loan Council, which oversees public capital expenditure in the Australian federation, compiles a loan programme based on submissions from the states and then allocates loan funds *by state* rather than by project or by functional area. We shall return to this aspect later.

The point has frequently been made in chapters 6 and 7 that there is little in the way of a formal connection between the mechanisms affecting vertical fiscal imbalance and those which affect horizontal fiscal imbalance. (It is, of course, true that the mechanism for tax sharing take some account of both horizontal and vertical imbalances and they represent the major transfer item.) Indeed we have observed that, in both federations, there are in fact various formulae and processes which impact upon horizontal imbalance depending on the nature of the function. Each programme seems to have a different methodology for this purpose, and they, in turn, differ from the basic equalization programmes achieved in Australia through the operations of the Commonwealth Grants Commission and in Canada through the formal Equalization formulae. There is no way horizontal equalization can be applied separately to individual components of a consolidated budget: it has to be done for the budget as a whole, covering both revenue and expenditure. It can, of course, be done for separate subbudgets with revenue earmarked for specified functions.

Finally there is, of course, no consistent connection between intergovernmental funding which is unconditional and that which is conditional. The former tends to change from year to year in a smoother pattern primarily because it is based on formulae negotiated to cover long term periods, as with the net tax-sharing agreements in Australia. By contrast the conditional funding is, as we have seen, prone to severe fluctuations year to year, especially the capital element of it. It is quite apparent that the process for determining conditional funding is, generally speaking, more short term and more political. What is of particular importance is the fact that we have uncovered no evidence to suggest that, in determining the level and nature of conditional funding, there is automatic consideration of the level of unconditional funding. The states/provinces must seek the one type of funding through quite different channels from the ones through which they pursue the other type. The only time an automatic link is forged between unconditional and conditional funding is when an attempt is made to offset some movement in conditional funding by a commensurate change in unconditional funding, as for example, when a national government shifts its funding from single programmes into block grants, or takes over some government function from the subnational units, or for ideological or other political reasons simply decides to fund certain aspects of state/provincial activity in one way rather than the other as happened in Canada with the Established Programs Financing arrangements. This is another example of a problem not unique to federal forms of government but exacerbated by them.

These then are some of the main factors which emerged out of our analysis of federal finance in Australia and Canada. They are evidence of a very piecemeal and fragmented pattern of priority determination and resource allocation, and so present severe obstacles to the implementation of the envisaged planning system. We did, of course, encounter some countervailing forces. A portion of the intergovernmental fiscal transfers is considered on a long term basis. In Australia the old Financial Assistance Grants, and the tax-sharing arrangements which replaced them, have been negotiated for five year periods, although it has not been uncommon for them to be supplemented in some years on an ad hoc basis reflecting political opportunism. Some Australian conditional funding, and a good deal of Canadian conditional funding, is negotiated on a formula basis applicable over three or five years with a lengthy period stipulated as being required if one unit of government wishes to withdraw. This, of course, reflects the fact that conditional funding is often associated with intergovernmental agreements. The very mechanisms of correcting horizontal imbalance through equalization programmes must create something of an air of certainty for a subnational unit of government, in the sense of a net or backstop should anything untoward occur in its revenue-raising or expenditure capabilities.

This leaves only the general debate about conditional funding to consider. This debate warrants separate attention because it loomed so large in responses from interviewees employed in subnational governments who saw it as perhaps the prime obstacle to attainment of public sector planning, especially at their level of government. The arguments against conditional funding and the descriptive data about them in both federations were presented comprehensively earlier. It must naturally be conceded that any type of conditional funding will make decision making by a subnational government more complicated. This is especially so for a central budget agency like a state treasury which will need to be able to compute, for government estimates, the amount of expenditure from the state's own revenue which will be required for every functional area. If some of those functional areas are to be the subject of intergovernmental funding as well as local funding, this will obviously change the level of local funding required.

If it were a complete substitution of intergovernmental funding for local funding (that is with no matching or other requirements for a contribution by the recipient government), that need not be of concern to the recipient government, because if it is for the same amount which the recipient government would have spent anyway, the recipient government is able to free that amount of funds for spending elsewhere. If it is for an amount less than would have been spent by the recipient government on that function, the recipient government is always able to deploy some of its own revenue to top up the intergovernmental transfers being given for that function. If the intergovernmental funding is for an amount greater than would have been spent by the recipient government then that is obviously of no fiscal concern to the recipient government, although it may be of political concern in that it creates a higher expectation on the part of those benefiting from the expenditure, and an expectation that the higher level of funding will always continue even if the intergovernmental funding should cease or diminish. Such is the lack of sophistication and natural human reaction of beneficiaries of public expenditure. However, the point to be made is that in terms of our discussion of planning, involving priorities which we define to mean choices, none of the possible methods of conditional funding under this scenario really affect the priorities of subnational governments.

A somewhat different picture emerges if the government giving the conditional funding, which in Australia and Canada means the national government, attaches some kind of matching or other constraint to its funding. We have seen that the most common type of fiscal condition in these two countries is that which requires the recipient government to match the intergovernmental transfer to some degree. If those conditions only result in the recipient government devoting the same, or a lesser amount, of their own revenue to a particular function compared with what it would have spent on that function in the absence of the intergovernmental transfer, then there has surely been no effective interference with the priorities of the recipient government. This will depend on whether the subnational government has any choice as to how much it will match. If it has a choice, then the marginal cost to the subnational government of variations in the level of the service is reduced by the national government's contribution. However we can readily agree with the arguments advanced by interviewees and in the literature, that if the conditions of the intergovernmental transfer result in the recipient government devoting more of its own revenue to a function than it would have devoted in the absence of the intergovernmental transfer, a priority distortion has taken place for the recipient government. We can also readily agree that if, because of the nature of the matching or other conditions, the recipient (say subnational) government is able to draw more intergovernmental funds for a particular function than the donor (say national) government had intended it would spend on that function, then a priority distortion has again taken place, this time for the donor government. The former situation is claimed to have occurred in both federations, especially in those situations where there were governments in power at the national level with a conflicting ideology with that of any incumbent subnational government, particularly in functions like public housing, land purchasing and some quasi-welfare payments. The latter situation has also occurred in both federations, though more so in Canada, where runaway provincial spending in conditional programme areas causing escalating national government spending through matching conditions, was partly responsible for the new components of the Established Programs Financing package which now places a ceiling on national government contributions. In Australia there were similar occurrences, though to a lesser extent, with public hospital funding causing the national government to review its open-ended commitment to meet fifty per cent of the costs involved in that function. There is a conflict, from the viewpoint of the economic theory of efficient resource allocation, between placing a ceiling on the national government's contributions, and offering a subsidy to the subnational government in recognition of the spillover benefits of expenditure undertaken by the latter. However it is doubtful whether any attempt at measuring the spillovers has ever influenced the ratio of the matching requirement.

Thus we can accept the argument that such priority distortion can and does occur. But what is unclear is the scale on which it occurs in both federations.

There is no evidence to suggest that it is a problem of great magnitude. No respondent in the interviews associated with this study was prepared to place a figure on the proportion of intergovernmental transfers so affected, and as we saw earlier, the Australian author who has conducted the most research in this area, Robert Jay, was not able to provide such a figure either. The basic reason is that it is impossible to compute because of the manner in which public finance data is presented; because of the poor overview and research capacity of the central coordinating institutions at both national and subnational levels in the two federations, which have failed to tackle this question; as well as the real probability that the problem is a relatively insignificant one anyway. Indeed, all the evidence which is available suggests that the proportion of intergovernmental funding affected by the priority distortion phenomena is very low indeed.

For a start, conditional funding has always represented less than half of all the intergovernmental transfers in Australia. In the case of Canada, whilst conditional funding exceeds unconditional funding, it has generally represented less than two-thirds of the total mixture. This allows latitude for the topping up process, referred to earlier, from unconditional funds into conditionally funded functions. This has been referred to elsewhere as the "bottles analogy",[1] whereby the various bottles, that is, functions of subnational governments, are filled by the donor government to the levels it desires through its conditional funding devices, and the subnational governments then top up those bottles which they think should be filled to a higher level with the use of their considerable reservoir of unconditional intergovernmental transfers, as well as with their own revenue. Once again we can see that this analogy breaks down if any bottle is filled by the donor government to a higher level than the subnational government would have wished in the first place; or if the donor government produces a bottle which the recipient government would not have even placed in the line-up at all if given the choice. It must also be conceded that the evidence adduced from the tables in Chapter 8, for both Australia and Canada, revealed a very erratic pattern of overall conditional funding for many functional areas from year to year, and it has to be agreed that this would cause some uncertainty about whether the flow into each bottle would be a trickle or a flood each year. This, of course, is more of an administrative problem revolving around communications between politicians and public administrators at both levels of government.

Secondly, it is obvious from the data in Chapter 8 that the level of dependence on intergovernmental transfers varies greatly from state to state in Australia, and from province to province in Canada. There is a definite pattern in both federations that the more populous the state or province, the lower its dependence on intergovernmental transfers, or to put it the other way around, the more autonomous it is in that it provides a higher proportion of its expenditure needs from its own revenue sources. There is also something of a pattern in existence, especially in Canada, whereby the more populous subnational units received a greater share of their intergovernmental funding in the conditional form mainly because the unconditional element of intergovernmental fiscal transfers in each country has a strong horizontal equalization component. So those subnational units with the greatest accent on conditional funding in their profile of intergovernmental receipts are precisely those units which have more fiscal autonomy in general, and are therefore logically better placed to offset any priority distortion effects. To take some extreme cases for the purpose of illustration: Ontario in Canada receives 96 per cent of its intergovernmental funding in the conditional form; the Alberta figure is 88 per cent, but those transfers represent only 17 per cent of all the revenue coming to the province of Ontario and only 10 per cent of all the revenue coming to Alberta. Considering that the priority distortion element would only be a fraction of that 17 per cent and 10 per cent, its overall impact is most likely to be negligible. In the Australian case, Victoria receives 45 per cent of its intergovernmental funding in the conditional form and New South Wales the same, but it can be estimated that those transfers represent only 16 per cent of all Victoria's revenue and 17 per cent of that of New South Wales.

In view of these figures it is difficult to find much sympathy for the priority distortion argument in the more populous states and provinces. It seems therefore, on the surface at least, to be more of a problem for the less populous states and provinces. However, in their situation, the pattern of intergovernmental funding acts to rectify the situation. In both Australia and Canada, especially Canada, the smaller states and provinces are definitely more dependent overall on intergovernmental funding, but the profile of that funding has a much smaller proportion of conditional funding in it. So even in Prince Edward Island, the most fiscally dependent Canadian province (over 55 per cent of its total revenue comes from intergovernmental transfers), the conditional funding from the national government represents only 25 per cent of the revenue coming to the province from all sources because that province receives only about half of all its intergovernmental transfers in the conditional form.

In Australia, Tasmania, the smallest state, receives only 33 per cent of all its intergovernmental funding in the conditional form, and that would represent only 18 per cent of all the state's revenue receipts from all sources. Consequently, even in the most fiscally dependent subnational units, their intergovernmental conditional funding represents 25 per cent (Prince Edward Island) and 18 per cent (Tasmania) of their total revenue. Once again the priority distortion element of that conditional funding is likely to be only a fraction of the total. If it amounted to even a fifth of all the conditional funding that would still represent only 5 per cent and 3.5 per cent respectively of the province/state's total revenue from all sources. (The statistics would be more meaningful if we could segregate conditional grants with a matching requirement, but no separate data of this kind is provided for either federation.)

Another way of attempting to come to grips with the extent to which the priority of subnational units might have been distorted is to examine those priorities as reflected in the proportion of state or provincial expenditure devoted to each functional area over a period of time. Any significant changes might, superficially at least, indicate the difficulty they have in maintaining such priorities, and the lack of any substantial variation could indicate a capacity on their part to weather all vagaries, including fluctuations in intergovernmental funding, particularly conditional funding. This is not an easy task to perform because of the lack of comparable data for each country between states or provinces, especially data on a functional basis. The state or provincial governments themselves do not provide such data, and so we are forced to rely on derived data presented by the government statisticians in both countries, as well as the Commonwealth Grants Commission in Australia. It should be noted also that the presentation of this data differs from the presentation used for conditional funding, so that it is not possible to compare directly fluctuations in conditional funding for a function with total state/local spending on that function.

A trend analysis was performed of the functional breakdown of fiscal consumption expenditure for Australian state and local authorities. (Local authorities were lumped with state authorities for this purpose because of the fact that there is a difference between the Australian states in the distribution of government functions between state and local authorities.) Considering that this analysis represented a ten year period, there was a reasonable consistency in the proportion of consumption spending allocated to each function, and this is true for every state, even though the proportion allocated to a particular function would vary from state to state. In other words, even though priorities differ from state to state, each state has maintained its priority pattern more consistently that might be expected given the pronounced fluctuations in intergovernmental transfers on which the states are so dependent. It can be noted that this was the case through a period (1972–75) when conditional funding to all states increased very rapidly. So there is obviously sufficient flexibility in the system of Australian public finance to allow priorities to differ from state to state, and also to allow each state to maintain its priorities.

Some qualifications do need to be made to this broad conclusion. First-ly, figures for consumption expenditure are "net" amounts of spending after deducting the recoupment of fees, charges, sales, and so on, in that public function. The definition of final consumption expenditure employed by the Australian Bureau of Statistics includes: "Fees and charges for services rendered and sales of goods and services by general government bodies have been offset against . . . gross expenditure, together with recoveries from other governments, to give final consumption expenditure by general governments".[2] Thus, in the allocation of consumption expenditure to various government functions, state and local authorities must take account of intergovernmental transfers into that function as well as generated revenue. This may account for some of the difference between the expenditure profile from state to state because one state may make charges for a particular government service whilst another may not. For example, there has until recently been no direct charge to patients at public hospitals in Queensland, whereas all other states have made such a charge, which will result in a "netting off" process in all states except Queensland. This factor also accounts for the major exception to our generalization about the consistency of expenditure profile within each state, namely, the item "hospital and clinic services". It was discovered that all states recorded an appreciable increase in the share of consumption expenditure on this function in the latter part of the period under review as a result of the new boosted hospital cost-sharing arrangements introduced in the mid 1970s. Of course the very process of "netting" does not negate the general tenor of our conclusion. Indeed the possibility of using offsetting revenue adds another important element of flexibility for state/local governments. It is mentioned here because it explains to some extent the general conclusion we have drawn about lack of priority consistency between states, but consistency within states. Yet another point to be made is that the bulk of "final consumption expenditure" constitutes wages, salaries, and supplements. Supplements include "contributions by general government bodies to superannuation funds and accruing superannuation liability of public enterprises", but "direct payment of pensions etc. to former employees by way of unfunded retirement benefits schemes are treated as transfer payments". Given the nature of such consumption expenditure it would be reasonable to expect a fair degree of consistency within any unit of government because items such as wages, salaries, and supplements are generally determined by formulae or quasi-formulae, or at least some arbitral process, which produces escalation of a stable kind. This stability is further compounded by the comparative inflexibility of the government employment staffing establishment itself, at least in the short run.

A similar breakdown was analysed for expenditure on fixed assets. Once again there is a different pattern of priorities from state to state. The consistency of priorities within each state is reasonably high though not as constant as was the case for consumption expenditure. To some extent greater fluctuations might be expected in relation to capital expenditure than for recurrent expenditure because of the commencement and termination of major projects. Western Australia and Tasmania have the least consistent patterns of priority but even in those states the changes are confined to just a few functions. Thus in the field of capital expenditure, a vital aspect of public sector planning, the national system is also flexible enough to allow different state priorities, but a fair maintenance of priorities within states. Indeed the differences in priorities from state to state are less than they were in the case of consumption expenditure.

A few pitfalls of this kind of analysis should be elaborated upon. The statistician's definition of expenditure on new fixed assets includes all spending whether for replacement or additions. He admits the impossibility of maintaining a satisfactory and consistent distinction between new construction and maintenance, and, for example, expenditure on maintenance of roads is treated as capital. This does not affect our general conclusion as long as the statistician's figures are presented on a consistent basis, but in the case of roads and any other items involving maintenance, it means that we cannot be privy to the pattern of resource allocation by state/local governments as *between* new construction and maintenance. In other words a state government could, in any year, have spent a quite different mixture of funding between new construction and maintenance, but the figures available to us would not reveal that shift in priorities. A practical example of the "netting" aspect occurs, for example, when the statistician's definition of expenditure on construction of dwellings for rental purposes by state housing authorities makes provision for a deduction of the book value of previously rented dwellings sold to tenants (expenditure on houses built for sale is excluded). Once again this disguises a little of the priority shift at the state level as between sale/rental of public housing, but it does give state governments an added degree of flexibility in their priority determination. It unquestionably accounts for a part of the priority difference between states.

Tables which are compiled by the Commonwealth Grants Commission relating to social service expenditure, give a more detailed breakdown of functions than do the statisticians' data, and always reveal quite significant priority differences between the Australian states. The amount of expenditure allocated to particular functions can vary substantially from state to state and there is hardly an individual function where variation of some kind does not occur between the states. When we distinguish between current and capital outlays in each state, states have experienced a progressive trend towards a greater emphasis on current outlays since 1964–65. The mixture of current and capital outlays is reasonably similar between states but within each state there have been quite different rates of increase from year to year. The variation in those increases, though significant, has been nothing like the pronounced variations we observed earlier in relation to intergovernmental fiscal transfers. In other words, the annual changes in state current and capital outlays in Australia are smoother than the changes in federal transfers. The year 1974–75 stands out as an aberration to all these generalizations, but it proved to be a temporary phenomenon, and the trends which had been in existence soon were resumed.

Little similar data is available for Canada, and it is not as useful because it relates only to very broad functional areas, and only for a few recent years. It shows significant differences between provinces in the annual variations of expenditure in most functions. It also reveals, within all provinces, some sharp variations in the pattern of annual changes in expenditure on each function. This would, superficially at least, tend to indicate a different priority pattern from province to province and a less consistent priority pattern within provinces than was the case in the Australian states.

However, taking Australian and Canadian figures together, this data seems to indicate either (1) that the flow of intergovernmental funding in both countries does not significantly shift the priorities of the states or provinces — because the mere fact that priorities do differ between subnational units indicates flexibility to manoeuvre, whereas a fair degree of consistency of priorities within units indicates stability within that system; or (2) that states and provinces have a remarkable and resilient capacity to adapt to changing patterns of intergovernmental funding in order to maintain their priorities. Whichever explanation is closer to the truth, these factors tend to suggest a much lower priority distortion effect than was claimed by respondents in the interviews, or authors in the literature which we surveyed. How else can one explain a situation of marked fluctuations in intergovernmental funding to the states and provinces, as evident from many of the tables in Chapter 8, and greater stability in priorities, as evident from the foregoing analysis?

A comment needs to be made on one other particular aspect of the conditional funding debate outlined in Chapter 8, namely, the argument that if a state or province does not wish to be influenced by conditional funding it can refuse to accept the relevant funds. We saw in Chapter 8 that states and provinces have refused conditional funds from time to time. Indeed the Canadian statistics on participation by provinces in conditional grants and shared-cost programmes reveal a pronounced asymmetry in the geographical impact of conditional funding; probably much greater than would apply in Australia. The overall situation in Canada is quite different, in that the possibility of "opting out" of federal programmes and receiving tax points in lieu, has been an alternative in theory and in practice. That alternative has not really existed in Australia since the introduction of uniform taxation, and it wasn't such a possibility before then, partly because of the constitutional requirement in Australia that all direct and indirect taxes levied by the Australian national government have to be uniform across the whole continent. As we observed in Chapter 8, refusal of conditional funding is always technically possible but it is not often politically possible. There are many small conditional grants in Australia that the states could and occasionally have refused. It depends very much on the scale of the programme involved. Clearly the potential for refusing conditional funding for the hospital or school system is vastly different from that for refusal of such funds for historic monuments. Where large amounts of potential funding are involved, refusal would be more obvious to the electorate, and would cause more havoc with a state or province's public finance, especially as the taxpayers from that state or province would be contributing to a programme from which their state or provincial government would be receiving no return. In the case of the smaller programmes, the situation would depend on how effective the state or provincial opposition or pressure groups were in pointing out to the electorate that money was going begging. This, in turn, would be influenced by the extent to which a state or provincial government wanted to share the kudos for a programme with the national government, since it must be conceded that national governments frame many programmes with conditional rather than unconditional funding to gain votes, and especially to honour election pledges. That is only natural. Given the level of dependence of the Australian states on intergovernmental transfers, it is unlikely that they could reject any substantial intergovernmental transfer for very long. Given the nature of both state and provincial functions in both countries, together with their relatively less lucrative taxation bases, there will always be substantial pressure to accept conditional funding. And given the political necessity for states or provinces to keep their own taxes and fees relatively close to those of their counterparts, the possibility of accepting or rejecting conditional funds by lowering or raising their own levels of taxation becomes more remote.

This leads us presumably into the somewhat philosophical question of whether conditional funding is a control exerted by the national government over the subnational units, or merely an inducement. Suffice to say, that if the division of powers including revenue-raising capacities, and the overall constraints of taxation levels in the community, are sufficient to make it economically impossible for a state or province to do without an intergovernmental transfer, an inducement becomes a control. If it is only political pressures which are at work, as for example when the amount of the funding is small but symbolic, inducements remain mere inducements.

Obviously we have not confronted all of the points raised about conditional funding. Many of them should be regarded as technical or administrative matters related to the meddlesome nature of the strictures connected to them. These have been discounted here as artificial constraints rather than fundamental ones. That is not to say that they aren't important or a hindrance to planning attempts; but they are not an intrinsic part of the conceptual problem associated with conditional funding. We might reasonably conclude this aspect by simply observing that (1) the fiscal powers under the constitutions of both countries do override the formal power division elsewhere in the constitution; (2) conditional funding is intended to be a means whereby national governments do impose their own priorities; (3) whether those priorities conflict with priorities of the subnational units will depend on the nature of the funding used; (4) some of that funding will interfere with subnational governments' priorities; (5) there is no evidence to suggest that the degree of such interference in either country is particularly significant, and indeed all the evidence points the other way; (6) some of the claims about priority distortion stem from a poor coordinating capacity in the subnational unit of government itself, and particularly the absence of an overview of all intergovernmental fiscal transfers; (7) political factors are key elements in conditional funding and it is natural that donor and recipient should vie for any political mileage to be gained in such spending; (8) this political process is affected by the degree of understanding in the electorate, as to the division of powers and the exigencies of such funding, and the operation of federal finance in general; (9) given that the largest conditionally funded programmes in Australia and Canada are for the largest functions allocated to the states and provinces under the constitution, it is inevitable that there will continue to be debate about conditional funding.

Intergovernmental Agreements

There are some elements of federal finance which are related to the observations made about intergovernmental agreements in Chapter 6. Many of the hindrances presented by intergovernmental agreements were administrative and technical. Many reflected an intergovernmental communication and bargaining structure which posed obstacles to harmonization of national and provincial priorities. We shall comment on this aspect soon. However, many intergovernmental agreements in both countries, but especially Canada, reflected a feature common to some conditional funding programmes. That feature is the fact that many single agreements and programmes have been handled in a process that closely resembles our planning system. As we have already observed in Chapter 6, the bulk of intergovernmental agreements are negotiated for a fixed term longer than one year; there are objectives spelt out within the agreement; the mechanisms which are devised to implement each agreement provide for allocation of responsibility between levels or units and the sharing or transfer of resources; and often (especially in Canada) there is a sunset clause providing for a review of the agreement close to its termination. Canadian data presented in Chapter 6 indicated that the vast majority of intergovernmental agreements in that federation are for very long time spans (greater than ten years). We also noted, however, that there is no common time frame for all agreements, and only rarely is there a common originating or terminating year. This means that the forecasting, implementation, and review processes are conducted individually for each agreement, and not across all agreements, or even across groups of them, in the same field.

We seem to be faced therefore with a situation where definite potential exists for the application of our planning system to individual intergovernmental agreements and individual federal fiscal programmes, but the potential appears to evaporate when more than one agreement or fiscal transfer is contemplated. Then matters begin to arise, such as fiscal asymmetry between states or provinces, divergences between capital and recurrent funding, differing locations in the administrative structure, and so on. In other words, the *potential for planning in such intergovernmental relations appears to be inversely related to the range and scale of fiscal and administrative contact encountered.* Scale is a serious inhibiting factor because the greater the amount of resources involved, the larger the impact on the internal activities of the participating governments. *Range* is possibly even more significant, because the greater the number of individual agreements or programmes considered, the more variegated the pattern of intergovernmental relations becomes, predominantly because of the observable lack of uniformity between agreements and programmes in these two federations.

These matters tend to suggest that public sector planning in a federation can therefore be bedevilled by complexity, which, in turn, focuses our attention on the mechanisms for coordination of intergovernmental arrangements *within* and *between* the units of government in these federations. From the evidence available, canvassed in both Chapters 6 and 8, both kinds of coordinating capacity are very weak, though becoming stronger. The rise of the central coordinating agency for intergovernmental relations has only been a recent phenomenon in both Canada and Australia, although established earlier in Canada. In particular, the *coordinating machinery within each level of government does not at present have the capacity to undertake the type of overview, and control, which would be required for the adoption of our planning system right across the plane of that government's intergovernmental relations.* Consider the present limited availability of data to such central agencies on all intergovernmental fiscal transfers and agreements, together with the limited degree of their involvement in the actual negotiation of such intergovernmental matters. Add to this the tensions which exist between such central agencies and the operating or functional departments, exacerbated by the cabinet system in these Westminster model governments which generally dispenses power throughout a level of government, and it would simply be impossible for such central agencies in either country at the present time to engage in a system of forecasting, determination of priorities, allocation of resources, implementation, and review, of the whole spectrum of intergovernmental fiscal transfers and agreements. The situation is not helped by the fact that there is, in most Australian states and Canadian provinces, as well as in the Australian and Canadian national governments, a fragmentation of coordination between several central agencies for different kinds of resources, for example, treasuries or ministries of finance for government funding, public service boards or commissions for manpower, attorney generals' offices for legal matters, and prime ministers' or premiers' departments for policy. To add yet another complicating factor we can note that, within each unit of government in both federations, coordination is still impeded by the presence of crown corporations and various statutory or semi-government organizations which tend to escape encapsulation in the budget or provisions of the public service acts. There is also often a fragmentation of government finance into different accounts, including trust funds, and an artificial separation of current from capital funding, all of which tend to make allocation of resources within each unit an exceedingly complex task. We might reasonably conclude that for the introduction of planning the coordinating capacity required for *intergovernmental relations* is intimately related to the coordinating capacity *within* each of the units of government participating in those relations. Weaknesses in such internal coordinating processes will singularly frustrate attempts to coordinate the relations of the unit of government with others in the federation. Such internal coordination has not been a prime focus of this study but its inadequacies have surfaced often throughout our earlier discussion.

From these remarks a suggestion immediately emerges that the perfect political and administrative pattern to underpin our proposed planning system would be one in which a single and powerful coordinating agency existed in each unit of government in the federation, to control all elements of that unit's intergovernmental relations. Then intergovernmental relations would become a matter of negotiations between the politicians and administrators of those seven (Australian) or eleven (Canadian) superagencies. That would, indeed, provide a potential for the introduction of planning in intergovernmental relations, because all the elements of our planning system could be handled in the one set of institutions, although all of the theoretical and pragmatic problems of federalism revealed earlier would still have to be overcome. Such a move would also encounter the problem of accountability which was revealed so potently in our analysis of intergovernmental agreements, namely, that the tighter the intergovernmental arrangements, the more binding and predictable they are, the less democratic they become because of the natural tendency of governments to attempt to place them outside the usual channels of public scrutiny. If that is true of single intergovernmental agreements we can imagine that it would be intensified under any system which controlled a wide range of such agreements. (We shall return to this aspect.) Perhaps the main lesson arising from these points is simply a reinforcement of one of the key elements of the discussion in Chapter 1, namely, the vital importance of coordination in any planning system.

In relation to coordination, we have also considered at some length the processes of *coordination of intergovernmental relations* in the two federations. In relation to intergovernmental agreements, we considered the lessons of the literature and interview responses concerning ten types of intergovernmental machinery. The results of that analysis, simply stated, seemed to be that despite the growing frequency of intergovernmental contact by both politicians and administrators, or perhaps because of it, no portion of such machinery possessed the potential for handling the type of planning we have envisaged. Indeed most of the parts of this machinery seem to have come into being on an ad hoc basis in response to periodic tensions in intergovernmental relations. One significant by-product of the proliferation of such machinery seems to be a belated recognition of the prominent role of the administrator in intergovernmental relations, and especially the transformation of that role from that of "facilitator" of such relations to a more modern day role of "frustrator" of intergovernmental relations, to the extent that the public servant involved in negotiating intergovernmental agreements or fiscal transfers has come to identify with the political views of the unit of government he represents, rather than attempting to take a national perspective.

Of particular significance to this aspect is the fact, observed in Chapters 6 and 7, that the intergovernmental machinery which does exist in the two federations still treats each fiscal transfer and each government in isolation, rather than as a portion of an overall pattern of intergovernmental relationships. Indeed, the Australian experience, in particular, suggests that the only type of common approach occurs with the rise and fall of political tensions between a state government and the national government. Thus, if the *prevailing* mood between a government and the national government is hostile (whatever the cause), there will be a tendency for all intergovernmental negotiations occurring at that time to become soured, and for obstacles to arise. This prevailing mood need not necessarily involve complete governments; it can be the result of a straight clash of personalities between say a state premier and the prime minister. It can also arise out of tensions surrounding an election, or by-election, especially when there are different parties in office at the national and state level, and even when the same party rules at both levels, because the one government may expect even greater concessions to be made by the other at that time. Since both national and state governments in Australia are elected for only three year terms, the periods between an election of some kind are relatively short. Thus if the planning of intergovernmental relations requires a cool period of political relationships to prevail, this will not be easy to achieve. It is difficult to conceive of the elements of our planning system being introduced or functioning smoothly *across the whole gamut* of intergovernmental relations in periods of severe political storms between the units of government in these federations, if those storms are persistent.

The lessons from the conclusions drawn thus far are that there are impediments to the reconciliation of planning and federalism which are reflected in both the structure of intergovernmental relations, and the political process which takes place within and surrounding that structure. Therefore the introduction of a planning system, such as the one envisaged, would require reforms to both the structure and functioning of both federations. Our emphasis will be on structural reform because it is an axiom of politics that changes in process tend to require, to a large extent, changes in the institutional framework within which the process takes place. To alter a politician or public servant's attitude, and method, one tends to have to change his actual behaviour through some rule changes. Nonetheless we shall have some separate comments to make about process later.

If we consider the structural aspects of both federations first, there are a number of basic aspects that have emerged from our analysis of the division of powers and the two main elements which bridge that division — intergovernmental relations and financial relationships.

Division of Powers

The introduction of public sector planning into intergovernmental relations would ideally require a number of changes in the way powers are currently formally divided in Australia and Canada. It would obviously help if some new method of power division could be devised which facilitated coordination between levels of government rather than conflict. Some radical solutions present themselves, as with the West German model of horizontal distribution of powers which segregates the functions of levels of government according to which level has the policy function and which has the implementation function,[3] or the Indian model which superimposes a planning framework over the existing federal division of powers.[4] But changes of this kind would require radical reform and, unquestionably, constitutional amendments. They would also drastically alter the whole shape and character of the Australian and Canadian federations, whereas our task is to measure the potential for planning within the existing federal framework.

The basic problem which we have identified with the present power division in these two federations is that it is out of step with modern day linkages between government functions, and the scale and nature of government activity itself. It does not recognize, or make allowance for, the interdependence of governments which arises out of the interdependence of the community itself. Most significantly, it refuses to acknowledge the impracticability of dividing single public functions discretely between self-contained units of government. Clearly then the challenge is to devise a division of powers which can take account of these factors, and at the same time provide the potential for sufficient coordination between the units of government to allow planning to proceed. The obvious method is, in the first instance, to produce *criteria* for the division of powers.

However, there are even hindrances to the process of criteria development. They include recognition of the following points at least. Even when criteria are formulated there will then be disagreement about the meaning of the criteria themselves, such is the inadequacy of our language and the necessary vagueness of criteria. Serious consideration will have to be given to allocating fiscal powers prior to, or at least in conjunction with, public expenditure; or assigning regulatory functions for a variety of reasons, not the least of which is the potential for any severe degree of vertical fiscal imbalance to see financial powers connected with transfers of funds override constitutional power allocation, as we have seen currently occurs in both Australia and Canada. A decision needs to be made as to whether it is actual functions which will be allocated or also the objectives of those functions, and this means an attempt at broad rather than narrow definitions of government functions; where necessary a function may have to be broken into its subelements. The matter of the asymmetry of the federation will arise and there needs to be a resolution of whether all the subnational units need to perform the same range of functions, or whether the national government or a neighbouring subnational unit could provide any functions in the smaller units of the federation. In this, and other respects, the question of the sovereignty of the federal units has to be seriously considered because it may be that the governments and peoples of states or provinces may believe that sovereignty only exists if that government has the full range of powers in its arsenal. Finally, whatever criteria emerge, it must be realized that there will probably have to be a trade-off between the criteria themselves, because it is inevitable that the application of various criteria to the federal allocation of functions will suggest placement of the same function at a different level. This trade-off is political in nature, and should be made by the political process and not the legal or administrative process.

In the pursuit of such criteria there are, of course, lessons to be learnt from the literature and practice of federalism in Australia and Canada, and our interviews also produced some valuable notions in this area, as canvassed in Chapter 5. The major shortcoming of these criteria was that they tended to relate directly to the layer cake model of federalism envisaged by the founding fathers of both federations. The criteria for allocation which they adopted can still be expected to be of at least some relevance today, though they must obviously be modified to take account of factors mentioned previously. The old "layer cake" criteria included the following aspects:

1. Where a function is indivisible by nature and must spread across the whole geographical entity, that is a function for a national government. This was seen to apply to defence, diplomacy, immigration, international economic relations, dealings with the British Empire (at the time of constitution), and any area where the nation had to speak with one single voice.

2. Functions which should apply uniformly across the nation are generally regarded as being appropriate to a higher government. However, it must be stated immediately that there has always been a debate about the merits of uniformity itself, many writers pointing out

that one of the main virtues of federalism is meant to be the possibility of achieving a lack of uniformity. Then there are also many who claim that uniformity can just as readily be achieved by the subnational units acting in concert. Suffice to point out here that the desire for uniformity in Australia in relation to weights and measures, currency, coinage, marriage laws, and other functions, resulted in those functions being given to the national government, and it might be inferred that failure to allocate other functions such as railways, education, law and order, and so on, meant that there was no overwhelming desire for uniformity in those matters. Of course, a distinction can be made between those functions where a case can be made for national responsibility mainly, or even wholly, on the cost or efficiency advantages of national provision (for example, in the fields of transport and communication), and those where the case for national responsibility rests mainly, even wholly, on the desirability of a uniform level of service or uniform regulation (for example, age pensions and company law).

3. Those matters on which units of government at the same level cannot agree should pass to a higher level of government. Since the national level is the only level at which there is but one government, this inevitably means that it sweeps up all such functions in relation to the states in the same way that states have kept to themselves those functions which cause dissension between local governments. Whilst this principle is widely accepted in the literature, there is still dispute as to whether it means that the higher level of government should actually assume the function in question, or solely act as the arbiter of disputes from lower levels which would retain the function. In any event Australian functions, like customs and excise, were given to the national government on this basis, as was provision for the Interstate Commission to settle disputes about interstate transport and trade. State governments have controlled provision and distribution of certain utilities on the same grounds.

4. Where government regulation is required over resources or entities that are mobile, it is generally believed that that function should be given to the highest level of government that can embrace such mobility. Thus for example, the functions of trade, industrial disputes, and navigation regulation, and later civil aviation, were split in the Australian Constitution into their intrastate and interstate elements, and power over the latter assigned to the national government. Clearly it is physically impossible for a subnational unit of government to control activity the moment it has crossed a particular border. It is important to emphasize this point because many writers argue that mobility can be catered for most of the time by cooperation between subnational units, but the actual act of crossing a political boundary cannot be controlled by any unit of government on either side of that boundary.

5. In those functions where nationwide equality of opportunity and equality of standards in public service are required, these functions are generally regarded as being for the proper exercise of a national government. And a similar argument is made for functions where it is felt necessary that statewide equality be allotted to that level. Obviously there is enormous scope for difference of viewpoint here as equity is probably the most elusive political criterion ever conceptualized. In Australia it would seem that citizens believe opportunities and standards in a variety of welfare services should be nationwide as they have been allocated to the national level, whereas the allocation of education, law and order, and health to the states, and not to local government, can be partially explained as a desire to see statewide equality of services in those functions. This criterion has also been invoked to give higher levels power over functions which lower levels might use to discriminate against certain inhabitants of their units, for example, racial or religious minorities.

6. Where there are "spillovers" the function should go to a higher level of government. Many people assume that this is simply an economic term dealing with external economies where the actions of one unit deliberately or inadvertently affect a neighbouring unit. However, it is just as much a political term because the unique political characteristic of federalism is that all citizens elect all three levels of government. Or, to put it more explicitly, both state and national governments represent the interests of the people of the state in the same way that both state and local governments represent the interests of the citizens of a local authority area. The aim here then, whenever a function arises which contains inherent externalities or spillovers, is to transfer the function to a level high enough to capture all the spillover effects, so that it can remove or at least mitigate them. The Australian formal federal structure does not contain many examples of this, although it is partly exemplified by state government retention of ultimate control over town planning, and the provision of some basic resources the natural catchment area of which spans a number of local authorities. It is also present again in the parts of the constitution which allowed the commonwealth government to regulate interstate mobility of commodities, people, and ideas.

7. Where the resources of a unit of government are not ample enough to allow it to fulfil a function adequately, there is a case for allocating that function higher. This criterion is a very loaded one because the question immediately arises as to why the resources could not be made available from the higher to the lower level to carry out the function, rather than take away the function itself. However, this line of argument usually refers to those functions which have significant economies of scale, such as research activity, or construction of very large capital projects. Or it may really be beyond its resources

because of the size of the unit of government, so that states could not sponsor international airlines or shipping companies or armed forces.

8. Levels of government should be allocated those functions appropriate to the revenue sources at their disposal. The assumption made here is that certain taxes and levies are collected for particular purposes, and the government which collects them should be charged with meeting those purposes. The best example of this is the literature relating to local government, which says quite forcibly that if local government is to have property taxes as its main source of revenue, it should be required to undertake all those public functions which are related to servicing property. It is an extremely relevant, though not very useful, criterion here because it pre-empts once again the question of whether revenue sources or functions should be allocated first. The danger in its pure application can be seen in the current Australian situation of a high level of vertical fiscal imbalance, whereupon the logic of this argument would mean transferring a substantial array of functions to the commonwealth government for the sole reason that it controls most of the direct and the most important indirect taxes. It also overlooks the fact that it is common for two, and even three, levels of government to tax the same person, company, or property.

9. It was a maxim at confederation in most federations that those levels of government which had built up expertise and administrative efficiency in a particular function should retain that function. Thus this is largely an "ex-post" criterion, but it could also presumably apply in any rational allocation of functions from first principles, that the allocation would take strong account of the existing levels of expertise (or lack of it) in a particular level. The alternative of a reshuffle of the relevant public servants between levels has occurred in Australian history (census and statistics, and income tax collection), but it seems a remote possibility now, as does the prospect of a completely unified public service for two or even the three levels of Australian government.

10. There are a number of criteria which are brought into play to delineate functions which should not be given to a higher (national) level of government, although, as will be seen, each of them leaves open the question of whether it should be the state or local government which should perform them. Thus in Australia, Canada, and America, it was generally believed that functions should be reserved for subnational units, which involved:
    * knowledge of "local" conditions
    * experimentation
    * variety
    * home or family life
    * private rights
    * everyday life
    * close participation and constant accountability

* affecting only that particular geographical area
* scope for public spirit and "local" patriotism
* close supervision
* varying with different "localities" or "parallels of latitude"
* internal affairs
* "local" options and choice among the "local" options
* access to "local" sources of information
* speedy action
* responsiveness

These sorts of criteria are not defined at all well and tend to be expressed more in sentimental phrases, such as the following from the debates of the founding fathers: "to the state everything that is local and relating to one state", "federal powers must be uniform and general, state powers local and particular", "the inner life of each community to the states", "a power that must be exercised differentially is not a federal power", and "to the less remote government the powers that are nearer their homes and closer their affections".

These are, for the most part, spatial notions and they often hinge on a definition of the word "local", the meaning of which may be often clear to the author, but is not conveyed to the reader. They are countered by many other authors who argue that any level of government can operate in a decentralized manner, so that even a national government which had a remote centre could still meet these requirements by decentralizing its physical administration as well as its decision-making processes. This is, of course, countered by the argument that what is envisaged is political decentralization, not administrative decentralization, on the principle that the politicians who are elected solely by a locality will be fully responsive to that locality alone, as well as the more fundamental point that unless "local" communities have to pay for their differential requirements there is no effective way of discerning their real preferences. In turn, this is accompanied by a warning from others, who point to the danger of allocating a function so low that it ends up in a unit of government unduly dominated by particular groups who can then discriminate in the conduct of that function. In other words, when does close, intimate, responsive government become corrupt government?

It must be stressed that these criteria are not necessarily those which were used by the architects of the constitutions studied. As mentioned earlier, we don't know what their actual criteria were because they never gave them explicitly. The criteria outlined have come from commentators inferring the basis of allocation from the lists contained in the constitution, or simply engaging in polemic. That polemic, like the criteria listed, arises out of a belief in coordinate or layer cake federalism irrespective of which particular level, if any, an author favours.

The basic faults of these criteria have already been touched upon, including their inability to recognize explicit and implicit linkages between various government functions, and the frequent emergence of "override" criteria which can dominate any national debate about the division of powers. This is part of the move from coordinate federalism to organic federalism. The modern literature of political science and public administration accepts for the most part that a return to coordinate federalism is not possible. It is simply not practicable to secure levels of government into watertight compartments together with their electors and clients. It does not necessarily mean that all functions of government will be shared by two or three levels, but it is likely that the most expensive ones, which touch the most people, will be, as well as many other related functions. *The question now becomes that of determining criteria to allocate the role that each level of government will perform in the shared responsibilities.* There has, then, been a shift in thinking on two grounds:

1. We are now speaking of the allocation of roles in a single function, responsibility for which will be shared between two or three levels, rather than the allocation of discrete government functions between levels. Accepting this fact, the exercise becomes one of determining which level of government should have the primary role in that function, which level should have the secondary role, and maybe which should have the tertiary role.

2. We are now speaking more in terms of the "roles" of levels of government, rather than in terms of tasks or physical activities of levels of government. In other words, the emphasis is more on the objective of government functions rather than the functions themselves. The literature has very little to say about how to define roles of levels of government. For example, as noted earlier, the Bailey task force on coordination in welfare and health, and to some extent the Holmes committee on care of the aged and infirm, spoke in terms of the commonwealth having a role of watching over the welfare/health field, eliminating overlapping, plugging gaps, initiating, and so on — in other words, a policy and surveillance "role". The state and local governments would have mainly a delivery "role", including decisions and their implementation on the location, timing, and manner of delivery. By contrast, Harris, in an assessment of the material pertaining to the Bland inquiry, formulates a schematic illustration of responsibility division. He ascribes to the commonwealth a "role" incorporating goal formulation, identification of objectives, study of alternative courses of action, and periodic review of the outcomes of a programme in terms of the objectives; whereas the state governments would be concerned with evaluation of alternative projects and developments by reference to costs and benefits, and action through public expenditure, or aid to private expenditure.[5]

Most of the old criteria which applied to coordinate federalism, listed earlier, will still be applicable, since the main distinguishing characteristic between the three levels of government is still the spatial one. In other words, even where levels of government are sharing responsibility for a single government function, the role of each level will still be determined very much by geographical factors. In consideration of a federalism that is both dynamic and organic, the following appear to be criteria for allocation of responsibilities between levels:

1. If uniformity across the nation in a particular function is regarded as essential, there seems to be a weight of opinion in favour of giving the national government a preponderant control of the function; if not total control. This also applies to state governments being given a major say in functions that should be uniform state-wide. The question arises as to whether the same result cannot be achieved by subunits acting together. The arrangements for provinces in Canada to opt out of past national programmes which were meant to be uniform is held to demonstrate that a province, acting alone, could keep its policies uniform with those of other provinces without having to hand over the primary responsibility for the function itself. It has to be said, however, that in Australia it has been immensely difficult to get six state governments of different political persuasions to voluntarily establish uniform legislation and keep it uniform. The delays in getting uniform company law are a case in point. To adapt the words of John Adams, it is extremely difficult to get six clocks to strike at the same moment. Also there are certain functions, like immigration, where a bird's eye view of the whole nation is required constantly, and it seems likely that all states could not plug all the gaps as fast as they appeared. There is also the point made in relation to local government, that if uniformity is desired in functions like education and police, they could not be given to local government if they were to be financed solely from existing local government revenue because the services will be unevenly provided — best in affluent areas and worst in poor areas. It could be countered that the higher level of government could theoretically provide equalized grants to the lower levels to perform the function, but then we might properly observe that the higher level would have the primary role in that function anyway. (And this is not practical given the difficulty, mentioned earlier, of equalizing for particular public functions.) We might as well at this point raise the obverse, which is that in those functions where variety or lack of uniformity, and indeed some experimentation, is desirable, the main responsibility for the function should be allocated as low as practicable.

2. This leads to the question of portability, and virtually the same arguments apply as in the first criterion, so that in those functions where portability is required between various geographical areas falling within different subnational units, the primary role in that function is for the higher, national government.

3. It could be stated in a bland way that the role of horizontal equalization is one for the level of government higher than the level in which the units are to be equalized. It can be argued, of course, quite persuasively that a single level of government can quite ably equalize

itself, as occurs in some federations. However, it has to be admitted that there must be more trust between the units of the same level of government that exists in Australia, where units of government at one level look to a higher level to arbitrate their cases and equalize their standards. It may be a tautology, but it is worth saying, that horizontal equalization between units of government only becomes necessary because there is a division of powers between levels of government in the first place. If there were only one government in the nation all equalization would be interpersonal equalization of some kind. Experience does point to one unintended consequence of handing over the role of equalization to a national government. This occurs where a national government is responsible for its own territories, and implements its own standards and priorities in those territories, for example, ACT or Northern Territory, and that choice produces consequent pressures on state governments to follow suit.

4. It is generally agreed in the modern literature that where national standards have to be set in a particular function the primary role for that function should go to the national government. However, the degree of involvement of the national government is in dispute. It is not clear how much it should become involved in the fine detail of standard setting or of auditing and monitoring those standards. For example, the unanimous view of the state submissions to the Bland Committee was that the commonwealth government should not become involved in the details, and should determine the composition of programmes but not projects. The means of achieving a standard in providing a function will vary according to localities, they said, and so will the desirable mixture of projects to meet the standards; so the fine detail was better left to the states. There are two comments to be made about this, and the first is that the states seem noticeably reluctant to adopt the same principle in their responsibility sharing with local governments. Secondly, it seems unavoidable, in most cases, that if a national standard is desired the national government will have to set that standard in reasonably fine detail or otherwise it ceases to be a truly national standard.

5. This leads to two further criteria, one of which is that the higher level of government should confine itself to policy making, and the actual administration of a function should be performed by the lowest level capable of performing it. Many will object that this begins to look like the famous old dichotomy between policy and administration which has been proved to be unworkable in practice, but nevertheless it seems to be the only practical method of responsibility sharing. A corollary is that the higher level should perform most if not all of the research which goes into determination of policy making. None of this means that the lower level, now mainly the administrative agent, should have no voice in policy. Indeed the reverse is likely to be true because the literature of public administration tells us that it is the

official who has to implement the policy, and deal with those it affects, who will be the first to detect flaws and virtues in the policy itself. But it does mean that, in the crunch, the final power over policy determination must go to the higher level. Recent noise regulation procedures are of relevance here, whereby state governments have determined broad policies on noise levels and definitions of noise, but the regulation of noise and the determination of the hours in which it will be permitted, are left to local authorities to determine according to their local climate and social conditions.

6. The second criterion which is an outcome of our fourth point is that primary responsibility in functions should be allocated to the level of government which already possesses the expertise in that field. On the face of it this is bound, in Australia at least, to favour the state level, since it is the oldest level and possesses most of the public servants. But the argument would still hold good where a state wanted to enter a field like international relations or water supply, functions in which another level of government had the expertise.

7. The question of spillovers arises again and the same arguments seem to apply, that the primary role must go to that level of government capable of catching and minimizing or eliminating all the spillovers. This argument is based on the assumption that a lower unit of government would either be unaware of the externalities involved, or if it were, because of political motivation would seek to "do in" its neighbours where the spillovers favoured it, and appeal to a higher level anyway if the spillovers were against it. It ought to be said here that it is very easy to espouse this criterion or principle but difficult to implement it, if only because for example, in border areas, there are very few functions performed by a state or local government that do not affect other state or local governments respectively. An extension of the spillover criteria occurs in cases where lower units are simply in dispute over a function and the higher level has to be the arbiter. Mathews and Jay go so far as to say that the fact that cooperation is needed between states on any function is, ipso facto, proof that it should be a commonwealth function, which may be so, but there would still need to be a secondary interest in the function for the states.[6] Another, more interesting case occurs where, because of circumstances, one state is in a position to manipulate another. The latter was a fear expressed by Western Australia when it sought national government control of the transcontinental railway, fearing that otherwise South Australia could manipulate traffic between Western Australia and the eastern states. The same fear is expressed by the maritime provinces in Canada when Quebec starts talking about a corridor tax for goods passing from central Canada to the east, and the plea is for the higher, dominion level to be the regulator of interprovincial traffic.

8. It is widely held that the level of government which has the best infor-

mation sources in relation to a function, and therefore is in the best position to make appropriate decisions, should have primary responsibility for that function. This is not a conclusive criterion however, as there is some dispute as to whether a higher level of government acting in an administratively decentralized manner is able to gain access to information as easily as the unit of government at that spatial level. This argument is often put in relation to state versus commonwealth powers in Australia, when it is pointed out that the commonwealth can, given the desire, decentralize its operations quite well (for example, Australia Post, or Social Security offices). Therefore the assessment of which level has the best information network is best handled technically, realizing that all levels have politicians in the field as well as public servants, although the telling factor may be that in any given spatial area there will always be more local politicians than state than national, although this need not be true of the numbers of public servants. It is also slightly more imperative for the lower level of government to listen carefully to the information it receives within its area of government. A corollary of this "information" criterion is that of "promptness" or "responsiveness" in the sense that the primary role in a function should go to the level of government which will handle it most quickly, and then all the arguments just raised again come into play.

9. Once again the question of mobility of resources arises and the previous arguments apply. So many disparate entities are mobile, including germs, criminals, professional people, school children, electricity, etc., and they all have a habit of crossing political boundaries of subnational units. There can be no doubt that higher levels of government are best able to handle functions of government which attempt to regulate things which are mobile, but in this case the question of degree arises, and past Australian experience shows that it has only been in relation to things which are *highly* or *frequently* mobile that a complete transfer of function to the national government has been necessary, as for example with some diseases, pensioners, unemployed, and so on. Otherwise the slower and slightly more cumbersome procedure of cooperation between the lower units at the same level is the manner of coping with mobility. This question has arisen in recent years in relation to the very serious problems of different standards applying to training for professional people (lawyers, doctors, nurses, etc.) who do move around the country. Consider for example the doctor who cannot sign a death certificate in the state of his practice because he didn't gain his qualification in that state. Again it could be stressed that it is impossible for any unit of government to regulate the mobility or movement across its own borders to another unit of the same level of government.

10. Those functions in which the nation, as a nation, needs to make an impression on the world, or speak with one voice, or appease national

guilt, are conceded by all writers to belong to the national government. Even the Australian states after the gloom of the last olympics were prepared to recognize a primary responsibility for the commonwealth government in the encouragement of sport. But all of this is really not much more than saying that where there are distinctively national aspirations and symbols to maintain, it is the national government which is responsible. That does not take us very far, since not all citizens of any federation see their role as citizens of the nation taking precedence over their role as citizens of a state or province.

11. Now one of the most contentious criteria concerns the old question of matching allocation of the function to allocation of the finances in the federation. Thus Mr Whitlam could say that the commonwealth should have the main role in the provision of those functions where it provided the bulk of the finance. He also stated that if a function were desired to grow in importance it should be "hitched to the star" of the commonwealth government.[7] It would be easy to forget this criterion and say that the allocation of revenue ought not to predetermine the allocation of functions, or even argue that the reverse should be the case, were it not for the fact that state governments have resisted a number of offers to allow them back into the larger revenue fields. In a similar way local government in Australia is singularly unimaginative in the revenue sources it pursues, and the argument for neglecting the revenue allocation becomes that much weaker. Nonetheless the argument must finally be rejected here, mainly because it is not a consideration of allocation of functions from first principles, but also because, if taken to its extreme, it would be a cumulative or self-perpetuating process, so that the richer level of government would progresively gather up all the functions, the most expensive first, and then be in a position to manipulate spending on those functions in order to keep it growing richer still. Moreover, if the functions it took over in the early stages were the potentially more expensive ones, it could plead a case to the people of the nation to allocate to it an even larger share of the revenue. Even the theories of dynamic or organic federalism envisage a continuance of fairly evenly matched bargaining power between the levels of government; or what is left is not federalism at all. Naturally enough this problem is raised more acutely in the Australian federation than the Canadian with its lower degree of vertical fiscal imbalance.

12. Where equality of opportunity or access to a government service is especially important or where it is necessary to protect the interests of minorities, that function is best monitored and even controlled by the higher level of government. This arises too in respect of health and welfare services, and both the recent Bailey and Holmes reports see a definite role for the commonwealth government in protecting the interests of the nongovernment recipients of national grants, despite the fact that both reports favour the commonwealth handing over all pro-

grammes which can be effectively implemented at a lower level — and as low as possible. Another associated criterion is that if the government function involves the corporation, or indeed sole use, of voluntary labour in its delivery, then it ought to be allocated to as low a level as possible.

13. Whilst dealing with the Bailey and Holmes reports, and similar Canadian literature in particular, it is now widely accepted that there is a proper role for a national government as an initiator, or prodder, or stimulator. In other words, where there is a felt need within a government function for innovation, usually connected with research, that role belongs to the national level, and presumably that reasoning can apply to any responsibilities shared between state and local governments which would see state governments in a similar posture. It is worth noting in this connection that it is stated, though not proven, in the literature, that openness to change increases the higher the level of government. The explanation offered is that it is easier for a pressure group desiring change to lobby one government than six, although some case material available showed the dexterity of some industries in swaying smaller states with little vested interest in that industry to change their policies, thereby bringing moral pressure on other states — for example, successful attempts in the late 1970s by lobbyists for the margarine industry to change consumer legislation affecting margarine in Tasmania (despite the fact that no margarine was manufactured in Tasmania) thereby forcing other states to follow suit.

14. Simplicity and comprehensiveness combine as criteria to say that where one level of government is already heavily involved in functions of a kind similar to the one being considered, every effort should be made to allocate that function to the same level. However, there is definitely considered to be a predominant role for the higher level of government in monitoring the comprehensiveness of the programme coverage in functional fields where it has some involvement.

15. Functions which cannot be fragmented to achieve their purpose have to be national functions. This would include control and regulation of the lower units of government, functions with pronounced economies of scale, and research and experimentation.

16. Although it is a conservative criterion in itself the disturbance to the status quo must figure in considering reallocation of a function. If it is going to cost a lot in dollars or anguish to transfer, say, the payment of pensions to another level, it is not worth the move even though other factors may suggest it.

17. There is a criterion which says that a level of government should be equipped with powers to handle any problem it will have to confront. Stated like that it doesn't mean much, but it becomes clearer when an attempt is made to view the allocation of powers from the point of view of a business or individual trying to escape government regulation altogether. That business will probably have a vested interest in

pressing for all functions affecting it to be allocated as low as possible, or at least to argue for as much dispersal of power as possible. If there is not adequate coordination between levels there will develop what has been described in the literature as "zones of anarchy" where no necessary government regulation exists. The reverse case can also be cited where there could be too much regulation and even duplication of regulation in the one function. In both cases monitoring is required and it has to be done by the level of government which can match the entity being regulated. Since the entity will undoubtedly have a bird's eye view at any moment in time across the whole nation, it can only be matched by the national level of government.

18. There remain a number of vague criteria which are important but difficult to encapsulate in a pragmatic way. These include an admonition that primary roles should be given to functions whose levels are:

    (a) more democratic;

    (b) more effective;

    (c) least corrupt or least likely to be corrupt or dominated by vested interests;

    (d) best able to give a lead or set an example;

    (e) possessing the best career opportunities for public servants, and so will be able to attract the best calibre officials to perform the function;

    (f) best able to integrate the function with logical partner functions, for example, sea, land, air, and rail transport.

Finally it has to be said that those writers who either advocate organic federalism and/or believe it to be inevitable anyway, are all quick to point out that responsibility sharing, that is, the acknowledgment of an interest for more than one level of government in a government function, must be accompanied by appropriate ongoing intergovernmental machinery for the allocation and constant review of roles for each level. The question only now being confronted, especially in the Canadian literature and constitutional review, is how to make this machinery more accountable to each level and to the public in general, who must obviously find it harder to read a recipe for a marble cake than one for a layer cake.

Some Lateral Thinking

We might question whether it is necessary for the federal relationship to be symmetrical throughout all its parts. In other words, is it necessary for every state to have the same relationship with the national government or for every local authority to have the same relationship with a state government? If not, then it is likely that there will be different criteria regarding the allocation of functions for different individual relationships. This is, of course, forbidden in relation to federal/state revenue sharing because, as we have seen, the Australian constitution stipulates clearly that the commonwealth government cannot discriminate between states or parts of states. However that need not necessarily apply to functions of government. Indeed it does not apply already with respect to railways, Tasmania having handed over its railways to the commonwealth, and South Australia a portion of its rail system. There is also the point raised in the Canadian literature, cited herein, that large provinces may wish to, and be able to, carry on certain functions, but smaller provinces might well prefer the dominion government to conduct the function in the province. It is likely that any asymmetry will be disturbed along this distinguishing line of large versus small units. From our earlier analysis it is clear that larger subnational units have an inherently different political relationship with the national government than do smaller ones, because being a larger part of the whole federation their interests are likely to be more similar to those of the national government, they can exert more influence on the national government, and the national government in framing its policies (especially the uniform ones), is likely to base its policy making more closely on conditions in larger states. Of course this principle is already much better known to local government where it is not uncommon to see some local governments in a different relationship to the state government from that of others, the result being that the functions being performed by one local government will differ from those being performed by another.

It has been suggested, as an extreme measure, that if federalism is dynamic, the best solution to the allocation question is to give each level of government the power to amend its own powers; that is, to discard or take on functions at will. This would force political compromises between levels of government over functions and parts of functions.

A more urgent and more practical alternative is to regard the criteria for allocation of functions as having to be flexible in themselves and altering with changing circumstances. The solution then becomes one of establishing new and better intergovernmental machinery for reviewing and monitoring and adjusting the criteria. It is the Canadians who have addressed this problem most directly because "executive federalism", as Smiley termed it, is more of an issue there. In fact, proposed constitutional amendments in the late 1970s sought to enshrine the meetings of first ministers (the equivalent of the Australian Premiers Conferences) in the constitution itself so that they would become a mandatory part of the machinery of government. Space does not permit here a full discussion of the sort of formal machinery Australia could consider to perform this task. We already have an elected Senate which is supposed to be a states house connected to a national house; we have the Premiers Conference and various ministerial and executive councils; we have a number of advisory statutory commissions which look after intergovernmental relations in a particular functional area; we have commonwealth and state grants commissions; we have arrangements for public servants of one level to also carry out functions for another level; we have state departments for local government; we have a host of nongovernment professional and social bodies whose membership includes people from all levels of government, and we have the Advisory Council for Inter-government Relations. Surely out of all these bodies which span the levels of government some machinery could be moulded to perform a task like that envisaged. The main problem, of course, is how to make it accountable to each level and to the public at large. As Reid has said of Australia, the institutions of cooperative federalism diminish ministerial responsibility in direct relationships to the binding power of their decisions.[8]

Another lateral approach is to consider the effect of the separation of powers on the division of powers. Whether a certain function is to be given to a particular government unit may well be strongly influenced by the degree to which the executive or judiciary dominates the legislature. Or if a unit of government has decided to abdicate its policy-making role in a function and hand it to a statutory body, this may be important. To illustrate this in the extreme: could a rational discussion of conventional criteria for allocation of functions take place between one level of government where the policy on that function was made in parliament, and another level where it was the prerogative of a public servant or judicial commission? Probably not.

Some would say that the existing attitudes of the public should be considered in allocation of functions. For example, a significant body of literature tells us that the public do not care which level performs it as long as it is efficiently and effectively handled. Still other literature suggests that some people think a particular level of government performs all government functions anyway. Still more people confuse the levels of government which perform particular services, as witnessed in Australia by the number of federal members of parliament who receive complaints about property rates, and the number of aldermen who handle grievances about pensions of various kinds. Now this is quite a serious matter and it is of profound importance in determining criteria for the allocation of functions. Two immediate solutions spring to mind, one being to educate the public as to which level of government provides which service and why, or to accept public ignorance and indifference and attempt to unify or coordinate the delivery of services by the three levels of government. The first has been very poorly handled in Australia, especially regarding citizenship education in state government education curricula. There have been some promising experiments in recent years regarding the second, including a one-stop welfare shop for all three levels of government, current initiatives by the commonwealth ombudsman to share offices and the same telephone number with the state ombudsman, and close liaison in regional centres between public servants of the three levels. However, the fundamental question here is whether governments should legislate or act to make people aware of reality, or attempt to bring government action more in line with people's perceptions of reality.

Another method of approaching this problem is to consider some sort of unification of the public services of the various levels, in the direction of the Indian model, or the West German. The Advisory Council for Inter-government Relations has already begun valuable exploratory work on the interchange of personnel, but that does not overcome the basic difficulty that public servants are held accountable through only one of the three levels of government. A completely unified system would at least make public servants feel that they were equally responsible to three levels. This might overcome the problem, which we observed in the review of the Canadian literature, of public servants deliberately aiding politicians in obscuring their accountability in order to bolster their level of government and therefore their own career prospects. (In the succinct words of one of the authors we encountered, some people would rather be on top of a two-foot dung hill, than a third of the way up a six-foot dung hill.) It might also make for speedier government action if public servants from three levels of government did not have to take a symbolic amount of time scrutinizing proposals and information from other levels of government simply to accentuate the sovereignty of their own level. It would also make buck-passing that much more difficult. These arguments are connected in an obtuse way to the view, often expressed, that a basic consideration in parcelling out functions is that a level of government has to have enough total power and enough variety of tasks to attract officials of a high calibre. We might also extend the discussion to consideration of whether the whole legal system could not be unified in Australia. Similar, and some additional, aspects arise.

Since politics is conducted largely in symbols, and some government functions are significantly more visible than others, and some carry more prestige than others, it seems inevitable, therefore, that when levels of government discuss the allocation of a function they will, at least psychologically, perceive the function from a symbolic viewpoint and hence desire it or shun it as the case may be.

There are a number of other considerations which spring to mind which are also not readily answered because of the way spatial considerations have dominated the approach to the definition of criteria for allocating functions. Perhaps they are best postulated as open-ended questions.

Should the potential of a power or function be a determinant of where it is placed?

Should we give powers over *new* functions of government to one particular level consistently?

Does all the allocation have to be vertical or could there be some specialization of tasks within the one level of government so that one unit of a level would provide a function for all the other units in that level? (This might be appropriate where one spatial unit possessed most of the national phenomena which had to be regulated.)

Could horizontal reallocation of functions include delegation of functions by one unit of government to another unit of the same level?

Could functions be allocated but financial limitations be placed on the expenditure of that function?

Should functions be categorized according to the extent to which they invade the liberty of individuals, and in particular their privacy, as a basis for subsequent allocation?

If one subnational unit of government has all the resources related to a particular function, is it not a question of that unit versus the rest of the whole nation rather than a dispute between all of that unit's level and other levels?

In vast areas, sparsely populated, can there be such a thing as a "local interest" if there is nobody there to foster it, and which level should then be regarded as responsible for functions in that area?

Will a government act as rationally in relation to a function in which it is only indirectly involved, say through funding, as it would if it had the function itself? And will it tend to make decisions on its participation on a better or worse pool of information?

The criteria which have been outlined must be considered in any attempt to allocate functions between levels of government. The trade-off between them cannot, however, be prescribed. It is a matter of individual political preferences which, with some good fortune, when accumulated may result in a majority of opinion with regard to shifting functions towards particular levels. The trade-off will be more likely, and be achieved considerably faster, if all parties agree to adopt the concept of speaking in terms of primary and secondary interests in most government functions for the levels of government, rather than attempting to allot sole responsibility to a particular level. A few points need to be added in relation to the Australian situation. The first is that it seems doubtful whether there could ever be a completely rational discussion between the three levels of government about the allocation of functions, whilst the degree of vertical fiscal imbalance remains so high.

It should seriously be considered whether the size of the units of government could not be reviewed before any final decision is made to allocate a function. It would seem that most of the proposals on new states, or regionalism, have come to grief because it was always thought that the new units would have exactly the same functions as the units from which they would be extracted. There is a link between function and size so fundamental that one just cannot be considered without the other.

In view of citizen perceptions and cultural attitudes towards governments in Australia, it might not be so much a question of which level should perform which function, but more a question of whether the citizen is prepared to trust any government at all. This in itself might emphasize the fact, that in the short term at least, it may be better to aim at setting up a process for governments to shift functions around within the existing constitutional framework. There are already clear procedures for a referral of power, or the alternative could be to declare more powers to be concurrent.

It seems highly likely, given our relatively brief experience with organic federalism, that the criteria for allocation of functions will change absolutely, and relatively to one another, as Australian federalism itself changes in its nature. In other words, the criteria themselves may well be dynamic, and a review of criteria for the allocation of roles should be updated and reviewed at frequent intervals.

Finally, the Australian political system has, until the present time, completely abdicated its responsibility for determining the criteria for allocating functions, and allowed the courts to conduct the exercise by default. That means that the legal system has performed a political task and hence has acted politically. To a political scientist, that is intolerable. For the political system to address itself to this question the single most dominant theme is that the process should be conducted democratically. Since democracy means participation and openness, that suggests that any review of the criteria for the allocation of functions of government between the levels of government in the Australian federal system should incorporate some form of public participation. That might best be achieved through the establishment of some kind of intergovernmental machinery for a constant review of government functions in the light of the criteria developed.

Steps such as those which have been outlined should overcome many of the obstacles to planning presented by the division of powers to the extent that they would provide for a more rational allocation of roles, rather than discrete functions. They would recognize the importance of responsibility sharing in a federation. They would reorient the institutional channels of communication between levels of government giving a firmer basis for intergovernmental negotiations to determine priorities, allocate resources, and implement the attendant decisions — the three core elements of our planning system. They would go some way towards recognizing the linkages through the interrelatedness of government activity, and hence provide a clearer overview for coordinating bodies within and between governments in the two federations, and they would recognize the need to incorporate provisions to maintain political accountability.

Intergovernmental Agreements

It has been our main contention throughout this study that the mechanism of intergovernmental agreements offers the greatest potential for the introduction of public sector planning into the federal systems under review. Primarily this is because it is the most explicit and tangible bridge across the division of powers. *Intergovernmental agreements between the sovereign units of a federation are formal recognition of a fusing or sharing of some of that sovereignty.* This is extremely important because, as we have observed, the splitting of sovereignty is the main political hallmark of federation and its most divisive factor. Hence it lays the foundation for a variety of political obstacles to coordination between the levels of government.

We have already noted earlier a number of aspects of intergovernmental agreements in Australia and Canada which pose difficulties for the introduction of public sector planning, but it will be recalled that these were related mainly to the problems inherent in coordinating a wide range of agreements of varying scales. Another fundamental problem which we noted in Chapter 6 was the difficulty of maintaining accountability of units of government for their participation in such agreements. Indeed it must be recognized that the very nature of such agreements (for example, their long term framework, their binding nature, and the secrecy of the processes whereby they are negotiated), makes them an inherently undemocratic instrument, and so a challenge is immediately presented to devise ways of recognizing and countering this chronic condition.

In a political system the basic prerequisite for determining accountability is that the role of each actor in the process must be clear. To this extent any attempt to ensure clarification of the role of each unit of government in intergovernmental agreements would have to be preceded by the review of the division of powers mentioned earlier. Given the binding nature of agreements in a constantly changing federal environment there is a need for a regular review of agreements, even though they are long-term agreements themselves — perhaps a decennial review process, instigated by a neutral body independent of any one level of government, as for example the Australian Advisory Council on Inter-government Relations for which there is no strict Canadian equivalent.

Ideally, all intergovernmental agreements should be tabled as a green paper in each provincial/state legislature and the national parliament for debate before final ratification. However, it would seem that the best forum for in-depth analysis of these agreements is the Australian and Canadian Senates which were, after all, meant to be Houses of Parliament reflecting geographical interests. (This would require a new-look Canadian Senate, with better representation of all provinces than in the past.) Such small houses could well establish a standing committee to examine all intergovernmental agreements and submit reports for full debate in that chamber. If scrutiny prior to ratification of agreements proves difficult at times for reasons of time constraints, confidentiality, security, or the sheer mechanics of the situation, such agreements should definitely be investigated and debated after ratification, and to this end they might well contain a standard "sunset" clause and maybe an intergovernmental impact statement. The Senate should also be given the power to subpoena state/provincial public servants for examination on these aspects.

In order to conduct the parliamentary scrutiny just outlined a more high-powered, advisory network is needed. The Canadian Federal-Provincial Relations Office is a model which could well be upgraded for the purpose, and it would, of course, need its composition changed to include permanent representation of provincial and municipal public servants on its staff. Such a body would serve well as a research agency to back up Senate and provincial parliamentary inquiry into intergovernmental agreements.

The next logical step is a better codification of intergovernmental agreements and a consequent breaking down of the secrecy associated with them. Any attempt to define the status of federal-provincial conferences would assist in this process. The arguments for and against codification of intergovernmental agreements have been well canvassed elsewhere and it must be conceded that there is no guarantee that it would, of itself, ensure any less political posturing. The factor which appears to tip the balance is that if agreements are formalized, a formal situation requires some sort of trade-off. If the actors in the bargaining process, in this case public servants, know that there ultimately has to be a trade-off, it is easier to achieve one. At present, in describing intergovernmental agreements the Federal-Provincial Relations Office gives the following information: name of the agreement, time frame, objectives, financing and operation, payments, and whom to contact for further information. The recent Royal Commission on Australian Government Administration, in an analysis of seven intergovernmental arrangements, provided a longer and complementary list.[9] The sort of codification envisaged would be an amalgam of the two lists, which would be constantly updated and sent to all federal and state members of parliament and made readily available to local governments, and pressure groups, and deposited in public libraries, and so on. It is really reprehensible that no level of government in either federation has a central repository and index of all intergovernmental arrangements entered into by that government.

In order to combine flexibility with openness there may well be a case for moving towards broader agreements rather than a plethora of individual, detailed, highly technical documents. Current Australian moves for greater use of the interchange of powers under the constitution, including transfer of powers *both* ways, could also add a welcome note of flexibility. But that serves to highlight again the need for the constant monitoring and debating devices that were outlined earlier.

It must be stressed that these suggestions are only incremental ones requiring no fundamental constitutional changes, and are merely a simple refinement and rearrangement of existing administrative machinery. The basic dilemma of how to make the area of intergovernmental agreements more open to democratic accountability remains. That presupposes public participation, which, in its turn presupposes public understanding of, and interest in, the role of governments. The reforms suggested would seek to enhance that understanding so that citizens could hold each level of government correctly to account for its part in the process. But institutional reforms alone will not do this. It needs a massive onslaught through the education system to acquaint the public, and particularly the young people who will be the electorate of the future, about how they are governed. Yet the curricula in both Canadian and Australian primary and secondary schools are deficient in this area of citizen education. Of course, education is the clear prerogative of state/provincial governments, so initiative is theirs. Naturally, it will take quite a while to educate citizens about the role of each level of government let alone what happens when they interact. In the meantime, it may be as well to accept public ignorance about intergovernmental agreements as given and compensate for it. To this end simple reforms, as already mentioned, like joint location of government offices would be a welcome start; or one-stop welfare shops for the three levels of government are interesting; or the moves by the federal ombudsman in Australia to share office space and the same telephonist and inquiry desk with his state counterpart. If people cannot identify the chef who baked the marble cake or the committee which concocted the recipe, they might at least know which shop sells it so that they can go back to that shop if the cake is too sour, too sweet, too rich, or too old.

A few more questions arise in relation to these aspects. Should guidelines for intergovernmental agreement negotiations be laid down for the benefit of public servants? The recent Australian task force on coordination in welfare and health suggested that a successful consultative process would include: defined scope of deliberation, clear goal definition, trust, continuity and flexibility, openness of discussion, concentration on real issues, some influence on policy, suitably representative membership, and availability of resources.

Can there ever be a completely rational discussion between the three levels of government about intergovernmental agreements while there is such a large degree of vertical fiscal imbalance? This is especially true in Australia. Similarly, should we not seriously consider the size of the units of government before any review of intergovernmental agreements is undertaken? Developments in Canada and Australia in recent years toward regionalism at the subnational level (for example, the Council of Western Premiers and the Council of Maritime Premiers) and at the subprovincial level (regions for various educational, social, and economic development purposes) might well be taken as superficial evidence that the very structure of the federal system is faulty. This is not surprising when it is realized that the political boundaries often have only historical significance. Can there be meaningful discussion about intergovernmental agreements when some of the participating units of government are barely economically viable?

The role of the public servant would be made so much easier if the emphasis of each government on its sovereignty were downplayed. One cannot begin any process of agreement or negotiation if each level of government regards itself as sacrosanct or untouchable. If we cannot clarify the responsibilities of each level of government under intergovernmental agreements then the only alternative is for all levels to be held equally responsible for every agreement they enter.

Federal Finance

We have already examined many elements of the federal financial relationships in Australia and Canada, especially the debate about unconditional and conditional fiscal transfers. It has become patently clear throughout this discussion that the structure of federal finance in the two federations, especially Australia, is not at all conducive to the adoption of public sector planning, predominantly because of the degree and nature of the existing vertical fiscal imbalance. This breaks a number of important linkages, including the connection between taxation and expenditure decisions, between capital and current funding, between vertical and horizontal imbalance, between conditional and unconditional funding, and between associated government functions. We might, for the purposes of illustration, focus on the Australian intergovernmental mechanisms for the allocation of funds for capital expenditure, namely, the Australian Loan Council. In a nation like Australia, which is still developing, public capital expenditure assumes a particular importance for planning because it relates to the laying down of the infrastructure which will, in turn, determine the future fiscal and spatial direction of further public and private expenditure. The process of decision making in the Australian Loan Council, if we can oversimplify it a little, is that each state government presents a proposed loan programme on behalf of its own instrumentalities, its semigovernment authorities, and its local governments. The commonwealth may also submit a loan programme. The size of the total loan programme is negotiated between the states and the commonwealth with the commonwealth having the upper hand for a variety of reasons, but mainly because of its financial domination and the fact that it underwrites state loan programmes. It controls the exchange rate, interest rates, the banking system, and monetary policy in general. The actual voting mechanism on this aspect of Loan Council decisions also gives the commonwealth two votes and a casting vote. But the distribution of the final loan programme is a spatial one, that is, by states and to the commonwealth government. That is to say, no attempt is made to rank in order the various *projects* or elements which make up the loan programme, irrespective of their location, which would have to occur under any rational system of intergovernmental public sector planning. This is because the matter of sovereignty again arises, and the determination of priorities and allocation of resources in this instance is performed as an exercise between separate sovereign entities in a manner which allows each to retain its identity throughout. In fact it is stretching a point quite a long way to regard Loan Council deliberations as a "determination of priorities" — it is more of the nature of a spatial squabble in a fowlyard. The very existence of a backstop provision reinforces this tendency, whereby if the participants cannot agree there has to be a reversion to a formula which is the average distribution which has occurred between the spatial units over the past five years. We might reasonably conclude that the Australian Loan Council is a totally inappropriate institution for the facilitation of public sector planning in intergovernmental relations in Australia and presents a major obstacle to the introduction of such planning. For it to become useful, in this respect, the loan programme would have to be considered on a functional, in addition to a spatial basis, the capital expenditure would need to be related to the federal distribution of recurrent funding, and both would have to be considered on a forward projection basis — possibly a five year rolling programme. (The recent changes to the operations of the Australian Loan Council in relation to infrastructure projects provides evidence of the capacity of that body to break away, at least to a small extent, from its hidebound spatial orientation, even though the voting structure still gives the commonwealth a veto, since in any majority decision, that majority must include the commonwealth.)

This last-mentioned point introduces the other major Australian institution for handling federal financial relations, the Premiers Conference. (Canada has a close equivalent in its Conference of First Ministers.) However, the Premiers Conference suffers from exactly the same impediments to planning which are present in the Loan Council, though in relation to the distribution of recurrent finance which is its main concern. Again the allocation process is a spatial one and in this case there is no attempt to relate it to the capital expenditure distribution. There has been a five year formula for the tax-sharing element, the major element, but that has been subject to many ad hoc additions in the nature of pork-barrelling from year to year. It has become the subject of so much politicization and accentuation of sovereignty of the units of the federation as to make the achievement of the key elements of our planning system, that is, determination of priorities, allocation of resources, and long term implementation, well nigh impossible. So both the Loan Council and the Premiers Conference are fundamental impediments to the attainment of public sector planning because of the nature of their composition and decision making, as is the very fact that they do not coexist but rather artificially divide the federal distribution of funds for capital purposes from the distribution of funds for recurrent purposes. Moreover the actual decision-making process of both bodies is secret, particularly that of the Loan Council, making the whole process unaccountable, especially as the decisions of both bodies are not tabled or debated in either national or state parliaments. In addition, in the case of the Loan Council the Australian Constitution (Section 105 and 105A) tends to place the deliberations of the Loan Council permanently outside parliamentary scrutiny. These points about the Loan Council and Premiers Conference apply with equal force to the vast array of interministerial conferences which take place in both Australia and Canada, the number and range of which we observed earlier.

Consequently any move towards public sector planning of fiscal matters in the Australian and Canadian federations would require fundamental reform of the structure and process of federal financial relations, in particular the operations of the major political institutions responsible for vertical and horizontal fiscal balance. As already mentioned, one of the major changes would have to be for a consideration of fiscal resource allocation on a sectoral rather than a spatial basis, but because of the intense contemporary political emphasis on the sovereignty of subnational units in both the Australian and Canadian federations, such a shift of emphasis would not be easily achieved. It would have to be accompanied, or preceded by a number of other changes, and those changes would have to be akin to the kind of reforms suggested in relation to the division of powers and intergovernmental agreements.

Those changes would have to include, among other things, a clearer presentation of the effects of federal financial resource allocation in relation to some objectives or criteria. This would at least involve the proposal of Lane's that the purposes of each intergovernmental transfer should be clearly identified and that the amount so transferred should be classified in relation to those purposes.[10] For example, tax-sharing grants and many specific purpose grants contain both horizontal and vertical adjustment objectives but the total amount of the grants does not differentiate between these two objectives. Clearly it should do so. The clarification process could be extended to encompass distinctions between capital and recurrent elements (especially in Canada where this distinction is rarely presented in official data); long term programmes and short term programmes (that is, the extent to which the amount under consideration is part of any ongoing commitment); the proportion of total intergovernmental transfers being devoted to the item, or function in question; and the growth in the amount compared with that of the previous year and in relation to movements in total outlays and GNP. Any mandatory requirement that such information be tabled should assist in the delineation of objectives of intergovernmental funding, and ideally that information should be debated in both national and subnational parliaments, preferably annually or even longer provided such a review were a regular feature of the parliamentary cycle even if biennial or triennial.

The political federal resource allocation process could also benefit in these respects from independent advice and analysis of such information. To that extent an "expert" body would seem most appropriate and the function of that body would be to assess the current and likely pattern of federal financial relations (revenue *and* responsibility sharing) in relation to the sorts of objectives just mentioned. This information would provide the basis for discussion at Premiers Conferences, Loan Councils, and interministerial meetings in particular functional areas. It would tend to make discussion at those meetings more rational, more coordinate, more informed, and probably more open, and thus be in the spirit of our planning system. (This is not to deny the opposing argument, often advanced in Canadian and Australian literature, that Premiers Conferences represent the extreme of the political bargaining process and should be used as an unfettered process of checks and balances. All that is being claimed here is that, if planning is desired, the processes of intergovernmental political meetings would have to change.) It could also serve as an advisory body to the national parliament, especially the senate, and also state parliaments where required. Its membership would need to reflect a federal participation, and so it could be composed of national, state, and local officials, permanent or seconded, together with outsiders. It could be a modified version of the Canadian Federal-Provincial Relations Office with a stronger fiscal reference, or an expanded and modified version of the Australian Commonwealth Grants Commission, such as occurred with the augmentation of that body to perform the analysis of fiscal relativities between the states. (The Grants Commission's present expertise lies in horizontal equalization and it is conceded that this new role also relates to vertical balance, and particularly the process of determining priorities between the expenditure and revenue components of the national and subnational governments.)

This whole process would also be aided by more inherent flexibility in federal fiscal arrangements, especially in relation to revenue sharing. This is particularly relevant for the Australian situation so characterized by vertical fiscal imbalance with attendant dependence of all the states on federal funding of one kind or other. The ideal solution to this problem (ideal in the sense of reconciling planning processes with federal power division), would be to move towards the Canadian system of greater explicit taxation for the states to levy, coupled with clear and unambiguous long term formulae for federal fiscal transfers. In other words, a specific portion of taxation would be designated as state taxation. The states would have the power to raise or lower that portion at their own behest, but their share of national government taxes would be fixed by formulae, although that particular share would be flexible enough to be altered if required by circumstances, on the advice of the institutional framework already outlined. The actual mechanisms of the process would depend on the particular taxes to be divided, and the taxes to be shared.

In Conclusion

The results of this study have reinforced the view that planning is basically incompatible with federalism. That has proved to be the case in both concept and practice, and in political terms the main factor is the divided sovereignty which is the essential ingredient of federalism. However our research has demonstrated also that the hindrances or obstacles which arise in any practical attempt to marry the two concepts are not necessarily insurmountable. The incompatibility can be mitigated by reforms which are practicable even within the constraints of the existing federal system.

The reforms which we have suggested for the federal system under review have been of three main kinds:

1. *Changes to the roles of the actors in the federal political process* principally in relation to the responsibilities of each level of government and the division of powers. This shift of emphasis to *roles rather than functions*, and the very division of those roles has been aimed at achieving

greater certainty in federal relations as well as more rationality and accountability — three vital ingredients of any planning system.

2. *Changes to the structure of federal relations* principally in relation to the major political institutions involved in the federal resource allocation process and its attendant coordination process. These changes have been aimed mainly at achieving smoother coordination and greater rationality in federal resource allocation; once again two vital ingredients for any planning system.

3. *Changes to the processes of federal relations* especially the way in which resource allocation is viewed, presented, debated, and decided. These are reforms aimed at achieving rationality accompanied by accountability.

Thus, in accordance with the stipulated aims of this study we have found that our planning system does not fit the federal systems particularly well. Hindrances have been identified and reforms suggested for the federal systems to make it more amenable to the sort of planning we have envisaged. The other main underlying element in these suggested reforms has been an attempt to achieve the maximum degree of accountability in such planning, and that has inevitably involved *taking the federal resource allocation process back to the politicians* for debate and decision, aided by more rational advice, in an open environment. This has not proved completely practicable either, for planning and democracy are basically incompatible. However, as Carl Friedrich observes:

> Planning is often involved in effective policy making as the very process of sorting out . . . alternatives. And the opinion which sees an insoluble conflict between planning and democracy is untenable. Experience has shown further that the voters have a sense of appreciation for objective achievements. The electorate at the same time recognizes that there are other than technical problems and it reacts sharply when the values and beliefs of the community are at stake. If the often-heard claim that planning is incompatible with democracy or with a free society is therefore untenable, contemporary evidence suggests that they both presuppose planning under contemporary conditions. Hence planning and public policy are least likely to be defective under such conditions as only democracy and freedom can provide.[11]

In the context of this study planning and federalism, like planning and democracy, are relatively, not absolutely, incompatible and thus the Australian and Canadian federal systems can be made more or less compatible with the planning system we have utilized. The extent to which the subnational units of these federations, or any other federation, can plan their activities will vary accordingly.

Notes

Introduction

1. Great Britain, The Plowden Committee, *Report of the Committee on the Control of Public Expenditure*, Command 1432 (London: HMSO, 1961).
2. R. Simeon, *Federal-Provincial Diplomacy. The Making of Recent Policy in Canada* (Toronto: University of Toronto Press, 1973).

Chapter 1

1. See for example, Morton A. Kaplan, "Systems Theory", in *Comparative Political Analysis*, ed. James C. Charlesworth (New York: Free Press, 1967), 150-51.
2. Oran Young, *Systems of Political Science* (New Jersey: Prentice-Hall, 1968), 98.
3. Ibid., 15.
4. Kaplan, "System Theory", 151. See also R.L. Sckoff, "Systems, Organisations, and Interdisciplinary Research", in *Systems Thinking*, ed. F.E. Emery (Harmondsworth, Middlesex: Penguin, 1978).
5. Herbert J. Spiro, "An Evaluation of Systems Theory", in *Comparative Political Analysis*, ed. Charlesworth, 164.
6. See J.D.B. Miller, *The Nature of Politics* (Harmondsworth, Middlesex: Pelican, 1965), chapter 11; and David Easton, *A Systems Analysis of Political Life* (New York: Wiley, 1965).
7. See for example, Gabriel Almond and James Coleman, eds., *The Politics of the Developing Areas* (Princeton: Princeton University Press, 1960).
8. See for example, Warren G. Bennis, "Organizational Developments and the Fate of Bureaucracy", in *Perspectives on Public Bureaucracy*, ed. Fred A. Kramer (Mass.: Winthrop, 1941), 161-84.
9. Karl W. Deutsch, *The Nerves of Government* (New York: Free Press-Macmillan Co., 1966).
10. See for example, the cautioning on this aspect given by David Easton, *Systems Analysis*, 18, and Herbert Spiro, "Systems Theory", 168-69.
11. Luther H. Gulick and Lyndall Urwick, eds., *Papers on the Science of Administration* (New York: Institute of Public Administration, 1937). See also, H. Fayol, *Administration Industrielle et Generale*, English edition (London: Pitman, 1955); L. Urwick, *The Elements of Administration*, 2nd ed. (London: Pitman, 1974); and F.W. Taylor, *Principles of Scientific Management* (New York: Harper and Row, 1911).
12. Luther H. Gulick, "Notes on the Theory of Organisation", in *Perspectives*, ed. Kramer, 33.
13. Ibid., 34.
14. Urwick, *Elements of Administration*, 27.
15. Ibid., 20.
16. Herbert A. Simon, *Administrative Behavior*, 2nd ed. (New York: Free Press, 1968), 20.
17. Ibid., 106.
18. Peter Self, *Administrative Theories and Politics* (London: George Allen and Unwin, 1977), 30.
19. Gerald E. Caiden, *The Dynamics of Public Administration* (Illinois: Dryden, 1971), 46.

20. See Harold Lasswell, *The Decision Process: Seven Categories of Functional Analysis* (College Park: University of Maryland Press, 1956).

21. David Braybrooke and Charles E. Lindblom, *A Strategy of Decision* (New York: Free Press, 1970), 74.

22. Ibid., 86-87.

23. Charles E. Lindblom, *The Policy-Making Process* (Englewood Cliffs, NJ: Prentice-Hall, 1968), 4.

24. See Charles E. Lindblom, "The Science of 'Muddling Through' ", *Public Administration Review* 19 (Spring 1959): 78-88; Yehezkel Dror, *Public Policymaking Reexamined* (San Francisco: Chandler, 1968), and *Design for Policy Sciences* (New York: American Elesevia, 1971); and Amitai Etzioni, "Mixed Scanning: A 'Third' Approach to Decision Making", *Public Administration Review* 27 (5), (December 1967): 385-92.

25. See Geoffrey Vickers, *Value Systems and Social Process* (Harmondsworth, Middlesex: Penguin, 1968), and also *The Art of Judgement* (Harmondsworth, Middlesex: Penguin, 1965).

26. Carl J. Friedrich, "Political Decision-Making, Public Policy and Planning", *Canadian Public Administration* 14 (I), (Spring 1971).

27. See Thomas R. Dye, *Policy Analysis* (Alabama: University of Alabama Press, 1976); and George C. Edwards III and Ira Sharkansky, *The Policy Predicament* (San Francisco: Freeman, 1978).

28. Richard Rose, ed., *The Dynamics of Public Policy* (London: Sage, 1976), chapter 1.

29. D. Waldo, "Scope and Theory of Public Administration" in *Theory and Practice of Public Administration: Scope, Objectives, and Methods*, monograph no. 8, ed. J.C. Charlesworth (Philadelphia: American Academy of Political and Social Science, 1968).

30. For works which give some insight into the New Public Administration, see F. Marini, *Towards a New Public Administration: The Minnow-Brook Perspective* (New York: Chandler, 1971); D. Waldo, ed., *Public Administration in a Time of Turbulence* (Scranton, Penn.: Chandler, 1971); Kramer, ed., *Perspectives*; and "The New Public Administration", *Public Management* 53 (11), (November 1971).

31. For a sample of public choice theorists, see Kenneth J. Arrow, *Social Choices and Individual Values* (New York: Wiley, 1951); Anthony Downs, *An Economic Theory of Democracy* (New York: Harper & Row, 1957); James M. Buchanan and Gordon Tullock, *The Calculus of Consent* (Ann Arbor: University of Michigan Press, 1962); William Niskanen, *Bureaucracy and Representative Government* (Chicago: Aldine, 1971); and Vincent Ostrom, *The Intellectual Crisis of American Public Administration* (Alabama: University of Alabama Press, 1973).

32. See for example, J. La Palombara, *Bureaucracy and Political Development* (Princeton: Princeton University Press, 1963); G. Almond and J.S. Coleman, eds., *The Politics of the Developing Areas* (Princeton: Princeton University Press, 1960); L.W. Pye, *Aspects of Political Development* (Boston: Little, Brown & Co., 1966); F.W. Riggs, *Administration in Developing Countries* (Boston: Houghton Mifflin, 1964); A.O. Hirschman, *The Strategy of Economic Development* (New Haven: Yale University Press, 1958); and M.J. Esman and J.D. Montgomery, "Systems Approaches to Technical Cooperation: The Role of Development Administration", *Public Administration Review* 29 (5), (September/October 1969).

33. Friedrich, "Political Decision-Making".

34. Andrew Shonfield, *Modern Capitalism* (London: Oxford University Press, 1969), 121.

35. Great Britain, *Report of the Committee on the Control of Public Expenditure*, Command 1432 (London: HMSO, 1961).

36. Sir Richard Clarke, *New Trends in Government* (London: HMSO, 1971).

37. Robert H. Haveman, "The Analysis and Evaluation of Public Expenditures: An Overview", *The PPB System*, vol. 1 (Washington: US Government Printing Office, 1969): 6.

38. See Kenneth F. Knight and Kenneth W. Wiltshire, *Formulating Government Budgets: Aspects of Australian and North American Experience* (St Lucia: University of Queensland Press, 1977), chapter 4.

39. Friedrich, "Political Decision-Making".

40. David Novick, ed., *Program Budgeting* (Cambridge, Mass.: Harvard University Press, 1965), 91 and 103.

41. Friedrich, "Political Decision-Making".
42. Peter Self, *Administrative Theories and Politics*, 157.
43. There is a long list of literature of a polemic nature on this theme, most of it related to the notion of economic planning for the whole economy or society, and a great deal of it written in response to the growth of totalitarian regimes in the first half of the twentieth century and the immediate postwar period. See for example, F.A. Hayek, *The Road to Serfdom* (London: Routledge and Kegan-Paul, 1944); L.C. Robbins, *Economic Planning and the International Order* (London: Macmillan, 1937); M. Polanyi, *The Concept of Freedom* (London: Watts, 1940); John Jewkes, *Ordeal by Planning* (London: Macmillan, 1948); Barbara Wootton, *Freedom under Planning* (London: Allen and Unwin, 1945).

Chapter 2

1. The concept of public works coordination had arrived much earlier in some states, as for example in Queensland, where a Bureau of Industry had been created in the early 1930s to fulfil this and other functions. See B.M. Molesworth, "The Bureau of Industry in Queensland", *The Economic Record* (June 1933): 105-8; and C. Lack, *Three Decades of Queensland Political History* (Brisbane: Government Printer, 1960).
2. E.O.G. Shann and D.B. Copland, *The Battle of the Plans* (Sydney: Angus and Robertson, 1931).
3. J.P. Abbott, "The Battle of the Plans", *Australian Quarterly* (14 September 1931): 111.
4. F.A. Bland and R.C. Mills, "Financial Reconstruction. An Examination of the Plan Adopted at the Premiers' Conference 1931", *The Economic Record* (November 1931): 166.
5. Hon. J.A. Lyons, "The National Plan — And After", *Australian Quarterly* (14 September 1931): 7-14.
6. See Allan G.B. Fisher, "Fundamental Presupposition for Successful Economic Planning", *The Economic Record* (October 1932): 88-98.
7. F.R.E. Mauldon, "Some Implications of Economic Planning", *Australian Quarterly* (14 June 1933): 92-100.
8. L.G. Melville, "Plans and Planners", *Australian Quarterly* (14 December 1934): 96-110.
9. F.A. Bland, *Planning the Modern State* (Sydney: Angus and Robertson, 1945).
10. T. Hytten, "Australian Public Finance Since 1930", *The Economic Record* (March 1935): 122-138.
11. C. Hartley Grattan, "The Future in Australia", *Australian Quarterly* (December 1938): 23-24. See also F.A. Bland, "Bigger and Better Budgets", *Australian Quarterly* (September 1936): 34-47; "Crisis Finance", *Australian Quarterly* (December 1939): 11-23; C.G.F. Simkin, "Budgetary Reform", *The Economic Record* (December 1941): 192-209; and Edward Masey, "Aspects of Planning", *Australian Quarterly* (10 June 1934): 82-92.
12. R.L. Mathews and W.R.C. Jay, *Federal Finance: Intergovernmental Finance Relations in Australia since Federation* (Melbourne: Nelson, 1972), 163 ff.
13. Paul Hasluck, *The Government and the People 1942-1945* (Canberra: Australian War Memorial, 1970), 511-12.
14. Mathews and Jay, *Federal Finance*, chapter 8.
15. Wilfred Prest, "War-time Controls and Post-war Planning", *The Economic Record* (1942): 211. For other perspectives on the 1939–45 period, see T. Hytten, "Wartime Financial Policy", *Australian Quarterly* (March 1940): 63-72; and E.J. Tapp, "Planning and Democracy", *Australian Quarterly* (September 1945): 75-83.
16. Prest, "War-time Controls and Post-war Planning": 213.
17. D.H. Merry and G.R. Bruns, "Full Employment: The British, Canadian and Australian White Papers", *The Economic Record* (December 1945): 223.
18. W.J. Waters, "Australian Labor's Full Employment Objective, 1942–45", *Australian Journal of Politics and History* 16 (1970): 64. However, it should be remembered that Copland was the government's economic adviser and played a major role in the development of the White Paper on full employment.

19. H.C. Coombs, "The Economic Aftermath of War", in *Post-War Reconstruction in Australia*, ed. D.A.S. Campbell (Sydney: Australasian Publishing Co., 1944), 78.

20. Ibid., 81.

21. Ibid., 98-99.

22. D.B. Copland, "The Change-Over to Peace" in *Post-War Reconstruction in Australia*, ed. Campbell.

23. For a discussion of the economic aspects of postwar reconstruction, especially the international aspects, see L.G. Melville et al., *Australia's Post-War Economy* (Sydney: Australasian Publishing Co., 1945); also Herbert Burton, "The Transition to a Peace Economy", *The Economic Record* (December 1945): 149-64; and A.J. Grenfeld, "A Plan of Reconstruction", *Australian Quarterly* (June 1946): 72-85.

24. D.B. Copland, "Professor Jewkes and the Alternative to Planning", *The Economic Record* (December 1948): 191-203.

25. G.D.H. Cole, quoted in F.R.E. Mauldon, "The Consumer in a Planned Economy", *The Economic Record* (June 1949): 1.

26. Mauldon, "The Consumer in a Planned Economy": 2.

27. Ibid., 3-4.

28. Ibid., 15.

29. *Sydney Morning Herald*, 6 May 1954.

30. H. Curtis, "Planning for National Development", *Australian Quarterly* (September 1954): 52-53.

31. *Report of the Committee of Economic Inquiry*, vol. 1 (Melbourne: Wilkie, 1965), 3.

32. Ibid., 432.

33. Ibid., 437.

34. Ibid., 450.

35. Ibid., 453.

36. Ibid., 242.

37. See "Policies for Economic Growth: The Vernon Report — A Review", *Australian Quarterly* (December 1965): 11-25. For an impassioned defence of economic planning and concern about the cost of state-rightism to economic growth, see R.O. Hieser, "Australian Economic Policy-Making", *Australian Quarterly* (December 1964): 36-48. For an economic appraisal of the assumptions in the Vernon Report, see B.L. Johns, "Growth Prospects for the Australian Economy to 1975", *Australian Quarterly* (March 1966): 26-44.

38. See *Planning, Programming, Budgeting and Control in the A.P.O.* (Canberra: Commonwealth Government Printer, June 1970).

39. For an account of the measures adopted in one state, Queensland, see Kenneth Wiltshire, *Portuguese Navy: The Establishment of the Queensland Department of Industrial Development* (Brisbane: Royal Institute of Public Administration, 1974).

40. A.J. Davies, "National Development", *Australian Quarterly* (December 1965): 51.

41. A.J. Davies, "Australian Federalism and National Development", *Australian Journal of Politics and History* 14 (1), (April 1968): 37-51.

42. E.G. Whitlam, "National Transport Planning: Political and Constitutional Problems", *Australian Quarterly* 40 (3), (September 1968): 40-54. For an earlier perspective on the same problem, see T. Hytten, "Some Problems of Australian Transport Development", *The Economic Record* (June 1947): 5-19.

43. Patrick Weller and James Cutt, *Treasury Control in Australia* (Sydney: Novak, 1976), 70.

44. James Cutt, "Program Budgeting", Royal Commission on Australian Government Administration", *Appendix Volume 1* (Canberra: AGPS, 1976): 83.

45. Commonwealth of Australia, Treasurer's Budget Speech 1973–74, *Statement No. 8 Changes in Budget Format and Presentation* (Canberra: AGPS, 1974).

46. *Treasury Submission to the Royal Commission on Australian Government Administration, Attachment B* (Canberra: Treasury): 23.

47. Cutt, "Program Budgeting": 83.

48. Commonwealth Treasury, *Problems in Preparing Forward Estimates of Australian Government Outlays* (Internal Paper), (Canberra: Treasury, 1974).

49. For a detailed description of the attempts at manpower forward estimates see Royal Commission on Australian Government Administration, *Appendix Volume 1* (Canberra: AGPS, 1976): 113-63.

50. *Review of the Continuing Expenditure Policies of the Previous Government* (Canberra: AGPS, June 1973).

51. Priorities Review Staff, *Goals and Strategies* (Interim Report), (Canberra: December 1973).

52. See C.P. Harris, *Relationships between Federal and State Governments in Australia* (Advisory Council for Inter-government Relations, information paper no. 6), (Canberra: AGPS, 1979).

53. For other more detailed comment on the problems of the forward estimates, see Weller and Cutt, *Treasury Control*, 70-73; and Patrick Weller, "Forward Estimates and the Allocation of Resources", in *Public Service Inquiries in Australia*, eds. R.F. Smith and P. Weller (St Lucia: University of Queensland Press, 1977), 203-18.

54. B.W. Fraser, "Recent Developments Affecting the Outlay Side of the Commonwealth's Budget", in *Recent Developments in Budgeting*, ed. R.L. Mathews (Canberra: Centre for Research on Federal Financial Relations, 1979), 1-10.

55. These developments are outlined briefly by R.G. Webster, "Recent Victorian Developments which affect Forward Works Planning", in *Recent Developments in Budgeting*, ed. Mathews, 15-20.

56. There were four reports of the Bland Inquiry titled *Report of the Board of Inquiry into the Victorian Public Service* (Melbourne: Government Printer). The first and second reports were in 1974, the third and fourth in 1975. For reviews of these reports see Jean Holmes, "The Victorian Inquiry", in *Public Service Inquiries in Australia*, eds. R.F. Smith and P. Weller (St Lucia: University of Queensland Press, 1978), 89-110.

57. Bland Inquiry, *First Report*: 44.

58. See, for example, Public Bodies Review Committee, *First Report to the Parliament on the Activities of the Public Bodies Review Committee* (Melbourne: Government Printer, December 1980).

59. See, for example, Dean Jaensch, "The South Australian Inquiry", in Smith and Weller, eds., *Public Service Inquiries*, 70-88.

60. R.D. Barnes, "Recent Developments in Budgeting in South Australia", in *Recent Developments in Budgeting*, ed. Mathews, 34.

61. For an analysis of the suggested NSW reforms see B. Moore, "Machinery of Government Changes in New South Wales", *Public Administration* (Sydney) 24 (2), (June 1975): 113-27.

62. N. Oakes, "Budget Developments in New South Wales", in *Recent Developments in Budgeting*, ed. Mathews, 11-14.

63. Interim Report of the Review of New South Wales Government Administration, *Directions for Change* (Sydney: Government Printer, 1977).

64. Ibid.: 39.

65. Ibid.: 44.

Chapter 3

1. S. Rufus Davis, *The Federal Principle* (Berkeley: University of California Press, 1978), 29-31.

2. Ibid., 41.

3. Ibid., 73.

4. Carl J. Friedrich, *Trends of Federalism in Theory and Practice* (London: Pall Mall, 1978), 8.

5. Geoffrey Sawer, *Modern Federalism* (Carlton: Pitman, 1976).

6. James Bryce, *American Commonwealth*, vol. 1 (London: Macmillan, 1914), 432.

7. Sawer, *Modern Federalism*, 7-8.

8. A.V. Dicey, *Introduction to the Study of Law of the Constitution*, 8th ed. (London: Macmillan, 1915), 171-72.

9. See K.C. Wheare, *Federal Government*, 4th ed. (London: Oxford University Press, 1963). (Wheare's concept of federalism owed much to Quick and Garran.)

10. See William Livingston, *Federalism and Constitutional Change* (Oxford: Clarendon Press, 1956); Ivor D. Duchacek, *Comparative Federalism. The Territorial Dimension of Politics* (New York: Holt, Rinehart & Winston, 1970); and William H. Riker, *Federalism, Origin, Operation, Significance* (Boston: Little, Brown & Co., 1964), chapter 2.

11. Anthony H. Birch, "Approaches to the Study of Federalism", in *American Federalism in Perspective*, ed. Aaron Wildavsky (Boston: Little, Brown & Co., 1967).

12. Morton Grodzins, "The Federal System", in *American Federalism*, ed. Wildavsky, 13-227.

13. See B.M. Sharma, *Federalism in Theory and Practice* (Chandausi: Bhargova & Sons, 1951), 99-109.

14. Wheare, *Federal Government*, 260.

15. Livingston, *Federalism and Constitutional Change*, 9.

16. Ibid., 10.

17. Sawer, *Modern Federalism*, 1.

18. Friedrich, *Trends of Federalism*, 10.

19. See Rufus Davis, "The 'Federal Principle' Reconsidered", in *American Federalism*, ed. Wildavsky, 3-32.

20. Ibid., 58.

21. See for example, Rameah Ritta Dikshit, *The Political Geography of Federalism* (London: Macmillan, 1975), 10; and Ivor D. Duchacek, *Comparative Federalism*, 12-14, and 192.

22. Morton Grodzins, "The Federal System", 256 ff.

23. Sawer, *Modern Federalism*, 1.

24. Ibid., 27.

25. Wheare, *Federal Government*, 58.

26. Livingston, *Federalism and Constitutional Change*, 10.

27. Sharma, *Federalism in Theory and Practice*, 35.

28. Paul A. Freund, "Umpiring the Federal System", in *Federalism Mature and Emergent*, ed. Arthur W. MacMahon (New York: Doubleday, 1955), 161.

29. Riker, *Federalism, Origin, Operation, Significance*, 136.

30. Sawer, *Modern Federalism*, 120-21.

31. Ronald L. Watts, *Administration in Federal Systems* (London: Hutchison, 1970), 14.

32. William S. Livingston, "Canada, Australia, and the United States, Variations on a Theme", in *Federalism Infinite Variety in Theory and Practice*, ed. Valerie Earle (Illinois: Peacock, 1968), 113-14.

33. Dicey, *Introduction to Study of Law of the Constitution*, 137.

34. Dikshit, *The Political Geography of Federalism*, 10.

35. Duchacek, *Comparative Federalism*, 207.

36. Ibid., 277-78.

37. Livingston, *Federalism and Constitutional Change*, 2.

38. R.L. Watts, *New Federations: Experiments in the Commonwealth* (Oxford: Clarendon Press, 1966), 67-69.

39. Livingston, "Federalism and Constitutional Change", in *American Perspective*, ed. Wildavsky, 46.

40. Friedrich, *Trends of Federalism*, 7.

41. Livingston, *Federalism and Constitutional Change*, 14.

42. Ibid.

43. Sawer, *Modern Federalism*, 1.

44. Wheare, *Federal Government*, 209.

45. Macmahon, ed., *Federalism, Mature and Emergent*, 18.

46. Watts, *Administration in Federal Systems*, 13.

47. Duchacek, *Comparative Federalism*, 207.

48. Livingston, *Federalism and Constitutional Change*, 10-11.

49. Sawer, *Modern Federalism*, 11.

50. Wheare, *Federal Government*, 88.

51. Duchacek, *Comparative Federalism*, 207.

52. Livingston, *Federalism and Constitutional Change*, 11.
53. Davis, *The Federal Principle*, 151.
54. Watts, *Administration in Federal Systems*, 115.
55. Wheare, *Federal Government*, 93.
56. Watts, *Administration in Federal Systems*, 10.
57. See Donald Smiley, *Canada in Question* (Toronto: McGraw-Hill Ryerson, 1976); Richard Simeon, *Federal-Provincial Diplomacy* (Toronto: University of Toronto Press, 1977); J.E. Richardson, *Patterns of Australian Federalism* monograph no. 1 (Canberra: Centre for Research on Federal Financial Relations, 1973); Kenneth Wiltshire, ed., *Administrative Federalism: Selected Documents in Australian Intergovernmental Relations* (St Lucia: University of Queensland Press, 1977).
58. Sawer, *Modern Federalism*, 14.
59. Friedrich, *Trends of Federalism in Theory and Practice*, 14.
60. Watts, *Administration in Federal Systems*, 99-100.
61. Riker, *Federalism, Origin, Operation, Significance*.
62. Wheare, *Federal Government*, 37.
63. Watts, *New Federations*, chapter 3.
64. Friedrich, *Trends of Federalism in Theory and Practice*, 173.

Chapter 4

1. See Kenneth Wiltshire, "Australian State Participation in Federal Decisions", in *Federalism in Australia and the Federal Republic of Germany*, ed. R.L. Mathews (Canberra: ANU Press, 1980), 65-138; see also J.R. Odgers, *Australian Senate Practice* (Canberra: AGPS, 1972); L.F. Crisp, *Australian National Government* (Melbourne: Longman, 1973); Campbell Sharman, "The Australian Senate as a States' House", in *The Politics of New Federalism*, ed. Dean Jaensch (Adelaide: APSA, 1977), 64-75.
2. Under the Fraser government's "new federalism" arrangements the states received a fixed percentage share of net personal income tax, eventually about forty per cent, but this was passed on to them only after it had been collected by the national government. Under the new arrangements in the early 1980s it was changed to a little over twenty per cent of a basket of net commonwealth taxes. For a detailed history of these changes see "Payments to or for the States, the Northern Territory and Local Government Authorities", *Budget Paper No. 7* (Commonwealth Treasury): (1981-82) chapter 2 and appendix, and (1982-83) chapter 2.
3. Section 51 subsection 37 gives the national government power over: "Matters referred to the Parliament of the Commonwealth by the Parliament or Parliaments of any State or States, but so that the law shall extend only to States by whose Parliaments the matter is referred, or which afterwards adopt the law". For an analysis of the operation of this section and other attempts to refer powers between levels see J.E. Richardson, *Patterns of Australian Federalism*, monograph no. 1 (Canberra: Centre for Research on Federal Financial Relations, 1973), 92-97.
4. For elaboration on some difficulties in the conduct of this relativity review exercise see R. Else-Mitchell, "Fiscal Equality between the States: The New Role of the Commonwealth Grants Commission", *Australian Journal of Public Administration* 28 (2), (June 1979): 157-67; Russell Mathews, *Australian Federalism 1979* (Canberra: Centre for Research on Federal Financial Relations, 1981); R. Else-Mitchell, "The Australian Federal Grants System and its Impact on Fiscal Relations of the Federal Government with State and Local Governments", reprint no. 38 (Canberra: Centre for Research on Federal Financial Relations, 1980); Russell Mathews, *The Distribution of Tax Sharing Entitlements among the States*, reprint no. 31 (Canberra: Centre for Research on Federal Financial Relations, 1979); Russell Mathews, *Regional Disparities and Fiscal Equalisation in Australia*, reprint no. 30 (Canberra: Centre for Research on Federal Financial Relations, 1979). See also Commonwealth Grants Commission, *Report on State Tax Sharing Entitlements* (Canberra: AGPS,

1981); Commonwealth Grants Commission, Report on State Tax Sharing and Health Grants (Canberra: AGPS, 1982); and "Payments to or for the States, the Northern Territory and Local Government Authorities", *Budget Paper No. 7* (Canberra: AGPS, 1981–82 and 1984–85).

5. For an analysis of the operations of the Interstate Commission see Richardson, *Patterns of Australian Federalism*: 71-82. Section 101 of the Australian Constitution says: "There shall be an Interstate Commission, with such powers of adjudication and administration as the Parliament deems necessary for the execution and maintenance, within the Commonwealth, of the provision of this Constitution relating to trade and commerce, and of all laws made thereunder". For a thorough analysis of interstate mobility in Canada and other federations see John A. Hayes, *Economic Mobility in Canada* (Ottawa: CGPS, 1982).

Chapter 5

1. K.C. Wheare, *Federal Government* (London: Oxford University Press, 1963), 10.
2. William H. Riker, *Federalism, Origin, Operation, Significance* (Boston: Little, Brown & Co., 1964), 5.
3. Geoffrey Sawer, *Modern Federalism* (London: Pitman, 1976), 2.
4. Daniel J. Elazar, *Federalism*, International Encyclopedia of the Social Sciences (New York: MacMillan Co., 1967).
5. S. Rufus Davis, *The Federal Principle* (Berkeley: University of California Press, 1978), 142-43.
6. G.V. Portus, ed., *Studies in the Australian Constitution* (Sydney: Angus and Robertson, 1933), 34-35.
7. *Report of the Royal Commission on Dominion-Provincial Relations*, book 1 (Canada: 1867–1939), (Ottawa: Queen's Printer, 1940), 30-31.
8. R. Else-Mitchell, "National Planning and Intergovernmental Relations: Constitutional and Legal Issues", *Public Administration* (Sydney), 28 (1), (March 1969): 20.
9. The Hon. Sir John Quick, *The Legislative Powers of the Commonwealth and the States of Australia with Proposed Amendments* (Sydney: Law Book Co., 1919), 308-10.
10. Quoted in R. Norris, *The Emergent Commonwealth* (Melbourne: Melbourne University Press, 1975), 4.
11. Ibid., 4-5.
12. John Quick and Robert Randolph Garran, *The Constitution of the Australian Commonwealth* (Sydney: Angus and Robertson, 1901), 81.
13. Ibid., 125-26.
14. J. Quick and R.R. Garran, *The Annotated Constitution of the Australian Commonwealth* (Sydney: Angus and Robertson, 1901), 157.
15. Ibid., 195.
16. Quick, *Legislative Powers*, 268-69.
17. Quick and Garran, *The Constitution*, 339-40.
18. Alfred Deakin, *Federated Australia* (Melbourne: Melbourne University Press, 1968), 56-66.
19. Norris, *The Emergent Commonwealth*, 180.
20. Quick and Garran, *The Constitution*, 340.
21. Donald Creighton, *The Road to Confederation* (Toronto: Macmillan, 1964), 118.
22. Wilfred Eggleston, *The Road to Nationhood* (Toronto: Oxford University Press, 1946), 38-42.
23. G.P. Browne, *Documents on the Confederation of British North America* (Toronto: McClelland and Stewart, 1969), xxviii.
24. Quoted in G.F.G. Stanley, "Act or Pact? Another Look at Confederation", in *Confederation*, ed. D.G. Creighton et al. (Toronto: University of Toronto Press, 1967), 115.
25. Ibid.
26. D.V. Smiley, *Canada in Question* (Toronto: McGraw-Hill Ryerson, 1976), 5.
27. See Commonwealth of Australia, *Report of the Royal Commission on the Constitution*

(Canberra: Government Printer, 1929): 74, 173-74, 204, 206-7, 223-27; and Parliament of the Commonwealth of Australia, *Report of the Joint Committee on Constitutional Review* (Canberra: Government Printer, 1959): 60-61.

28. See for example, R.L. Mathews, ed., *Fiscal Federalism: Retrospect and Prospect*, research monograph 7 (Canberra: Centre for Research on Federal Financial Relations, 1974): 115-16.

29. See for example, Commonwealth, *Report of Commission on Constitution*: 151, 153, 244, 247.

30. See J.A. Corry, *Difficulties of Divided Jurisdiction*, A Study prepared for the Royal Commission on Dominion-Provincial Relations, appendix 7 (Ottawa: Queen's Printer, 1939): 7-9.

31. See Commonwealth, *Report of Commission on Constitution*: 221; Mathews, ed., *Fiscal Federalism*, 117-18; Portus, ed., *Australian Constitution*, 34-39.

32. Commonwealth, *Report of Commission on Constitution*, 244; Mathews, *Fiscal Federalism*, 114-20.

33. Mathews, *Fiscal Federalism*, 119; Corry, *Divided Jurisdiction*, 8-9.

34. Corry, *Divided Jurisdiction*, 9-10.

35. See *Proceedings of the Australian Constitution Convention* (Sydney: Government Printer, 1973), 278; Gordon Greenwood, *The Future of Australian Federalism*, 2nd ed. (St Lucia: University of Queensland Press, 1976); Corry, *Divided Jurisdiction*, 8-9.

36. See *Report on Dominion-Provincial Relations*, book 1, 31; MacGregor-Dawson, *The Government of Canada* (Toronto: University of Toronto Press, 1967), 90-93; J.R. Mallory, *Social Credit and the Federal Power in Canada* (Toronto: University of Toronto Press, 1954), 25; and Mathews, *Fiscal Federalism*, 115.

37. See for example, Commonwealth, *Report of Commission on Constitution*, 86, 173-74, 204, 206-7, 208-12, 219-20; Portus, *Australian Constitution*, 57; Parliament, *Report on Constitutional Review*, 60-61, 112, 113; Sidney Sax, "Australian Health Services — Development and Problems", *Public Administration* (Sydney) 34 (3), (September 1975): 227-30; Geoffrey Sawer, "Seventy-Five Years of Australian Federalism", *Australian Journal of Public Administration* 36 (1), (March 1977): 8-11; *Constitutional Convention*, 278; E.G. Whitlam, "National Transport Planning: Political and Constitutional Problems", *Australian Quarterly* (September 1968): 46; C. Sanders, "Higher Education — State or Commonwealth?" *Australian Quarterly* (December 1950): 41-49.

38. Smiley, *Canada in Question*, 54.

39. See for example, Richard Simeon, *Federal-Provincial Diplomacy* (Toronto: University of Toronto Press, 1973), 41; Edwin R. Black, *Divided Loyalties, Canadian Concepts of Federalism* (McGill, Montreal: Queen's University Press, 1975), 2; J. Peter Meekison, ed., *Canadian Federalism: Myth or Reality* (Toronto: Methuen, 1963); Paul Fox, *Politics: Canada*, 2nd ed. (Toronto: McGraw-Hill, 1966).

40. R.L. Mathews, "Innovations and Developments in Australian Federalism", *Publius* 7 (3), (Summer 1977): 16-17.

41. R.L. Mathews, ed., *Intergovernmental Relations in Australia* (Sydney: Angus and Robertson, 1974), 23.

42. See for example, L.F. Crisp, *Australian National Government* (Melbourne: Longman, 1970); see Robert Menzies, *Central Power in the Australian Commonwealth* (London: Cassell, 1967); Geoffrey Sawer, *Australian Federalism in the Courts* (Melbourne: Melbourne University Press, 1967) and *Federation under Strain* (Melbourne: Melbourne University Press, 1977); C.A.N. Hawker, "Towards Federal Equilibrium", *Australian Quarterly* (September 1937): 57-66; R.N. Spann, *Government Administration in Australia* (Sydney: Allen and Unwin, 1979); K.W. Knight, "Federalism and Administrative Efficacy", in R.L. Mathews, ed., *Intergovernmental Relations in Australia*, 43-55; and L.F. Giblin, "Federation and Finance", *The Economic Record* (November 1926): 145-60.

43. Some of these have been familiar in Australia for many years. See for example, Commonwealth, *Report of Commission on Constitution*: 86-87.

44. See for example, A.J. Davies, "Australian Federalism and National Development", *Australian Journal of Politics and History*, 14 (1), (April 1968): 37-51; Allan Peachment, "Patterns of Conflict Resolution in Australian Federalism", *Politics* 6 (2), (November

1971): 137-47; R. MacGregor Dawson, *The Government of Canada* (Toronto: University of Toronto Press, 1967); Hon. Mr Justice Else-Mitchell, *Essays on the Australian Constitution* (Sydney: Law Book Co., 1961); P.R. Heydon, "Cooperative Administration in Immigration", *Public Administration* (Sydney) 24 (47), (March 1965): 47-59; Articles "National Planning and Intergovernmental Relations", *Public Administration* (Sydney) 28 (1), (March 1969).

45. Australia, Task Force on Coordination in Welfare and Health (P. Bailey, Chairman), *Second Report* (Canberra: AGPS, 1978); Committee on Care of the Aged and the Inform (A.S. Holmes, Chairman), *Report* (Canberra: AGPS, 1977). (The Bland Report was never published.)

46. Australian Institute of Political Science, *Federalism in Australia* (Melbourne: Cheshire, 1949), 151.

47. Mathews, *Fiscal Federalism*, 115-16.

Chapter 6

1. Federal-Provincial Relations Office, *Federal-Provincial Programs and Activities: A Descriptive Inventory* (Ottawa: April 1983), i.

2. See Kenneth Wiltshire, "Australian State Participation in Federal Decisions", in *Federalism in Australia and the Federal Republic of Germany*, ed. R.L. Mathews (Canberra: ANU Press, 1979), 65-138.

3. Richard Simeon, *Federal-Provincial Diplomacy. The Making of Recent Policy in Canada* (Toronto: University of Toronto Press, 1973), 302-4.

4. Ibid., 304.

5. D.V. Smiley, *Canada in Question: Federalism in the Seventies* (Toronto: McGraw-Hill, 1976), 59.

6. Ibid.

7. *Report of the Committee on Care of the Aged and the Infirm* (Canberra: AGPS, 1977): 23.

8. *Administrative Federalism, Selected Documents in Australian Intergovernmental Relations*, ed. Kenneth Wiltshire (St Lucia: University of Queensland Press, 1977).

9. Department of the Prime Minister and Cabinet, *Australian-State Cooperative Arrangements, Joint Consultative and Planning Arrangements* (Canberra: July 1975): Foreword.

10. Smiley, *Canada in Question*, 61-62.

11. See for example, Royal Institute of Public Administration (Queensland), *Mass Media in the Seventies — Their Impact on Public Administration* Brisbane: 1973).

12. Task Force on Coordination in Welfare and Health (P. Bailey, Chairman), *Second Report Consultative Arrangements and the Coordination of Social Policy Development* (Canberra: 1978): 25-27.

13. G.S. Reid, "Political Decentralization, Cooperative Federalism and Responsible Government", in *Intergovernmental Relations in Australia*, ed. R.L. Mathews (Sydney: Angus and Robertson, 1974), 28.

14. See Smiley, *Canada, 57*.

15. For an analysis of Australian Premiers Conferences see C. Sharman, *The Premiers Conference: An Essay in Federal State Interaction* (Canberra: ANU, RSSS, 1977); D.A. Dixon, "The Premiers' Conference, February, 1970, A View of Federal-State Financial Relations in Australia", *Australian Quarterly* (June 1970): 47-60; and Wiltshire, "State Participation in Federal Decisions". Financial aspects of particular premiers conferences can be found in R.L. Mathews and W.R.C. Jay, *Federal Finance: Intergovernmental Relations in Australia Since Federation* (Melbourne: Nelson, 1972). The Canadian Conference of First Ministers is analysed in Smiley, *Canada*; Simeon, *Federal-Provincial Diplomacy*; Edgar Gallant and R.M. Burns, articles on "The Machinery of Federal-Provincial Relations", *Canadian Public Administration* vol. 7 (4), (1965): 525-26; and Donald V. Smiley, "Public Administration and Canadian Federalism", *Canadian Public Administration* vol. 7 (1964): 371-88.

16. See the Canadian references in note 15 plus G. Veilleux, *Les Relations Intergovernmentales au Canada 1867–1967: Les Mecanismes du Cooperation (Montreal: Quebec University Press, 1971)*; R. Dyck, "Canada Assistance Plan: The Ultimate in Cooperative Federation", *Canadian Public Administration*, vol. 19 (1976); R. Lindenfield, "Hospital Insurance in Canada: An Example in Federal Provincial Relations", *Social Science Review* vol. 33 (June 1959); R. Schultz, "Intergovernmental Cooperation, Regulatory Agencies and Transportation Regulation in Canada: The Case of Part III of the National Transportation Act", *Canadian Public Administration* vol. 19 (1976): 183-207.

17. See Appendix in R.L. Mathews, ed., *Federalism in Australia and the Federal Republic of Germany* (Canberra: ANU Press, 1980).

18. R.H. Leach, *Interstate Relations in Australia* (Lexington: Kentucky University Press, 1965).

19. See for example, G. Starr, "America's Federalism without Washington, Australia's Missing Link", *Australian Quarterly* (September 1976): 62-72.

20. Gerard Veilleux, "L'évolution des Mécanismes de Liaison Intergovernmentale", in *Confrontation and Collaboration — Intergovernmental Relations in Canada Today*, ed. Richard Simeon (Toronto: IPAC, 1979), 39.

21. K.W. Taylor, "Coordination in Administration", *Proceedings of the Ninth Annual Conference of the Institute of Public Administration of Canada* (Toronto, 1957).

22. Edgar Gallant, "The Machinery of Federal-Provincial Relations: I", *Canadian Public Administration* (8), (1965): 518.

23. Ibid.: 526.

24. R.M. Burns, "The Machinery of Federal-Provincial Relations: II", *Canadian Public Administration* (8), (1965): 530.

25. Gordon Robertson, "The Role of Interministerial Conferences in the Decision-Making Process", in *Confrontation and Collaboration — Intergovernmental Relations in Canada Today*, ed. Richard Simeon (Toronto: Institute of Public Administration of Canada, 1979), 78-88.

26. Stevenson, "The Role of Intergovernmental Conferences in the Decision-Making Process", in *Confrontation and Collaboration*, ed. Simeon, 89-98.

27. Department of the Prime Minister and Cabinet, *Australian-State Government Cooperative Arrangements* (Canberra: May 1975).

28. Veilleux, "L'évolution des Mécanismes de Liaison Intergovernmentale", 44.

29. Kenneth Kernaghan, *The Power and Responsibility of Intergovernmental Officials in Canada*, Paper delivered to the Annual Conference of the Institute of Public Administration of Canada (Winnipeg: 1979): 22-23.

30. Colin Campbell and George J. Szablowski, *The Superbureaucrats* (Toronto: Macmillan, 1979), 49-51.

31. Veilleux, "L'évolution des Mécanismes de Liaison Intergovernmentale", 42-45.

32. Richard Simeon, "The Federal-Provincial Decision-Making Process", in *Intergovernmental Relations, Issues and Alternatives, 1977*, Ontario Economic Council (Toronto: 1977): 31-32.

33. Stevenson, "Intergovernmental Conferences", 93.

34. Kernaghan, *Intergovernmental Officials in Canada*: 4-5.

35. Richard Simeon, *Federal-Provincial Diplomacy* (Toronto: University of Toronto Press, 1977).

36. See for example, Kernaghan's references to two unpublished Ph.D. Theses, viz., Richard John Schultz, *Federalism, Bureaucracy and Public Policy: A Case Study of the Making of Transportation Policy* (Toronto: York University, April 1976) and Simon McInnes, *Federal-Provincial Negotiation: Family Allowances 1970-76* (Ottawa: Carleton University, April 1978).

37. Kernaghan, *Intergovernmental Officials in Canada*: 10.

38. New South Wales Premier's Department, *The Financial Relationships of the Commonwealth and the States: A Statement by the Premiers of all the States* (Sydney: 1970).

39. For an attempt to explain the lack of emphasis on full interprovincial liaison in Canada, see Richard H. Leach, "Interprovincial Cooperation: Neglected Aspect of Canadian Federalism", *Canadian Public Administration* vol. 2 (1959): 83-99; and Smiley, *Canada*, 64-67.

40. Kernaghan, *Intergovernment Officials in Canada*: 11.

41. Robertson, "Interministerial Conferences", 85.

42. Stevenson, "Intergovernmental Conferences, 93.

Chapter 7

1. The only significant shift of a taxing power to occur in Australia in the postwar period has been the transfer of payroll tax from the commonwealth government to the state governments in 1971, but this was in response to the loss by the states of receipts duties following a constitutional challenge. For a history and analysis of those events see R.L. Mathews, ed., *State and Local Taxation* (Canberra: ANU Press, 1977), 259-70.

2. For a history of uniform income taxation and state reaction to it see R.L. Mathews and W.R.C. Jay, *Federal Finance: Intergovernmental Financial Relations in Australia since Federation* (Melbourne: Nelson, 1972); and J.E. Richardson, *Patterns of Australian Federalism*, monograph no. 1 (Canberra: Centre for Research on Federal Financial Relations, 1973).

3. For a history of the changes to name and content of the taxation reimbursement grants see Leo A. Hielscher, *The Financial Assistance Grant*, occasional paper no. 1 (Canberra: Centre for Research on Federal Financial Relations, 1976): appendix A.

4. For differing perspectives on the evolution of federal fiscal relations in Canada see J.R. Mallory, *The Structure of Canadian Government* (Toronto: Macmillan, 1971); D.V. Smiley, *Canada in Question: Federalism in the Seventies*, 2nd ed. (Toronto: McGraw-Hill Ryerson, 1976); G. Stevenson, *Unfulfilled Union* (Toronto: Macmillan of Canada, 1979).

5. For a further description, including specific details of taxes, ceilings, limitations, and methods of measurement, see Federal-Provincial Relations Office, *Federal-Provincial Programs and Activities* (Ottawa).

6. See *State and Local Government Finance*, Canberra, Australian Bureau of Statistics.

7. For some expositions of this view in relation to the Australian states see Hielscher, *The Financial Assistant Grant* and *The Financial Relationships of the Commonwealth and the States*, a statement by the premiers of all the states to the 1970 Premiers Conference, 19 January 1970; T.L. Lewis, "Making Federalism Work: Problems of the States", in *Making Federalism Work: Towards a More Efficient, Equitable and Responsive Federal System*, ed. Russell Mathews (Canberra: Centre for Research on Federal Financial Relations, 1976), 203-13.

8. See for example, Mathews and Jay, *Federal Finance*; R.L. Mathews, ed., *Fiscal Federalism: Retrospect and Prospect*, monograph no. 7 (Canberra: Centre for Research on Federal Financial Relations, 1974), chapter 10; Russell Mathews, *Revenue Sharing in Federal Systems*, monograph no. 31 (Canberra: Centre for Research on Federal Financial Relations, 1980); Russell Mathews, "The Future of Government Finance", *Public Administration* (Sydney), 32 (2), (June 1973): 1-15.

9. For some comments on the potential for increased exploitation of the tax base of the Australian states, see R.C. Gates, "The Search for a State Growth Tax", in R.L. Mathews, *Intergovernmental Relations in Australia* (Sydney: Angus and Robertson, 1974), 159-77; and R.L. Mathews, ed., *State and Local Taxation*, part three.

Chapter 8

1. The term "conditional funding" is being used here in an extremely broad sense to cover vertical transfers of funds with any form of condition attached to the *manner in which they must be spent*. This definition thus excludes the tax sharing (formerly Financial Assistance) grants in Australia even though they are given on condition that the states do not levy an income tax. For Canada this definition would exclude the equalization grants. For various definitions of conditional funding, most of them narrower than the definition employed here, see Russell Mathews, *Revenue Sharing in Federal Systems* (Canberra: Centre for Research on Federal Financial Relations, 1980), 25; James A. Maxwell, "Federal Grants in Canada, Australia and the United States", *Publius*, 4 (2), (Spring 1974): 63-76; J.S.H. Hunter, *Federalism and Fiscal Balance* (Canberra: ANU Press, 1977), 62; Garth Stevenson, *Unfulfilled Union* (Toronto: Macmillan, 1979), 156-58; Robert Jay, "The Shift to Specific Purpose Grants: From Revenue Sharing to Cost Sharing", in *Responsibility*

Sharing in a Federal System, ed. R.L. Mathews, monograph no. 8 (Canberra: Centre for Research on Federal Financial Relations, 1975): 41; A.J. Robinson, *Federalism and Efficiency: A Proposal to Improve the Economic Efficiency of the Canadian and Australian Federal Systems*, occasional paper 14 (Canberra: Centre for Research on Federal Financial Relations, 1980): 16.

2. For a complete inventory of the perceived objectives of conditional funding see B.S. Grewal, "Specific Purpose Grants in a Federal System: Overseas Experience", in *Responsibility Sharing*, ed. Mathews: 122; Jay, "Specific Purpose Grants"; Stevenson, *Unfulfilled Union*, 158; Mathews, *Revenue Sharing*, 27; Mathews, "The Future of Government Finance", *Australian Journal of Public Administration* 32 (2), (June 1973): 12; Hunter, *Federalism and Fiscal Balance*, 58-60; R.L. Mathews and W.R.C. Jay, *Federal Finance: Intergovernmental Financial Relations in Australia since Federation* (Melbourne: Nelson, 1972), 314; Russell Mathews, *Regional Disparities and Fiscal Equalisation in Australia*, reprint no. 30 (Canberra: Centre for Research on Federal Financial Relations, 1979): 46-47; R. Else-Mitchell, "The Australian Federal Grants System and its Impact on Fiscal Relations of the Federal Government with State and Local Governments", *Australian Law Journal* 54 (August 1980): 486-87; Ontario Economic Council, *Intergovernmental Relations* (Toronto: 1977), 40 ff.' Ross Cranston, "From Co-operative to Coercive Federalism and Back?", *Federal Law Review* 10 (2), (June 1979): 128-36; W.R. Lane, "Financial Relationships and Section 96", *Public Administration* (Sydney), 34 (1), (March 1975): 50-61.

3. Lane, "Financial Relationships and Section 96".

4. D.V. Smiley, "The Rowell-Sirois Report. Provincial Autonomy and Post-War Canadian Federalism", *Canadian Journal of Economics and Political Science* 28 (1), (1962): 61-62.

5. Mathews, *Revenue Sharing*, 34.

6. R.L. Mathews, ed., *Intergovernmental Relations in Australia* (Sydney: Angus and Robertson, 1974), 226-27.

7. Ibid., 171.

8. Sir Henry Bolte, *Ministerial Statement on Commonwealth and State Financial Relationships*, Victorian Parliamentary Debates (Melbourne: 10 March 1970): 25-27.

9. Pierre Elliott Trudeau, *Federal-Provincial Grants and the Spending Power of Parliament* (Ottawa: Queen's Printer, 1969), 19-20.

10. D.V. Smiley, *Canada in Question* (Toronto: McGraw-Hill Ryerson, 1976), 139-40.

11. George E. Carter, *New Directions in Financing Canadian Federalism*, occasional paper 13 (Canberra: Centre for Research on Federal Financial Relations, 1980): 16-17.

12. Stevenson, *Unfulfilled Union*, 158.

13. Grewal, "Specific Purpose Grants", 142.

14. P.B. Wade, "Recent Developments in Fiscal Federalism in Australia, with Special Reference to Revenue Sharing and Fiscal Equalization", in *Fiscal Federalism: Retrospect and Prospect*, ed. R.L. Mathews, monograph no. 7 (Canberra: Centre for Research on Federal Financial Relations, 1974): 69.

15. J.S.H. Hunter, *Federalism and Fiscal Balance*, 60.

16. G.F. Berkeley, *Financing Education in Queensland: The State-Commonwealth Mix*, occasional paper no. 2 (Canberra: Centre for Research on Federal Financial Relations, 1976).

17. Douglas A.L. Auld, *Contemporary and Historical Economic Dimensions of Canadian Confederation*, occasional paper no. 12 (Canberra: Centre for Research on Federal Financial Relations, 1979): 30-31.

18. J. Holmes and C. Sharman, *The Australian Federal System* (Sydney: George Allen & Unwin, 1977), 150.

19. Ibid., 164.

20. Mathews, *Revenue Sharing*, 35.

21. R.M. Burns, *Intergovernmental Fiscal Transfers: Canadian and Australian Experiences*, monograph no. 22 (Canberra: Centre for Research on Federal Financial Relations, 1977), 59.

22. Stevenson, *Unfulfilled Union*, 173.

23. Ministry of Treasury, Economics, and Intergovernmental Affairs, *Federal-Provincial Shared-Cost Programs in Ontario*, Ontario tax studies 8 (Toronto: 1972): 10.

24. Ibid.: 12-13.

25. Hon. Donald W. Craik, *Notes for a Statement on Shared Costs or Unconditional Grants*, IPAC national conference (Winnipeg: 30.8.1979).
26. Wade, "Fiscal Federation": 58-60.
27. Berkeley, *Financing Education in Queensland*: 15.
28. C.P. Harris, *Relationships between Federal and State Governments in Australia*, information paper no. 6 (Canberra: Advisory Council for Inter-government Relations, 1979): 72-74.
29. See E.G. Whitlam, "The Future of Australian Federalism — A Labor View", in *Intergovernmental Relations*, ed. Mathews, 301-6.
30. Ibid., 306.
31. Russell Mathews, "Federal Balance and Economic Stability", *The Economic Record* 54 (146), (August 1978), reprint no. 26 (Canberra: Centre for Research on Federal Financial Relations): 16-18.
32. Russell Mathews, *Philosophical, Political and Economic Conflicts in Australian Federalism*, reprint no. 23 (Canberra: Centre for Research on Federal Financial Relations, 1977): 16-17.
33. R. Mathews, *Regional Disparities and Fiscal Equalisation*: 48-49.
34. Else-Mitchell, "Australian Federal Grants System".
35. Lane, "Financial Relationships": 64-65.
36. P. Weller and R.F.I. Smith, "Setting National Priorities: The Role of the Australian Government in Public Policy", in *Making Federalism Work: Towards a More Efficient, Equitable and Responsive Federal System*, ed. R.L. Mathews (Canberra: Centre for Research on Federal Financial Relations, 1976): 88-89.
37. R. Mathews, "The Future of Government Finance", *Public Administration* (Sydney), 32 (2), (June 1973): 12-13.
38. Cranston, "Co-operative to Coercive Federalism": 130 ff.
39. J.A. Hayes, "Federal-Provincial Coordination and Consultation in Canada", in *Making Federalism Work*, ed. Mathews, 47-48.
40. Wade, "Fiscal Federalism": 69.
41. New South Wales Premier's Department, *The Financial Relationships of the Commonwealth and the States* (Sydney: Government Printer, 1970). See also comments along similar lines in Harris, *Relations Between Federal and State Governments*, 70 ff.
42. Berkeley, *Financing Education in Queensland*: 14.
43. See Carter, *Financing Canadian Federalism*: 17-18.
44. G. Young, "Federal-Provincial Grants and Equalisation", in *Intergovernmental Relations*, Ontario Economic Council (Toronto: 1977): 40-41.
45. Robinson, *Federalism*, 17.
46. Else-Mitchell, "Australian Federal Grants System": 486.
47. See Hunter, *Federalism and Fiscal Balance*, 64; Lane, "Financial Relationships and Section 96", *Intergovernmental Relations*, ed. Mathews, 141-43; W.R.C. Jay, "Implication of Specific Purpose Grants for Equalisation Policies", in *Fiscal Equalisation in a Federal System*, ed. R.L. Mathews, monograph no. 4 (Canberra: Centre for Research on Federal Financial Relations, 1974): 85-112; Grewal, "Specific Purpose Grants", 143; Harris, *Relations between Federal and State Governments*: 70 ff.
48. Holmes and Sharman, *Australian Federal System*, 136.
49. This problem was, of course, particularly in evidence with the introduction of the Canadian EPF arrangements, which produced protracted negotiations about the horizontal equalization arrangements which would have to accompany the national government's partial withdrawal from the associated, massive, conditionally-funded programmes. The tensions were obviously mainly between the affluent and poorer provinces. For more detailed elaboration of this point see R. Mathews, "Issues in Australian Federalism", *Economic Papers*, no. 58, March 1978, reprint no. 24 (Canberra: Centre for Research on Federal Financial Relations, 1978): 40 ff.; R. Else-Mitchell, "The Rise and Demise of Coercive Federalism", *Australian Journal of Public Administration*, 36 (2), (June 1977), reprint no. 20 (Canberra: Centre for Research on Federal Financial Relations, 1977): 117 ff.; *1975 Report of the Centre for Research on Federal Financial Relations*, Canberra; and C. Saunders and K. Wiltshire, "Fraser's New Federalism 1975–80; An Evaluation", *Australian Journal of Politics and History* 26 (3), (December 1980): 355-71.

50. Trudeau, *Federal-Provincial Grants*, 16.
51. Hayes, "Federal-Provincial Coordination", 47.
52. Stevenson, *Unfulfilled Union*, 170 ff.
53. Young, "Federal-Provincial Grants": 41-42.
54. See for example, Else-Mitchell, "Australian Federal Grants System"; also G. Sawer and C.A. Saunders, "The Development of the Commonwealth Spending Power", *Melbourne University Law Review* (1978): 11.
55. Holmes and Sharman, *Australian Federal System*, 139-40.
56. See Harris, *Relations between Federal and State Governments*: 70 ff.
57. Cranston, "Cooperative to Coercive Federalism": 129-30.
58. Ibid.: 134.
59. Trudeau, *Federal-Provincial Grants*, 20-22.
60. Burns, *Fiscal Transfers*: 60.
61. Stevenson, *Unfulfilled Union*, 157.
62. For a brief analysis of the impact of this trend on individual states see K. Wiltshire, "New Federalisms — The State Perspective", in *The Politics of New Federalism*, ed. Dean Jaensch (Adelaide: APSA, 1977), 76-86.
63. New South Wales Premier's Department, *The Financial Relationships of the Commonwealth and the States*: 7.
64. Hielscher, *The Financial Assistance Grant*: 2-3.
65. W. Prest, "Tax Sharing and Coordination", in *Making Federalism Work*, ed. Mathews, 141. On this general point see also data presented in R. Cotton, "The Future of Australian Federalism — A Liberal View", in *Intergovernmental Relations*, ed. Mathews, 281-94.
66. Holmes and Sharman, *Australian Federal System*, 153-54 and 157-58.
67. Mathews and Jay, *Federal Finance*, 293. See also Lane, "Direct Taxes in Relation to the Division of Fiscal Powers", in *Intergovernmental Relations*, ed. Mathews, 135; and Prest, "Tax Sharing", 193-98.
68. Hayes, "Federal-Provincial Coordination", 41.
69. Trudeau, *Federal-Provincial Grants*, 24.
70. R.L. Mathews, ed., *Fiscal Federalism: Retrospect and Prospect*, research monograph no. 7 (Canberra: Centre for Research on Federal Financial Relations, 1974): 219-20.
71. Mathews, ed., *Intergovernmental Relations*, 226-27. (Similar arguments are advanced by Gates in this volume.)
72. Wade, "Fiscal Federalism": 68-69.
73. Jay, "Specific Purpose Funding", 43 ff.
74. See also Jay, "Specific Purpose Grants", 85-112.
75. Prest, "Tax Sharing and Coordination", 194.
76. See also Hunter, *Federalism and Fiscal Balance*, 61 ff; Harris, *Relations Between Federal and State Governments*, 56 ff.
77. Grewal, "Specific Purpose Grants", 140-41.
78. See Carter, *Financing Canadian Federalism*, 12; and Hayes, "Federal-Provincial Coordination", 46 ff.
79. See Mathews, *Revenue Sharing*, 33-34.
80. Robinson, *Federalism*, 17.
81. T.L. Lewis, "Making Federalism Work: Problems of the States", in *Making Federalism Work*, ed. Mathews: 206.
82. Mathews, *Regional Disparities and Fiscal Equalisation in Australia*: 46-47.
83. Cranston, "Cooperative to Coercive Federalism": 132-36.
84. Weller and Smith, "Setting National Priorities", 94.
85. Holmes and Sharman, *Australian Federalism System*, 150.
86. R. Mathews, *Philosophical, Political and Economic Conflicts in Australian Federalism*, reprint no. 23 (Canberra: Centre for Research on Federal Financial Relations, 1977): 14.
87. Jay, "The Shift to Specific Purpose Funding": 120.
88. New South Wales Premier's Department, *The Financial Relationship of the Commonwealth and the States*: 8.
89. Stevenson, *Unfulfilled Union*, 170.

90. Else-Mitchell, "Australian Federal Grants System": 487.
91. Stevenson, *Unfulfilled Union*, 161-62.
92. Hunter, *Federalism and Fiscal Balance*, 60.
93. R. Mathews, *Regional Disparities and Fiscal Equalisation in Australia*: 47.
94. Stevenson, *Unfulfilled Union*, 157-58.
95. See Australian Medical Association, *Submission to the Commission of Inquiry into the Efficiency and Administration of Hospitals* (Canberra: November 1979): 11-18.
96. W.R. Lane, "Financial Relationships and Section 96": 61.

Chapter 9

1.   R.L. Mathews, ed., *Making Federalism Work: Towards a More Efficient, Equitable and Responsive Federal System* (Canberra: Centre for Research on Federal Financial Relations, 1976): 124.
2.   See Australian Bureau of Statistics, *Public Authority Finance*, State and Local Authorities (Canberra).
3.   See for example, P. Bernd Spahn, ed., *Principles of Federal Policy Coordination in the Federal Republic of Germany*, monograph no. 25 (Canberra: Centre for Research on Federal Financial Relations, 1978); and R.L. Mathews, ed., *Federalism in Australia and the Federal Republic of Germany* (Canberra: ANU Press, 1980).
4.   See B.S. Grewal, *Centre-State Financial Relations in India* (Patiala: Punjabi University Press, 1975); and B.S. Grewal, *Fiscal Federalism in India*, monograph no. 3 (Canberra: Centre for Research on Federal Financial Relations, 1974).
5.   C.P. Harris, *Relationships between Federal and State Governments in Australia*, information paper no. 6 (Canberra: Advisory Council for Inter-government Relations, 1979).
6.   See R.L. Mathews and W.R.C. Jay, *Federal Finance: Intergovernmental Financial Relations in Australia since Federation* (Melbourne: Nelson, 1972), chapter 1.
7.   E.G. Whitlam, *On Australia's Constitution* (Melbourne: Widescope, 1977), 270.
8.   R.L. Mathews, ed., *Intergovernmental Relations in Australia* (Sydney: Angus and Robertson, 1974), 28.
9.   Royal Commission on Australian Government Administration, *Appendixes to Report Volume Two* (Canberra: AGPS, 1976): 425-56.
10. W.R. Lane, "Financial Relationships and Section 96", *Public Administration* (Sydney), 34 (1), (March 1975): 45-72.
11. Carl J. Friedrich, "Political Decision Making, Public Policy and Planning", *Canadian Public Administration*, 14 (1), (Spring 1971): 15.

Index

Other Titles in the Scholars' Library